HELPING THOSE
EXPERIENCING LOSS

HELPING THOSE EXPERIENCING LOSS

A Guide to Grieving Resources

ROBERT J. GROVER AND SUSAN G. FOWLER

LIBRARIES UNLIMITED

AN IMPRINT OF ABC-CLIO, LLC
Santa Barbara, California • Denver, Colorado • Oxford, England

Library of Congress Cataloging-in-Publication Data

Grover, Robert, 1942–
  Helping those experiencing loss : a guide to grieving resources / Robert J. Grover and Susan G. Fowler.
      p. ; cm.
  Includes bibliographical references and index.
  ISBN 978-1-59884-826-7 (pbk. : alk. paper) — ISBN 978-1-59884-827-4 (E-ISBN) 1. Grief—Information resources. 2. Grief. I. Fowler, Susan G., 1958– II. Title.
  [DNLM: 1. Grief—Resource Guides. 2. Grief. BF 575.G7]
  BF575.G7G776   2011
  155.9'3—dc22   2011010835

ISBN: 978-1-59884-826-7
EISBN: 978-1-59884-827-4

15 14 13 12 11   1 2 3 4 5

This book is also available on the World Wide Web as an eBook.
Visit www.abc-clio.com for details.

Libraries Unlimited
An Imprint of ABC-CLIO, LLC

ABC-CLIO, LLC
130 Cremona Drive, P.O. Box 1911
Santa Barbara, California 93116-1911

This book is printed on acid-free paper ∞

Manufactured in the United States of America

*We dedicate this book to Susan's mother,
Jo Anne Fowler, whose grief journey following
the death of Susan's father has been conducted
with uncommon grace and faith.*

CONTENTS

ACKNOWLEDGMENTS

We are grateful for the support of our editor, Blanche Woolls. She provided us guidance as we submitted our proposal and was quick to respond when we had questions. We can't imagine a more congenial, professional, knowledgeable person with whom to work.

We thank Margaret Fowler and Carlee Wilson, two mental health professionals with a lifetime's experience working with children and adults dealing with life's crises, who read and gave feedback on our manuscript.

The review media below graciously provided permission to quote from their reviews:

Booklist: Bill Ott, Editor and Publisher, American Library Association, 50 E. Huron, Chicago IL 60611

Choice: Reprinted with permission from CHOICE http://www.cro2.org, copyright by the American Library Association. Francine Graf, Editorial Director, 575 Main St., Suite 300, Middletown, CT 06457

Kirkus Reviews: Eric Liebetrau, Managing Editor and Nonfiction Editor, Kirkus Reviews/Kirkus Media, 479 Old Carolina Court, Mt. Pleasant, SC 29464

Library Journal and *School Library Journal:* Library Journals LLC, a wholly owned subsidiary of Media Source, Inc. No redistribution permitted. Brian Kenney, Editorial Director, 160 Varick St., 11th Floor, New York, NY 10013

Voice of Youth Advocates: Edward Kurdyla, Publisher, and RoseMary Honnold, Editor in Chief, E. L. Kurdyla Publishing, LLC

Finally, we thank the many people who have shown interest in this project, and those who daily engage in helping others deal with loss. Grief is a shared human experience that our society prefers to avoid. We are grateful for the brave men and women who are helping to change this trend, and in so doing, help to heal our world.

1

INTRODUCTION TO THE BOOK

CHAPTER OVERVIEW

This chapter is an overview of this guide to grief literature with a statement of need for the book as well as a statement of purpose, intended audience, and scope of resources included. Criteria for selecting recommended resources are outlined, along with suggestions for using this guide. Each book chapter is briefly introduced.

NEED FOR THIS BOOK

Death and loss are integral parts of the life experience. Throughout our lives we must face the loss of friends who move away, relatives, friends, and pets who die, and loss of possessions we hold dear. As we mature, we become aware that we lose relationships and physical abilities. Eventually we lose our mobility and our world becomes smaller. Ultimately, we lose our lives.

Children and young adults may experience loss of parents or grandparents, siblings, and friends. The death of a pet can be a devastating loss to young people. In addition, other experiences that cause grieving for youth include: adoption and the feeling of loss of birth parents and identity, divorce and the loss of stability, foster care and loss similar to that of divorce, and the loss of friends when a family moves. Grieving can also be caused by developmental changes and by abusive situations.

Despite the inevitability of loss and grieving, our society tends to avoid discussion of loss. In the 1970s the work of Elisabeth Kübler-Ross and the hospice movement brought death and dying to the public's attention in direct ways that we had not encountered before. Kübler-Ross identified five stages of grieving, and the hospice movement presented a new paradigm for end-of-life care; whereas the medical profession is focused on the preservation of life, hospice care is most concerned with preserving the dignity of the dying person and the emotional well-being of the dying person's loved ones. The dying person and loved ones are counseled on the stages of dying and the emotional consequences of the dying person and family and friends.

During the last 40 years, the movement to view death and dying as a natural part of the life experience has fostered research and publication of an increasing volume of popular literature for youth and adults. The result has been a deluge of books, videos, and audio recordings on death, dying, and grieving. While the availability of these resources is welcome, the general public has been without a reliable guide to these resources. This book is an effort to address that need.

PURPOSE AND AUDIENCE

The purpose of this book is to introduce librarians, teachers, mental health professionals, and parents to major issues related to grief and grieving and to recommended print and nonprint resources to assist adults and youth who are grieving. More than a bibliography, this guide provides the reader guidance on key issues with suggestions for approaching and assisting persons who identify themselves as grieving; however, we make no attempt to provide the counseling that can best be provided only by professionally certified counselors.

This guide is limited to English language resources and includes selected books, audio recordings, a limited number of video recordings, websites, and national organizations. Emphasis is placed on recent (2000–present) publications in English, although older but important resources also are included. With the exception of websites and organizations, all recommended resources were favorably reviewed by at least one respected reviewing source or by the authors.

Books, audio recordings, and video recordings were identified by searching *Books in Print Online,* which provides publication information, annotations, author information, and reviews from numerous review media. In addition, the following catalogs were consulted for recommended books on adoption, bereavement, death, divorce, foster care, and suicide:

- *Children's Catalog* (2006), 19th edition and 2007, 2008, and 2009 supplements
- *Middle and Junior High Core Collection* (2009), 10th edition
- *Senior High Core Collection: A Selection Guide* (2007), 17th edition and 2008 and 2009 supplements

The audience for resources recommended in this guide includes children, preschool through age 12; young adults, ages 13–18; and adults. The intended users of this guide are librarians, teachers, mental health professionals, and parents.

SELECTION OF RESOURCES LISTED

Each chapter of the guide introduces the topic under consideration, emphasizing important issues and implications for service, followed by a listing of resources with critical annotations. Ordering information available at the time of publication is included, along with citations for review excerpts. Most titles recommended are in print (available for purchase) at the time of the writing.

In addition to books, this guide lists eBooks, audio recordings, and videos that are recommended for use by an audience identified in the annotation. Recommended age of users is based on review recommendations and the judgment of the authors. We recognize that suggested age of audience varies by the reading ability and interests of the individual reader; therefore the adult reader should use his or her professional discretion when selecting resources for individual children.

Only nonfiction titles were considered for recommended adult resources; however, a large number of fiction books were considered and are listed in the children's and young adult sections (chapters 3 and 4). Fiction that relates realistic problems and emotions can provide models for grieving youth and can help them to understand their circumstance through the experiences of fictional peers. Youth sometimes feel that they are alone in their grieving experience, and fiction can provide them an informed perspective on their situation.

Resources were identified using *Books in Print Online*, a reliable, current source of resources in print with annotations and accompanied by published reviews. Only those titles reviewed by the author or favorably reviewed by one respected reviewing source are included in our recommended lists. Review sources consulted and excerpted reviews are used with the permission of these respected review media: *Booklist, Choice, Kirkus Reviews, Library Journal, School Library Journal,* and *Voice of Youth Advocates.*

The authors also consulted with a panel of mental health professionals to assure that the book is grounded in issues relevant to the intended audience.

Annotations were written by the authors and based on reviews and, whenever possible, their examination of titles. A large number of resources related to grief and grieving are available to the public, and this guide does not attempt a comprehensive listing of materials. Instead, it is a guide to helpful resources evaluated by professionals and considered appropriate for the intended audience. The authors selected the recommended resources based on these criteria:

1. The intended audience is clearly stated.
2. The resource (book, video, website, audio recording) is appropriate for its intended audience. The vocabulary and treatment of the subject are clear, accurate, and current.
3. Fiction is factually correct, based on accepted theories and research on bereavement and treatment of grieving children, youth, and adults.
4. The topic is treated even-handedly; no bias is evident.
5. Organization of the material is logical.
6. Supplementary materials such as graphics, chronologies, appendices, and other materials are appropriate and useful to the intended audience.
7. For nonfiction, the table of contents and index provide easy access to the topics included.
8. Whenever possible, available resources are listed; out-of-print titles are listed when they are unique, and pertinent to the topic at hand.

HOW TO USE THIS GUIDE

Each chapter begins with an overview of the topic, for example, the grieving process. The reader is advised to peruse this prefatory material to understand better the cognitive, emotional, and physical reactions that accompany grief. This understanding also will assist in both the selection of resources for the child or adult needing help and the communication with the bereaved person. The chapter introductions

are based on literature that is cited, with complete citations at the end of the chapter. Included are suggestions for interacting with grieving adults and youth.
Following is a description of entries.

Book Entry Elements

Each book entry includes the following information in order: Author's last name, first name. **Title.** City where published: Publisher, imprint, date released. Number of pages. Price [pa indicates paper cover]. ISBN numbers.

Sample Entry: Single Author

Carson, Jo. **You Hold Me and I'll Hold You.** New York: Scholastic, Orchard Books, 1997. 32p. $6.95pa. ISBN 0-531-07088-3; 978-0-531-07088-8.

> **Note:** Assume the book is a hardback edition unless noted after price—"pa" indicates paperback.

Sample Entry: Two Authors

Gellman, Marc, and Thomas Hartman. **Lost and Found: A Kid's Book for Living through Loss.** New York: HarperCollins, 1999. 176p. $15.99. ISBN 0-688-15752-1; 978-0-688-15752-4.

Multimedia Entries

Each media entry includes the following information: Author last name, first. **Title.** Format. Running time. Price. ISBN numbers.

Sample Entry for a Multimedia Package

Cochran, Bill. **The Forever Dog.** Holmes, NY: Spoken Arts, 2007. Compact disc or cassette and hardcover. 27 min. $29.95 CD; $27.95 cassette. ISBN 0-8045-4177-9, 978-0-8045-4177-0 CD; 0-8045-6955-X, 978-0-8045-6955-2 cassette.

ANNOTATIONS

Book and media descriptions are based on authors' examination of the titles or by publishers' descriptions and reviews. The authors have selected informative and evaluative statements from published reviews to provide additional authoritative information about the resource. For picture books, the name of the illustrator is cited in the annotation. A suggested age range is given for children's (chapter 3) and young adult (chapter 4) resources.

Example

Curtis, Jamie Lee. **Tell Me Again about the Night I Was Born.** New York: HarperCollins, Joanna Cotler Books, 1996. 40p. $16.99. ISBN 0-06-024528-X; 978-0-06-024528-3.

> Actor Curtis tells the story of a young girl who asks her parents to tell her again the family story of her birth and adoption. "Curtis' use of an ingenuous childlike

narrator is just as successful here as it was in *When I Was Little* (1993), and so are [Laura] Cornell's comical, exuberant illustrations, which have great child appeal" (*Booklist* Oct. 15, 1996). Ages 4–8.

ARRANGEMENT OF ENTRIES

With the exception of the children's resources (chapter 3) and the young adult resources (chapter 4), recommended books and other resources are arranged alphabetically by author's last name.

Chapters 3, children's resources, are intended for children to and including age 12. Chapter 4, resources for young adults, lists items intended for youth ages 13–18. Both chapters are organized by topic, then alphabetically by author. Following are the topic subdivisions:

- Adoption
- Death—general (chapter 3 only)
- Death of a friend
- Death of a parent
- Death of a sibling
- Divorce
- Foster care
- Grieving (chapter 4 only)
- Suicide (chapter 4 only)

The reader is advised that there is overlap between some titles for older children listed in chapter 3 and titles for younger adolescents in chapter 4. Both chapters should be consulted when working with youth in upper elementary and middle schools.

OUTLINE OF CHAPTERS

This guide to the literature of grieving is organized by age or developmental level of the audience. Research indicates that developmental stages bring different challenges and perspectives for living. Among children, the developmental stages change within a short number of years, accompanied by physical, intellectual, and emotional development. The adult years are more static, yet the changes in perspective do occur. The book uses these life stages to outline the changing perspectives on grieving.

Chapter 1 is an overview of the guide with a statement of purpose, intended audience, scope of resources included, how to use the book, and an introduction to the chapters.

Chapter 2 describes the grieving process. The authors cite professional literature to introduce the feelings that accompany loss. Grieving is defined in broad terms to include various types of loss, including death of parents, friends, companion animals, and children. Grieving is also associated with changes in relationships— adoption, assignment to a foster home, divorce, and moving. Models for examining the grieving process by identifying stages or common attributes of grieving are examined, along with recommended strategies for addressing grief. A section of the chapter is addressed to librarians, teachers, mental health professionals, and parents, suggesting strategies for establishing a rapport while helping grieving children and adults. Key resources to help bereaved individuals are listed with annotations.

Chapter 3 focuses on children and loss. The introduction summarizes key issues from the literature to show how children's developmental stages influence how they grieve in order to help librarians, teachers, mental health professionals, and parents to understand the psychology of loss among children. Included are suggestions for assisting children in a supportive manner. Resources for adults who help grieving children are followed by fiction and nonfiction books, recordings, and websites for children listed by age categories—early childhood (ages 0–4), middle childhood (ages 5–8), and late childhood (ages 9–12).

Chapter 4 concentrates on young adults—ages 13–18. Adolescents are seeking their own identities, and loss of relatives or friends present additional challenges at a time when each day is a challenge. In this chapter we cite literature in the behavioral and social sciences that describe the grieving process of young adults so that librarians, teachers, parents, and mental health professionals can better understand the psychology underlying young adult behaviors. We then suggest ways that librarians and teachers can assist adolescents as they confront major loss and recommend resources appropriate for older children and young adults, and for the adults who work closely with them.

Chapter 5 discusses the grave emotional reactions to loss of a child. Beginning with a personal account to frame the trauma that accompanies loss of a child, we discuss the causes of prenatal and infant deaths and the psychological trauma that will accompany the loss of a child, no matter the age. The psychological effect of a child's death on siblings and other family members is followed by suggestions for parents and service providers so that they can effectively assist grieving youth. A number of books, recordings, and websites are recommended as resources.

Chapter 6 addresses death of a spouse. This chapter provides a description of the emotions and challenges that accompany the loss of a life partner, with implications for library staff who work with grieving widows and widowers. An annotated bibliography of suggested resources concludes the chapter.

Chapter 7 discusses grieving as we age. The aging process causes changes in one's perspective on grieving, and it is helpful for service professionals to understand how the aging process influences perspectives on death and grieving. The impact of grieving on health is followed by suggestions for serving aging bereaved adults and for recommended resources.

Chapter 8 investigates the role of spirituality on grieving. Research on grieving indicates that faith plays a vital role in healing. The role of faith is briefly explained, and titles that provide a faith perspective are presented.

The index provides access by author, title, and subject to each of the information sources cited or reviewed.

SOURCES CONSULTED

The following resources were consulted to identify resources and reviews:

Barber, Raymond W., and Patrice Bartell, eds. *Senior high core collection: A selection guide.* 2007. 17th ed. and 2008, 2009, and 2010 supplements. New York: H. W. Wilson.

Books in print with reviews. New Providence, NJ: R. R. Bowker, 2001–. http://www.book sinprint.com.

Price, Anne, ed. *Children's catalog.* 2006. 19th ed. and 2007, 2008, and 2009 supplements. Standard Catalog Series. New York: H. W. Wilson.

Price, Anne, ed. *Middle and junior high core collection.* 2009. 10th ed. and 2010 supplement. New York: H. W. Wilson.

Price, Anne, and Marguerita Rowland, eds. *Children's core collection.* 20th ed. New York: H. W. Wilson, 2010.

2

———◆◈◆———

A PORTRAIT OF GRIEF

CHAPTER OVERVIEW

The authors cite professional literature to introduce the grieving process and to define terms. Feelings associated with grief are described, along with factors that influence the depth of grieving. The strategies for addressing grief and factors of resilience that can influence the depth of grieving and physical impact are explored. A section of the chapter is addressed to librarians, teachers, and parents, suggesting strategies for establishing a rapport in helping grieving children and adults. Key recommended resources are listed with descriptive annotations.

DEFINING GRIEF AND MOURNING

Loss is a prominent and enduring part of life. Kübler-Ross and Kessler (2000) provide a commonly held attitude toward loss:

> We eventually lose everything we have, yet what ultimately matters can never be lost. Our houses, cars, jobs, and money, our youth and even our loved ones, are just on loan to us. Like everything else our loved ones are not ours to keep. But realizing this truth does not have to sadden us. To the contrary, it can give us a greater appreciation for the many wonderful experiences and things we have during our time here. (75)

Loss is closely associated with grieving, and we begin by defining *mourning* and *grief*:

Mourning is the external part of loss. It is the actions we take, the rituals and the customs. *Grief* is the internal part of loss, how we feel. The internal work of grief is a process, a journey. It does not end on a certain day or date. It is as individual as each of us. Mourning can occur over loss of a relationship or such things as a home, job, or country (Kübler-Ross and Kessler 2005; Hooyman and Kramer 2006).

Although we usually associate *grieving* with death, the definition is much broader. Archer (1999, 1) defines grief as follows:

> We normally think of grief as occurring in the context of bereavement, the loss of a loved one through death, but a broadly similar reaction can occur when a close relationship is ended through separation, or when a person is forced to give up some aspect of life that was important.

As Archer suggests, grieving is associated with losses beyond the death of a loved one, including divorce, death of a pet, moving, starting school, death of a former spouse, marriage, graduation, end of addictions, major health changes, retirement, financial changes (positive or negative), holidays, legal problems, and empty nest. Often they are not seen as grieving events, but we grieve for the loss of all relationships we consider significant (James and Friedman 2009).

Grief is a natural human reaction because it is a universal feature of life and transcends culture, although the form and intensity of its expression can vary considerably. Archer (1999) also points out that grieving occurs in other social mammals and birds after loss of a parent, offspring, or mate. Indeed, animals and young children show similar responses to temporary separations and permanent losses.

As noted above, grief applies to much more than the death of a loved one. It is related to any aspect of our identity. While it can be a loved one, it can also be a job, a limb, or anything intimately associated with identity. Psychology theorists see grief as a complex process because we develop our identities based on complex sets of ideas that are closely linked to those aspects of life that are most important to us, such as family, home, friendships, job, beliefs, and possessions. These ideas are emotionally charged and resistant to change (Archer 1999).

EXPLORING GRIEF

People grieve because they have lost an essential part of how they think about themselves. Consequently, they must change their outlook about identity in order to match the new reality emerging from the loss. This new sense of identity must be incorporated into the world as they perceive it.

Grief is pervasive, affecting a person's entire being. "It is experienced psychologically and cognitively through painful feelings, thoughts, and attitudes; socially through behavior with others; and physiologically through health and bodily symptoms" (Hooyman and Kramer 2006, 16). Grief is based on one's individual perspective on a loss. It is not necessary for a loss to be recognized by others for us to grieve.

Some losses are not accompanied by grieving because the attachment was not strong, for example, death of a divorced spouse after a bad marriage or after a particularly long and difficult period of caregiving.

In our childhood we are taught to acquire things—parents' praise, toys for being good, and high grades in school. "While we have learned much about acquiring things, we have precious little accurate information on what to do when we lose them" (James and Friedman 2009, 24).

Sometimes loss is predictable and inevitable, yet we receive no training in how to respond to these events that are certain to cause pain. We are even told not to talk about it. Many children are told, "Don't cry." (Don't feel bad.) "On Saturd: we'll get you a new dog." (Replace the loss.) "If you're going to cry, go to you. room." (Grieve alone.) "Time heals all wounds." (Just give it time.) "We have to be strong for..." (Be strong for others.) "You have to keep busy." (Keep busy.) None of these myths help a person deal with loss and the feelings that accompany it (James and Friedman 2009, 26–35).

Cultural Differences

The cultural context of an individual and a community shapes the perception of responses to the grieving process. Cultural differences in grieving behavior patterns reflect the culture's view of what is healthy and appropriate following a loss.

In Western cultures, individuals are expected to recover quickly from grief. "Most Americans are uncomfortable around others' sadness and tears and so want a quick solution to grief. In our culture, pain is seen as something that can and should be avoided, instead of being viewed as an inescapable part of being human" (Hooyman and Kramer 2006, 19).

Although it may appear that crying is a universal response to grief, Hooyman and Kramer (2006) cite the Balinese custom to appear unruffled, even happy because they believe that the gods will ignore their prayers if they are not calm.

Understanding the Grieving Process

Grief can be addressed if it is understood. A model for describing the facets of dying and applied to grief was introduced by Elisabeth Kübler-Ross (1969, 1981), who acknowledged that grief is as individual as our lives. The five stages devised by Kübler-Ross are tools to help us understand the feelings associated with grieving; a person may not go through all of them, and may not go through them in a certain order. The five stages are frequently found in counseling and popular literature about grieving. Below is a description of these stages.

1. *Denial* occurs when one cannot believe that he/she won't see the loved one again. Denial helps the survivor to survive the loss. The griever has difficulty believing what happened. Could it have been prevented? As they accept the loss, they are beginning the healing process, and the denial starts to fade. In this process, the feelings they were denying start to surface.
2. *Anger* may be directed at the deceased loved ones for not taking care of themselves, at the doctors, or at the surviving spouse for what they did not do. They may be angry that they are left alone. These feelings may not be logical, but they are legitimate feelings. Other feelings that may emerge are panic, sadness, hurt, and loneliness, which become stronger as they begin to function normally again. They may have feelings of guilt, which is anger directed inward. In fact, the survivor did what they could, and they could not have done more to save their loved one.
3. *Bargaining* occurs as the survivor realizes an impending loss or experiences a recent loss. They want the other person to be restored, and they elicit any number of "if...then" scenarios to bring the loved one back. For example, they want to find the cause of the illness to prevent it; they want to see the doctor sooner; they want to prevent the accident from happening. "Guilt is

often bargaining's companion. The 'if onlys' cause us to find fault with ourselves and what we 'think' we could have done differently" (Kübler-Ross and
Kessler 2005, 17)

4. *Depression* is the deep, empty feeling of loss. Life seems pointless. A person doesn't feel like getting out of bed. They may not feel like eating or
going anywhere. Kübler-Ross and Kessler (2005) describe this depression
as a "heavy, dark feeling." Depression in grief is a way of protecting the
grieving individual by shutting down their nervous system so that they can
begin to adapt to something that they feel incapable of handling at the
time.

5. *Acceptance* is *not* being all right with the loss of a loved one—most people never feel okay about it. "This stage is about accepting the reality that
our loved one is physically gone and recognizing that this new reality is the
permanent reality." We learn to live with this new reality (Kübler-Ross and
Kessler 2005, 24–25).

Although the Kübler-Ross Model has been cited in professional literature for
many years, a review of bereavement literature by the Institute of Medicine cau-
tioned against using the concept of bereavement stages, noting it "might lead
people to expect the bereaved to proceed from one clearly identifiable reaction to
another in a more orderly fashion than usually occurs. It might also result in hasty
assessment of where individuals are, or ought to be in the grieving process" (Wortman and Silver 1990, 229).

James and Friedman emphatically state that grief should not be regarded in terms
of stages. "The nature and intensity of feelings caused by a loss relate to the indi-
viduality and uniqueness of the relationship" (James and Friedman 2009, 11–12).

Hooyman and Kramer (2006, 37) agree: "Whether applied to the dying person
or the bereaved, grief does not proceed in a linear fashion but reappears again
and again to be reworked, with the emotional reactions to death varying greatly"
(Hooyman and Kramer 2006, 39). Researchers generally agree on the following
three phases of the grieving process:

1. Avoidance encompasses shock, numbness, disbelief, and denial, which all
function to buffer the painful reality of loss. Other feelings may be fear, anxiety, dread, disorganization, and an inability to comprehend the situation.
Some people want to be with others; some prefer to be alone. Some prefer
to focus on tasks to keep grief at a distance, for example, making funeral or
financial arrangements or preparing meals.

2. Confrontation is the intense realization that the loved one is gone. Common
feelings are sadness, guilt or blaming others or self, helplessness, panic, confusion, anger, despair, loss of faith, and disillusionment.

3. Accommodation occurs when the bereaved person gradually moves on, re-
entering the everyday world and lives with the loss of the loved one (Hooyman and Kramer 2006, 40).

The authors note that because of the widespread use of the Kübler-Ross five-step
model and its clarity, it is valuable as a mechanism for understanding the grieving
process. Furthermore, Kübler-Ross (2005) herself states that the model is not linear, and some bereaved individuals do not attend to all five stages.

GRIEF AND STRESS

Following the death of his wife, Lewis (1961) describes the conflicted feelings of grief: it's like the feelings of fear—fluttering in the stomach, restlessness, yawning. Sometimes he felt "mildly drunk or concussed."

> There is a sort of invisible blanket between the world and me. I find it hard to take in what anyone says. Or perhaps, hard to want to take it in. It is so uninteresting. Yet I want the others to be about me. I dread the moments when the house is empty. If only they would talk to one another and not to me. (Lewis 1961, 3)

The feelings that Lewis eloquently expressed in his writing are the physical manifestations of stress, caused by a loss.

Stress

Stress is an internal alarm within our bodies that sends a strong message: "A change is taking place; begin adjusting now." Various external events can trigger stress symptoms; Moody and Arcangel (2001, 29) rate levels of stress:

- *Lowest:* environmental changes that require unconscious adjustments: change in light causes eye dilation, fluctuation in temperature affects respiration
- *Higher:* challenges like unexpected phone calls, uninvited guests, traffic jams
- *More intense:* canceled appointments, unmet deadlines, and late arrival at meetings
- *Greater levels:* holidays, serious legal problems
- *Still higher:* personal or family illness, job change, retirement, change in residence
- *Second highest:* divorce, separation, serious illness
- *Highest:* death of a loved one

Moody and Arcangel assert that while the above scale is universal, people experience events with different intensity, that is, no two people respond to the death of a loved one or to other stressors with the same intensity. Every loss is novel.

Physical Manifestations of Stress

Moody and Arcangel (2001, 30–33) describe the various indicators and manifestations of stress as follows:

- The first stage of stress is alarm, when the brain perceives a problem. Immediately the body responds: heart rate, breathing, perspiration, and blood circulation elevate, and muscles tense. The result is a burst of energy.
- Initial cognitive symptoms of grief-related stress are depression, decreased concentration, distorted concerns, exaggerated worry, headaches, increased irritability, mental fatigue, memory loss, mood swings, obsessive thoughts, sleep disorders. These symptoms are often referred to as shock.
- The first symptom of stress or shock is usually an inability to function mentally at the usual level. The person claims to feel in a fog and has the feeling of being

overwhelmed, perhaps questioning her/his sanity. The human system usually returns to normal in six to eight weeks.

- If stress is prolonged, the alarm phase advances to resistance—the second phase. The physical response can be allergies, asthma attacks, backaches, heart disease, headaches, hypertension, immune disorders, migraines, and skin disorders. Health care professionals report that 75 to 90 percent of their patients' illnesses are stress-related.

- If stress is prolonged still further, it advances to the third stage—exhaustion. A variety of physical symptoms accompany exhaustion, for example, allergies, appetite disturbance, blood pressure elevation, breathing difficulties, digestive problems, dizziness, fainting spells, fatigue, headaches, heart palpitations, colds and infections, insomnia, nightmares, numb or tingling extremities, worsening of previous medical conditions, shortness of breath, sleep deprivation, sweating, substance abuse, urinary infections, vomiting, and weight change.

- Behavioral symptoms include frowning, grimacing, grinding teeth, negative attitude, nervousness (foot tapping, nail biting, finger drumming, etc.), sighing, sulking, changes in speed of walking and talking.

- Emotional changes include angry outbursts, anxiety, crying spells, discouragement, fear, frustration, helplessness, hypersensitivity, joylessness, moodiness, nightmares, panic, tearfulness, and worry.

- Intellectual symptoms include the following: boredom, lack of concentration, confusion, difficulty making decisions, increased errors, forgetfulness, indecisiveness, irrational thoughts, poor judgment, lack of focus, errors in language, lethargy, memory loss, obsessive thoughts, low productivity, and low self-esteem.

- Following are social symptoms of stress: critical attitude, distrust, intolerance, jealousy, lack of intimate connection, loneliness, nagging, relationship disturbances, resentfulness, self-centeredness, sexual dysfunction, withdrawal.

- Spiritual symptoms include apathy, cynicism, distrust, doubt, emptiness, judgmentalism, loss of direction, martyrdom, and unforgiveness.

Bereaved individuals are at greater risk of death because each person is predisposed to certain illnesses. Prolonged, intense stress can affect a weak organ. While grief does not cause death, chronic stress kills through stroke, heart attack, suicide, and perhaps cancer. Given this tendency, stress of grief should not last more than one year.

Mental, emotional, physical, and spiritual health are major factors in a person's ability to cope with loss. If persons are already in crisis (serious health problem or facing surgery), they may postpone mourning until their condition has stabilized. Appearance is not a reliable measure of a person's mourning (Moody and Arcangel 2001).

DISENFRANCHISED GRIEF

Every society establishes norms for grieving. These norms include expected behaviors and rules for how one is to feel and think. The rules also govern what losses one should grieve, how one grieves them, who should grieve the loss, and to whom others should respond with sympathy (Doka 2002).

Organizations, such as businesses, are expected to be fair, functional, and rational, and they may limit acknowledgement of loss only to family members. These policies reflect societal recognition and support by sanctioning the primacy of the family relationship.

Funerals play a vital role in enfranchising grief. A funeral is the vehicle by which grief is acknowledged and sanctioned, and support is rendered. Consequently, the funeral testifies publicly to the right to grieve.

In a diverse society, loss disenfranchised by the larger society may be acknowledged within a smaller subsociety. An example would be the death of a same-sex lover who may be recognized within the gay community, but not by the family or coworkers. Grieving rules differ between cultures (Doka 2002, 9).

Doka (2002) has postulated five categories of disenfranchised grief:

1. The relationship is not recognized. Nontraditional relationships may not be socially sanctioned, for example, extramarital affairs, cohabitating unmarried couples, homosexual relationships, and children of these relationships.
2. Past relationships such as ex-spouses, past lovers, or former friends may bring grief, but the right to grieve is not extended by society.
3. The loss is not acknowledged. It may not be considered significant. Perinatal deaths may bring strong reactions of grief, but people generally consider such losses minor. Loss of a fetus through abortion, placing children for adoption or foster care, and loss of a companion animal also may be overlooked as significant losses.
4. Yet another loss that causes grief but is unrecognized by society is substantial change in a persona caused by mental illness or a serious accident. Secondary losses also can be severe, for example, loss of a job, infertility, loss of reputation, aging, and developmental losses. The griever is excluded. People defined by society as incapable of grief include the very old, the very young, the developmentally disabled, and the mentally ill.
5. Circumstances of the death are a factor in the social acceptance of grieving. Certain types of death are not accepted by society, causing embarrassment of survivors. Included in these types of shunned death are suicide, homicides, persons executed, and the death of alcoholics.

Doka (2002) declares that disenfranchising grief may exacerbate bereavement by intensifying the emotions associated with normal grief. Also, individuals in unsanctioned relationships and other disenfranchised individuals may be excluded from caregiving of the dying and attendance at rituals. Furthermore, disenfranchised grief precludes social support; there is no role in which the mourner can exercise his right to mourn. Disenfranchised mourners cannot ask to be excused from work, and they do not receive expressions of sympathy.

Disenfranchised grief is a growing issue spurred by higher percentages of divorced people; and the prevalence of AIDS means that large numbers of homosexuals experience losses in their relationships.

OTHER TYPES OF GRIEF

Deserving recognition are several specialized types of grief, which are discussed below: anticipatory grief, loss of a sibling, and loss of a companion animal.

cipatory Grief

ipatory grief occurs before the death of a loved one. We may go through
ie or all of the stages of grief, but that does not stop our going through them
i again when our loved one dies. Anticipatory grief may be experienced in that
iimbo when loved ones are not getting better but are not dying. "Forewarned is
not always forearmed. Experiencing anticipatory grief may or may not make the
grieving process easier or shorten it" (Kübler-Ross and Kessler 2005, 4).

When anticipation of loss may encompass several years because of a long-term
illness like multiple sclerosis (MS) or Alzheimer's disease, a person may experience
all five stages of grief before the loved one's death.

> In some cases, anticipatory grief may happen months or years before the loss.
> It is important for us to remember that this anticipatory grief stands alone
> from the grief we feel after a loss. For many, anticipatory grief is just a prelude
> to the painful process we face, a double grief that will ultimately bring heal-
> ing. (Kübler-Ross and Kessler 2005, 5)

Sibling Loss

When a brother or sister dies, surviving siblings may receive little support or even
recognition of their pain. Parents are so grief-stricken at the loss of a child that they
often find themselves unable to cope with the needs of their surviving children.
With family and friends concentrating on the parents' tragedy, the suffering of
siblings often goes unnoticed (Donnelly 1988).

Animal Loss

The relationship between animals and humans links us to the natural world and
bonds us to other living beings that can provide us with what we want from other
humans. Pets become a part of their owners' lives, and their loss is felt deeply; however, Western culture does not recognize the loss as worthy of grieving. "In general,
animals' roles are undervalued unless the animals are of direct use to people and
society. An example of this attitude is the great emphasis placed on dogs who assist
people who are blind, deaf, use wheelchairs, or have epilepsy" (Meyers 2002, 251).

The human-animal relationship is not a substitute for human companionship.
"The human-animal relationship stands on its own, possessing unique properties
that distinguish it from others. It is not more or less important than other relationships; it is simply different—worthy of affirmation, validation, and respect" (Meyers 2002, 252).

DEALING WITH GRIEF

Since grieving is a frequent aspect of the life experience, how can healthy individuals cope with the feelings that accompany grief? How can one reach closure?

Closure

The concept of closure was adopted from the medical profession to indicate the
healing or closing of a wound. However, grieving does not end abruptly or perma-
nently, as this term suggests.

Kübler-Ross and Kessler (2005) assert that there are two closures to grief: (1) the unrealistic conclusion after a loss, a quick wrap-up so that we can move on, and (2) doing things that help put the loss in perspective by reviewing what happened and why it happened.

> In grieving we mistakenly think we can finish everything, but grief is not a project with a beginning and an end. It is a reflection of a loss that never goes away. We simply learn to live with it, both in the foreground and in the background. Where grief fits in our lives is an individual *thing*, often based on how far we have come in integrating the loss. (Kübler-Ross and Kessler 2005, 158)

Terms like *reformulation* and *integration* seem more descriptive of the process than *resolution* or *recovery* or *closure* because loss produces permanent changes, and grieving has no definite end. The intent is not to revert to life before the loss but to learn to integrate a loss into a new social context and identity.

A model for grief integration is the R Process Model, formulated by Therese Rando (1983, 1988), which is useful for professionals and the bereaved. This model integrates much of the research and writing about grief phases or tasks:

- Recognizing and accepting the reality of the loss. Many individuals try to deny the loss. Common feelings during this phase are fear, panic, feeling overwhelmed. They may feel they are losing their minds.

- Reacting to, experiencing, and expressing the pain of separation. In this second phase the bereaved give up control and resign themselves to the feeling of chaos. Short-term avoidance and distraction are not necessarily maladaptive, that is, some avoid memories or immerse themselves in work, travel, or generally keeping busy. However, denying the feeling of pain, idealizing the dead, neglecting one's health, or using alcohol or drugs are not helpful.

- Reminiscing. Telling and retelling memories is a way of keeping loved ones alive. Telling or writing stories and sharing photographs is an important step in finding meaning for loss. Dreaming is also a way of working through an emotional loss; telling dreams to a friend or writing them down can provide insight.

- Relinquishing old attachments. While research indicates that bereaved individuals maintain a bond with the deceased, the challenge is to form new attachments and love other people.

- Readjusting and reinvesting. One must learn from his experiences and grief, recognize the interplay between life and death, and learn to live in an imperfect world. Through readjustment, we can emerge stronger through greater self-knowledge, empathy, and compassion toward others. (Hooyman and Kramer 2006, 43–50)

It is commonly said that time is a healer. In reality, time doesn't heal, but the process that occurs during time is what resolves grief. The healing process includes remembering and reorganizing. The bereaved must realize that it was the loved one's time to die, although it was sooner than wanted. As Kübler-Ross and Kessler (2005) note, the more that the bereaved's self-identity was connected to the loved one, the more difficult it is to make this adjustment. Acceptance takes time—usually years instead of weeks or months.

Summarizing recent research on grieving and intervention, Hooyman and Kramer (2006) conclude that grief is not a singular event to get over as quickly as possible. Instead, it is a complex process that entails making meaning of the grieving person's loss and new place in the world.

Even when a person has fully mourned, grief may recur on anniversaries of the death or on important shared occasions, or in seasons, weeks, or years that recall the relationship. Grief on these occasions may become muted as time passes.

The most common form of unresolved grief is absence of grief, when we defend ourselves from the painful feelings accompanying loss. We may appear to be healthy and recovered, but the emotions associated with grief have been repressed. In our society we celebrate the stoicism of heroes like Clint Eastwood and John Wayne. "Failure to mourn is the emotional equivalent of failing to care for a broken bone" (Volkan and Zintl 1993, 66).

Resilience

Hooyman and Kramer (2006, 66) define resilience: "[T]he behavioral patterns, functional competence, and cultural capacities that individuals, families, and communities use under adverse circumstances (in this case, loss) and the ability to make adversity (e.g., loss) into a catalyst for growth and development." In layman's language, resilience consists of all those personal and social characteristics that enable people to cope with and overcome loss so that they can move on with their lives.

Studies reveal certain personality characteristics common to those who are resilient in the face of serious losses. The ability to address a loss in a determined and optimistic way is followed by lower distress after bereavement. The degree to which a person has a purpose in life and establishes goals is associated with more positive outcomes following bereavement. Other reasons for resilience include strong religious beliefs and social support by family or community (Parkes 1986).

Hooyman and Kramer identify four elements of resilience:

1. Certain background characteristics, which include gender, age, race/ethnicity and culture, developmental phase of life, and family structure. These characteristics influence the ways that people integrate loss in their lives.
2. Adversity, including nature of the loss and prior losses.
3. Personal, family, social, cultural, and community resources of the grieving person.
4. Mental and physical well-being. (Hooyman and Kramer 2006, 66)

Spirituality

Spirituality is an element of personal capacities that affects the grieving process, helping individuals to deal with loss and death, life's meaning, and rituals. Spirituality—believing in a superior being—can be practiced with or without church affiliation. The lives of spiritual people are guided by principles that are part of their belief system.

Research supports this contention, although a death may cause people to question their beliefs—"Why did God allow this to happen?" Religion can assist in the grieving process by easing the grieving and by providing a support group through the church. In some cases, strict religious beliefs can stand in the way of grieving (Moody and Arcangel 2001).

The Griever's Story

Following the death of a loved one, the bereaved may tell the story of their loved one's illness or accident over and over before and after the funeral. That telling of the story is an important part of their coping with the shocking change in their lives, and it is part of the healing process. "You must get it out. Grief must be witnessed to be healed. Grief shared is grief abated" (Kübler-Ross and Kessler 2005, 63).

Support and bereavement groups allow the bereaved to associate with others who have experienced loss, and they provide a forum for telling the story of loss—reinforcing the fact that their loss matters. Telling the story over time may provide feedback and perhaps fill in details, providing missing pieces to the puzzle or providing insight.

When someone is telling their story over and over, they are trying to figure something out. In such cases, ask questions or give your reaction to help the person to find the missing part that is puzzling them.

Tears

Tears are a way of relieving sadness.

The worst thing you can do is to stop short of really letting it out. Uncried tears have a way of filling the well of sadness even more deeply. If you have a half hour of crying to do, don't stop at 20 minutes. Let yourself cry it all out. It will stop on its own. If you cry till your last tear, you will feel released (Kübler-Ross and Kessler 2005, 43).

Roberts writes about her recovery following the death of her husband:

> The healing will never happen quickly enough. Your pain will never stop soon enough. Your loss will always remain with you, as will your special memories. Your life will be changed forever by death. But, in spite of your loss, there will be a new depth and richness about you. And it will come one day at a time, one step at a time. (Roberts 2002, 94–95)

HELPING THE BEREAVED

For the most disturbed bereaved individuals, professional support may be needed. Grief facilitators can ease a person's grief by educating them and helping them work through their thoughts and feelings.

When encountering a mourner, consider the circumstance. Immediately after a loss, mourners' emotions are raw, and they often are just trying to make it through the day. It is best not to walk up and ask about their loss. Greet any bereaved person as you normally would, and let that person determine the direction of the conversation.

Immediately after a loss, survivors usually need physical and emotional care. They need chauffeuring of relatives to the airport, lawn mowing, caring for pets, or sitting with the mourner.

Sympathizers are usually well-intentioned, but they may say things that are offensive or hurtful. Communication problems are less likely to occur when sympathy is offered at the appropriate place and time. Sensitivity is the key for interacting with the bereaved. Genuine sympathy requires entering the other person's world without judging or advising, but closure statements incorporate all three. Moody and Arcangel (2001) suggest sending a card or letter to express sympathy and continuing to stay in touch by phone or e-mail.

Some people are naïve or insensitive about loss. Saying, "Don't grieve; I can't bear it" shows an intention to avoid their own discomfort. Statements like, "You're young and can marry again," "But you have other children," and "Well, just go get another dog" give the distinct impression that the lost ones are dispensable (Moody and Arcangel 2001).

Clichés like "She isn't suffering any more," "Be happy you had him that long," "Be happy she is with God Now," or "You'll heal in time," demean the loss and can produce shame. They suggest, "You're wrong to grieve." Moody and Arcangel (201) explain that sympathizers tend to say what *they* need to hear.

Expressions such as, "You need to take it easy," "You need to stop working so hard," or "You must exercise" are projections—the speakers are expressing their own needs. Instead, a person might more correctly say, "I need for you to take it easy," "I wish you would stop working so hard," or "I think you should exercise more."

Staudacher (1987) suggests the following ways to help a grieving person:

- Accept the bereaved as the person is. Statements like these help:
  - Don't worry if you cry in front of me. It's hard not to cry when you feel so sad.
  - It's natural to cry, and I hope you do not feel embarrassed or sorry doing it.
- Listen to these persons. They need to retell the story of the relationship and the loved one's final weeks or months and to express their feelings.
- Be patient. People grieve at their own pace. Don't expect rapid recovery.
- Provide practical help. For example, deliver meals, babysit, mow the lawn or work in the garden, feed the pets, bring fresh flowers, write notes expressing love and encouragement, accompany the survivor(s) to the cemetery, house sit, make phone calls, shop for groceries, give the survivor(s) reading on grief, do their laundry, wash their car.
- Provide social support by being sensitive to the survivors' reluctance to go out in public and offering to accompany them in public.

Following the break of a relationship, the work of mourning includes a review of the relationship—what it meant and what was lost. Elements of the relationship are replayed in daydreams, memories, and dreams. The purpose of the review is to find a way to reach acceptance of the way things were (Volkan and Zintl 1993, 27).

In recent years a number of domains have been created by and for the bereaved. Survivors can create online memorials for their loved ones at sites like Link for Lights, Angel Babies, A Place to Remember, and GriefNet that provide free online memorials, chat rooms, e-mail support, directories, and other services.

Additional recommended print and online sources are found below.

SUMMARY

Mourning is the external part of loss—the actions we take, the rituals, and the customs. *Grief* refers to the feelings that accompany a loss. Feelings associated with grief are described, along with factors that influence the depth of grieving. Cultural differences in grieving behavior patterns reflect the culture's view of what is healthy and appropriate loss. Research indicates that grief does not proceed through fixed tasks.

Every society establishes norms and rules for grieving. These rules govern what losses one should grieve, how one grieves them, who should grieve the loss, and to whom others should respond with sympathy. Individuals in socially unsanctioned relationships may be excluded from caregiving of the dying and attendance at rituals, and disenfranchised grief precludes social support in which the mourner can exercise his right to mourn.

Resilience consists of all those personal and social characteristics that enable people to cope with and overcome loss so that they can move on with their lives. Included are such personal characteristics as gender, age, race/ethnicity and culture, developmental phase of life, and family structure. Other factors influencing resilience are nature of the loss and prior losses; personal, family, social, cultural, and community resources; and mental and physical well-being.

When assisting a mourner, it is very important to consider the circumstance and provide any physical and emotional care that might be needed. Suggestions are given for librarians, teachers, mental health professionals, and parents to establish rapport in helping bereaved individuals. Recommended resources on bereavement follow.

RECOMMENDED RESOURCES

Becvar, Dorothy Stroh. **In the Presence of Grief: Helping Family Members Resolve Death, Dying, and Bereavement Issues.** New York: Guilford, 2003. 284p. $30.00pa. ISBN 1-57230-937-7; 978-1-57230-937-1.

> A marital and family therapist and clinical social worker, Becvar offers her insights on dealing with the bereaved, drawing on illustrations from her experience with clients. Becvar states that healing after a loss is an ongoing process with grief a constant companion. For those assisting the bereaved, this book is a guide to help the bereaved navigate the grieving process. Recommended for undergraduate and graduate students, as well as professionals who work with bereaved individuals.

Boss, Pauline. **Ambiguous Loss: Learning to Live with Unresolved Grief.** Cambridge, MA: Harvard University Press, 2000. 176p. $21.00pa. ISBN 0-674-00381-0; 978-0-674-00381-1.

> Presents what Boss (University of Minnesota and family therapist) has learned from many years of treating individuals and families suffering from uncertain or incomplete loss, such as the gradual loss of a family member to Alzheimer's disease, immigration, adoption, chronic illness, or a family whose son is reported missing in action. Boss suggests strategies for coping with the pain to help persons come to terms with their grief. Case stories offer narratives of people who learned to cope with various types of ambiguous loss. "A compassionate exploration of the effects of ambiguous loss and how those experiencing it handle this most devastating of losses" (*Kirkus Reviews* Mar. 15, 1999).

Braestrup, Kate. **Here If You Need Me: A True Story.** New York: Little, Brown, 2007. E-book. $13.99. ISBN 0-316-06630-3; 978-0-316-06630-3.

> After the author's husband was killed in a car accident, Braestrup decided to follow her husband's dream to enter the ministry. Upon completion of divinity school, she became a chaplain for the Maine Wildlife and Game Service, giving comfort to people whose loved ones were missing, and to the staff who had to deal with tragedies. "Braestrup's strength is evident throughout the memoir, which is by turns funny, tender, and frightening, yet always reinforced by the undercurrent of great love. *Here If You Need Me* is recommended for public libraries" (*Library Journal* April 15, 2007).

Callanan, Maggie, and Patricia Kelley. **Final Gifts: Understanding the Special Awareness, Needs, and Communications of the Dying.** New York: Bantam Books, 1992 (reissued 1997). 256p. $17.00pa. ISBN: 978-0-553-37876-4; 0-553-37876-7.

> Authored by two nurses with vast experience in end-of-life care, *Final Gifts* describes the mental and emotional state of persons experiencing Near Death Awareness—the knowledge that they are near death and have needs for a peaceful death. The dying process is described. Case studies illuminate the understanding and communication skills needed by caregivers and family members to assist both the dying and survivors. Advice for helping the dying is provided for caregivers, family, and friends. Recommended for all adults encountering elderly or slowly dying individuals.

Canfield, Jack, and Mark Victor Hansen. **Chicken Soup for the Grieving Soul: Stories about Life, Death and Overcoming the Loss of a Loved One.** Chicken Soup for the Soul Series. Deerfield Beach, FL: Health Communications, 2003. 272p. $14.95pa. ISBN 1-55874-902-0; 978-1-55874-902-3.

> A collection of short essays and some poetry relating personal stories of loss, including spouses, children, and parents. The pieces are short (3–5 pages), providing opportunities for a quick, quiet read with reflection. The stories are well written and poignant, but the titles often do not suggest the topic addressed. There is no index, but this book is recommended for young adults and adults who have recently experienced loss of a loved one.

Carter, Abigail. **The Alchemy of Loss: A Young Widow's Transformation.** Deerfield Beach, FL: Health Communications, 2008. 304p. $24.95. ISBN 0-7573-0790-6; 978-0-7573-0790-4.

> Carter's husband was killed in the World Trade Center on September 11, 2001. She recalls her agonizing grief and her coping with two small children. She likens her grieving stages to the three stages of an alchemist's process to turn lead into gold—the blackening (disorientation), whitening (reawakening), and reddening (enlightenment). She eventually is able to assess her situation and begins a new life in Seattle. "Readers coping with their own losses will appreciate Carter's candor as she travels beyond some well-trod territory" (*Booklist* Sept. 1, 2008).

Church, Forrest. **Love and Death: My Journey through the Valley of the Shadow.** Boston: Beacon Press, 2008. 165p. $22.00. ISBN 0-8070-7293-1; 978-0-8070-7293-6.

> Diagnosed with terminal cancer, this pastor and author of several books on history and spiritual guidance revisits in his last book several of his sermons to explore the meaning of life and love. He draws upon his vast experience counseling congregants who have lost loved ones, adding his own thoughts and feelings as he faces

imminent death. "Church speaks directly to the heart with a message of certain solace to virtually anyone facing the loss of a loved one" (*Booklist* Sept. 1, 2008).

Davenport, Donna S. **Singing Mother Home: A Psychologist's Journey through Anticipatory Grief.** Denton, TX: University of North Texas Press, 2003. 184p. $26.95. ISBN 1-57441-162-4; 978-1-57441-162-1.

A professor of counseling psychology (Texas A&M University) offers an account of her experiences coping with the loss of her mother. Davenport reviews her experience, applying theories of anticipatory grief and grieving, and offers the reader insight into the process. The concluding chapters describe psychological approaches to grief and recommend further reading.

Dennis, Dixie. **Living, Dying, Grieving.** Sudbury, MA: Jones & Bartlett, 2008. 227p. $69.95pa. ISBN 0-7637-4326-7.

This textbook includes such topics as aging, end-of-life planning, and coping with dying, death, and bereavement, and does so from the perspective of adults, children, and religious and cultural perspectives. Dennis, an administrator at Austin Peay State University, presents such controversial issues as physician-assisted suicide, when to allow a person to die, and deaths caused by risky behavior or violence. Since it is to be used with mature students, the text includes critical thinking questions, class activities, a glossary, and additional related print and nonprint resources. Recommended for advanced secondary and college students. (Review Source: *Reference & Research Book News* May 1, 2009).

DeSpelder, Lynne Ann, and Albert Lee Strickland. **The Last Dance: Encountering Death and Dying.** 8th ed. New York: McGraw-Hill Professional Publishing, 2009. 672p. $94.25. ISBN 0-07-340546-9; 978-0-07-340546-9.

This eighth edition of a standard college-level textbook is an interdisciplinary introduction to death, dying, and bereavement. Included are discussions of ethical principles, financial planning, and caregiver-patient relationships. Grounded in theory and research, this book also provides practical application for students. (Review Source: *Reference & Research Book News* Aug. 1, 2009.)

DeVita-Raeburn, Elizabeth. **The Empty Room: Surviving the Loss of a Brother or Sister at Any Age.** New York: Scribner, 2004. 240p. $14.00pa. ISBN-10: 0-7432-0152-3; ISBN-13: 978-0-7432-0152-0.

One morning when she is 6, DeVita-Raeburn wakes up, and her older brother Ted is gone. Her parents explain that he went to the hospital for "a while," which turns out to be eight years in a plastic bubble. He dies of a rare autoimmune disease at age 17. The author recalls her life with Ted, while exploring the impact of a sister's or brother's death on their siblings. DeVita-Raeburn draws on interviews of more than two hundred survivors of sibling loss to present and understand the lifelong impact of a sibling's death and strategies for healing and moving ahead in life. A dramatic story recommended for young adults and adults.

Doka, Kenneth J., ed. **Disenfranchised Grief: New Directions, Challenges, and Strategies for Practice.** Champaign, IL: Research Press, 2004. 470p. $29.95pa. ISBN 0-87822-427-0; 978-0-87822-427-2.

Doka (gerontology, College of New Rochelle, NY) has assembled essays by 26 experts in this field to provide theoretical, empirical, clinical, and educational discussions of disenfranchised grief for mental health professionals, students, and a sophisticated public. Chapters discuss how many types of loss can be addressed via grief therapy, support groups, and ritual.

Doka, Kenneth J., ed. **Living with Grief: Loss in Later Life.** Living with Grief Series. Washington, DC: Hospice Foundation of America, 2002. 353p. $24.95. ISBN 1-893349-03-9.

Compiled following the September 11, 2001, attacks, this book by Hospice Foundation of America concerns a number of issues related to loss, including growing old and facing death, issues related to hospice care, spiritual care as death approaches, effects of grief on a survivor's health, loss of a significant other, and suicide in older people. Chapters are written by authorities in their fields.

Doka, Kenneth J., and Amy Tucci, eds. **Living with Grief: Before and after the Death.** Living with Grief Series. Washington, DC: Hospice Foundation of America, 2007. 366p. $24.95pa. ISBN 1-893349-08-X; 978-1-893349-08-7.

Explores through articles by professionals in the counseling field such topics as anticipatory grief and mourning, disenfranchised grief, parental bereavement, adult loss of a parent, working with children, self-help, and family counseling. Also included are several essays by grieving individuals, implications for practice, and self-care for the professional. "This book will be useful primarily to professionals, but it is accessible to interested lay readers as well; it nicely complements other books in the series and J. William Worden's *Grief Counseling and Grief Therapy: A Handbook for the Mental Health Practitioner*" (*Library Journal* May 1, 2007).

Dornstein, Ken. **The Boy Who Fell Out of the Sky: A True Story.** New York: Knopf Doubleday, 2007. 352p. $13.95pa. ISBN 0-375-70769-7; 978-0-375-70769-8.

The author recounts his grieving following the death of his older brother, killed along with all on board Pan Am flight 103, when a terrorist's bomb downed the plane near Lockerbie, Scotland, in December 1988. Although six years apart in age, the two brothers were very close, and Dornstein, age 19 when his brother died, recalls in detail his uncovering his brother's erratic life and failed attempt to become a successful author. This account will help grieving teens and adults to understand better the emotional turmoil of grief. "The healing process for Dornstein, as he alternately approaches and retreats from this self-assigned task, is laid out with dogged thoroughness. His journey in moving beyond an intractable knot of bereavement is depicted with blunt yet graceful sensitivity" (*School Library Journal* July 1, 2006).

Edelman, Hope. **Motherless Daughters: The Legacy of Loss.** Cambridge, MA: Da Capo Press, 2006. 432p. $15.95pa. ISBN 0-7382-1026-9; 978-0-7382-1026-1.

Edelman's mother died when she was 17. First published a decade ago, this book builds on interviews with hundreds of mother-loss survivors, and the author reflects on her personal experience to explore the ways that losing a mother can affect almost every aspect of a woman's life. "Her insights on the psychological development of motherless daughters, their relationships with family members and with others, and their life choices should be very useful to women who have experienced a similar loss. Recommended for popular psychology collections" (*Library Journal* Aug. 1, 1995).

Ellis, Thomas M. **This Thing Called Grief: New Understandings of Loss.** Minneapolis, MN: Syren Book Company, 2006. 111p. $14.95pa. ISBN 0-929636-64-3; 978-0-929636-64-1.

Ellis explains that grief and pain have the potential to transform a person's life in a healing way. A marriage and family therapist, Ellis uses many stories of loss from his therapy practice to illustrate grieving, and shows how a bereaved person can learn from the experience of loss and work toward a healing transition. "His [Ellis's] short, excellent, and readable book—perfect for someone experiencing grief and sadness—is recommended for all libraries" (*Library Journal* July 1, 2006).

Fanslow-Brunjes, Cathleen. **Using the Power of Hope to Cope with Dying: The Four Stages of Hope.** Fresno, CA: Quill Driver Books, 2008. 140p. $25.00. ISBN 1-884956-80-7; 978-1-884956-80-5.

An authority in the care of the dying and their families, Fanslow-Brunjes defines and explains her four-stage process for engendering hope when death is inevitable. Written for both the dying and those who support them, the reader is guided in the use of the power of hope to face the inevitable. The author has worked with the dying for more than 40 years and claims that more than 40,000 dying individuals have been helped with this system.

Hooyman, Nancy R., and Betty J. Kramer. **Living Through Loss: Interventions Across the Life Span.** New York: Columbia University Press, 2006. 452p. $90.00; $29.50pa. ISBN 978-0-231-12246-7; 978-0-231-12247-4 pa.

A research-based report of loss and grieving by two social work researchers and teachers who have done extensive work in this area. Different types of losses are defined along with a discussion of the grieving process. Clinical and research-based models to explain grieving are discussed. Grieving and loss at several stages in life are explained with suggested intervention techniques. A current, scholarly source for students and professionals in the social work and psychology fields.

James, John W., and Russell Friedman. **The Grief Recovery Handbook; The Action Program for Moving Beyond Death, Divorce, and Other Losses.** 20th Anniversary Expanded Edition. New York: HarperCollins, 2009. 208p. $16.99. ISBN 0-06-095273-3; 0-06-019279-8

James founded the Grief Recovery Institute more than 30 years ago, an agency that offers grief counseling and support in the United States and Canada. First published in 1988, this edition has been revised and updated to provide an easily understood guide for grief recovery. "A practical guide to coping with the grief of death or divorce, complemented by excellent exercises for finding peace and regaining energy. Highly recommended for public library and other self-help collections" (*Library Journal* March 2, 2009).

Kasher, Asa, ed. **Dying and Death: Inter-Disciplinary Perspectives.** Kenilworth, NY: Rodopi, 2007. 232p. $64.00 pa. ISBN 90-420-2245-0; 978-90-420-2245-4.

Professor of professional ethics and philosophy of practice at Tel Aviv University, Kasher has compiled 15 essays on death and dying by multidisciplinary authors from around the world. Recommended for scholars and professionals.

Keeley, Maureen P., and Julie M. Yingling. **Final Conversations: Helping the Living and the Dying Talk to Each Other.** Acton, MA: VanderWyk & Burnham, 2007. 234p. $24.95. ISBN 1-889242-30-6; 978-1-889242-30-9.

Last interactions with a dying loved one leave lifelong memories. The authors are communication experts who combine the stories of contributors with their own advice. "The directness is refreshing, especially in the emphasis on the strong relationship a final conversation both represents and creates. Recommended for all public libraries" (*Library Journal* Mar. 15, 2007).

Koman, Aleta. **How to Mend a Broken Heart: Letting Go and Moving On.** New York: McGraw-Hill Trade, Contemporary Books, 1997. 240p. $19.95. ISBN 0-8092-3172-7; 978-0-8092-3172-0.

Koman, a therapist and teacher, presents a detailed, step-by-step plan for anyone dealing with loss. Not confined to death of a loved one, the book addresses such topics as loss of a job, divorce, separation, breakup, and end of a friendship. "Recommended for public libraries and counseling centers" (*Library Journal* May 15, 1997).

Kübler-Ross, Elisabeth. **On Death and Dying: What the Dying Have to Teach Doctors, Nurses, Clergy and Their Own Families.** New York: Routledge, 2008. 264p. $37.95pa. ISBN 0-415-46399-8; 978-0-415-46399-7.

The five stages of grief (denial, anger, bargaining, depression, and acceptance) were formulated by Kübler-Ross 40 years ago when she worked with dying patients at the University of Chicago. Most people facing death were observed to pass through these stages. Over time, the stages have become part of our understanding of loss of any kind. This classic text is reissued with a new introduction that reviews its influence on thought and practice in care for the dying. It is recommended for those whose work brings them into contact with the dying and for any adult wishing to know how to cope with a significant loss.

Kübler-Ross, Elisabeth, and Kessler, David. **Life Lessons: Two Experts on Death and Dying Teach Us about the Mysteries of Life and Living.** New York: Scribner/Touchstone, 2000. 224p. $15.00pa. ISBN 0-684-87074-6; 0-684-87075-4.

Kübler-Ross, the author of many books on death and dying, joins with Kessler, an end-of-life expert, to outline important lessons one should learn in a lifetime. Among the 14 lessons are relationships, loss, guilt, fear, anger, patience, forgiveness, and happiness. This read would be inspirational to a grieving adult and is recommended for young adults as well as adults.

Kübler-Ross, Elisabeth, and David Kessler. 2005. **On Grief and Grieving: Finding the Meaning of Grief through the Five Stages of Loss.** New York: Simon & Schuster, 2005. 256p. $25.00; $15.00pa, e-book. ISBN-10: 0743266293; ISBN-13: 9780743266291.

Kübler-Ross, an authority on death and dying, died in 2004, leaving us this book coauthored by Kessler, an expert on hospice and palliative care. The Kübler-Ross five-stage model of dying is applied to the grieving process with a detailed discussion of the deep, sometimes conflicting emotions that accompany loss of a loved one. The impact of anniversaries, health, finances, and age are among other aspects explored, along with a chapter on specific circumstances for grief—children, multiple losses, disasters, suicide, Alzheimer's disease, and sudden death. An excellent overview of grieving, applicable to many types of loss.

Leick, Nini, and Marianne Davidsen-Nielsen. David L. Stoner, trans. **Healing Pain: Attachment, Loss, and Grief Therapy.** New York: Routledge, 1991. 192p. $37.50. ISBN 0-415-04795-1; 978-0-415-04795-1.

Grief may be triggered by many situations besides the death of a loved one, for example, divorce, severe illness, physical injury, or the birth of a handicapped child. The authors investigate why the process of grief can be a dramatic turning point. It describes the treatment methods developed by the authors and gives practical advice on how to work with normal grief in individual or group settings. "This moving book will be of great value not only to professionals such as therapists, physicians, nurses, and social workers, but also to those encountering grief in themselves or others; indeed, anyone who has hesitated or felt unsure in approaching a friend or colleague who has recently experienced a loss would benefit from reading this excellent book" (*Choice* Nov. 1, 1991).

Levy, Alexander. **Orphaned Adult: Understanding and Coping with Grief and Change after the Death of Our Parents.** Diane Publishing, 1999. 190p. $24.00. ISBN 0-7567-5605-7; 978-0-7567-5605-5.

Losing a parent after we have become adults is expected but usually more difficult than we imagined it would be. This book validates the disorienting emotions that can accompany the death of parents and guides the reader through the transition from the sudden onset of sorrow to subtle changes in identity, new friendship patterns, shifts of roles within the surviving family, and recognition of one's own mortality. "Incorporating his own personal experience with the accounts of others who have lost their parents, psychologist Levy examines this profound life-changing event with compassion and understanding. . . . This wise and caring book is recommended for all collections" (*Library Journal* Sept. 15, 1999).

McCabe, Marilyn. **The Paradox of Loss: Toward a Relational Theory of Grief.** Santa Barbara, CA: Praeger, 2003. 240p. $43.48. ISBN 0-275-97986-5; 978-0-275-97986-7.

Explains a theory of grief and loss designed to represent the realities not addressed in conventional views of grief. This relational theory embraces the reality that the lost one remains with the grieving individual, and a major aspect of grieving is the reintegration of our lives around the loss. The experience proceeds as part of the griever's dynamic relationship with the lost loved one and others as the griever reconstitutes life in her/his new reality. Useful to scholars and practitioners whose work brings them in touch with death and grieving.

Mallon, Brenda. **Dying, Death, and Grief: Working with Adult Bereavement.** London: Sage, 2008. 208p. $42.95. ISBN 978-1-4129-3415-2; 131-4129-3415-X.

Links loss, grief, and bereavement to counseling skills, providing the theoretical background along with case studies, exercises, and personal accounts of loss. Written for anyone who provides support to adults following bereavement, including professionals and volunteers in hospitals, nursing homes, and hospices. "Highly recommended. Upper-division undergraduates and above" (*Choice* Aug.1, 2009).

Miller, Sally Downham. **Mourning and Dancing: A Memoir of Grief and Recovery.** Deerfield Beach, FL: Health Communications, 1999. 215p. $10.95. ISBN 1-55874-671-4.

Miller, now an educator, consultant, and speaker in the area of grief and loss, describes the sudden death of her first husband, who died of cancer at the age of 24. A widow with two small children, she recalls the 30 years since that loss, sharing her feelings about learning how to live with pain, to incorporate loss into our lives, to heal, and to regain hope. It is an emotional and inspirational story of value to all who have lost a dear one unexpectedly.

Moody, Raymond A., Jr., and Dianne Arcangel. **Life after Loss: Conquering Grief and Finding Hope.** New York: HarperSanFrancisco, 2001. 228p. $14.95pa. ISBN 0-06-251729-5; 0-06-251730-9pa.

Written for those experiencing grief, this is an authoritative, easily readable discussion of the stress and emotions of grief with suggestions for giving and receiving sympathy. Both functional and dysfunctional grief responses are described as well as suggestions for coping and adjusting to loss. The book concludes with an uplifting chapter, "We Will See Them Again." Moody is an M.D. and author of *Life after Life;* Arcangel is formerly a hospice chaplain and director of the Elisabeth Kübler-Ross Center of Houston.

Parkes, Colin Murray. **Bereavement: Studies of Grief in Adult Life.** 3d ed. New York: Routledge, 2001. 288p. $21.95pa. ISBN 1-58391-127-8; 978-1-58391-127-3.

> First published in 1972, this updated third edition examines the emotions and symptoms that people experience after a loss. The book is useful to those who lack a specialist's knowledge of psychology, although scientific and technical data are included. For those doctors, clergy, lawyers, nurses, teachers, mental health professionals, librarians, and others whose work brings them into the lives of the bereaved, the book also can be recommended to bereaved people who want to understand their grief. "Relying on psychodynamic, behavioral, and social systems models for understanding grief, Parkes does a fine job in synthesizing complex theoretical and conceptual frameworks without becoming too general or diffuse" (*Choice* June 1, 1988).

Rufus, Anneli. **The Farewell Chronicles: On How We Really Respond to Death.** Cambridge, MA: Da Capo Press, 2005. 320p. $14.95pa. ISBN 1-56924-381-6; 978-1-56924-381-7. Out of print.

> Revisiting the deaths of many people she has known, journalist and author Rufus describes her response to death in personal scenarios. "With wry humor and brutal candor couched in gorgeous prose, Rufus depicts perverse responses to death as well as the more conventional trappings and expressions of grief. This wise and forthright book is recommended for large public and university libraries" (*Library Journal* July 1, 2005).

Sanders, Catherine M. **Surviving Grief…and Learning to Live Again.** Hoboken, NJ: Wiley, 1992. 240p. $29.95pa. ISBN 0-471-53471-4; 978-0-471-53471-6.

> Dr. Sanders, a therapist and researcher specializing in bereavement issues, draws directly from her own experiences and those of her clients and her research to help the reader to understand that the feelings associated with loss are part of a natural process of readjustment and renewal. She delves deeply into the different experiences of grief, and talks about what it means to lose a mate, a parent, or a child. "Sanders details the emotions that accompany each phase and offers practical suggestions for dealing with them. The author's straightforward approach and skillful blend of anecdotes, pragmatism, and philosophy make for an exceptionally readable and reassuring book" (*Library Journal* June 15, 1992).

Shaw, Eva. **What to Do When a Loved One Dies: A Practical and Compassionate Guide to Dealing with Death on Life's Terms.** 2nd ed. Carlsbad, CA: Writeriffic, 2003. 408p. $28.95; $24.95pa. ISBN 0-97057583-1.

> A comprehensive source for understanding the emotions of grieving and the practical tasks to accomplish when a loved one dies. Included are immediate actions to take, making arrangements after the death, costs, wills, hospice, and grief, along with discussions of suicide, stillbirth, and AIDS. There are also sections on "Where to Get Help" that recommend self-help books, support groups, or organizations that can be of assistance. The practical information is detailed, and suggestions of additional resources make this a very useful source book for families.

Sheehy, Gail. **Passages in Caregiving: Turning Chaos into Confidence.** New York: HarperCollins, William Morrow, 2010. 396p. $27.99. ISBN 978-0-06-166120-4.

> The noted author of *Passages, New Passages,* and 13 other books, describes her experience caring for her husband, Clay Felker. Much more than a memoir, this artfully

written personal account is also a manual for caregivers. Sheehy identifies eight stages of caregiving and provides advice for navigating each stage. Included is a list of hotlines, organizations, and palliative care programs for caregivers.

Sheeler, Jim. **Final Salute: A Story of Unfinished Lives.** New York: Penguin, 2008. 280p. $25.95. ISBN 978-1-59420-165-3.

Pulitzer Prize-winning journalist Jim Sheeler conveys the stories of soldiers killed in Iraq and the grieving families left behind. Sheeler shadows Marine Major Steve Beck for two years and other service personnel assigned the responsibility of notifying next of kin when a soldier has fallen. Although he received no training for his role, Beck's efforts to assist grieving families are heroic.

Staudacher, Carol. **Beyond Grief: A Guide for Recovering from the Death of a Loved One.** Oakland, CA: New Harbinger, 1987. 244p. $10.95. ISBN 0-934986-43-6.

The author, a grief consultant and author of several books on grieving, presents a guide for anyone surviving the death of a loved one. Included are chapters on loss of a spouse, parent, or child, and loss of a loved one through accidental death, suicide, and murder. Written for both the bereaved and the helping professional, it combines personal stories with explicit suggestions for recovery.

Valentine, Christine. **Bereavement Narratives: Continuing Bonds in the 21st Century.** New York: Routledge, 2008. 198p. $45.95. ISBN 0-415-45730-0; 978-0-415-45730-9.

Based on a study of 25 cases of bereavement, the meanings that bereaved people gave to their experiences of losing a loved one are examined with an analysis of what those experiences reveal about societal values. Close attention is paid to the dying person's final moments and the reactions of loved ones. The resulting conclusions are especially beneficial to professionals working with grieving relatives.

Van Praagh, James. **Healing Grief: Reclaiming Life after Any Loss.** Collingdale, PA: Diane Publishing, 2000. 286p. $24.00. ISBN 0-7567-5920-X; 978-0-7567-5920-9.

The author discusses loss broadly to include loss of a loved one, divorce, coping with a terminal illness, midlife problems, losing a home or job, or aging. Van Praagh explains how the devastating sorrow of a loss can be transformed into opportunities for growth and warns against trying to conform our grief to the expectations of others. He offers guidance through each step of the grieving process. "Through his readings with various clients, death is demystified, grief is shown to be a natural response to death, healing comes with the realization that one day we'll be together again with our loved ones, and love is the only ageless power in the cosmos.... This book goes to great lengths to examine healthy and destructive ways of handling grief as well as how to discuss the subject of death with children" (*Library Journal* May 15, 2001).

Walsh, Froma, and Monica McGoldrick. **Living Beyond Loss: Death in the Family.** 2nd ed. New York: Norton, 2004. 480p. $29.95pa. ISBN 0-393-70438-6; 978-0-393-70438-9.

Chapters by leading authorities reveal how the family response to loss affects all members and their relationships across the life cycle. An update of the 1991 edition, new chapters address such topics as spirituality, gender issues, suicide and other traumatic deaths, and unacknowledged losses. Provides readers guidelines for working with loss and end-of-life dilemmas, the immediate aftermath of traumatic loss, and long-term complications.

Welshons, John E. **Awakening from Grief: Finding the Way Back to Joy.** Little Falls, NJ: Open Heart Seminars, 2000. $14.95pa. ISBN 1-928732-57-7; 978-1-928732-57-0.

Welshons, a counselor and teacher, asserts that our society avoids grief, resulting in detraction from our ability to embrace life's ups and downs. By embracing tragedy and disappointment, we can lay the foundation for growth and insight. Topics include how to deal with aging and dying parents; how to heal from the loss of a child, spouse, or friend; and how to heal a relationship. "Welshons, a student of Elisabeth Kubler-Ross, previously self-published this title and sold 17,000 copies; his clear, direct style will hook readers. Highly recommended for all libraries" (*Library Journal* July 1, 2003).

Wickersham, Joan. **The Suicide Index: Putting My Father's Death in Order.** Boston: Houghton Mifflin Harcourt, 2009. 336p. $14.95pa. ISBN 0-15-603380-1; 978-0-15-603380-0.

One winter morning in 1991, Joan Wickersham's father shot himself in the head. As she follows her father's suicide chronologically from his death through a passage of 15 years, she traces family history using an index format. "Wickersham's memoir unravels the twisted branches of family ties in the aftermath of her father's suicide as she attempts to answer the question, 'Why did he do it?' Certainly no book, as she herself admits, could answer a question at once so metaphysical and so very personal, but Wickersham's effort is worth the read" (*Library Journal* Apr. 1, 2008).

Worden, J. William. **Grief Counseling and Grief Therapy: A Handbook for the Mental Health Practitioner.** 4th ed. New York: Springer, 2008. 328p. $45.00. ISBN 0-8261-0120-8; 978-0-8261-0120-4.

The author is a fellow of the American Psychological Association and holds academic appointments at the Harvard Medical School and at the Rosemead Graduate School of Psychology in California. This handbook has become a standard for grief therapy, and this update presents Worden's most recent thinking on bereavement drawn from extensive research, clinical work, and the new literature in the field.

SOURCES CONSULTED

Archer, John. 1999. *The nature of grief: The evolution and psychology of reactions to loss.* London and New York: Routledge.

Doka, Kenneth J., ed. 2002. *Disenfranchised grief: New directions, challenges, and strategies for practice.* Champaign, IL: Research Press.

Donnelly, Katherine Fair. 2000. *Recovering from the loss of a sibling: When a brother or sister dies.* New York: Dodd, Mead, 1988; iUniverse, 2000.

Hooyman, Nancy R., and Betty J. Kramer. 2006. *Living through loss: Interventions across the life span.* New York: Columbia University Press.

James, John W., and Russell Friedman. 2009. *The grief recovery handbook: The action program for moving beyond death, divorce, and other losses.* 20th Anniversary Expanded Edition. New York: HarperCollins.

Kavanaugh, R. E. 1972. *Facing death.* Baltimore: Penguin Books.

Kübler-Ross, Elisabeth. 1969. *On death and dying.* New York: Macmillan.

Kübler-Ross, Elisabeth. 1981. *Living with death and dying.* New York: Macmillan.

Kübler-Ross, Elisabeth, and David Kessler. 2000. *Life lessons: Two experts on death and dying teach us about the mysteries of life and living.* New York: Scribner/Touchstone.

Kübler-Ross, Elisabeth, and David Kessler. 2005. *On grief and grieving; Finding the meaning of grief through the five stages of loss.* New York: Simon & Schuster.

Leming, Michael R., and George E. Dickinson. 2002. *Understanding dying, death, and bereavement.* 6th ed. Belmont, CA: Thomson Wadsworth.

Lewis, C. S. 1961. *A grief observed.* London: Faber and Faber.

Meyers, Barbara. 2002. Disenfranchised grief and the loss of an animal companion. In *Disenfranchised grief: New directions, challenges, and strategies for practice,* ed. Kenneth J. Doka, 251–64. Champaign, IL: Research Press.

Moody, Raymond A., Jr., and Dianne Arcangel. 2001. *Life after loss: Conquering grief and finding hope.* New York: HarperSanFrancisco.

Parkes, C. M. 1972. *Bereavement: Studies of grief in adult life.* New York: Tavistock.

Parkes, C. M. 1986. *Bereavement: Studies of grief in adult life.* 2nd ed. New York: Tavistock.

Rando, Theresa A. 1983. "An investigation of grief and adaptation in parents whose children have died from cancer." *Journal of Pediatric Psychology* 8: 3–20.

Rando, Theresa A. 1988. *Grieving: How to go on living when someone you love dies.* Lexington, MA: Lexington Books.

Roberts, Barbara K. 2002. *Death without denial, grief without apology: A guide for facing death and loss.* Troutdale, OR: NewSage Press.

Sanders, Catherine M. 1989. *Grief, the mourning after: Dealing with adult bereavement.* New York: Wiley.

Shear, Katherine. 2003. Medical treatment may reduce the pain of grief. In *Death and dying,* ed. James Haley, 104–12. Opposing Viewpoints Series. San Diego: Greenhaven Press.

Staudacher, Carol. 1987. *Beyond grief: A guide for recovering from the death of a loved one.* Oakland, CA: New Harbinger Publications.

Volkan, Vamik, and Elizabeth Zintl. 1993. *Life after loss: The lessons of grief.* New York: Scribner's.

Worden, J. William. 1991. *Grief counseling and grief therapy: A handbook for the mental health practitioner.* New York: Springer.

Wortman, Camille B., and Roxanne Cohen Silver. 1990. Successful mastery of bereavement and widowhood: A life-course perspective. In *Successful aging: Perspectives from the behavioral sciences,* ed. Paul B. Baltes and Margret M. Baltes, 225–37. Cambridge: Cambridge University Press.

3

CHILDREN AND LOSS

CHAPTER OVERVIEW

Our contemporary society does not prepare children for grieving, nor does it prepare adults for helping children grieve. In this chapter we cite research literature in the behavioral and social sciences that describe the grieving process of children so that librarians, teachers, mental health professionals, and parents can better understand the psychology underlying children's behaviors. We then suggest ways that professionals and parents can assist children as they confront major loss, and we recommend resources appropriate for children and for adults who work closely with them.

THE GRIEVING PROCESS OF CHILDREN

Children are taught to acquire things—parents' praise, toys, or other gifts—for behaving, for earning good grades in school, and for developing healthy habits for eating and hygiene. Unfortunately, we give children little direction for dealing with losses and the emotions associated with them. Loss in life is predictable and inevitable, yet we typically provide little or no training for responding effectively to those events that are certain to cause pain. Some adults even tell children *not* to talk about it.

The feelings associated with loss begin early. In fact, clinicians and researchers report a substantial amount of evidence that intrauterine events can leave lasting impressions on people. In other words, a person's first experience with grief could have occurred before birth, leaving impressions that may be carried through childhood and perhaps beyond. Also, the birth process can play a role in the development of our early psyches because of the separation from the womb and accompanying feelings (Moody and Arcangel 2001).

Loss leads to grieving and, for children, requires intervention. We first discuss how children grieve, followed by strategies for intervening and assisting the child in the grieving process.

Each Child Grieves Differently

Children react differently to loss. Moody and Arcangel (2001), writing about the loss of a parent, introduce these differences:

> No two snowflakes falling from the winter sky will ever be alike. Similarly, no two survivors adapt to loss in exactly the same way. Identical twins do not mourn the death of their mother identically because each is unique in thoughts, feelings, beliefs, personality, and the relationship held with the mother. (58)

There is general agreement that a child's developmental stage is a major factor influencing grief, as described below. Adults working with children must be knowledgeable of these developmental stages as they confront grief with children.

Developmental Stages and Grieving

Children in early childhood (0–4 years), middle childhood (5–8 years) and late childhood (9–12 years) grieve differently because of their developmental level. Cognitive and language ability, communication style, developmental tasks, and emotional stability are more important among children than any other age group for understanding loss (Hooyman and Kramer 2006, 87–88).

Early Childhood (0–4 years)

Infants and toddlers cannot express their feelings in words, but they show their stress by their fussy behavior or withdrawal. When infants are separated from their mothers, they cry out in grief. Moody and Arcangel (2001, 11) explain the gravity of this separation:

> Even though their separation may be only temporary, or even imagined, it can be intensely devastating. No behaviors are powered by stronger emotions than grief, and they do not disappear with infancy.

Children may encounter death before the age of four. In earlier times, people were not sheltered from death because it was a natural part of their lives. In our youth-focused culture, many people do not discuss death, and television is now the predominant way death is presented. "Unfortunately, the violent scenes presented there teach nothing wholesome about dying. Death is not portrayed as real, nor is any sense of sorrow for the bereaved" (Moody and Arcangel 2001).

During the second and third years of a child's life, they begin to understand their feelings and are able to express them. However, few adults understand that children have a need for attachment and a need to express their sorrow when separated. Instead, many adults implore children to ignore their emotions by saying something like, "Big boys/girls don't cry," or "I'll give you something to cry about!" (Moody and Arcangel 2001, 11). Children should be told when parents are leaving and their return assured. This will help children not to feel abandoned.

Young children (ages 2–4) have not attained the cognitive ability to understand the permanence of death and divorce, and they lack the language ability to describe their emotions, although by age 4 they can label emotions like "sad." When they grieve, children in this age group assume that others know their feelings and generally are unable to draw comfort from spoken statements of support. By the time children are four or five years, they are beginning to develop empathy, and most can see a situation from the other person's viewpoint.

Middle Childhood (Ages 5–8)

Children in middle childhood are less able than younger children to distract themselves from their emotions. They state directly their feelings; they may think they killed their parent or loved one through their anger or negative thoughts. Children in middle childhood develop relationships outside the home, spend more time socializing, and compare their home life to that of other children their age. They may be jealous of friends who have a home life without the stresses of a critically ill parent or sibling.

During this age period, children become capable of more complex thought and ask many questions about the cause of a parent's or loved one's illness and death. These children should be presented the truth in a gentle and respectful manner.

> They need a gentle honesty, information appropriate to their age and developmental level, the ability to grieve in their own way, loving, supportive adults, someone to listen no matter the hour, respect for their feelings, limits on behavior, consistency as much as is possible, and time to be a child. (Sweder 1995, 59)

Late Childhood (Ages 9–12)

Because of their more sophisticated concrete logical-operational thinking and problem-solving skills, older children are generally able to move ahead after a few months following a major loss, such as divorce or a parent's death. They are more capable of articulating their feelings and needs, seeking support, and making meaning of their loss. In late childhood their anger is less intense than adolescents' and they do not feel the overwhelming sadness of younger children (Hooyman and Kramer 2006).

Research suggests that children of all ages experience grief, but they are able to tolerate strong grief reactions only for short periods. After a short period of grieving, they then turn back to play or some other safe activity (Corr 2000, 28).

Supporting children through loss has long-term effects. Childhood experiences with death and grieving can help or hinder individuals when they encounter losses as adults. A child's introduction to death and early separations creates an internal pattern for adjusting to loss, and they hold onto their early feelings about their mortality (Moody and Arcangel, 2001).

Disenfranchised Grief of Children

Society establishes norms for grieving. These norms include expected behaviors and rules for how one is to feel and think. The rules also govern what losses one should grieve, how one grieves them, who should grieve the loss, and to whom others should respond with sympathy (Doka 2002). When the societal rules are violated, the grief is disenfranchised.

The grief of children is sometimes disenfranchised because (1) the relationship is not recognized, (2) the loss is not recognized, (3) the griever is not recognized, or (4) the type of death is not recognized by society (Crenshaw 2002). Adults may underestimate the degree of attachment a child may have for a teacher, friend, pet, or playmate who has died or from whom the child is separated. Losses unrelated to death may not be recognized as causing grief, for example, divorce, adoption, foster care placement, moving to a new school or community, and incarceration of a parent. Unfortunately, some adults do not understand that children are capable and need to grieve their losses, and these adults do not support children in their grieving. Siblings or parents who might have died from AIDS or suicide, or a family member killed while committing a crime, pose instances when a family is too embarrassed to grieve, leaving children disenfranchised as well.

In the section that follows, various types of loss, including losses sometimes disenfranchised, are discussed.

TYPES OF LOSS EXPERIENCED BY CHILDREN

A number of losses by children should be given special consideration by professionals and parents helping children to experience these losses. These types of loses are described below.

Sibling Death

When a brother or sister dies, surviving siblings may receive little support or even recognition of their pain. Parents may be so grief-stricken at the loss of a child that they often find themselves unable to cope with the needs of their surviving children. (See also chapter 5, "Loss of a Child.") With family and friends concentrating on the parents' tragedy, the suffering of siblings often goes unnoticed. These children need the attention of a caring adult, using appropriate strategies as outlined below.

Divorce

Divorce is a common occurrence in American families. The divorce rate in the United States has quadrupled in the past 20 years (Hooyman and Kramer 2006, 103), and the U.S. Census Bureau (2002) has reported that half of first marriages end in divorce. Reaction to divorce is similar to children's reaction to a parent's death; however, the stress factor is different. In a divorce children experience anger and sadness because of divided loyalties. These children also may experience the hurt caused by conflict, loss of economic support, guilt feelings, and a feeling of rejection.

Children in early childhood have more difficulty adjusting to divorce because they do not have the cognitive ability to understand divorce, even believing they will not see the missing parent again. In their egocentrism, young children may believe they are the cause of the divorce. Adolescents, especially girls, have difficulty dealing with divorce.

Because children may have no warning that a divorce is planned, their initial response often is disbelief or denial. They may create fantasies or explanations for their parent's absence—for example, Dad or Mom went on a trip and will come back. Children may have feelings of anger, anxiety, powerlessness, and a sense of personal failure long after the divorce (Hooyman and Kramer 2006).

Adoption

Even when adopted children are in loving, supporting homes, they experience the loss of their biological parents, their families, and their history. International adoptees also lose their country and their culture. Loss of their mother is most difficult for any adopted child. "All adopted children, regardless of the age of relinquishment, grieve for their mother, since at some level they were connected with her throughout her pregnancy." The trauma of separation from the birth mother varies with the degree of attachment (Hooyman and Kramer 2006, l06).

Adopted children who do not resemble their adoptive parents may face questions from other children and from strangers about their differences.

> When the adopted parents are asked whether they have any biological children or children of "their own," the adoptee, who is very much biological and their own, experiences yet another negation of who he or she is. Our language of "biological," "real," and "own" can compound the losses experienced by adoptive children. (Hooyman and Kramer 2006, 107)

Younger adopted children may fantasize that their birth family is perfect, unlike their adoptive family who sets rules and disciplines them. Such fantasies are more likely to emerge when the children are disappointed or angry with the adoptive parents.

Hooyman and Kramer (2006) point out that feelings of loss surface typically at ages 11, 13, and 18—just before they become independent. These adopted children romanticize their birth families during these times and may express hatred toward their adoptive parents and themselves. They may think about suicide, and they may experiment with risky behaviors.

Foster Children

Foster children, like adopted children, experience loss of their birth parents. Sometimes these children are taken from their homes with little warning or with little explanation and opportunity to say good-by.

Two emotional themes common to most foster children are pain from their separation from family and hope for the future. Some children may be placed in successive homes, each placement causing grief. If foster children are unable to mourn, or they lack support to do so, they may act out in order to be rejected by their foster families. Those foster children who are able to bond with their foster families usually are in homes where foster parents are supportive, caring, and patient.

With each new placement, foster children lose their families and often their friends as well. Their development is characterized by discontinuity, never knowing when they will be moved. Children of color often are placed in white homes, thereby losing their culture as well.

Foster children must contend not only with the usual issues associated with growing up, they must also cope with the loss of home, friends, and schools. They must undergo these losses for reasons that are beyond their control, and they have no assurance that their foster home situation has permanence.

Pet Death

Death of a pet poses serious problems for children. While parents may not realize the seriousness and impact of an animal death for a child, there is also a tendency among many adults to undervalue a household pet. Meyers, a human-animal bond consultant and certified grief therapist, states the following:

> In general, animals' roles are undervalued unless the animals are of direct use to people and society. An example of this attitude is the great emphasis placed on dogs who assist people who are blind, deaf, use wheelchairs, or have epilepsy. (Meyers 2002, 251)

The bond between children and animals can be especially strong. It is important not to replace the animal too quickly. Doing so may complicate the grieving process and inadvertently teach children that animal life is cheap and can be replaced. Children's loss of a family pet can be as traumatic as other types of loss, and adults should be aware and implement appropriate strategies to help children grieve.

STRATEGIES FOR HELPING CHILDREN GRIEVE

Should teachers and librarians leave discussions about death to parents, clergy, or psychologists? Bertman insists that educators should take an active role because they are present when a student's parent or sibling dies, when a pet dies, when a divorce occurs, or when a celebrity or political leader is killed.

> If she [the teacher or librarian] detaches herself from the situation, she will only create a void for her students when they are confused and most in need of help. The teacher *is* the professional. She must also be able to assess the needs of all the students, be aware of her own limitations, and above all have the appropriate resources available when referral is necessary. (Bertman 1995, 222)

As noted earlier, American society tends to protect children from death and from rituals related to death. Although such protection is well intentioned, depriving children of discussion and rituals inhibits their ability to accommodate loss and to learn coping skills for future losses. Such protection also may block a child's efforts to overcome the loss—to engage in grief tasks.

Grief Tasks

Librarians, teachers, mental health professionals, and parents can help children accomplish grief tasks. Worden has identified four tasks that must be accomplished in order for children to adapt to loss. The tasks do not have to be completed in any order, and they can be revisited and reworked by the grieving person over time. Worden asserts that the tasks apply to children but can be understood only in terms of the emotional, cognitive, and social development of the child. Loss through death is experienced in different ways in the different developmental phases; therefore, the tasks have been adapted to take into account the age and developmental level of the child (Worden 1996, 12–16).

Task 1: To accept the reality of the loss. To accomplish this task, children must be told about the death in ways that are accurate and in vocabulary appropriate for the stage of development. They must also be told repeatedly. As children develop cognitively, they are able to understand the finality of the loss.

Task 2: To experience the pain or emotional aspects of the loss. Children need to engage in this task gradually because their ability to cope is less than that of an adult. Their feelings are like those of adults—sadness, guilt, anger, and anxiety. A child's ability to experience the pain is influenced by the modeling of adults in the child's life. If these adults are able to articulate their feelings without being overwhelmed, the child will be able to address this task more effectively. Worden also notes that feelings of ambivalence in the relationship with the deceased adult may lead to feelings of abandonment and lead younger children to feel responsible for the death.

Task 3: To adjust to an environment in which the deceased is missing. This adjustment is influenced by the roles and closeness of the deceased person in the child's life. For example, mothers typically are the emotional caretakers in a family, and their loss has a substantial and lasting impact on a child. Mourning for a childhood loss can be revived later in life during important life events; for example, a girl who loses her father will experience renewed grief as she plans for her wedding and her father is not present to share the event.

Task 4: To relocate the dead person within one's life and find ways to memorialize the person. This task does not mean that the child gives up the relationship; instead, she or he finds a new place for the deceased person in her or his emotional life. Children need help to transform the role of the deceased person so that there is recognition that the person is dead physically but remains in one's memory and heart.

These tasks can be accomplished most effectively through interventions led by adults. Possible strategies are discussed below.

Professional Intervention for Grieving Children

Some children's grief is particularly complicated, and special training is needed to help them. Professional help should be sought for children who exhibit one or more of the following changes if they continue:

- Prolonged depression
- Difficulty relaxing
- Less concern about appearance
- Avoidance of social contact or activities previously enjoyed
- Expressed feelings of worthlessness
- Nightmares or other sleep disturbances
- Difficulty with schoolwork
- Behavioral problems in school
- Eating disorders
- Regressive behaviors (Hooyman and Kramer 2006, 112)

Professional grief facilitators can ease a child's grief by educating them and help-ing them work through their thoughts and feelings.

Talking with Grieving Children

Many adults are reluctant to talk about death with children, yet adults should be encouraged to teach children about death as a natural and inevitable fact of life. Books and recordings can provide opportunities for these discussions. Recom-mended resources are found at the end of this chapter.

Before talking with grieving children, it is advisable for professionals to gather some preliminary knowledge of the children and their loss:

- Get as much information about the loss as possible from the child's surviving parent, friend, or relative.
- Ask the family how the school could be most helpful to the child.
- Learn of the funeral rituals and whether classmates can be appropriately involved.
- Tell the grieving child's class what happened and allow them to react; suggest ways for the class to help the grieving child.
- Talk with the bereaved child and listen to the child's story (see specific sugges-tions below).
- Be aware that children react to grief in age-specific ways (as described above).
- Recognize that bereaved children may be upset for a long time.
- Create a quiet place in the school where children can retreat for grieving or any reason.
- Create a peer group with teachers to discuss concerns about dealing with griev-ing. (Adapted from Silverman 2000, 226–27)

The way children are informed of a death can complicate or facilitate their bereavement. Sometimes parents ask school personnel to tell their children of a death if they are overcome with their own grief. Schreder (1995), a pioneer in grieving and death, recommends the following approaches and activities to help youth deal with loss. These approaches can be used with individuals, families, or small groups "but must be used with sensitivity, understanding, and awareness of how powerfully we as adults affect and influence young people" (Schreder 1995, 204).

1. Create a safe environment that gives children support. Validate the child's crisis and pain, but let the child know that you cannot make things better. Don't rush the child. Help him feel at ease with some of the following, de-pending on his developmental level:
   a. Have a supply of stuffed animals to be her friend. If she feels comfortable, talk to her about why she made that choice.
   b. Ask the child to draw what's on his mind—feelings, family, whatever.
   c. Puppets and dolls can be a vehicle for children to talk about themselves through the puppets.
   d. Clay can be used to provide an artistic and emotional outlet.

e. Music can be used for expression. For us to ask children and adolescents to talk about their favorite music and why they like it helps us to understand them. They can be encouraged to write words to popular songs or to create their own songs.

f. In a group session, discussion can begin with the events that brought them here (Schreder 1995, 204–5).

2. Acknowledge and validate their feelings. Adults sometimes use clichés like, "You're too young to understand," "Don't talk about it and it will be all right," or "Don't cry; you need to be brave." All of these statements minimize the child's pain. Help children identify their feelings and recognize them as normal.

3. Provide activities to give children opportunities to talk about memories and times shared with the person who is dying or has died.

a. Encourage children to bring in objects associated with the loved one and allow them to talk about the person.

b. Ask children to draw a picture of their loved one and ask them to talk about it.

c. Read a book together and discuss the child's reaction.

d. Let the child choose a stone to carry around. It becomes a worry rock and absorbs some of the pain, giving back strength and courage.

e. Children may select or make their own puppets to prepare puppet shows.

f. Ask the children which colors describe how they feel. What does that color mean or feel like to them?

g. Provide snacks as a break in intense conversations; a snack can be a comfort for children and a release from anxiety they may be experiencing. (Adapted from Schreder 1995, 207–8)

Be aware that grieving is a long journey. People of all ages need ample time, support, acknowledgement, and permission to grieve. Grief ebbs and flows; it is brought to the surface by anniversaries, holidays, birthdays, date of death, and special events or memories of the deceased person. While talking and comforting a child are important aspects in the child's grieving process, rituals also can serve to assist grieving.

Rituals

Research indicates that children who participate in rituals following a death are less likely to exhibit psychological distress than children who do not. Funerals and other forms of bereavement rituals may ease the grief experience if children are prepared, given support during the event, and provided follow-up (Hooyman and Kramer 2006).

Besides funerals, children and their families may participate in other rituals. Librarians and teachers may assist children by considering the following:

• Rituals should be devised as children share the story of their loss and should not be imposed.

• Rituals should involve objects with symbolic value, such as a letter, song, flower, or picture.

- Rituals should lead to thought and discussion about the participants' feelings and thoughts.
- Rituals are also important following death of a pet. A formal burial, lighting a candle, or other rituals are advised.

Rituals can be conducted in groups. For example, a tree can be planted in memory of a child's loved one. The ritual can include discussion of the loved one when alive and what the child will miss. Releasing a balloon or writing a poem at the anniversary of a death—or any number of such events—can assist a grieving child.

SUMMARY

Adults, including teachers and librarians, may be reluctant to engage grieving children in grief tasks, expecting parents or mental health professionals to do this; however, teachers and librarians are frequently in contact with these children on a daily basis in the school and can very effectively assist them in their grieving.

Children grieve from a variety of situations, including death of a parent or sibling, death of a pet, divorce, adoption, placement in foster care, and other traumatic events. After learning some of the background of the child's loss, teachers and librarians can help a grieving child by encouraging them:

- To have their grief made legitimate
- To learn about the death or other major loss in segments so that they are not overwhelmed
- To learn a vocabulary so that they can describe the changes in their lives
- To talk about both negative and positive qualities of the person who died
- To find ways of honoring the dead
- To be included in the family drama as it plays out after the loss (Silverman 2000, 226)

A teacher or other adult can interact with a child in a sensitive manner, using language appropriate to the child's developmental level. Grieving lasts over a prolonged period of time and can be stimulated by anniversaries and reminder events. Rituals can be encouraged as a means for addressing the loss and expressing emotions associated with it.

ADULT RESOURCES

In this section we provide adult books to help parents, teachers, librarians, and health care professions interact with children experiencing loss. We also list in a separate section resources for children to help them understand loss and how to deal with it.

Askeland, Lori, ed. **Children and Youth in Adoption, Orphanages, and Foster Care: A Historical Handbook and Guide.** Children and Youth Series: History and Culture. Portsmouth, NH: Greenwood, 2005. 222p. $62.95. ISBN 0-313-33183-9; 978-0-313-33183-1.

A collection of essays that reviews the practice of adoption, orphanage placement, and foster care from the colonial period to the present, with a focus on such

20th-century issues as interracial and international adoption. "Editor Askeland has done an admirable job of giving depth and scope to this complex and all-too-often neglected aspect of American childhood. Summing Up: Highly recommended. Collections with a focus on family studies, legal studies, social work, and teacher education, serving lower-level undergraduates and above; public libraries" (*Choice* June 1, 2006).

Bergquist, Kathleen Ja Sook, M. Elizabeth Vonk, Dong Soo Kim, and Marvin D. Feit, eds. **International Korean Adoption: A Fifty-Year History of Policy and Practice.** New York: Routledge, 2007. 409p. $150.00. ISBN 0-7890-3064-0; 978-0-7890-3064-1.

Examines the sociohistorical background, the forming of new families, reflections on Korean adoption, birth country perspectives, global perspectives, implications for practice, and archival and historical resources on Korean adoption. Viewpoints and research are discussed from the academic disciplines of psychology, ethnic studies, sociology, social work, and anthropology. "Sure to become the indispensable starting point for anyone seeking to navigate the complex currents of Korean international adoption. Summing Up: Essential. All levels/libraries" (*Choice* Dec. 1, 2007).

Blatt, Susan McNair. **A Guidebook for Raising Foster Children.** Portsmouth, NH: Greenwood, Bergin & Garvey, 2000. 240p. $91.95. ISBN 0-89789-653-X; 978-0-89789-653-5.

Blatt, a pediatrician and director of a child welfare agency, provides guidance to enhance the experience of foster families. The book presents helpful information about health, behavior, school, and many other aspects of a foster child's life. Intended as a resource for families with foster children and anyone involved with the foster care system.

Blomquist, Barbara Taylor. **Insight into Adoption: Uncovering and Understanding the Heart of Adoption.** 2nd ed. Springfield, IL: Charles C. Thomas, 2009. 212p. $27.95pa. ISBN 0-398-07846-7; 978-0-398-07846-1.

An adoption consultant with two adopted children, Blomquist offers advice on emotional and adjustment issues faced by most adoptive parents and adopted children. As in the first edition, the focus is on the adopted child's thinking and feelings. Recommended for parents, social workers, mental health professionals, teachers, and librarians.

Brodzinsky, David M., and Jesus Palacios, eds. **Psychological Issues in Adoption: Research and Practice.** Portsmouth, NH: Greenwood, Praeger, 2005. 336 p. $119.95. ISBN 0-275-97970-9; 978-0-275-97970-6.

A collection of 12 articles by leading researchers from North America, Netherlands, Spain, and Scandinavia. These experts detail how the practice of adoption has changed both in North America and Europe in recent decades, influenced by such factors as a falling rate of domestically born infants placed for adoption, a rise in international adoption, children of color placed with Caucasian parents, increased foster care, and special needs adoptions. This volume augments the first author's earlier book *The Psychology of Adoption,* coedited with Marshall Schechter (1990). "Anyone doing research on adoptions will want to have this volume, which saves the time and trouble of scouring through countless journal articles and governmental reports. And in this respect, the volume fails; by unwisely pricing this work at $115, its publisher may force some scholars to rely on local libraries for access to this important and indispensable work" (*Choice* Mar. 1, 2006).

Chin, Ava. **Split: Stories from a Generation Raised on Divorce.** New York: McGraw-Hill, 2002. 256p. $14.95pa. ISBN 0-07-139106-1; 978-0-07-139106-1.

Generation X writers share their personal reflections on growing up as children of divorce. These 15 stories articulate some of the most difficult emotional aspects of growing up in a home split by divorce. "Many adults in their twenties and thirties were raised on divorce, and this brave and insightful collection of essays gives them a long-awaited platform. Each essay is unique in its tone and setting, but many common themes run throughout the book: the family's inability to talk openly about the divorce, the shuffling back and forth between parents' homes, and frustrations of living with stepparents." Recommended for any adults working with children (*Booklist* Aug. 1, 2002).

Coughlin, Amy, and Caryn Abramowitz. **Cross-Cultural Adoption: How to Answer Questions from Family, Friends, and Community.** Washington, DC: Regnery, 2004. 160p. $18.95. ISBN 0-89526-092-1; 978-0-89526-092-5.

The authors, both attorneys, draw from their experiences as adoptive parents of foreign-born children to help relatives and friends of adoptive families address important, frequently asked questions about cross-cultural adoptions.

Davies, Betty. **Shadows in the Sun: The Experiences of Sibling Bereavement in Childhood.** Series in Death, Dying and Bereavement. Philadelphia, PA: Brunner-Routledge, 1998. 368p. $62.96/$35.96pa. ISBN 978-0-87630-912-4; 978-0-87630-911-7.

Discusses the immediate, short- and long-term effects of sibling bereavement and the variables that influence them. Practical guidelines are offered for those who seek to help grieving siblings, children, and families. The author has extensive experience in bereavement counseling.

Doka, Kenneth J., ed. **Living with Grief: Children and Adolescents.** 2008. Washington, DC: Hospice Foundation of America. 420p. $34.95. ISBN 978-1-893349-09-4.

An authoritative book of readings by experts on children and adolescents experiencing loss. Provides research results and a theoretical overview with practical advice for teachers, parents, and mental health professionals. Parental loss, sibling loss, and loss of a friend are each addressed in their own chapters. Other chapters examine play therapy, protocols for schools, use of the Internet as a coping tool, and recommendations for reading for children and adolescents.

Dyregrov, Atle. **Grief in Children: A Handbook for Adults.** Philadelphia, PA: Jessica Kingsley, 2008. 207p. $24.95pa. ISBN 1-84310-612-4; 978-1-84310-612-8.

In this revision of the 1991 English edition, clinical psychologist Dyregrov (Center for Crisis Psychology, Bergen, Norway) discusses children's grief by age and gender. Dyregrov deals with a range of common physical and psychological responses and describes methods of approaching grief in children. He gives advice on how loss and bereavement should be handled at school, explains when it is appropriate to involve expert professional help, and discusses the value of bereavement groups for children. Illustrated with case studies and incorporating current research, this book is recommended for parents, mental health professionals, teachers, librarians, and all concerned with the welfare of bereaved children. Recommended resources also are included.

Emswiler, Mary Ann, and James P. Emswiler. **Guiding Your Child through Grief.** New York: Bantam, 2000. 304p. $15.00pa. ISBN 0-553-38025-7; 978-0-553-38025-5.

Drawing upon research and personal narratives, the Emswilers explain children's usual reactions when they lose someone near to them. Included is an age-appropriate reading list. There are helpful suggestions for parents, mental health professionals, teachers, librarians, health care professionals, and others who work closely with children.

Fiorini, Jody J., and Jodi Ann Mullen. **Counseling Children and Adolescents through Grief and Loss.** Champaign, IL: Research Press, 2006. 232p. ISBN 0-87822-553-6; 987-0-87822-553-8.

A synthesis of current research and best practices for counseling youth, with guidelines for selecting appropriate counseling strategies. The authors, university professors with extensive counseling experience, describe children's and adolescents' emotional, cognitive, and behavioral responses to various kinds of loss. Types of loss examined with case studies include death, moving, divorce, loss of childhood, school transitions, family life changes, and such tragic and stigmatizing losses as a sudden death, natural disasters, and abuse. Intended for mental health professionals in schools and other settings; however, the clear explanations and comprehensive coverage also make this a useful resource for teachers and librarians.

Fogarty, James A. **The Magical Thoughts of Grieving Children: Treating Children with Complicated Mourning and Advice for Parents.** Amityville, NY: Baywood, 2000. 194p. $42.95/$39.95pa. ISBN 0-89503-205-8; 0-89503-206-6.

Fogarty, a psychologist and consultant on family bereavement, explains how children's grief-related magical thinking can inhibit their recovery and create personality disorders. The book provides therapeutic techniques for healing grieving children. Intended for mental health professionals, educators, nurses, and others who assist children grieving the death of a loved one,

Foster, Celia. **Big Steps for Little People: Parenting Your Adopted Child.** London: Jessica Kingsley, 2008. 216p. $19.99pa. ISBN 1-84310-620-5; 978-1-84310-620-3.

Drawing on the wisdom gained in her own family life, this mother of two adopted sons offers an account of life with adopted children and examines the issues that many adoptive families encounter, including children with attachment problems and how to tackle a variety of behavioral issues.

Gerstenzang, Sarah. **Another Mother: Co-Parenting with the Foster Care System.** Nashville, TN: Vanderbilt University Press, 2007. 224p. $59.95. ISBN 0-8265-1548-7; 978-0-8265-1548-3.

The author, a social worker, discovered while raising a foster child that coparenting in the New York City foster care system was a complex and frustrating process. Gerstenzang offers new or prospective foster parents advice on coping with the system, living as a multiracial family, learning new cultures, and advocating for the child.

Goldman, Linda. **Breaking the Silence: A Guide to Help Children with Complicated Grief—Suicide, Homicide, AIDS, Violence, and Abuse.** 2nd ed. New York: Brunner-Routledge, 2001. 304p. $29.25pa. ISBN 978-1-58391-312-3.

This second edition provides techniques for working with children in various areas of complicated grief. Among topics included are suicide, AIDS, homicide, and other violent crime, abuse, and bullying. A new chapter is "Communities Grieve: Involvement with Children and Trauma." Specific suggestions for talking with and caring for grieving students are provided with numerous examples. A useful guide for librarians as well as educators, health professionals, and parents/caregivers.

Grollman, Earl A., ed. **Bereaved Children and Teens: A Support Guide for Parents and Professionals.** Boston: Beacon Press, 1995. 256p. $17.00. ISBN 978-080702307-5.

Chapters are by experts in grieving children and adolescents. Early chapters explain how to introduce the concept of death to children, and other chapters are devoted to sibling death, the impact of culture on youth grieving, care for dying and bereaved children, and use of stories, films, and drama. A useful guide for parents, teachers, health care professionals, and librarians working with children.

Grollman, Earl A. **Talking about Death: A Dialogue between Parent and Child.** Boston. 3rd ed. Beacon Press, 1990. 128p. $20.00pa. ISBN 0-8070-2364-7; 978-080702363-1.

The first section of this book is a read-along for parents to read to children. The dialog is accompanied by clear black and white illustrations. The language is direct, and the vocabulary is controlled for preschool and primary grade children. An appended section for the adult provides explanation for segments of the children's read-along and discusses issues and emotions related to children who face the death of loved ones. A valuable resource for parents, teachers, and librarians to read to individual students.

Grollman, Earl A., Ralph Klicker, and Joey O'Connor. **A Place Prepared: Helping Children Understand Death and Heaven.** Orleans, MA: Paraclete Press, 2006. DVD. 40 min. $29.95. ISBN 9781557253828.

Experts in the field of death and family issues offer practical suggestions and insightful tips for helping children to come to terms with this difficult topic. The video is divided into four segments: being honest with ourselves, as adults, about death; understanding death and children's emotional response to it; talking with children about funerals; and talking with children about heaven. "Parents and educators will find emotional support and honest answers to children's questions about death in this thought-provoking title. An excellent product for both group and individual viewing, it will be useful for parenting seminars, continuing education programs, and general population viewing" (*School Library Journal* July 1, 2000).

Holland, John. **Lost for Words: Loss and Bereavement Awareness Training.** Philadelphia, PA: Jessica Kingsley, 2005. 128p. $55.00. ISBN 1-84310-324-9; 978-1-84310-324-0.

Psychologist Holland has designed a training package designed for staff supporting children experiencing bereavement in schools and other settings. The book includes materials and instructions for group activities, templates for transparencies, and handouts. Training sessions encompass such issues as children's behavior changes subsequent to a loss and their concept of death. Recommended for teachers, librarians, and other professionals working with children.

Humphrey, Keren M. **Counseling Strategies for Loss and Grief.** American Counseling Association, 2009. 260p. $48.95. ISBN 978-1-55620-246-9.

This practice-oriented book describes a range of effective counseling strategies appropriate for the treatment of diverse loss and grief issues commonly presented in individual, family, and group psychotherapy settings. Based on contemporary understandings of the nature of personal and interpersonal loss and the ways in which people integrate loss and grief into their lives, this innovative book focuses on tailoring interventions to the uniqueness of the griever's experience.

James, John W., and Russell Friedman with Dr. Leslie Landon Matthews. **When Children Grieve: For Adults to Help Children Deal with Death, Divorce, Pet Loss, Moving, and Other Losses.** New York: HarperCollins, 2001. 268p. $24.00. ISBN 0-06-019613-0.

The authors of *The Grief Recovery Handbook* team with psychotherapist Matthews to dispel several myths of grieving (e.g., don't feel bad, you can replace the loss) and to provide causes for children's grief, suggestions for helping children, and applications of these strategies in real case studies. A readable book for any adult wanting to help children recover from loss.

Jeynes, William. **Divorce, Family Structure and the Academic Success of Children.** New York: Routledge, 2002. 228p. $39.95. ISBN 0-7890-1487-4; 978-0-7890-1487-0.

A single-volume reference on the history, methodology, and current theory on this social issue. "Divorce, separation, remarriage, living with neither parent, and other domestic relationships are explored in detail. The information presented is important because knowing the effects of family structure on academic performance can help teachers help their students perform to the best of their abilities" (*Library Journal* Feb. 15, 2002).

Johnson, Paul, and Bruce St. Thomas. **Empowering Children through Art and Expression: Culturally Sensitive Ways of Healing Trauma and Grief.** Philadelphia, PA: Jessica Kingsley, 2007. 175p. $29.95pa. ISBN 1-84310-789-9; 978-1-84310-789-7.

Johnson, a licensed clinical social worker, and St. Thomas, a practicing art therapist, examine use of arts and expressive therapies with children who have experienced loss, especially those whose lives have been disrupted by forced relocation with their families to a different culture or community. The book explores how children express and resolve unspoken feelings in play and other creative activities. The authors combine personal and professional perspectives, using case examples as well as the authors' own childhood experiences, to demonstrate practical strategies with such art forms as drama, the visual arts, storytelling, and sculpting with clay. It also equips the reader with knowledge of the theory behind these intervention techniques. Recommended for professionals working with traumatized children who have experienced loss, grief, relocation, and other kinds of trauma.

Kübler-Ross, Elisabeth. **On Children and Death.** New York: Simon & Schuster, 1997. 288p. $13.95pa. ISBN 0684839393; 9780684839394.

The author of *On Death and Dying,* and several other books on bereavement, addresses the question, "How are children different from adults when faced with terminal illness?" Based on a decade of working with dying children, this book offers the families of dead and dying children the practical help they need to deal with one of life's most tragic circumstances, the death of a child. Many examples are given to illustrate problems that families face, along with advice for providing the love and support the ill child and other family members require. Written for parents but useful for other adults who have a close relationship with dying children.

Lieberman, Alicia F., Nancy C. Compton, Patricia Van Horn, and Chandra Ghosh Ippen. **Losing a Parent to Death in the Early Years: Guidelines for the Treatment of Traumatic Bereavement in Infancy and Early Childhood.** Herndon, VA: Zero To Three Press, 2003. 143p. $39.95. ISBN 0-943657-72-5; 978-0-943657-72-1.

Four therapists at the San Francisco General Hospital's Child Trauma Research Project provide a practical guide for the assessment and treatment of young children who have experienced the death of a parent or primary caregiver. Intended for mental health professionals, educators, and child care professionals. "Overall, the volume provides solid guidance, supported by both research and concrete examples for those working with—or hoping to work with—children" (*Choice* May 1, 2004).

Lewis, Paddy Greenwall, and Jessica G. Lippman. **Helping Children Cope with the Death of a Parent: A Guide for the First Year.** Contemporary Psychology Series. Santa Barbara, CA: Praeger, 2004. 184p. $38.95/$20.00pa/$38.49 e-book. ISBN 0-275-98097-9; 0-313-36155-Xpa; 0-313-03925-9 e-book.

The first year following a parent's death is often the most difficult—the first birthday, holiday, spring, summer, autumn, and winter spent without the loved one often revives the pain. This guide by two child psychologists chronologically leads the reader through a child's first year of mourning the loss of a parent, beginning with helping the child anticipate the death, if it is expected, or through the initial shock of unexpected death. It is intended to help the families, teachers, librarians, and community members surrounding a child to anticipate and cope with the many difficulties that arise.

Marta, Suzy Yehl. **Healing the Hurt, Restoring the Hope: How to Guide Children and Teens through Times of Divorce, Death, and Crisis with the RAIN-BOWS Approach.** Saw Robin Press, 2006. 341p. $16.95. ISBN 1427607427; 978-1427607423. 1-57954-591-2.

Finding no support groups for children of divorced parents, Marta founded RAINBOWS in 1983, an international nonprofit organization to support children, teens, and adults recovering from a major loss. This book is based on the experiences of the volunteers, participants, and parents who have successfully bridged the gap between adults and grieving children. Marta identifies the causes of grief and the signals of children's grieving, and suggests a variety of activities to help children cope with their grief. Recommended for parents and any adults who work with children.

Meese, Ruth Lyn. **Children of Intercountry Adoptions in School: A Primer for Parents and Professionals.** Portsmouth, NH: Greenwood, 2002. 208p. $51.95. ISBN 0-89789-841-9; 978-0-89789-841-6.

Children adopted from other countries have complex histories that place them at high risk for failure in school. Meese, professor of special education at Longwood (Virginia) University, explains those needs and offers suggestions for educators to help these children reach their potential. Included are the stories of children adopted from Romania, Russia, and China, and their interactions in U.S. schools. Intended for teachers, mental health professionals, librarians, and all who work with children in schools.

Maskew, Trish. **Our Own: Adopting and Parenting the Older Child.** Morton Grove, IL: Snowcap Press, 1999. 283p. $23.95. ISBN 0-9669701-2-8; 978-0-9669701-2-8.

The author, a mother of three, including two adopted boys, draws on her experiences and interviews with dozens of adoptive families and professionals to cover such topics as attachment, family adjustment, dealing with difficult behaviors, birth family and cultural ties, grief, and other adoption issues. "Raising adopted children is not the same as raising birthchildren, as Maskew knows, and she offers ideas and advice that are both practical and extensive.... Excellent for all public libraries" (*Library Journal* Sept. 1, 1999).

Moe, Barbara A. **Adoption: A Reference Handbook.** 2nd ed. Contemporary World Issues Series. Santa Barbara, CA: ABC-CLIO, 2007. 342p. $55.00. ISBN 1-59884-029-0; 978-1-59884-029-2.

Explores the current issues surrounding adoption in the United States. Following an overview of the topic, it chronicles the milestones in adoption history with biographical sketches of individuals who have had a major influence on child welfare and adoption philosophies and practices. Recommended for use by parents, adoption agencies, social workers, and policy makers.

Oxhorn-Ringwood, Lynne, Louise Oxhorn, and Marjorie Krausz. **Stepwives: Ten Steps to Help Ex-Wives and Step-Mothers End the Struggle and Put the Kids First.** New York: Simon & Schuster, Fireside, 2002. 288p. $13.00pa. ISBN 0-7432-2246-6; 978-0-7432-2246-4.

Lynne and Louise for 10 years were stepwives—the ex-wife and current wife of the same man and the mother and stepmother to the same child. While they managed a civil relationship, each was seething with anger on the inside. With the guidance of marriage and family therapist Marjorie Krausz, Oxhorn-Ringwood and Oxhorn developed a 10-step program that can help women begin to work together effectively for the sake of their children. "Based on the authors' own experiences and illustrated with quotes from their diaries, the book offers practical suggestions for developing empathy and learning to lessen tension and support the children caught in a divorce. While their suggestions are commonsensical (e.g., the mother should refrain from calling when the child is with the stepmother), their sense of optimism and cooperative approach are highly unique" (*Library Journal* April 15, 2002).

Pavao, Joyce Maguire. **The Family of Adoption.** Rev. ed. Boston: Beacon Press, 2005. 144p. $16.00pa. ISBN 0-8070-2827-4; 978-0-8070-2827-8.

Pavao argues that there are predictable and understandable developmental stages and challenges for every adoptee, and she believes that adoptive parents, teachers, therapists, and all who work with children must understand these developmental stages as normal. "Pavao's book is a worthy addition to the literature on adoptions. An adoptee herself and a 20-year veteran of a clinical practice aimed at helping adoptive families, Pavao has been able to distill from these experiences an overview on adoptions that is both sensitive and insightful" (*Choice* January 1, 1999).

Sammons, William A., and Jennifer M. Lewis. **Don't Divorce Your Children: Protecting Their Rights and Your Happiness.** New York: McGraw-Hill, 1999. 304p. $14.95pa. ISBN 0-8092-2793-2; 978-0-8092-2793-8.

The authors, both pediatricians, offer advice on how to prevent the painful physical and emotional distancing that can occur between divorced parents and their children. Fictional diary entries drawn from the authors' experience illustrate both parents' and children's perspectives as they deal with divorce. "Lewis and Sammons answer concerns about how to tell children about a pending divorce, how to help the child make the adjustment, and how to continue being a caring and involved parent beyond the divorce. This is a valuable source for people with children seeking advice about divorce" (*Booklist* July 1, 1999).

Savarese, Ralph James. **Reasonable People: A Memoir of Autism and Adoption. On the Meaning of Family and the Politics of Neurological Difference.** New York: Other Press, 2007. 496p. $25.95. ISBN 1-59051-129-8; 978-1-59051-129-9.

This memoir traces the development of DJ, a boy considered profoundly retarded and who now, six years later, earns all A's at a regular school. Savarese argues for a reasonable commitment to human possibility and caring. "Savarese's careful melding of memoir and passionate advocacy for the disabled informs and inspires" (*Booklist* Apr. 1, 2007).

Schaefer, Dan, and Christine Lyons. **How Do We Tell the Children? A Step-by-Step Guide for Helping Children Two to Teen Cope When Someone Dies.** 3rd ed. New York: Newmarket Press, 2002. 203p. $24.95. ISBN 1-55704-430-9; 978-1-55704-430-3.

Schaefer, a psychologist and former funeral home director, and journalist Lyons explain how to inform children about the realities of death. Now in its third edition, this guide is expanded to include new material on dealing with trauma, violence in schools, and an enlarged "Crisis Section" with scripts, answers, and messages for children.

Schwartz, Lita Linzer, and Florence Whiteman Kaslow, eds. **Welcome Home! An International and Nontraditional Adoption Reader.** New York: Routledge, 2003. 247p. $170.00. ISBN 0-7890-1773-3; 978-0-7890-1773-4.

A guide to the process as well as pros and cons of adopting children with special needs from outside the United States and from a different racial/cultural background. Parents and adoptees offer firsthand perspectives on the cautions and benefits of nontraditional adoption. "An outgrowth of the editors' research in the Northeast-Northwest Collaborative Adoption Projects (which seeks to study a large sample of adoptive families), this is highly recommended for adoptive parents and especially prospective adoptive parents. Academic researchers may also find it useful given the current research and references" (*Library Journal* Nov. 1, 2003).

Sember, Brette. **Complete Adoption and Fertility Legal Guide.** Naperville, IL: Sourcebooks, Sphinx Publishing, 2004. 368p. $22.95pa. ISBN 1-57248-373-3; 978-1-57248-373-6.

Sember offers a guide for those struggling with fertility issues and contemplating adoption. Addressing adoption, she explains responsibilities and legal issues for birth mothers and adoptive parents and explains the various types of adoption and includes guidelines for single-parent as well as gay and lesbian adoptions. In the second part of the book, she examines infertility treatment. "Attorney Sember manages to address albeit in a glancing fashion the major areas of adoption, both legal and emotional. . . . Highly recommended for all public libraries" (*Library Journal* Aug. 1, 2004).

Shulman, Diana. **Co-Parenting after Divorce: How to Raise Happy, Healthy Children in Two-Home Families.** Sherman Oaks, CA: WinnSpeed Press, 1997. 136p. $12.95pa. ISBN 0-9656907-0-9; 978-0-9656907-0-6.

This guide by a psychotherapist provides advice to help divorced parents create a healthy environment that produces well-adjusted children. "Shulman provides practical, straightforward capsules often broken down into useful steps. Though this is most suitable for divorced parents as a 'ready reference' guide for thinking quickly on one's feet, public libraries would certainly do patrons a service by adding it to their collections" (*Library Journal* Aug. 1, 1997).

Silber, Kathleen, and Patricia M. Dorner. **Children of Open Adoption.** San Antonio, TX: Corona, 1990. 193p. $10.95pa. ISBN 0-931722-78-0; 978-0-931722-78-3.

The authors have extensive experience studying open adoption and implementing open adoption policies, which include both the birthparents and adoptive parents sharing information and having access to a child. The authors' study indicated positive results of such an arrangement. "All participants in open adoption in-terviewed by the authors reported positive, loving experiences that benefited all concerned. A timely and readable study" (*Booklist* Mar. 15, 1990).

Silverman, Phyllis R. **Never Too Young to Know: Death in Children's Lives.** New York: Oxford University Press, 1999. 288p. $27.95pa. ISBN 0-19-510955-4; 978-0-19-510955-9.

Using stories of children's own experiences and supported by research, Silverman explains the effects of loss upon children, the challenges they face as they grieve, and ways of supporting them as they grow in the bereavement process. Part 1 centers on making meaning of death and grief; part 2 examines children's responses to the death of a parent, sibling, child, or friend; and part 3 is devoted to helping mourners, supportive services, and resources. "The book highlights useful theory, research, and experiential information for mental health professionals and others who work with bereaved youth" (*Choice* May 1, 2000).

Silverman, Phyllis R., and Madelyn Kelly. **A Parent's Guide to Raising Grieving Children: Rebuilding Your Family after the Death of a Loved One.** New York: Oxford University Press, 2009. 272p. $16.95pa. ISBN 0-19-532884-1; 978-0-19-532884-4.

Silverman is an internationally recognized leader in the field of bereavement and Kelly is a writer and television news producer. The authors offer guidance on such aspects of childhood loss as living with someone who's dying, preparing for the funeral, explaining death to a two-year-old, addressing the moods of a grieving teenager, learning how and where to get help from therapists and bereavement groups, developing a new sense of self, and continuing a relationship with the person who died. The authors advocate an open, honest approach, suggesting that our instinct to protect children from the reality of death may be more harmful than helpful. Included are pertinent accounts and advice on grieving from children, teenagers, young adults, and parents who have experienced family losses. "A useful resource for parents and professionals that work with families who are experiencing a loss" (*Library Journal* May 5, 2009).

Simon, Rita J., and Sarah Hernandez. **Native American Transracial Adoptees Tell Their Stories.** Lanham, MD: Lexington Books, 2008. 380p. $ 80.00. ISBN 0-7391-2492-7; 978-0-7391-2492-5. Paperback: $36.95. ISBN 0-7391-2493-5; 978-0-7391-2493-2.

This study of 20 Native American transracial adoptees reveals their struggle to establish a sense of cultural identity while raised in non-Native homes. Most participants agreed that adoptive parents can help their adoptive child by nurturing a connection with their child's tribal community. Suggested for graduate students and faculty, professionals, and interested adults. "The book is important because it tackles an ignored subject. However, it is also frustrating, for while it challenges readers' ignorance and apathy about Native American adoptees in the latter 20th century, the book does little to help readers know what to do with this new knowledge" (*Choice* Mar. 1 2009).

Simon, Rita James, and Rhonda Roorda. **In Their Own Voices: Transracial Adoptees Tell Their Stories.** New York: Columbia University Press, 2000. 408p. $54.00. ISBN 0-231-11828-7; 978-0-231-11828-6.

Simon is a professor in the American University College of Law and School of Public Affairs. This book is a collection of 24 interviews conducted with black and biracial young adults who were adopted by white parents representing a wide range of religious, economic, political, and professional backgrounds. Results of the interviews are analyzed and compared with earlier studies. The book also includes a brief history of transracial adoption and its current legal status.

Sinclair, Ian, Kate Wilson, and Ian Gibbs. **Foster Placements: Why They Succeed and Why They Fail.** Supporting Parents Series. London: Jessica Kingsley, 2004. 272p. $34.95pa. ISBN 1-84310-173-4; 978-1-84310-173-4.

Based on exhaustive research sponsored by a British government funded initiative, the authors, social researchers at the University of York and University of Nottingham, discuss the primary concerns in foster placement planning. The authors indicate that the contribution of the school, social workers, the child's family, and the individual characteristics of the child are major factors in determining the types of support most beneficial to the child's placement. Recommended for mental health professionals, policy makers, foster families, and those interested in foster child care.

Smart, Carol, Bren Neale, and Amanda Wade. **The Changing Experience of Childhood: Families and Divorce.** Cambridge, UK: Polity Press, 2001. 232p. $34.95pa. ISBN 0-7456-2400-6; 978-0-7456-2400-6.

Smart, Neale, and Wade, all faculty members at the University of Leeds, explore children's values, principles, and feelings about family life. The book explores children's own accounts of family life after divorce and allows the reader to see these changes from their point of view. Recommended for all who are concerned about children and the family.

Straub, Sandra Helene. **Pet Death.** Amityville, NY: Baywood, 2004. 174p. $40.95. ISBN 0-89503-282-1; 978-0-89503-282-9.

Personal stories by pet owners augment the discussion of such issues as telling a child a pet has died, the grieving process, and coping with the loss of a pet. "Straub, a grief counselor in private practice who has lived with many cats, has written a lachrymose but practical guide for grieving pet owners as well as mental health professionals, teachers, clergy, medical personnel, and veterinarians" (*Reference & Research Book News Review* Aug. 1, 2004).

Weinberg, Lois A. **The Systematic Mistreatment of Children in the Foster Care System: Through the Cracks.** New York: Routledge, 2007. 360p. $102.95. ISBN 0-7890-2392-X; 978-0-7890-2392-6.

Relates the stories of 10 children in the foster care system from diverse ethnic and cultural backgrounds and the efforts by advocates to find them permanent places to live, appropriate schooling, and other essentials they need. The case studies reveal how social service agencies frequently fail to meet their obligations to children in the system and what can be done to address these failures. "Weinberg provides practical advice for advocating for children and their educational needs with educational systems and outside agencies.... The book talks about efforts at the federal, state, and regional levels to correct these cracks in the child placement systems" (*Choice* Sept. 1, 2008).

Wolf, Anthony E. **Why Did You Have to Get a Divorce: A Guide to Parenting through Divorce.** New York: Farrar, Straus & Giroux, 1998. 256p. $16.00pa. ISBN 0-374-52568-4; 978-0-374-52568-2.

Dr. Wolf argues that divorce does not have to do long-term damage to a child. Based on case material, he shows parents how to steer children through the pain and the complex feelings engendered by divorce—feelings that can create continuing problems for a child. "Ultimately, he reassures divorcing parents that being good parents whenever they are with their children is the key to giving children nice lives, despite divorce" (*Booklist* Sept. 1, 1998).

RESOURCES FOR CHILDREN

Resources listed below are recommended for children up to age 12. The reader is also urged to consult chapter 4 for additional resources for older children.

The arrangement of titles below is by the major categories of grief: adoption, death (general), death of a friend, death of a parent or grandparent, death of a pet, death of a sibling, divorce, and foster care.

Adoption

Atinsky, Steve. **Trophy Kid: Or How I Was Adopted by the Rich and Famous.** New York: Random House Children's Books, Delacorte, 2008. 192p. $15.99. ISBN 0-385-73049-7; 978-0-385-73049-5.

Since his adoption at age three by Hollywood movie stars, 13-year-old Joe's life in the public eye has hidden the isolation he feels at home, and his longing to know more about his Croatian birth parents. To publicize Joe's progress and their help to him, his adoptive parents hire writer Tom Dolan to ghost write his autobiography to show them in a positive light as his father begins a campaign for the U.S. Senate. "Readers will most likely see before Joe does that his parents are guilty of nothing more than self-absorption, a flaw not limited to movie stars. But they will appreciate the widening of Joe's world as he makes friends with 'ordinary people' connected to Tom and begins to see his parents through the eyes of others" (*School Library Journal* Aug. 1, 2008). Ages 9–12.

Bergren, Lisa T. **God Found Us You.** HarperBlessings Series. New York: HarperCollins, 2009. 40p. $10.99. ISBN 0-06-113176-8; 978-0-06-113176-9.

By the creators of *God Gave Us You* (2000). Little Fox asks his mother to tell his favorite story, and Mama Fox recalls her praying for a pup, and God delivered him to her. "The gentle text tells of the adult fox's longing to become a mother, her long period of waiting and her prayers and faith in God, with the birth mother and her place in the story also gracefully acknowledged" (*Kirkus Reviews* May 15, 2009). "[Laura J.] Bryant's appealing images, mostly gentle pastels, are sweet but not saccharine, portraying these anthropomorphous animals as intelligent, loving, and wonderfully matched. A nice introduction to adoption for any child, adopted or not" (*Booklist* May 1, 2009). Ages 3–7.

Bunting, Eve. **Jin Woo.** New York: Houghton Mifflin Harcourt Trade & Reference, Clarion Books, 2001. 32p. $16.00. ISBN 0-395-93872-4; 978-0-395-93872-0.

David is uncertain about his new little brother who is arriving from Korea. He is alternately sad, hopeful, unbelieving, and excited at this change in his life, which is an accurate portrayal of the whirlwind of feelings that surround any new big brother. The child, Jin Woo, soon wins his heart. This picture book exploration of the arrival of an adopted Korean baby is the second collaboration by Bunting and illustrator Chris K. Soentpiet (*So Far From the Sea*, 1998) and as a Korean adoptee himself, the talented Soentpiet is particularly well-qualified to illustrate this one. "A solid choice for adoption shelves, especially for those looking for material on international adoption" (*Booklist* Mar. 15, 2001). Ages 5–8.

Bunting, Eve. **Train to Somewhere.** St Louis, MO: San Val, 2000. 32p. $17.15. ISBN 0-613-28679-0; 978-0-613-28679-4. Logan, IA: Perfection Learning Corporation, 2000. 32p. $14.60. ISBN 0-7569-4260-8; 978-0-7569-4260-1.

Marianne is in a group of 14 homeless children traveling with a guardian from New York to the Midwest in 1878 in search of families to adopt them. Marianne is the one nobody wants. She's older than the others, not as cute as the little girls, not as muscular as the boys, and not manipulative. Marianne is taken, finally, by an elderly couple. They really wanted a boy, but they like her, and they're kind. Illustrated by Ronald Himler. Ages 5–8.

Carlson, Nancy. **My Family Is Forever.** New York: Penguin Group, Puffin, 2006. 32p. $5.99pa. ISBN 0-14-240561-2; 978-0-14-240561-1.

An Asian girl tells the story of her adoption by an American couple and states that family members need not look alike in order to share common experiences and love. "Decorated with upbeat, brightly colored pictures portraying a supportive, loving family, this cozy picture book will have great appeal for many youngsters, though adoptees, and kids from blended families, single-parent homes, or any nontraditional family, will feel a special connection" (*Booklist* Apr. 1, 2004). Ages 4–7.

Cummings, Mary: **Three Names of Me.** Park Ridge, IL: Albert Whitman, 2006. 40p. $15.95. ISBN 0-8075-7903-3; 978-0-8075-7903-9.

This story of international adoption is told by a young girl who has three names. She was named Wang Bin, "gentle and refined princess," by her caregivers at her Chinese orphanage; her American parents gave her the name Ada; and her Chinese birth mother gave her a third name. "Soft and delicate, the realistic illustrations capture the mood of the story and reveal Ada's thoughts about who she is and where she came from. The warmth and simplicity of this story, plus the positive message on adoption, should appeal to most readers" (*School Library Journal* Oct. 1, 2006). Ages 7–9.

Curtis, Jamie Lee. **Tell Me Again about the Night I Was Born.** New York: HarperCollins, Joanna Cotler Books, 1996. 40p. $16.99. ISBN 0-06-024528-X; 978-0-06-024528-3.

Actor Curtis tells the story of a young girl who asks her parents to tell her again the family story of her birth and adoption. "Curtis' use of an ingenuous childlike narrator is just as successful here as it was in *When I Was Little* (1993), and so are [Laura] Cornell's comical, exuberant illustrations, which have great child appeal" (*Booklist* Oct. 15, 1996). Ages 4–8.

dePaola, Tomie. **A New Barker in the House.** New York: Penguin, 2004. 32p. $5.99pa. ISBN 0-14-240141-2; 978-0-14-240141-5.

In this sequel to *Meet the Barkers,* Barker twins Morgie and Moffie meet their adopted brother, Marcos, who is three years old and only speaks Spanish. "Brimming with dePaola's characteristic charm and clarity, full page art and panel illustrations move the tale along visually. In addition to being an upbeat portrayal of international adoption, this is also a subtle lesson in diplomacy for any age" (*Booklist* July 1, 2002). Ages 5–8.

Friedman, Darlene. **Star of the Week: A Story of Love, Adoption, and Brownies with Sprinkles.** New York: HarperCollins, 2009. 32p. $18.89. ISBN 0-06-114137-2; 978-0-06-114137-9.

Cassidy-Li was adopted from China when she was a baby. When it is her turn to be "Star of the Week" in her kindergarten class, she makes brownies and assembles a poster with pictures of her family, friends, and pets, but she doesn't have a photo of her birth parents. With help from her family, she finds a way to include them.

Illustrated by Roger Roth. "The pictures add character and a light touch to a story, which, while upbeat, deals forthrightly with the uncertainties of adoptees. Cassidy-Li's thoughts and questions about her birth family will resonate with adopted children and serve as a springboard for discussion in homes and classrooms" (*School Library Journal* June 1, 2009). Ages 5–8.

Heo, Yumi. **Ten Days and Nine Nights: An Adoption Story.** New York: Random House Children's Books, Schwartz & Wade Books, 2009. 40p. $19.99. ISBN 0-375-94715-9; 978-0-375-94715-5.

A young Korean-American girl eagerly awaits the arrival of her newly adopted sister from Korea, while her whole family prepares. Meanwhile, the girl's mother flies to Korea to meet the baby and bring her home. "Heo's stylized artwork fills the pages with family warmth in this welcome and endearing addition to adoption books" (*Booklist* Apr. 1, 2009). Ages 4–8.

Hicks, Betty. **Get Real.** New York: Roaring Brook Press, 2006. 192p. $16.95. ISBN 1-59643-089-3; 978-1-59643-089-1.

Thirteen-year-old Destiny feels alienated in her messy, haphazard family, and helps her adopted best friend Jil when she finds her birth mother and decides to have a relationship with her. "The girls' friendship is a successful vehicle for unearthing the complexities of adopted children's emotions and their families' dilemmas. More than that, though, Hicks offers a solid YA novel featuring strong characters, deep friendships, supportive families, and the joy and pain of growing up" (*Booklist* Oct. 15, 2006). Ages 10–14.

Keller, Holly. **Horace.** New York: HarperCollins, 1995. 32p. $4.95pa. ISBN 0-688-11844-5; 978-0-688-11844-0.

Horace, a leopard, is the adopted son of tiger parents. Every night at bedtime his mother tiger tells him how he came to be their child. As Horace grows older, he wonders whether he belongs with his adoptive family. After a search for a family that looks more like him, he comes to realize his adoptive family is his real family and where he belongs. "The warmth and security from which Horace ventures forth to discover the relationship between his roots and his allegiances are confirmed in every well-chosen word of Keller's simple text and in each line of her affectionate, carefully composed illustrations" (*Kirkus Reviews* April 1, 1991). Ages 4–8.

Kent, Rose. **Kimchi and Calamari.** New York: HarperCollins, 2007. 240p. $16.89. ISBN 0-06-083770-5; 978-0-06-083770-9.

Fourteen-year-old Joseph Calderaro was adopted from Korea, but his adoptive Italian parents refuse to divulge any details regarding his birth parents or his Korean heritage. After his social studies teacher assigns an essay on cultural heritage, Joseph fabricates a story about his ancestry. When his essay is selected for entry in a national contest, his lie is revealed, and he makes a concerted effort to discover the truth about his birth family. "Kent has done an excellent job of creating a likable protagonist whose confusion about his status is touching, and also funny. This is one of the best of the recent spate of books about adolescent adoptees facing quests to establish their identities" (*School Library Journal* May 1, 2007). Ages 8–12.

Kidd, Diana. **Onion Tears.** New York: Scholastic, Orchard Books, 1991. 62p. $15.95pa. ISBN 0-531-05870-0; 978-0-531-05870-1.

Nam-Huong, a young Vietnamese girl, tries to overcome her grief after the loss of her family and adjust to her new life with the Australian family with whom she lives. With the help of her understanding teacher and her friend Chu Minh, she is able to come to terms with her past and accept her new life. "The story is sympathetic and well told, giving children an idea of how noncombatants, in this case a little girl, suffered during the Vietnam Conflict" (*School Library Journal* June 1, 1991). "Simple, concrete, and matter-of-fact, the writing makes the book convincing as a child's first-person narrative and, ultimately, moving as an expression of the resilience of the human spirit. While this short book is accessible to third-graders, it would also be a good selection for English-as-a-second-language students" (*Booklist* Mar. 15, 1991). Ages 7–10.

Klein, Adria F. **Max and the Adoption Day Party.** Read-It! Readers Series. Mankato, MN: Picture Window Books, 2006. 24p. $19.99. ISBN 1-4048-3145-2; 978-1-4048-3145-2.

Max brings a special present to his friend Jose's adoption day party. The first book in the Read-It! Readers Series, "These books all use simple words and sentence patterns to help children who are just beginning to read. Average-quality, brightly colored cartoons [by Mernie Gallagher-Cole] fill most of the pages" (*School Library Journal* July 1, 2007). Ages 5–7.

Krementz, Jill. **How It Feels to Be Adopted.** St. Louis, MO: San Val, Turtle Books, 1982. ISBN: 0-606-03821-3; ISBN 13: 978-0-606-03821-8. Out of print.

Nineteen adoptees between ages 8 and 16 share their views, feelings, and personal experiences in three-page monologues that Krementz accompanics with photos of the kids in solo portraits and in adoptive-family groups. Some of the kids have been contacted by their birth mothers and are glad to know them, but consider their adoptive mothers their real ones. As for their birth fathers, few give them a thought. "Comments range from the automatic defense—Krementz isn't one for probing—'It's not different, it's special' to 'It makes me stick out from other people. I'm not ordinary.' The statements are pretty much skimmed from the surface, but they have a calculable draw, and not only for other adoptees" (*Kirkus Reviews* Nov. 11, 1982). Ages 8–16.

Krishnaswami, Uma. **Bringing Asha Home.** New York: Lee & Low Books, 2006. 32p. $13.22. ISBN 1-58430-259-3; 978-1-58430-259-9.

Eight-year-old Arun, an Asian Indian American boy, waits impatiently while international adoption paperwork is completed before he can meet his new baby sister from India. "Chalk pastel illustrations follow the text closely, but the dark palette of blues and grays sets a somber tone for the joyful story. Arun's tale presents an authentic slice of East Indian American life and provides a fresh perspective in adoption stories" (*Booklist* Oct. 15, 2006). Ages 4–8.

Lewis, Rose. **Every Year on Your Birthday.** New York: Little, Brown Books for Young Readers, 2007. 32p. $16.99. ISBN 0-316-52552-9; 978-0-316-52552-7.

On each birthday of her adopted Chinese daughter, a mother recalls the highlights of the times they have shared. "Delicately expressive watercolors [by Jane Dyer] capture the girl's excitement and happiness. Beautifully designed with framed scenes and boxed sequences of her growth, this loving portrait of a single mother and an adopted child gently accentuates the importance of incorporating the child's culture into her new life" (*Booklist* June 1, 2007). Ages 3–6.

Lewis, Rose A. **I Love You Like Crazy Cakes.** New York: Little, Brown Books for Young Readers, 2000. 32p. $16.99. ISBN:0-316-52538-3; ISBN 13:978-0-316-52538-1.

This story of a woman who travels to China to adopt a baby girl, based on the author's own experiences, is a celebration of the love and joy a baby brings into the home. Illustrated by Jane Dyer. "The illustrations are done in light-drenched colors, clear and rosy hues that match the bubbling joy of the text....Sure to delight many families whose own children may have come to this country, and to their families, by the same means, this is also a lovely way to introduce others to the concept of foreign-born adoption" (*Kirkus Reviews* Aug. 9, 2000). Ages 4–8.

Lewis, Rose. **I Love You Like Crazy Cakes.** Norwalk, CT: Weston Woods Studios, 2004. Mixed media; hardcover & CD-ROM. 7 hrs. 42 min. $ 29.95. ISBN 1-55592-135-3. Mixed media; hHard cover & audio cassette. $24.95. ISBN 1-55592-095-0; 978-1-55592-095-1. Compact Disc. $ 12.95. ISBN 1-55592-936-2; 978-1-55592-936-7.

"Actress Mia Farrow narrates the tale in a gentle, measured tone that perfectly meshes with the text. The video scans Jane Dyer's tender watercolors, rightly focusing on the expressive faces of the characters" (*School Library Journal* Sept. 1, 2002). Ages 4–8.

Little, Jean. **Emma's Strange Pet.** I Can Read Books: Level 3. New York: HarperCollins, Harper Trophy, 2004. 64p. $3.99pa. ISBN 0-06-444259-4; 978-0-06-444259-6.

Max, an adopted child, wants a dog, but his sister Emma is allergic to fur, and they decide that a lizard is a good compromise. Caring for their pet brings the children closer and helps to resolve issues related to Max's status as a newly adopted family member. "Little portrays real characters who bring everyday problems to satisfying conclusions. Simple, full-color line-and-watercolor illustrations [by Jennifer Plecas] do a great job of capturing expressions of confusion, worry, anger, and joy" (*School Library Journal* Sept. 1, 2003). Ages 5–8.

Little, Jean. **Emma's Yucky Brother.** New York: HarperCollins, 2001. 64p. $14.95. ISBN 0-06-028348-3; 978-0-06-028348-3. Out of Print.

Emma finds out how hard it is to be a big sister when her family adopts a four-year-old boy named Max. Emma has always wanted a little brother. Now her family is adopting Max, and Emma is sure he will be the best brother ever. But Max has his own ideas. He thinks sisters are yucky, and that Emma is the yuckiest! "Little's simple words and [Jennifer] Plecas' clear, expressive line-and-watercolor illustrations tell an intense story that goes beyond direct messages to show both siblings' hurt, anger, and displacement and, finally, their bonding. An excellent book to introduce new readers to the idea that a good story can show many sides" (*Booklist* Dec. 1, 2000). Ages 4–8.

McKay, Hilary. **Saffy's Angel.** New York: Simon & Schuster Children's Publishing, 2002. 160p. $16.99. ISBN 0-689-84933-8; 978-0-689-84933-6.

Thirteen-year-old Saffron (Saffy) discovers she is adopted—her adoptive mother is the twin of her Italian mother who died in a car crash in Italy when Saffron was three. Saffy returns to Italy to search for a memento of her past, a stone angel in a garden in Italy. An award-winning book that "raises questions about belonging, attraction, and the subtle bonds that hold families and friends together" (*Booklist* May 15, 2002). Ages 8–12.

McKay, Hilary. **Saffy's Angel.** Casson Family Series, Book 1. New York: Random House Audio Publishing Group, Listening Library, 2004. 160p. Paperback & audio cassette, 3 vols., 4hrs. 43 min. $36.00. ISBN 0-8072-2098-1; 978-0-8072-2098-6.

"British actress Julia Sawalha wisely chooses not to attempt a distinct voice for each of the many characters, opting instead to allow her charmingly subtle vocal intonations to enhance the adept writing. This allows listeners to focus on description and mood, somehow making the story even funnier" (*School Library Journal* Nov. 1, 2002). Ages 8–12.

Newman, Lesleá. **Felicia's Favorite Story.** Ambler, PA: Two Lives Publishing, 2003. 24p. $9.95pa. ISBN 0-9674468-5-6; 978-0-9674468-5-1.

Felicia's favorite story is how her two mothers, Linda and Vanessa, adopted her from Guatemala. Illustrations by Adriana Romo. "This is a comforting book for children in alternative families as well as a pleasant tale for all children who rejoice in sharing their own life story" (*School Library Journal* Oct. 1, 2003). Ages 4–8.

Parr, Todd. **We Belong Together: A Book about Adoption and Families.** New York: Little, Brown Books for Young Readers, 2007. 32p. $15.99. ISBN 0-316-01668-3; 978-0-316-01668-1.

Writer and illustrator Parr introduces young children to adoption and ways that adoptive families come together. "As in Parr's *The Family Book* (2003), cheerful, friendly artwork, with thickly outlined forms and characters and a bold rainbow palette, inclusively depicts an array of children and families including one with a single parent and one with two dads and emphasizes the rewards of adoption for adults and children alike" (*Booklist* July 1, 2007). Ages 3–6.

Peacock, Carol Antoinette. **Mommy Far, Mommy Near: An Adoption Story.** Park Ridge, IL: Albert Whitman, 2000. 32p. $16.99. ISBN 0-8075-5234-8; 978-0-8075-5234-6.

Elizabeth, an adopted Chinese girl, sometimes wonders why her real mother gave her up. Her adoptive mother explains that although her Chinese mother loved Elizabeth and wanted to keep her, she couldn't because of China's laws. "The mother's tender support not only reassures Elizabeth but will also benefit other adoptees, especially those from Third World countries, as it reinforces the efforts of all loving, adoptive parents" (*Booklist* Mar. 15, 2000). "Confident brush strokes create fluid family scenes and thoughtful facial expressions. The illustrations [by Shawn Costello Brownell] make Elizabeth's intermittent vulnerability even more obvious" (*School Library Journal* May 1, 2000).

Polacco, Patricia. **In Our Mothers' House.** New York: Penguin Group, Philomel, 2009. 48p. $17.99. ISBN 0-399-25076-X; 978-0-399-25076-7.

Three young children experience the joys and challenges of being raised by two mothers. The narrator is a black girl who describes how her two Caucasian mothers, Marmee and Meema, adopted her, her Asian brother, and her red-headed sister. She describes the wonderful times they have growing in their home. "The energetic illustrations in pencil and marker, though perhaps not as well-rendered as in some previous works, teem with family activities and neighborhood festivity. Quieter moments radiate the love the mothers feel for their children and for each other" (*Booklist* May 1, 2009). Ages 5–8.

Stoeke, Janet Morgan. **Waiting for May.** New York: Penguin Group, Puffin, 2007. 32p. $5.99pa. ISBN 0-14-240853-0; 978-0-14-240853-7.

A young boy eagerly awaits the arrival of his new sister from China. As the weeks pass, his excitement builds until the family receives a photo of the new baby, but they must wait until May to go to China to bring her home. Ages 5–9.

Williams, Laura E. **Slant.** Minneapolis, MN: Milkweed Editions, 2008. 160p. $16.95. ISBN 1-57131-681-7; 978-1-57131-681-3.

Thirteen-year-old Lauren, a Korean-American adoptee, is taunted by kids calling her "slant" and other derogatory names. Her solution is to have an eye operation that will deepen the crease of her eyelids to make her more confident and popular. She resents her father's reluctance to grant permission for the surgery and his refusal to talk about her mother, who died several years earlier. She learns that her father has been shielding her from knowledge of her mother's depression and suicide. "Not all issues are resolved, but Lauren's voice and emotions ring true, realistically capturing the ups and downs of a contemporary young teen's life as well as exploring the dilemma of how to respond to blatant prejudice" (*Booklist* Dec. 1, 2008). Ages 8–13.

Wynne-Jones, Tim. **The Boat in the Tree.** Honesdale, PA: Boyds Mills Press, Front Street, 2007. 40p. $17.95. ISBN 1-932425-49-7; 978-1-932425-49-9.

A young boy dreams of sailing to Bongadongo after his younger brother is adopted. The boy finally has a means of escape but cannot use it without his brother's help. Illustrated by John Shelley. "The richly detailed vision will engage children, however, while the messages about working through sibling rivalry will hit home with many. One final note: it's nice to see a picture book about adoption in which the new arrival is an older child, rather than a baby" (*Booklist* Mar. 1, 2007). Ages 8–12.

Young, Ed. **My Mei Mei.** New York: Penguin Group, Philomel, 2006. 40p. $16.99. ISBN 0-399-24339-9; 978-0-399-24339-4.

Young's adopted daughter from China, Antonia, narrates this story of her own adoption and her wish to have a Mei Mei, a younger sister. The family travels to China to pick up the baby, but Antonia expresses conflicting emotions when her parents' attention is focused on the baby; however, Antonia's regret at having a sister gradually changes to sisterly love as Antonia learns the responsibilities of being a big sister. "Pencil-and-paint portraits of the girls and their parents float against open backgrounds of patterned fabric and paper, which evoke a sense of cozy domesticity in their resemblance to wallpaper while the wild swirls of flowers, vines, and shapes echo the story's emotional intensity. Families that have adopted multiple children will welcome this title, and children of all backgrounds will easily connect with Young's sensitive portrayal of how siblings move through jealousy and resentment and create the small moments that hold them fiercely together" (*Booklist* Jan. 1, 2006). Ages 4–8.

Xinran and Josee Masee. **Motherbridge of Love.** Cambridge, MA: Barefoot Books, 2007. 32p. $16.99. ISBN 1-84686-047-4; 978-1-84686-047-8.

This rhyming story celebrates the relationship between a parent and child through the exchanges between a little Chinese girl and her adoptive parent. "Masse's soothing paintings, predominantly in blues and greens, are exceptional, and infuse this lyrical poem with a sweet tenderness. While it is particularly relevant to adoptive children from China and their families, the story has resonance for anyone involved in an adoption" (*School Library Journal* Jan. 1, 2008). Ages 4–10.

Death (General)

Brallier, Jess M. **Tess's Tree.** New York: HarperCollins, 2009. 32p. $17.89. ISBN 0-06-168753-7; 978-0-06-168753-2.

Nine-year-old Tess invites her friends, family, and neighbors to celebrate her beloved maple tree's life before it must be cut down, and she discovers that it has meaning for many other people as well. "[Peter H.] Reynolds's soft watercolor vignettes extend the quiet story. Wispy lines portray a subtle vulnerability; washes of muted blue effectively provide emotional depth as Tess survives grief's powerful storm" (*Kirkus Reviews* Aug. 1, 2009).

Brown, Laurie Krasny. **When Dinosaurs Die: A Guide to Understanding Death.** New York: Little, Brown Books for Young Readers, 1996. $15.74. ISBN 0-316-10917-7; 978-0-316-10917-8 (Out of print). Saint Louis, MO: San Val, Turtleback, 1998. ISBN 0-606-17389-7; 978-0-606-17389-6 (Out of Print).

With the assistance of the dinosaurs from *Dinosaurs to the Rescue!* and *Dinosaurs Divorce,* the author and illustrator Marc Brown explain why death occurs and suggests strategies for coping with the resulting loneliness, anger, and fear. "The forthright approach makes the subject seem less mysterious and provides kids with plenty to think about and discuss with their parents. It's the brightly colored artwork, however, that will really enable children to relax with the concept" (*Booklist* Apr. 1, 1996). Ages 4–8.

Carson, Jo. **You Hold Me and I'll Hold You.** New York: Scholastic, Orchard Books, 1997. 32p. $6.95. ISBN 0-531-07088-3; 978-0-531-07088-8.

When a great-aunt dies, a young child finds comfort when her father holds her and tells her "You hold me, and I'll hold you." "Like the text, the illustrations [by Annie Cannon] allow rays of sun to dominate what could have been a dark subject. Realistic but nonthreatening, Carson's story charms as it comforts" (*School Library Journal* March 1, 1992). Ages 4–7.

Charles, Veronika Martenova. **The Birdman.** Montreal: Tundra Books, 2006. 32p. $17.95. ISBN: 88776-740-0; 978-0-88776-740-1.

Based on a true story, Noor Nobi is a tailor, making clothes to support his three children. When they are taken from him in an accident, he wanders Calcutta with no reason to live. Weeks after the accident, he goes to the market and for very little money, buys a sickly bird that he nurses back to health and sets free. This allows him to finally grieve for his children. He goes back to work, buys another bird, works to heal it and set it free. Eventually he becomes known as the Birdman of Calcultta, having found purpose in saving birds. "*The Birdman* is written in a vivid, poetic text, complemented by vibrant folk-art paintings, gloriously patterned with flowers, Hindu symbols, and soaring birds" (*Booklist*). Ages 5–8.

Coerr, Eleanor. **Sadako.** Lexington, KY: Book Wholesalers, 2002. Unp. $24.55. ISBN 0-7587-3544-8; 978-0-7587-3544-7.

Hospitalized with the dreaded atom bomb disease, leukemia, a child in Hiroshima races against time to fold one thousand paper cranes before she dies. This book is the same story as the author's *Sadako and the Thousand Paper Cranes* (Putnam, 1977), abbreviated and written for a younger audience. "Coerr uses a quiet, unsentimental voice in her retelling, letting the content of the story speak for itself. And it does, powerfully. [Illustrator Ed] Young amplifies the story's vision with his impressionistic pastel artwork illustrating scene after scene with narrative simplicity and emotional depth" (*Booklist* Nov. 1, 1993). Ages 5–8.

Coerr, Eleanor. **Sadako and the Thousand Paper Cranes.** Puffin Modern Classics. New York: Penguin, 2004. 80p. $5.99p and e-book. ISBN 978-0-14240-113-2.

This picture book is a rewrite of Coerr's book *Sadako and the Thousand Paper Cranes* (1977) for a younger audience and using pastel illustrations. Based on the real story of Sadako Sasaki, who was only two years old when an atom bomb was dropped on Hiroshima. When she is 12, several dizzy spells send Sadako to the doctor, and the budding school track star learns that she has leukemia. She races against time to fold one thousand paper cranes to verify the Japanese legend that by doing so a sick person will become healthy. She dies with 644 completed;

Sadako's classmates finish making the remaining cranes, and all 1,000 are buried with her. Ages 6–10.

Ganeri, Anita. **Journey's End: Death and Mourning.** Life Times Series. Columbus, OH: School Specialty Publishing, Peter Bedrick Books, 1999. 30p. $15.95. ISBN 0-87226-289-8; 978-0-87226-289-8.

Introduces briefly the customs and ceremonies surrounding death in the six major world religions: Hinduism, Buddhism, Sikhism, Judaism, Christianity, and Islam. "The ceremonies are captured with lavish color photography, and mythological stories are included and enhanced with dream-like watercolor illustrations by Jackie Morris. The fact file found at the end of each book has a chart with six facts about all of the religions" (*Voice of Youth Advocates* Dec. 1, 1999). Ages 10–12.

Gellman, Marc, and Thomas Hartman. **Lost and Found: A Kid's Book for Living Through Loss.** New York: HarperCollins, 1999. 176p. $15.99. ISBN 0-688-15752-1; 978-0-688-15752-4.

Rabbi Marc Gellman and Monsignor Thomas Hartman draw on years of counseling to describe different kinds of losses—possessions, competitions, health, and loss caused by death—with suggestions for coping with these losses. "With a few exceptions, such as a discussion of the soul, this is not a strictly religious book. Rather it is a practical, heartfelt exploration that emphasizes the idea of picking up after a loss and learning to look back with fondness and understanding" (*Booklist* May 15, 1999). Ages 9–14.

Goldman, Linda. **Children Also Grieve: Talking about Death and Healing.** Philadelphia, PA: Jessica Kingsley, 2006. 80p. $22.95 ISBN 1-84310-808-9; 978-1-84310-808-5.

An imaginative resource that offers support and reassurance to children dealing with the loss of a close friend or relative and to adults who are supporting them through their bereavement. Illustrated with color photographs, this book is designed to be read and worked through by children with an adult. The story tells of Henry, the dog of a family whose grandfather has died. During Henry's progress through the different stages of bereavement, he learns strategies for coping with his grief. At various stages of the story, Goldman provides readers with the opportunity to share their reactions to loss through words and pictures, using prompt questions that encourage the exploration of different facets of grief. "While some children might wonder why the dog is telling the story, this book will encourage dialogue and will aid children in dealing with loss and healing" (*School Library Journal* July 1, 2006). Ages 8–12.

Heegaard, Marge Eaton. **Coping with Death and Grief.** Minneapolis, MN: Lerner, 1990. 64p. $19.93. ISBN 0-8225-0043-4; 978-0-8225-0043-8.

Using case studies about children, this book discusses death as a natural occurrence, what happens when someone dies, and how to deal with feelings of loss and grief. "Grieving young people are reassured about their feelings and encouraged to express them; various outlets for their feelings are suggested. An excellent section discusses approaching others who are grieving" (*School Library Journal* Nov. 1, 1990). Ages 10–12.

Jeffers, Oliver. **The Heart and the Bottle.** New York: Penguin Group, Philomel, 2010. 32p. $17.99. ISBN 0-399-25452-8; 978-0-399-25452-9.

A girl and an unidentified man, possibly her grandfather, share a love of astronomy, oceanography, and life science. When the man dies, the girl puts her heart in a jar for safekeeping and abandons her studies. Then she meets someone who can release her heart. "The sophisticated palette creates a consistency across the pages, and the artwork, meticulously constructed and edited with a uniquely minimalist aesthetic, is signature Jeffers. Heartbreaking, witty and filled with hope, this will perhaps rings most true with children whose parents have recently suffered a loss" (*Kirkus Reviews* Feb. 15, 2010). "Aimed at an older audience than one would think at first glance, this allegory about grief and the futility of attempts at self-protection will resonate most with those who've suffered a loss. An unusual, original book" (*School Library Journal* Feb. 1, 2010). Ages 4–9.

Johnston, Marianne. **Let's Talk about Going to a Funeral.** The Let's Talk Library. New York: Rosen Publishing Group, 1997. 24p. $19.95. ISBN 0-8239-5038-7; 978-0-8239-5038-6.

Describes what happens before, during, and after a funeral and includes an explanation of grieving, the cemetery, the grave, and cremation. "This book deals with a confusing, sometimes frightening subject in a simple way, providing just enough information to answer many questions youngsters may have. It's an excellent book for classroom teachers, mental health professionals, and librarians to offer children and parents of children who have lost a loved one" (*School Library Journal* July 1, 1998). Ages 5–8.

Kadono, Eiko. **Grandpa's Soup.** Grand Rapids, MI: Eerdmans, 2009. 40p. $8.50pa. ISBN 0-8028-5347-1; 978-0-8028-5347-9.

After the death of his wife, an old man gradually realizes that making the soup she used to cook and sharing it with friends eases his loneliness. Ages 4–8.

Koss, Amy Goldman. **Stolen Words.** Middleton, WI: American Girl Publishing, 2001. 156p. $14.95. ISBN 1-58485-377-8; 978-1-58485-377-0. Paperback: 156p. $5.95. ISBN 1-58485-376-X; 978-1-58485-376-3. Both editions are out of print.

Eleven-year-old Robyn tries to recover from the death of her Aunt Beth by recording in her diary her family's visit to Austria. "Robyn is a true eleven-year-old girl, loving the small things she discovers in a foreign country, but also maturing as she deals with grief and her many fears. She is observant of human nature, funny, and endearing" (*Voice of Youth Advocates* Feb. 1, 2002). "Robyn's intimate, conversational entries in a new journal provide an engaging read as they realistically depict the grieving-healing process. Detailed, often humorous descriptions and commentary on the Austrian people and places alternate with poignant reflections on Aunt Beth and family experiences" (*Booklist* Oct. 15, 2001). Ages 9–12.

LaFleur, Suzanne. **Love, Aubrey.** New York: Random House Publishing Group, Delacorte Press, 2009. 272p. $18.99. ISBN 0-385-90686-2; 978-0-385-90686-9. Random House Publishing Group, Delacorte Press, 2011. 272p. $6.99pa. ISBN 0-375-85159-3; 978-0-375-85159-9.

While living with her grandmother in Vermont, 11-year-old Aubrey writes letters as a way of dealing with the loss of her father and sister in a car accident, and her abandonment by her mother. Her grandmother and some new friends provide comfort and support to help her overcome her denial of grief. "LaFleur captures the way everyday occurrences can trigger a sudden flood of memories and overwhelming feelings of renewed loss. She details the physical responses of the human body to emotional trauma with an immediacy that puts readers inside Aubrey's pain and loss" (*School Library Journal* Sept. 1, 2009). Ages 10–12.

LaFleur, Suzanne. **Love, Aubrey.** New York: Random House Audio Publishing Group, Listening Library, 2009. Compact disc. Unabridged. $30.00. ISBN 0-7393-8028-1; 978-0-7393-8028-4.

"Becca Battoe beautifully narrates this sensitive story of love, loss, and forgiveness, allowing listeners to experience a depth beyond what the written word can provide. As Aubrey comes face to face with the tough changes in her life, Battoe's voicing sounds firmer and more decisive" (*School Library Journal* Oct. 1, 2009). Ages 10–12.

Maddern, Eric, and Duncan Williamson. **Death in a Nut.** London: Frances Lincoln, 2005. 32p. $15.95. ISBN 1-84507-081-X; 978-1-84507-081-6.

Young Jack meets Death on the beach and stuffs it into a hazelnut shell that he throws into the sea. When he returns home, he finds his ill mother feeling much better, but eggs won't break, vegetables can't be sliced, and the butcher can't slaughter any livestock. Based on a Scottish folktale, this retelling is illustrated by Paul Hess. "Like Yugi Morales's *Just a Minute* (2003), this may help to make the Reaper a little less Grim for younger readers" (*Kirkus Reviews* Dec. 15, 2004). Ages 5–8.

Mills, Joyce C. **Gentle Willow: A Story for Children about Dying.** Washington, DC: American Psychological Association, 1993. 32p. $11.95. ISBN 0-945354-54-1; 978-0-945354-54-3. American Psychological Association, 2004. 32p. $9.95pa. ISBN 1-59147-072-2; 978-1-59147-072-4.

Amanda the squirrel is upset that she is going to lose her friend Gentle Willow, using the metaphor of a dying tree to show how the sadness and fear of death can be transformed by love and memory. Written for children who may not survive their illness or for the children who know them, this story addresses questions about cancer and its treatment, as well as the feelings of disbelief, anger, and sadness that accompany grief. Ages 4–8.

Murphy, Patricia J. **Death.** Tough Topics Series. Chicago: Heinemann-Raintree, 2007. 32p. $7.99pa. ISBN 1-4034-9783-4; 978-1-4034-9783-3.

Murphy discusses death, how it can happen, how it affects people, and funerals. The book explores how people feel when a loved one has died and how they can cope with grief, providing reassurance to any readers who have lost someone close to them. "Murphy gives an overview of the topic in a way that young readers can understand" (*School Library Journal* Dec. 1, 2007). Ages 4–8.

Nicholls, Sally. **Ways to Live Forever.** New York: Scholastic, 2008. 224p. $16.99. ISBN 0-545-06948-3; 978-0-545-06948-9.

Eleven-year-old Sam McQueen has leukemia and writes a book during the last three months of his life. He tells what he would like to accomplish, how he feels, and things that have happened to him. "Interspersed with Sam's lists, questions and odd bits of mortality facts on notebook paper, his narrative proceeds in short, candid chapters that reveal a boy who, though he's not ready to die, nevertheless can confront the reality with heartbreaking clarity" (*Kirkus Reviews* Sept. 1, 2008). Ages 9–12.

Portnoy, Mindy Avra. **Where Do People Go When They Die?** Minneapolis: Lerner, 2004. 24p. $15.95. ISBN 1-58013-081-X; 978-1-58013-081-3.

Young children ask family members, a teacher, and other adults the question in the title. Each reassuring answer is different, but they all lead back to: When people die, they go to God, who is everywhere. Portnoy, a rabbi, concludes with several suggestions for parents, advising them of other questions children might ask and possible answers. "Haas's muted watercolor illustrations help set the tone for this meaningful, much-needed book on a universal topic" (*School Library Journal* July 1, 2004). Ages 3–8.

Raschka, Chris. **The Purple Balloon.** New York: Random House Children's Books, Schwartz & Wade Books, 2007. 32p. $16.99. ISBN 0-375-84146-6; 978-0-375-84146-0.

Using a metaphor frequently found in the art of dying children, an image of a purple balloon floating free, the author uses balloon characters to discuss first the death of an old person, then a child's dying. "Raschka has turned a tough subject into a sensitive book that could be a useful tool for the right child with the right adult at the right time" (*Booklist* Apr. 1, 2007). "Streaked watercolor background washes change color with the mood, moving from blue to yellow on the final page describing 'what you can do to help.' Raschka's brief text avoids sentimentality and didacticism and is a good choice for those who want to provide assistance to children about this difficult subject" (*School Library Journal* June 1, 2007). Ages 3–8.

Rock, Lois. **When Goodbye Is Forever.** Intercourse, PA: Good Books, 2004. 32p. $7.95. ISBN 1-56148-449-0; 978-1-56148-449-2.

In life we learn to say many goodbyes. Some are easy, but some are very difficult to face. This book is intended to help young children understand different kinds of goodbyes, and to cope with bereavement. "The author has tackled a difficult topic with varying degrees of success. Some metaphors are rather awkward, but her sensitivity to the subject is apparent" (*School Library Journal* Mar. 1, 2005). Ages 3–8.

Rosen, Michael. **Michael Rosen's Sad Book.** Somerville, MA: Candlewick Press, 2005. 32p. $16.99. ISBN 0-7636-2597-3; 978-0-7636-2597-9.

The author shares his deep sadness following the death of his 18-year-old son, Eddie. Rosen writes about his sadness, how it affects him, and some of the things he does to cope with it. "This book tells them what they already intuit, and while you might not want to give it to a child who, at the moment, is happy, you would most certainly want to give it to one who is sad. It shows children that they are not alone, and it does so brilliantly" (*Booklist* May 15, 2005). Ages 5–10.

Rylant, Cynthia. **The Heavenly Village.** New York: Scholastic, 1999. 96p. $15.95. ISBN 0-439-04096-5; 978-0-439-04096-9.

Some people who go to heaven are not ready to give up their earthly understanding of time, their routines, or the loved ones they have left behind. For these people God created The Heavenly Village, where they can keep half a heart in heaven and the other half on earth until they are ready to move on. Rylant describes this quiet village and the stories of seven people passing through. "*The Heavenly Village* is a beautiful book—sad and joyful, pensive and intelligent, it is a pleasure to read" (*Voice of Youth Advocates* Feb. 1, 2000). Ages 10–14.

Salonen, Roxane Beauclair. **First Salmon.** Honesdale, PA: Boyds Mills Press, 2005. 29p. $15.95. ISBN 1-59078-171-6; 978-1-59078-171-5.

First Salmon is celebrated by the Northwest Pacific tribes to welcome back the salmon each year. During the event, Charlie remembers his late Uncle Joe—the things he learned from him, and the stories he told. By the story's end, he realizes that death is a part of nature's cycle, and as long as he has memories of his uncle, Joe will always be a part of him. "Libraries in the Pacific Northwest will want this title, and classes anywhere studying Native peoples could certainly benefit from this careful depiction of tradition" (*School Library Journal* Nov. 1, 2005). Ages 8–12.

Sloan, Christopher. **Bury the Dead: Tombs, Corpses, Mummies, Skeletons, and Rituals.** Washington, DC: National Geographic Society Children's Books, 2002. 64p. $18.95. ISBN 0-7922-7192-0; 978-0-7922-7192-5.

Examines the customs and practices of burial from ancient times to the present. The final chapter examines modern burials. "Sloan, an editor at National Geographic magazine and the author of two previous books for children, does a terrific job of providing an intriguing, reader-friendly text that is not overshadowed by the fabulous color photographs from the National Geographic Society's archives" (*Booklist* Dec. 1, 2002). "[B]oth thrill seekers and children seeking some perspective on death or grief will find this rewarding reading" (*Kirkus Reviews* Sept. 1, 2002). Ages 10–14.

Tomey, Ingrid. **Grandfather's Day.** Honesdale, PA: Boyds Mills Press, 2003. 64p. $9.95pa. ISBN 1-56397-947-0; 978-1-56397-947-7.

Raydeen, nine years old, tries to help her grandfather overcome his sadness after his wife's death. "While Raydeen, like most youngsters, cannot comprehend the pain of losing a lifetime companion, she instinctively responds to the need to fill the void in her grandfather's life and to build a loving relationship with him. [Robert A.] McKay's soft pencil sketches reflect the honesty and warmth of Tomey's caringly written approach to death and to renewed life" (*Booklist* Sept. 15, 1992). Ages 7–10.

Wood, Nancy C. **Old Coyote.** Somerville, MA: Candlewick Press, 2004. 32p. $16.99. ISBN 0-7636-1544-7; 978-0-7636-1544-4.

Realizing that he has come to the end of his days, Old Coyote knows it's time to move on to the next great adventure. He spends his last day reminiscing and saying goodbye to his family and friends. "Wood's sensitive narrative serves as a gentle introduction to a potentially difficult subject, and [Max] Grafe's mixed-media, earth-toned illustrations beautifully capture the essence of it all" (*Booklist* Dec. 1, 2004). Ages 5–8.

Death of a Friend

Bahr, Mary. **If Nathan Were Here.** Grand Rapids, MI: Eerdmans, 2004. 32p. $8.00pa. ISBN 0-8028-5235-1; 978-0-8028-5235-9.

Illustrated by Karen A. Jerome, *If Nathan Were Here* explores the grief of a young boy whose friend has died. He thinks of the happy times they shared, and the children at school talk about their remembrances of Nathan that they gather in a Memory Box. "The story offers no easy solution as it moves through the boy's anger and isolation to his rejoining life in gradual, unforced steps. The bright watercolors have a gentle, shining quality that enhances the book's hopeful message" (*Booklist* Apr. 15, 2000). Ages 5–8.

Bley, Anette. **And What Comes after a Thousand?** La Jolla, CA: Kane Miller, 2007. 32p. $15.95. ISBN 1-933605-27-8; 978-1-933605-27-2.

Describes the special friendship between a little girl named Lisa and an old man, Otto. After Otto dies, Lisa learns that he is present in her memory and with her forever in spirit. "True to the small child's viewpoint, this playful picture book, originally published in Germany, is also a heartfelt story of love, grief, and comfort.... What will hold and comfort even young preschoolers are the honesty of the loss and the enduring love, expressed in the exuberant pastel pictures of Lisa and Otto in the garden they both love" (*Booklist* May 15, 2007). Ages 4–8.

Brisson, Pat. **I Remember Miss Perry.** New York: Penguin Group, 2006. 32p. $16.99. ISBN 0-8037-2981-2; 978-0-8037-2981-0.

After his teacher, Miss Perry, is killed in a car accident, Stevie and his elementary school classmates share their memories of her. "[F]or children who are experiencing loss (even though this is one step removed from a family death), the story clearly makes the point that memory is an antidote for sadness. Sprightly ink-and-watercolor illustrations feature a multiethnic class, and capture Miss Perry with particular charm" (*Booklist* Feb. 1, 2006). Ages 4–7.

Carlstrom, Nancy White. **Blow Me a Kiss, Miss Lilly.** New York: HarperCollins, 1990. 32p. $13.00. ISBN 0-06-021012-5; 978-0-06-021012-0.

Sara and elderly Miss Lilly are best friends who share many happy times together. When they part, they blow kisses as their way of saying good-bye. Miss Lilly becomes ill and dies, leaving Sara in grief; however, the emphasis is on their friendship. "Deceptively simple, the language evokes deep emotion and vivid imagery. Schwartz's jubilant ink-wash illustrations capture the childlike innocence and serve as the perfect complement to the story" (*School Library Journal* July 1, 1990). Ages 4–8.

Edwards, Michelle. **Stinky Stern Forever: A Jackson Friends Book.** Boston: Houghton Mifflin Harcourt, 2005. 56p. $14.00. ISBN 0-15-216389-1; 978-0-15-216389-1. $5.95pa. ISBN 0-15-206101-0; 978-0-15-206101-2.

On her way home from school, second-grader Pa Lia sees her obnoxious classmate, "Stinky" Stern, hit by a van. Pa Lia and the students in her class face a difficult challenge: How should they remember the class bully? "While the subject matter is indeed serious and the tone, for the most part, somber, children who have experienced the loss of a classmate or friend will find hope in this honest presentation" (*School Library Journal* Oct. 1, 2005). Ages 5–8.

Monsell, Mary E., and Leslie Tryon. **Toohy and Wood.** New York: Simon & Schuster Children's Publishing, Atheneum, 1992. 80p. $12.95. ISBN 0-689-31721-2; 978-0-689-31721-7.

Wood, a poetic turtle, helps lizard Toohy accept the death of his best friend, a dove killed in a grass fire. "The characters and the writing have a serene, Pooh-like simplicity, and the layered humor will appeal to a range of sensibilities. Toohy's grief eases at the end in a believable way" (*School Library Journal* Oct. 1, 1992). Ages 7–10.

Nunes, Lygia Bojunga. **My Friend the Painter.** Trans. Giovanni Pontiero. San Diego, CA: Harcourt Trade Publishers, 1991. 96p. $13.95. ISBN 0-15-256340-7; 978-0-15-256340-0.

In this story from Brazil, 11-year-old Claudio remembers in his grief the good times he had with his painter friend, who has committed suicide. "Her [Nunes's] subtle transitions between present, past, and dream-world may not always be easy for young people to follow, and the focus on adults may not attract a wide following; but for the special reader, a rich, poetic glimpse of universal feelings filtered through an unfamiliar culture" (*Kirkus Reviews* May 1, 1991). Ages 10–12.

Nuzum, K. A. **The Leanin' Dog.** New York: HarperCollins, Joanna Cotler Books, 2008. 256p. $16.89. ISBN 0-06-113935-1; 978-0-06-113935-2.

> In a story set in Colorado during the 1930s, 11-year-old Dessa Dean mourns the death of her beloved mother, but the arrival of an injured dog and the friendship they form enables her to overcome her grief. "Dessa's sweet, simple narration, inflected with a bit of backwoods dialect, will draw preteen readers to this heart-warming tale of friendship between a dog who does not want to be confined and a girl who is afraid to leave her self-imposed confinement. The isolated setting, deep snow, and small cast of thoughtful, quiet characters combine to build a sub-dued atmosphere that is finally joyfully broken by the happy barks of The Leanin' Dog, as Dessa names her new friend" (*Voice of Youth Advocates* Dec. 1, 2008). Ages 9–12.

Paterson, Katherine. **Bridge to Terabithia.** New York: HarperCollins, 2007. 176p. $6.99pa. ISBN 0-06-122728-5; 978-0-06-122728-8. E-book: $6.99. ISBN 0-06-183267-7; 978-0-06-183267-3. ISBN 0-06-183269-3; 978-0-06-183269-7. CD Audiobook $25.95.

> The Newbery Medal-winning story of Jess Aarons and Leslie Burke who become friends and create the imaginary land of Terabithia. There they rule until Leslie drowns trying to reach their hideaway. Jesse struggles to accept the loss of his friend. Ages 10–12.

Smith, Doris Buchanan. **A Taste of Blackberries.** Logan, IA: Perfection Learning, 1992. 85p. $12.65. ISBN 0-8124-2284-8; 978-0-8124-2284-9.

> No one dreamed that Jamie's exuberance and a harmless prank could end in his sudden death. When it does, his friend must find the strength to bear his grief and his feeling that he might have saved his friend. Ages 9–12.

Death of a Parent or Grandparent

Austen, Catherine. **Walking Backward.** Custer, WA: Orca, 2009. 176p. $9.95pa. ISBN 1-55469-147-8; 978-1-55469-147-0.

> Twelve-year-old Josh's mother dies in a car crash, and his family falls apart. His father spends his time building a time machine to go back and prevent his wife from getting in the car. Josh's little brother talks to his Power Ranger as if it's his mother, and Josh tries to make sense of a world without his mother. "Given the subject matter, the story is never maudlin, and Josh's voice rings natural and true. An elegantly crafted volume of lasting power" (*Kirkus Reviews* Sept. 15, 2009). Ages 9–12.

Banks, Kate. **Dillon Dillon.** New York: Farrar, Straus & Giroux, Frances Foster Books, 2002. 160p. $16.00. ISBN 978-0-374-31786-7; 0-374-31786-0. New York: Far-rar, Straus & Giroux, Sunburst Paperbacks, 2005. 160p. $6.99pa. ISBN: 978-0-374-41715-4; 0-374-41715-6.

> Dillon Dillon has always wondered about his strange name, and during the sum-mer that he turns 10 years old, he learns that his parents were killed in a plane crash when he was 18 months old. They had named him Dillon, his mother's maiden name, and when her brother and sister-in-law adopted Dillon, they gave him their last name. This summer of discovery includes a relationship Dillon develops with three loons living on the lake near his family's New Hampshire cabin. They and his birthday gift of a rowboat provide the setting for Dillon to put the pieces of his life together. Ages 8–12.

Banks, Kathleen. **Dillon Dillon.** Prince Frederick, MD: Recorded Books, 2002. 3 audio cassettes 3 hrs. 30 min. $28.00. ISBN 1-4025-4136-8; 978-1-4025-4136-0.

"Scott Shina narrates Kate Banks' novel...clearly and deliberately, assuming different voices for each character. This audiobook would be useful in libraries and schools for leisure reading or as part of a reading or writing program" (*School Library Journal* Feb. 1, 2004).

Banerjee, Anjali. **Looking for Bapu.** New York: Random House Children's Books, Yearling, 2008. 176p. $6.50. ISBN 0-553-49425-2; 978-0-553-49425-9.

Eight-year-old Anu's grandfather Bapu moved from India to Anu's home in the Pacific Northwest when Anu was small, and Anu is overcome with grief when Bapu dies. Sensing the presence of Bapu's spirit, Anu is determined to find a way to bring him back through efforts that include superstition and magic. "Set in Seattle shortly after 9/11, Anu's narrative records incidents of prejudice, as when one emergency worker refers to him as a little Islam. With episodes that ring true to a boy's perspective, Banerjee's novel provides discussable issues and multicultural insights as well as humor and emotion" (*Booklist* Sept. 1, 2006). Ages 8–11.

Barron, T. A. **Where Is Grandpa?** New York: Philomel, 2000. 32p. $16.99/$6.99pa. ISBN 978-0-399-23037-0; 978-0-698-11904-8.

A boy listens as his family reminisces after the death of his grandfather, and he asks the question: "Where is Grandpa?" As the boy searches for an answer, he discover that his Grandpa is closer to home than he realized, enjoying all the beauties of nature that he loved. His grandfather is still with him in all the special places they shared. "A helpful introduction to death and the grieving process" (*School Library Journal* Feb. 1, 2000). "Because of the questions the story raises about death and religious teachings, this may be a choice best shared with parents" (*Booklist* May 1, 2000). Ages 4–8.

Clifford, Eth. **The Remembering Box.** St. Louis, MO: San Val, Turtleback, 1992. 59p. $12.95. ISBN 0-8335-9560-1; 978-0-8335-9560-7.

Nine-year-old Joshua enjoys his weekly visits to his grandmother on the Jewish Sabbath. Shortly before her death, she gives Joshua a "remembering box" in which she places artifacts from her life, giving him a sense of his heritage and helping him to cope with her death. "This warm and loving relationship between a boy and his grandmother is beautifully depicted and reminiscent of Mathis' *The Hundred Penny Box* (Viking, 1975). [Donna] Diamond's silhouettes, used for the stories that Grandma tells Joshua, are dramatic, and her meticulously detailed black-and-white illustrations of Joshua and his grandmother are both expressive and moving" (*School Library Journal* Dec. 1, 1985). Ages 8–12.

Cotton, Cynthia. **Fair Has Nothing to Do with It.** New York: Farrar, Straus & Giroux, 2007. 153p. $16.00. ISBN 0-374-39935-2; 978-0-374-39935-1.

When Grandpa dies suddenly immediately before Michael's visit, the loss hits 12-year-old Michael hard. His dad has no time for Michael, and when school starts, his math teacher seems to hate him and his friends are not around. Michael begins taking private art lessons with a retired art teacher, and the two become friends, but then Michael learns that his artist friend might be dying, too. "[T]he dramatic portrayal of Michael's grief, true to the child's viewpoint, is far from sentimental as he swings from denial to anger to sorrow, and, finally, to acceptance" (*Booklist* Apr. 1, 2007). Ages 10–12.

Crowe, Carole. **Turtle Girl.** Honesdale, PA: Boyds Mills Press, 2008. 30p. $16.95. ISBN 1-59078-262-3; 978-1-59078-262-0.

> Magdalena and her grandmother have a ritual of watching the sea turtles nest near her home. After her grandmother dies, Magdalena is very sad, but she feels that Grandma is with her again as she and her mother protect the new hatchlings while they scramble to the sea. "Combining lush art with a touching text, this book provides a gentle introduction to a discussion of grief and loss" (*School Library Journal* Apr. 1, 2008). Ages 5–8.

Davis, Katie. **The Curse of Addy McMahon.** New York: HarperCollins, 2008. 288p. $17.89. ISBN 0-06-128712-1; 978-0-06-128712-1.

> Sixth-grade aspiring writer Addy McMahon begins to believe in a family curse when her father dies of cancer, she temporarily loses her best friend, and her mother's boyfriend moves into the guest room of their house. Addy chronicles her life with a blend of diary entries and comic strips. "Davis re-creates all the pain, poignancy, and occasional satisfaction of sixth-grade life in this vivid first-person narrative" (*Booklist* July 1, 2008). "Peppered with authentic preteen conversations, the novel combines traditional narrative with graphic-novel stories, emails, and IMs. Though the happy ending is a bit too pat, the book is a fast-paced and interesting read" (*School Library Journal* July 1, 2008).

Dennison, Amy, Allie Dennison, and David Dennison. **Our Dad Died: The True Story of Three Kids Whose Lives Changed.** Minneapolis, MN: Free Spirit Publishing, 2004. 112p. $9.95. ISBN 1-57542-135-6; 978-1-57542-135-3.

> Twins Amy and Allie were eight years old and their brother David was four when their father suddenly died in his sleep. Encouraged by their mother, the children kept a journal for almost two years, writing about the night he died, the funeral, the first week, the first year, the cemetery, their thoughts and feelings, their sadness and grief, and the future. Later, they reflected on what they had written and added new reflections, offering suggestions for anyone who has experienced a similar loss. "[T]he book is a valuable resource not only for children who have lost a parent but also for the adults who interact with them" (*School Library Journal* Jan. 1, 2004).

dePaola, Tomie. **Nana Upstairs and Nana Downstairs.** Holmes, NY: Spoken Arts, 2006. Audio Cassette (7 min.) and paperback. $17.95. ISBN 0-8045-6943-6; 978-0-8045-6943-9.

> Originally published in 1973, this revised edition features new artwork accompanied by an audio recording read by the author. Every Sunday 4-year-old Tommy goes with his family to visit his grandparents. His grandmother lives downstairs, and his great-grandmother is always in bed upstairs because she is 94 years old. When his Nana upstairs dies, Tommy is devastated, but his mother provides comfort by explaining that Nana will come back in his memory when he thinks about her. "Sadness and love are heard in the different voices as he [dePaola] narrates the story that is based on his childhood. The instrumental background music fits the changing mood of the story" (*School Library Journal* Aug. 1, 2006). Ages 3–7.

Doyle, Roddy. **Her Mother's Face.** New York: Scholastic, 2008. $16.99. ISBN 0-439-81502-9; 978-0-439-81502-4.

> Ten-year-old Siobhán and her father continue to feel sad in the years following the death of Siobhán's mother. Seven years after the death, Siobhán can no longer remember her mother's face until she follows the advice of a mysterious woman. "This would not seem to be a book for every child, though it is certainly a tender

tale for those who have lost a parent. Yet Blackwood's wonderful watercolor-and-charcoal art, reminiscent of Patricia Polacco's pictures, has a lightness that, while not diminishing the story's heartbreaking core, adds a hopeful, soothing dimension" (*Booklist* Sept. 15, 2008). Ages 6–10.

Edwards, Michelle. **Papa's Latkes.** Somerville, MA: Candlewick Press, 2007. 32p. $6.99pa. ISBN: 0-7636-3563-4; ISBN 13: 978-0-7636-3563-3.

Only a few months after their mother's death, Selma and her sister Dora are facing their first Chanukah without their mother. With their father, they keep the traditional holiday celebration as their mother taught—except their father's attempt to make Mama's latkes only underscores how much they miss her. Beautifully illustrated by Stacey Schuett, this book speaks to anyone who has had to face an empty chair during the holidays. Ages 5–7.

Ewart, Claire. **The Giant.** New York: Walker, 2003. 32p. $16.95. ISBN 0-8027-8835-1; 978-0-8027-8835-1.

A young girl, grieving the loss of her mother, attempts to find the giant that her mother promised would look after her. While she dreams about this giant, life on the farm with her father goes on. The seasons change, crops are planted, summer turns to fall, and the harvest is brought in. As time passes, she discovers that the giant is her hardworking father. "Earth tones predominate in the paintings that emphasize the natural world, with scenes of fields, livestock, and weather as might be found on a Midwestern farm. The tone is somewhat somber, and the characters are idealized, but children will identify with the need to be cared for and protected, making this a good choice for one-on-one sharing or for Father's Day programs" (*Booklist* Apr. 15, 2003). Ages 3–8.

Going, K. L. **The Garden of Eve.** Boston, MA: Houghton Mifflin Harcourt, 2007. 240p. $17.00, $6.95pa. ISBN 9780152059866; 9780152066147.

Evie Adler, 10 years old, loses her mother to cancer and moves with her father from Michigan to an upstate New York country house with an apple orchard rumored to be cursed. Father throws himself into his work to bring the orchard back to life while Evie makes friends with Alex, who bears a strong resemblance to a recently deceased local boy. On her 11th birthday, Evie is given an apple seed by the sister of the orchard's original owner. The seed is the only thing to grow in the town in years, but only Evie and Alex can see the tree that grows—or go where the tree leads. "The theme of death is inescapable but the ending offers readers a sense of healing. In her fantastical setting, Going realistically portrays the different ways that people grieve and the emotions accompanying loss" (*School Library Journal* Dec. 1, 2007). Ages 8–12.

Goldman, Judy. **Uncle Monarch and the Day of the Dead.** Honesdale, PA: Boyds Mills Press, 2008. 32p. $16.96. ISBN 1-59078-425-1; 978-1-59078-425-9.

After the death of Lupita's Tío Urbano, who taught her that monarch butterflies are the souls of the dead, Lupita gains a deeper understanding of Día de los Muertos, the Day of the Dead, as it is observed in rural Mexico. Illustrated by Rene King Moreno. "The soft colored-pencil illustrations depict the arches of cempazuchitl flowers (marigolds as brightly orange as the butterflies), the cut-paper designs, or papel picado, and the funny skeletons and skulls, known as calacas, that decorate the houses and graveyards at this time in November. Multicultural customs and monarch butterflies are favorite subjects in classrooms, and this offering nicely combines the two" (*Kirkus Reviews* July 15, 2008). Ages 6–10.

Haynes, Max. **Grandma's Gone to Live in the Stars.** Concept Book Series. Park Ridge, IL: Albert Whitman, 2000. 32p. $15.95. ISBN 0-8075-3026-3; 978-0-8075-3026-9.

The story of a grandmother's death is told by Grandma herself as she says goodbye to her sleeping children and grandchildren and to all the earthly things she has loved. She then rises to her new home in the stars. Featuring pastel illustrations, this book is for all younger children (ages 4–8) and their families, regardless of religious beliefs. "[T]he story provides a way of looking at death as a passage and an afterlife as an extension of a full and loving life, a comforting view to grieving families who seek solace in a story or who wish to open a dialogue about death" (*School Library Journal* Dec. 1, 2000).

Henkes, Kevin. **Sun and Spoon.** Logan, IA: Perfection Learning, 1998. 135p. $12.65. ISBN 0-7807-8959-8; 978-0-7807-8959-3.

Spoon Gilmore's grandmother died, and he searches for a special memento so that he won't forget her. When he selects playing cards that she used, he must then reconcile his own needs with those of his grandfather. "A subject that could be overwhelmingly dark and cloudy is illuminated most comfortingly. Images of supportive parents and love between generations shine through without a heavy hand" (*School Library Journal* July 1, 1997). Ages 8–12.

Henkes, Kevin. **Sun and Spoon.** New York: Random House Audio Publishing Group, Listening Library, 1998. 135p. 2 audio cassettes, softcover. 1hr. 53 min. $28.00. ISBN 0-8072-8035-6; 978-0-8072-8035-5. Cassettes only: $23.00. ISBN 0-8072-8034-8; 978-0-8072-8034-8.

Read by Blair Brown. "Brown has a pleasant voice and interprets the characters well, reading with expression and sensitivity. The word-for-word narration is well-paced and well-recorded" (*School Library Journal* Dec. 1, 1998). Ages 8–12.

Hesse, Karen. **Poppy's Chair.** New York: Simon & Schuster Children's Publishing, 1993. 32p. $14.95. ISBN 0-02-743705-1; 978-0-02-743705-8.

Leah usually spends two weeks every summer with Gramm and Poppy, but this year Poppy is gone. Leah and her grandmother do the things they always do, but Leah doesn't want to talk about Poppy; she doesn't even want to sit in his chair. Finally, Leah learns from her grandmother how to accept her grandfather's death. "Hesse…skillfully chooses details that reveal her characters' feelings while epitomizing their loss" (*Kirkus Reviews* Feb. 15, 1993). Ages 5–8.

Hest, Amy. **Remembering Mrs. Rossi.** Somerville, MA: Candlewick Press, 2007. 192p. $14.99. ISBN 0-7636-2163-3; 978-0-7636-2163-6.

After her mother dies, eight-year-old Annie Rossi tries to cope, assisted by "Remembering Mrs. Rossi," a book of memories compiled by her mother's sixth-grade students. "Hest handles a delicate subject with compassion and understanding, without descending into maudlin emotion. Annie's reactions are perfectly in keeping with her age, and she is never presented as an example of the proper way to mourn" (*Kirkus Reviews* Dec. 15, 2006). Ages 8–12.

Holt, Kimberly Willis. **Keeper of the Night.** New York: Henry Holt Books For Young Readers, 2003. 180p. $16.95. ISBN 0-8050-6361-7; 978-0-8050-6361-5.

Presented in a series of vignettes, this is the story of 13-year-old Isabel, who lives on the island of Guam, and her family as they cope with the suicide death of Isabel's mother. "Holt, author of the award-winning *My Louisiana Sky* (Henry Holt,

1998/VOYA August 1998) and *When Zachary Beaver Came to Town* (1999/ VOYA December 1999), integrates the exotic setting and realistic characters into an easily read yet complex story of a girl growing up, family problems, and suicide" (*Voice of Youth Advocates* June 1, 2003). Ages 10–13.

Kennedy, Marlane. **Me and the Pumpkin Queen.** New York: HarperCollins, 2007. 192p. $15.99. ISBN 0-06-114022-8; 978-0-06-114022-8.

Eleven-year-old Mildred lives in Circleville, Ohio, site of a three-day pumpkin festival. When she was six, her mother, a former queen of the festival, passed away before fulfilling her dream of growing a giant pumpkin. Mildred decides to grow a prizewinner to honor her mother. "The psychologizing of Mildred's grief is unsubtly telegraphed, but withal it's a warmhearted and genuine offering that demands little and gives much" (*Kirkus Reviews* June 1, 2007). Ages 8–12.

Kornblatt, Marc. **Izzy's Place.** New York: Simon & Schuster Children's Publishing, Margaret K. McElderry, 2003. 128p. $16.95. ISBN 0-689-84639-8; 978-0-689-84639-7.

While spending the summer at his grandmother's Indiana home, fifth grader Henry Stone gets help from a new friend in coping with the recent death of his grandfather and the possibility of his parents getting divorced. "In straightforward language, Kornblatt writes a realistic, affecting account of the challenges of coming to terms with grief and family difficulties and the process of acceptance and healing. Henry is a likable, dimensional character that kids will relate to, and the problems he faces are sympathetically and sensitively portrayed" (*Booklist* June 1, 2003). Ages 9–12.

Krementz, Jill. **How It Feels When a Parent Dies.** New York: Knopf Doubleday Publishing Group, Knopf, 1988. 128p. $16.00. ISBN 0-394-75854-4; 978-0-394-75854-1.

Eighteen youth ages 7 to 16 discuss the questions and feelings they experienced when one of their parents died. The narratives are accompanied by photographs of the young people with their surviving parent and other family members. "There's a similarity of tone to all these accounts—perhaps it's the format—but the kids' individual reactions register nonetheless, as do their common pain and sense of loss. Others in the same situation may find comfort in their company and assurance that one does survive, stronger or not; kids who haven't lost a parent may be drawn to musing on the subject" (*Kirkus Reviews* May 29, 1981). Ages 7–12.

Lanton, Sandy. **Daddy's Chair.** Woodbury, NY: Lanton Haas Press, 2000. 32p. $14.95/$6.95pa. ISBN 0-9702482-1-0; 978-0-9702482-1-3.

Michael's father has died, and he can't believe that his father won't sit in his special chair again to read stories to him and play checkers. The story takes place during shiva, a period of mourning. "Realistic sepia-toned illustrations convey emotions appropriate to the text, capturing both the family unity and love, as well as the pervasive sense of sadness. A well-done book on a difficult subject" (*School Library Journal* July 1, 1991). Ages 4–8.

Layefsky, Virginia. **Impossible Things.** Tarrytown, NY: Marshall Cavendish, 1998. 208p. $14.95. ISBN 0-7614-5038-6; 978-0-7614-5038-2.

Twelve-year-old Brady would like to believe several impossible things, including that he can find his mother who was killed in an accident and that the dragonlike creature that has hatched in his secret hiding place really exists. He is also facing the impending remarriage of his father to a woman who wants to send him to military school. "Brady's ability to change some of the impossible things and accept the ones he cannot sends a comforting message to readers who have experienced similar problems, along with a captivating story" (*School Library Journal* Nov. 1, 1998). Ages 10–14.

Mathews, Eleanor. **The Linden Tree.** Minneapolis, MN: Milkweed Editions, 2007. 224p. $16.95. ISBN 1-57131-673-6; 978-1-57131-673-8.

When 9-year-old Katy Sue loses her mother to meningitis, she and her family must adjust to life without her. The arrival of Aunt Katherine brings further change, as she and Katy Sue's father gradually fall in love. "[T]he honest account of a family's journey of grieving and healing is well portrayed, and may be cathartic for children who have suffered their own losses" (*School Library Journal* Sept 1, 2007). Ages 8–12.

Mathews, Eleanor. **The Linden Tree.** Ashland, OR: Blackstone Audio, 2008. Compact Disc. 7 hrs. $60.00. ISBN 1-4332-2878-5; 978-1-4332-2878-0.

Read by Marguerite Gavin.

Miles, Miska. **Annie and the Old One.** Saint Louis, MO: San Val, Turtleback, 1971. 44p. $18.40. ISBN 0-8085-9209-2; 978-0-8085-9209-9. Saint Louis, MO: Phoenix Films & Video, 1976. 15 min. $99.00. VHS video. Closed-captioned.

Annie, an Indian child, tries to prevent her grandmother from dying. The "old one" had said she would return to Mother Earth when she finished helping Annie and her mother weave a new rug, and Annie tries to delay the project. Then her grandmother explains her beliefs, and Annie no longer attempts to delay. Illustrated by Peter Parnall. Ages 6–10.

Monk, Isabell. **Blackberry Stew.** Minneapolis, MN: Lerner, 2005. 32p. $15.95. ISBN 1-57505-605-4; 978-1-57505-605-0.

Hope is sad and angry that her Grandpa Jack has passed away. As she and Aunt Poogee remember the special times picking blackberries and other memories they shared with Grandpa Jack, Hope learns that as long as she has her memories, Grandpa Jack will live on. "The textured paintings nicely depict the child's emotions. Useful bibliotherapy for children dealing with the loss of a loved one" (*School Library Journal* June 1, 2005). Ages 4–8.

Myers, Anna. **Graveyard Girl.** Austin, TX: Eakin Press, 2007. 134p. $9.95pa. ISBN 1-934645-29-X; 978-1-934645-29-1.

Twelve-year-old Eli distances himself from people after he loses his mother and sister in the 1878 Memphis yellow fever epidemic. His father can't bear the tragedy and abandons his son. Eli meets Grace, the Graveyard Girl, who rings the bell for the dead and writes their names in the record. Grace helps Eli to learn that he can begin to overcome his grief when he helps others. "The situation provides tension as well as horrifying historical details about the epidemic itself. The book ends on a hopeful note, but its unrelenting sadness will be difficult for some readers" (*Kirkus Reviews* Oct. 1, 1995). Ages 8–12.

Napoli, Donna Jo. **Flamingo Dream.** New York: HarperCollins, 2002. 32p. $16.89. ISBN 0-688-17863-4; 978-0-688-17863-5.

A young girl grieves over her father's impending death from cancer, celebrating their last year together by making a memory book. Illustrated by Cathie Felstead. "Napoli's emphasis is on remembering the love that glues a relationship together, but she doesn't ignore the sadness and heartache that come with the loss of a loved one. The visually intense artwork, a mix of drawings by the narrator and collages comprising items related to the remembrances (an airplane wings pin or a feather), is very effective" (*Booklist*). Ages 5–8.

Pavlicin, Karen. **Perch, Mrs. Sackets, and Crow's Nest.** St. Paul, MN: Elva Resa, 2007. 160p. $16.95. ISBN 978-1-934617-00-7.

After his father's death, Andy does not look forward to spending a summer in rural upstate New York. As he does chores for his grandmother and her eccentric neighbor, and connects with his mother's childhood friend, he begins to accept that faith will help him deal with the changes that life brings, including his father's death. "This is an upbeat, positive story in which faith and resilience are accentuated in the face of life's dark clouds. The author breathes wise, hopeful life lessons into her novel with a subtle simplicity sure to touch hearts" (*School Library Journal* Dec. 1, 2007). Ages 8–10.

Perez, Amada Irma. **Nana's Big Surprise (Nana, ¡Que Sorpresa!).** San Francisco: Children's Book Press, 2007. 32p. $16.95. ISBN 0-89239-190-1; 978-0-89239-190-5.

In this story told in Spanish and English, Amada and her siblings eagerly await the arrival of their recently widowed grandmother from Mexico. The family hopes to cheer up Nana with a surprise gift of chicks like the ones Nana raised with their grandfather in Mexico. Illustrated by Maya Christina Gonzalez. "The sturdy, colorful illustrations are full of bright patterns, collage elements, and unusual perspectives that give them a magical edge. Although the busy backgrounds sometimes make the words difficult to read, this poignant tale of family love and grieving is ideal for reading aloud in either language, especially to children coping with deep losses of their own" (*Booklist* Mar. 15, 2007). Ages 6–9.

Polikoff, Barbara Garland. **Life's a Funny Proposition, Horatio.** New York: Henry Holt. Books For Young Readers, 1992. 144p. $14.95. ISBN 0-8050-1972-3; 978-0-8050-1972-8. Prince Frederick, MD: Recorded Books. E-book. $1.00. ISBN 1-4237-2448-8; 978-1-4237-2448-3.

After his father dies of lung cancer, 12-year-old Horatio and his mother move from Chicago to Wisconsin to be closer to other family members. Soon Horatio's grandfather and his dog move in with them. Unfortunately, the dog dies in an accident, precipitating further grieving by both Horatio and his grandfather. "Polikoff has carefully crafted a story that focuses on changes, personal growth, and relationships that build bridges among people of all ages and stages" (*School Library Journal* Aug. 1, 1992). Ages 9–12.

Polikoff, Barbara Garland. **Life's a Funny Proposition, Horatio.** Prince Frederick, MD: Recorded Books, 1992. Audio recording. $20.75 cassette; $30.75 CD. 2hrs., 30 min. ISBN 0-7887-9377-2; 978-0-7887-9377-6.

"Narrator Ramon de Ocampo offers a spirited yet soothing interpretation of Barbara Garland Polikoff's tender, somewhat uneven novel about a boy dealing with life after his father's death" (*School Library Journal* Apr. 1, 2002). Ages 9–12.

Pollet, Alison. **The Pity Party: 8th Grade in the Life of Me, Cass.** The Pity Party Series. New York: Scholastic, Orchard Books, 2005. 160p. $15.95. ISBN 0-439-68194-4; 978-0-439-68194-0.

In this sequel to *Nobody Was Here* (Scholastic, 2004), Cass is in eighth grade. Orphaned when she was eight, Cass is struggling to find her identity. When the school year begins, she is upset that she is stuck in classes without her closest friends Penelope and Tillie. After she becomes friends with Rod Punkin, she begins to understand herself. "She is able to come to terms with her parents' death, accept the benefits of counseling, and gain a sense of belonging. Inventive details, such as Cass's word lists, the comforting rhyming games she remembers playing with her mother, and the warm support of her art-collecting guardian and psychoanalyst aunt make this a first-rate purchase" (*School Library Journal* Sept. 1, 2005). Ages 9–13.

Ransom, Candice. **Finding Day's Bottom.** NetLibrary, 2006. E-Book. $15.95. ISBN 0-8225-7197-8; 978-0-8225-7197-1.

Jane-Ery, 11, is living in rural Virginia when her father dies in a sawmill accident and her grandfather leaves his mountain to help her and her mother survive. Grandpap's southern phrases abound, and his comment that one finds what one needs when one finds "Day's Bottom" sets Jane-Ery to thinking about her own search. "A novel full of insight and truth" (*School Library Journal* Sept. 1, 2006). Ages 10–12.

Ross, Adrienne. **In the Quiet.** New York: Random House Children's Books, Delacorte, 2000. 160p. $14.95. ISBN 0-385-32678-5; 978-0-385-32678-0.

Eleven-year-old Samantha and her father have not openly grieved the death of her mother; however, when Aunt Constance becomes part of the household, all three must face the loss they are experiencing. "Ross' first novel is peopled with quirky yet believable characters that readers will feel might never have connected but for the tragedy. Several subplots involving Samantha's best friend Bones (who has lost her father to divorce) and various unusual neighbors (each with secrets of their own) flesh out the action and keep the mood from becoming maudlin" (*Booklist* Mar. 1, 2000). Ages 8–12.

Rubright, Lynn. **Mama's Window.** St. Louis, MO: San Val, Turtleback, 2008. 89p. $19.60. ISBN 1-4178-1567-1; 978-1-4178-1567-8. Also available from New York: Lee & Low Books, 2005. 144 p. $16.95. ISBN 1-58430-160-0; 978-1-58430-160-8.

Based on the early 20th-century civil rights activist Owen Whitfield, this is the story of an orphaned African American boy who struggles to adapt to a new home with his uncle following his mother's death. Sugar hopes to fulfill his mother's dream of a stained-glass window for their church. Rubright's text "is filled with rich atmospheric and period detail. But what will affect readers most are Sugar's gradual, brave recovery from grief and the growing pride and love he shares with his new guardian" (*Booklist* July 1, 2005). Ages 10–13.

Rylant, Cynthia. **Missing May.** Logan, IA: Perfection Learning, 1992. $13.65. ISBN 0-7569-4591-7; 978-0-7569-4591-6. New York: Scholastic Paperbacks, 2004. 112p. $5.99pa. ISBN 0-439-61383-3; 978-0-439-61383-5. New York: Books on Tape, Inc., 2000. 2 cassettes, 2 hrs. 24 min. $18.00. ISBN 0-7366-9061-1; 978-0-7366-9061-4.

After the death of Aunt May, who raised her for six years, 12-year-old Summer and her uncle Ob leave their West Virginia trailer in search of the strength to go on living. Then Uncle Ob claims that May has sent a sign from the spirit world. "With homely detail, Rylant plunges readers into the middle of Summer's world, creating characters certain to live long in their memories. Her tightly woven plot wastes no words; May's death and the course of her husband and niece's grieving are both reflected in and illuminated by the state of Ob's mysteries and the course of that interrupted journey of discovery" (*School Library Journal* Mar. 1, 1992). Ages 10–14.

Seagraves, Donny Bailey. **Gone from These Woods.** Westminster, MD: Delacorte Press, 2009. 192p. $15.99. ISBN 0-385-73629-0; 978-0-385-73629-9.

> Eleven-year-old Daniel tries to cope with his guilt after accidentally killing his beloved uncle while hunting in the woods of North Georgia. Daniel's mother tries to hold the family together, and Mrs. Hardy, Daniel's guidance counselor, tries to help Daniel, but Daniel's alcoholic father makes the situation worse. "Although sometimes repetitive and slow-paced, with a quickly resolved ending and heavy-handed message about suicide, this satisfactory debut novel depicts a realistic portrayal of grief from a youth's perspective" (*Kirkus Reviews* July 1, 2009). Ages 9–12.

Slepian, Jan. **The Broccoli Tapes.** New York: Penguin Group, Philomel, 1989. 160p. $17.99. ISBN 0-399-21712-6; 978-0-399-21712-8. Out of print.

> During a stay of several months in Hawaii with her family, Sara reports her experiences by tape back to her sixth grade class in Boston. She reports adoption of a wild cat, Broccoli, a friendship with an Hawaiian boy, and the death of her grandmother. Broccoli also dies. "The fact that Sara's narration is addressed to her friends and teacher lends an immediacy and conversational tone which moves the story quickly. Characterization unfolds as quickly, remaining plausible and consistent throughout" (*School Library Journal* Apr. 1, 1989). Ages 10–12.

Smith, Hope Anita. **Mother Poems.** New York: Henry Holt Books For Young Readers, 2009. 80p. $16.95. ISBN 0-8050-8231-X; 978-0-8050-8231-9.

> Smith explores in poetry the death of a parent through the eyes of a child and a young woman. "Teens of all ages who have experienced the loss of a loved one will find comfort in this powerful and affecting book of poetry. The raw emotions sting and make the reader flinch, but they also bring the realization that memory is ultimately the gift that brings consolation" (*Voice of Youth Advocates* Apr. 1, 2009). "Like the poetry, Smith's simple, torn-paper collages in a folk-art style show the close embraces and vignettes without overwhelming the words" (*Booklist* Feb. 15, 2009). Ages 8–13.

Snyder, Zilpha Keatley. **Spyhole Secrets.** New York: Random House Children's Books, Delacorte, 2001. 192p. $17.99. ISBN 0-385-90016-3; 978-0-385-90016-4. Out of print.

> Hallie Meredith, 11 years old, is angry at God and feeling sorry for herself. Her father died in a car accident, her mother has had to find a job, and they moved to a cramped apartment in an old mansion, away from Hallie's friends and school. Hallie discovers the old mansion's attic, and a secret window where she can spy on another family. "This complex, appealing novel combines edgy Hitchcockian suspense with an insightful exploration of a young person's coping with loss, and the conversational prose intimately illustrates the effects of personal tragedy. Hallie is a likable, dimensional character, whose actions and thoughts subtly shift away from self-absorption as she regains her footing and faith" (*Booklist* May 1, 2001). Ages 9–12.

Spinelli, Jerry. **Eggs.** New York: Little, Brown, 2008. 240p. $5.99pa. ISBN 0-316-16647-2; 978-0-316-16647-8.

> After his mother's death, 9-year-old David lives with his salesman father, who is constantly on the road, and his grandmother. Primrose, 13, lives with her fortune-teller mother. David and Primrose forge a tumultuous friendship, helping each

other deal with the missing elements in their lives. "This book could be a comforting read for those who have lost an essential person in their lives. It will certainly be a tough sell for some teens, but those with younger siblings might be able to relate to Primrose and David's situation" (*Voice of Youth Advocates* June 1, 2007). Ages 9–14.

Tolan, Stephanie S. **Listen!** New York: HarperCollins, 2006. 208p. $16.89. ISBN 0-06-057936-6; 978-0-06-057936-4.

Charlene, known as Charley, is a sixth-grader recovering from the effects of a car accident and still unable to accept the death of her mother two years earlier. While hiking to strengthen her injured leg, Charley meets a stray dog she names Coyote. Through the process of training Coyote, Charley comes to terms with her feelings and her mother's death. "This is a sweet, gentle story of healing and the strong bond that can develop between humans and animals" (*School Library Journal* May 1, 2006). Ages 10–14.

Vigna, Judith. **Saying Goodbye to Daddy.** Park Ridge, IL: Albert Whitman, 1991. 32p. $16.99. ISBN 0-8075-7253-5; 978-0-8075-7253-5.

Clare's father is killed in a car accident, and she experiences the phases of grieving—denial, guilt, anger, fear, and acceptance. She is helped through the grieving process by her mother and grandfather. "[T]he subject [of grief] is addressed in a straightforward, accurate manner, and the book will suit those who need to explain the death of a parent. Acceptable for collections that can support another book on the grieving process" (*School Library Journal* Mar. 1, 1991). Ages 5–7.

Warner, Sally. **This Isn't about the Money.** New York: Penguin Group, Puffin, 2004. 224p. $5.99 pa. ISBN 0-14-240221-4; 978-0-14-240221-4.

Twelve-year-old Janey experiences trauma after a drunken driver runs into the family car, killing both of her parents. Janey must cope with her injuries, and she and her little sister must adjust to life with their great-aunt and grandfather in California, yet keep the spirit of their parents alive. "As always, Warner's dialog and characterization are rich and real" (*Booklist* Sept. 1, 2002). Ages 8–12.

Wiles, Deborah. **Each Little Bird that Sings.** Boston: Houghton Mifflin Harcourt, Sandpiper, 2006. 276p. $5.95pa. ISBN 0-15-205657-2; 978-0-15-205657-5. St. Louis, MO: San Val, Turtleback, 2006. 259p. $15.95. ISBN 1-4177-5432-X; 978-1-4177-5432-8. New York: Random House Audio Publishing Group, 2007. E-book. $38.25. ISBN 0-7393-4477-3; 978-0-7393-4477-4.

Comfort Snowberger, age 10, lives in the funeral home operated by her family in Snapfinger, Mississippi. Although well acquainted with death and funerals, she is shocked by the deaths of her great-uncle, great-great-aunt, and the disappearance of her beloved dog, Dismay, swept away during a flood. "Even aside from such happy extras as 'funeral food' recipes and Comfort's 'Top Ten Tips for First-Rate Funeral Behavior,' Wiles succeeds wonderfully in capturing 'the messy glory' of grief and life" (*Booklist* Mar. 1, 2005). Ages 9–12.

Wiles, Deborah. **Each Little Bird that Sings.** New York: Random House Audio Publishing Group, Listening Library, 2005. 5 CDs, 5 hrs. 11 min. $35.00. ISBN 0-307-28230-9; 978-0-307-28230-9. 3 cassettes, 4 hrs. 30 mins. $35.00. ISBN 0-307-28373-9; 978-0-307-28373-3.

"Kim Mai Guest brings a true southern lilt to the voice of Comfort, while creating distinct voices for Great Aunt Florentine, Great Uncle Edisto, Declaration

Johnson, and a myriad of other characters. This heartfelt, sometimes humorous story is a delight" (*School Library Journal* May 1, 2006). Ages 9–12.

Wiles, Deborah. **Love, Ruby Lavender.** New York: Random House Listening Library, 2004. 5 CDs or 3 audiocassettes, 3 hrs. 58 min.; paperback 216p. $36.00. ISBN 1-4000-8997-2, 978-1-4000-8997-0 CDs; 0-8072-2096-5; 978-0-8072-2096-2 cassettes.

Nine-year-old Ruby has not come to terms with her grandfather's death in a car accident last year, and now her grandmother is leaving for the summer. The two are kindred spirits and together steal chickens ready to be slaughtered. Miss Eula and Ruby continue their correspondence throughout the summer, and Miss Eula returns to find that Ruby has made new friends and adjusted to her grandfather's death. Read by Judith Ivey. "A rewarding read that perfectly blends the culture and the humor of the south, this not-to-be-missed title will be welcome in all collections that circulate audio books for children" (*School Library Journal* July 1, 2002). Ages 8–11.

Wood, Douglas. **Grandad's Prayers of the Earth.** Collingdale, PA: Diane, 2004. 28p. $17.00. ISBN 0-7567-7101-3; 978-0-7567-7101-0. Paperback edition: Somerville, MA: Candlewick Press, 2009. 32p. $6.99. 0-7636-4675-X; 978-0-7636-4675-2.

When a boy and his grandfather walk in the woods, the boy listens for the prayers of the earth and asks: "Are our prayers answered?" Long after his Grandad is gone, he understands Grandad's response: "If we listen very closely, a prayer is often its own answer." The boy, now a man, finds comfort in Granddad's explanation of how all things in the natural world pray and, in this way, add to the beauty of our world. Illustrated by P. J. Lynch. "Without mentioning any specific God or belief, the thoughtful text celebrates all creation and is perfectly complemented by the moving, expressive illustrations" (*School Library Journal* Jan. 1, 2000). Ages 5–8.

Woodson, Jacqueline. **Sweet, Sweet Memory.** New York: Hyperion Books for Children, 2007. 32p. $5.99pa. ISBN 1-4231-0680-6; 978-1-4231-0680-7.

Sarah lives with her grandparents, and she and her grandmother feel very sad when Grandpa dies. Sarah recalls Grandpa's belief that everything and everyone goes on and on. As time passes, memories of him make Sarah and her grandmother laugh and feel better. Sarah learns that stories and memories of loved ones are what keep everything and everyone going on and on. "The elegant text is matched by [Floyd] Cooper's images, which manage to be both dreamy and strong" (*Booklist* Feb. 15, 2001). Ages 5–9.

Ylvisaker, Anne. **Dear Papa.** Somerville, MA: Candlewick Press, 2007. 192p. $5.99pa. ISBN 0-7636-3402-6; 978-0-7636-3402-5. St. Louis, MO: San Val, Turtleback, 2007. 184p. $16.00. ISBN 1-4177-9062-8; 978-1-4177-9062-3.

One year after her father's death during World War II, 9-year-old Isabelle begins writing him letters, along with letters to other members of her family. The letters continue 14 years as she relates important events in her life and how she feels about them. Her mother remarries, and Isabelle wrestles with the acceptance of her stepfather. "The letters are personal and immediate, and the story is full of daily details that evoke the historical period and also dramatize the child's conflict between loyalty to her birth father and her growing love for the man who fathers her now. In her last letter to Papa in heaven, the adult Isabelle says of her stepdad, 'I love him most for letting me love you best'" (*Booklist* Aug. 1, 2002). Ages 9–12.

Death of a Pet

Allan, Nicholas. **Heaven.** London: Transworld Publishers, 2006. 32p. $9.99pa. ISBN 0-09-948814-0; 978-0-09-948814-9.

Dill the dog knows his time is up and packs his suitcase, telling his owner, Lily, that he is off to heaven. Dill describes his destination with many lampposts, lots of things to smell, and meaty bones. Lily disagrees and pictures heaven differently. She is sad when Dill is gone, but when she finds a puppy, she uses Dill's ideas to give the puppy a piece of heaven on earth. Ages 5–8.

Bunting, Eve. **The Summer of Riley.** Joanna Cotler Books. Logan, IA: Perfection Learning, 2002. 170p. $13.65. ISBN 0-7569-1366-7; 978-0-7569-1366-3. Prince Frederick, MD: Recorded Books, 2002. 4 CDs. 4 hrs. $46.75. ISBN 978-1-4025-2340-3. 3 cassettes. 4 hrs. $30.76. ISBN 978-0-7887-8975-5.

Riley the dog is a friend to 11-year-old William as he copes with his parents' separation, his father's engagement, and his grandfather's death. When Riley chases a prized horse, the law threatens to have Riley put to sleep. "Bunting's story will have strong appeal for middle-graders who will relish the bittersweet but satisfying resolution and the picture of a boy standing up to uncaring adults, bullies, and the system" (*Booklist* July 1, 2001). Ages 9–13.

Burleigh, Robert. **Good-Bye, Sheepie.** Tarrytown, NY: Marshall Cavendish, 2010. 32p. $16.99. ISBN 0-7614-5598-1; 978-0-7614-5598-1.

A father teaches his young son about death and remembering as he buries their beloved dog. Illustrated by Peter Catalanotto. "Although death is never mentioned nor is afterlife discussed readers will comprehend Sheepie's demise and accept the sensitively handled depiction of his burial. A thoughtful choice for one-on-one sharing, this should spark discussions about death and funeral customs" (*Booklist* Mar. 15, 2010). Ages 3–7.

Cochran, Bill. **The Forever Dog.** Holmes, NY: Spoken Arts, 2007. Compact disc or cassette and hardcover. $29.95 CD; $27.95 cassette. ISBN 0-8045-4177-9, 978-0-8045-4177-0 CD; 0-8045-6955-X, 978-0-8045-6955-2 cassette.

Mike and his dog, Corky, become best friends They are inseparable, and Mike makes a plan with Corky that they will do everything together forever. Mike's "Forever Plan" works until Corky becomes sick and dies, leaving Mike lonely and angry that Corky has broken his promise to be together always. Mike's mother explains to him that the Forever Plan would still work by Mike holding Corky in his heart forever. "This is a compassionate story that will help kids cope with a pet's death and death in general. A highlight is the appealing illustrations" (*Booklist* Apr. 1, 2007). Ages 4–8.

Cohen, Miriam. **Jim's Dog Muffins.** Long Island City, NY: Star Bright Books, 2008. 32p. $15.95. ISBN 1-59572-099-5; 978-1-59572-099-3. Star Bright Books, 2008. 32p. $5.95pa. ISBN 1-59572-100-2; 978-1-59572-100-6.

Jim's dog Muffins is hit by a garbage truck and killed, and the first-grade class sends him a condolence letter. When Jim returns to school, he withdraws from class activities, and the other first graders try to share his loss and ease his grief. "First published in 1984, this newly illustrated book does a fine job of showing the emotions of a child who loses his pet.... [Ronald] Himler's softly colored illustrations sensitively capture the nuances of classroom life" (*Booklist* Oct. 15, 2008). Ages 5–8.

Cohen, Miriam. **Jim's Dog Muffins.** Holmes, NY: Spoken Arts, 1990. Mixed media: paperback & 1 cassette, 7 min. $15.95. Spoken Arts, 1988. Mixed media: hardcover & 1 cassette. $13.90. Spoken Arts, 1991. VHS. 7 min. $44.95. ISBN 0-8045-9047-8; 978-0-8045-9047-1.

Demas, Corinne. **Saying Goodbye to Lulu.** New York: Little, Brown Books, 2009. 32p. $6.99pa. ISBN 0-316-04749-X; 978-0-316-04749-4.

> A young girl and her dog, Lulu, are the best of friends, but when Lulu grows older and becomes weak, the girl must face the possibility of losing her dear friend and eventually cope with its death. Over time the girl discovers that the memory of her beloved Lulu will live on in her heart. This story helps young children cope with the emotions that accompany loss of a loved one. "[Ard] Hoyt's expressive illustrations, ink-and-colored-pencil drawings washed with watercolors, reflect the tone of the text and show the child's sadness without sentimentality" (*Booklist* June 1, 2004). Ages 3–7.

DiSalvo-Ryan, DyAnne. **A Dog Like Jack.** Pine Plains, NY: Live Oak Media, 2006. Compact Disc; hardcover (Trade Cloth). $28.95. ISBN 1-59519-300-6; 978-1-59519-300-1. Pine Plains, NY: Live Oak Media, 2001. Audio Cassette; Softcover. 13 min. $25.95. ISBN 0-87499-759-3; 978-0-87499-759-0. North Kingstown, RI: BBC Audiobooks America, 2005. $16.95. Audio Cassette; Softcover. 13 min. ISBN 0-87499-758-5; 978-0-87499-758-3.

> Mike and his dog Jack share many years together, and when Jack dies, Mike grieves with his family and celebrates their life with the dog. "They talk about it, grieve together, celebrate Jack's life, and imagine a day when they will adopt another dog. This lovely story will help youngsters through the grief they are feeling if they have recently lost a pet or prepare them to face a pet's death" (*Booklist* Mar. 1, 1999). Ages 5–8.

Harris, Robie H. **Goodbye Mousie.** New York: Simon & Schuster Children's Publishing, Aladdin, 2004. 32p. $6.99. ISBN 0-689-87134-1; 978-0-689-87134-4.

> A boy finds that his pet, Mousie, won't wake up one morning. Mousie has died, and the boy feels disbelief, anger, and sadness. Burying Mousie and saying goodbye help the boy to feel better about his loss. "[Jan] Ormerod's understated art suits the subject matter, and the pictures express the child's changing feelings without upstaging or overpowering them. An excellent choice to help young readers deal with loss" (*School Library Journal* Sept. 1, 2001). Ages 3–7.

Hughes, Shirley. **Alfie and the Birthday Surprise.** Alfie Series. Bensalem, PA: Sandvik, 1999. 30p. $9.99. ISBN 1-58048-086-1; 978-1-58048-086-4. London: Retail Independent Publishers Group, 2007. 32p. $8.95pa. ISBN 0-09-920862-8; 978-0-09-920862-4.

> Bob McNally, the neighbor of Alfie and Annie Rose, is very sad because his old cat Smokey has died. Mr. McNally's family decides to hold a surprise party and give him a special present to cheer him up. Alfie is asked to look after the present until the party. "Preschoolers will appreciate the honest talk about the death of a pet, and they will love the story of the secret and the surprise. Hughes' line-and-watercolor pictures express the toddler's earnest body language—shoulders back, arms stiff, tummy out—and the tenderness between different ages across generations and across the street" (*Booklist* March 1, 1998). Ages 3–7.

Morehead, Debby. **A Special Place for Charlee: A Child's Companion Through Pet Loss.** Broomfield, CO: Partners In Publishing, 1996. 36p. $6.95. ISBN 0-9654049-0-0; 978-0-9654049-0-7.

> Charlee and Mark grew up together and were best friends. Many years later, Charlee is euthanized because of heart failure, and Mark's family mourns the dog's

death. Following their veterinarian's advice, Mark's family gathers to remember Charlee, makes a scrapbook to collect their memories, and plants a bush near Charlee's favorite place in the yard. Illustrated by Karen Cannon. "This simply told story is right on the mark in legitimizing a family's, and particularly a child's, grief over the loss of a pet. Its sound counsel and suggestions for coping are gently incorporated into the straightforward story line, and understated black-and-white drawings eloquently reflect the characters' emotions" (*Booklist* Nov. 15, 1996). Ages 9–12.

Newman, Leslea. **The Best Cat in the World.** Grand Rapids, MI: Eerdmans Books For Young Readers, 2004. 32p. $8.00. ISBN 0-8028-5294-7; 978-0-8028-5294-6.

Victor's "best cat in the world" dies, and, when he gets a new kitten, Shelley, he has difficulty accepting the differences between his first cat and this new kitten. "There are many books about the death of a pet, but Newman offers a much needed one about integrating a new animal into the home, a sensitive situation that she handles with tenderness and humor.... [Ronald] Himler's full-page water-color paintings usually focus on the humans in the story, but there are several images of Shelley that show her endearing ways" (*Booklist* Jan. 1, 2004). Ages 4–8.

Sachar, Louis. **Alone in His Teacher's House.** New York: Random House Children's Books, 1994. 96p. $11.99. ISBN 0-679-91949-X; 978-0-679-91949-0.

Marvin's third-grade teacher pays him to take care of her old dog, Waldo, while she's away. When Waldo dies, Marvin is upset and confused. Readers will "recognize Marvin's feelings, both the humor of having to confront your teacher as a person and the sorrow at the death of a beloved pet" (*Booklist* June 1, 1994). Ages 6–9.

Viorst, Judith. **The Tenth Good Thing about Barney.** New York: Simon & Schuster Children's Publishing, Atheneum, 1971. 32p. $15.95. ISBN 0-689-20688-7; 978-0-689-20688-7. New York: Simon & Schuster Children's Publishing, Aladdin, 1987. $5.99. 32p. ISBN 0-689-71203-0; 978-0-689-71203-6. Silver Spring, MD: AIMS Multimedia, 1987. VHS Video. 13 min. $49.95. ISBN 0-8068-9871-2; 978-0-8068-9871-1.

Illustrated by Erik Blegvad. At a backyard funeral, a little boy tries to think of ten good things to say about his cat, Barney—but can come up with only nine. Ages 4–8.

Wallace, Bill. **No Dogs Allowed!** Teachers Edition. New York: Holiday House, 2004. 214p. $16.95. ISBN 0-8234-1818-9; 978-0-8234-1818-3.

Fifth grader Kristine, struggling to accept the death of her beloved horse, finds it difficult to accept Mattie, the dog she receives for her birthday. "Kristine is likable and realistic as she struggles through her grief and resistance to emotional involvement with another pet. The book is written with humor and enough drama to keep readers interested, and they'll relate to the story and to Kristine's ultimate surrender to adorable Mattie" (*School Library Journal* Aug. 1, 2004). Ages 8–12.

Death of a Sibling

Conrad, Pam. **My Daniel.** New York: HarperCollins, 1989. 144p. $13.95. ISBN 0-06-021313-2; 978-0-06-021313-8. Logan, IA: Perfection Learning, 1991. 137p. $13.65. ISBN 0-8124-9825-9; 978-0-8124-9825-7.

Visiting the Natural History Museum with her grandchildren, Julia Creath feels the presence of her dead brother, Daniel, and remembers finding on the family farm the bones of the brontosaurus now on display in the museum. "Disarming candor, vivid descriptions, deeply felt characterizations, and a simple yet intricately crafted plot are all hallmarks of Conrad's narrative about Julia Creath Summerwaite and her younger brother Daniel" (*Booklist* Apr. 15, 1989). Ages 10–14.

Couloumbis, Audrey. **Getting Near to Baby.** New York: Random House Listening Library, 2004. 3 audiocassettes. 3 hrs. 54 min.; paperback 211p. $36.00. ISBN 0-8072-8876-4; 978-0-8072-8876-4.

Twelve-year-old Willa Jo Dean and Little Sister mourn the death of their baby sister. Over the course of a single day, Willa Jo mulls over her mother's depression, Little Sister's refusal to talk after the baby's death, and Aunt Patty's efforts to make things right by taking the girls into her home. Read by Mischa Barton. "This is an exceptional recording of an exceptional book that offers meaningful insights on some universal truths about grief and healing" (*School Library Journal* Aug. 1, 2001). Ages 9–12.

Elliott, Zetta. **Bird.** New York: Lee & Low Books, 2008. 48p. $19.95. ISBN 1-60060-241-X; 978-1-60060-241-2.

Mekhai, better known as Bird, is an artistic young African American boy who expresses himself through drawing as he struggles to understand his older brother's drug addiction and death. A family friend, Uncle Son, provides guidance and understanding. "In this beautiful picture book for older readers, Elliott and [Illustrator Shadra] Strickland tell a moving story in spare free verse and clear mixed-media pictures of an African American boy who loves to draw" (*Booklist* Nov. 1, 2008). Ages 6–10.

Erskine, Kathryn. **Mockingbird.** New York: Penguin Group, Philomel, 2010. 224p. $15.99. ISBN 0-399-25264-9; 978-0-399-25264-8.

Ten-year-old Caitlin has Asperger's Syndrome and struggles to understand emotions, to show empathy, and to make friends at school. Her older brother Devon is killed in a school shooting, and she and her father must deal with it. "Caitlin, her dad and her schoolmates try to cope, and it is the deep grief they all share that ultimately helps Caitlin get to empathy. As readers celebrate this milestone with Caitlin, they realize that they too have been developing empathy by walking a while in her shoes, experiencing the distinctive way that she sees and interacts with the world" (*Kirkus Reviews* Mar. 1, 2010). Ages 10–12.

Fletcher, Ralph J. **Fig Pudding.** Boston: Houghton Mifflin Harcourt, 1995. 144p. $15.00. ISBN 0-395-71125-8; 978-0-395-71125-5.

Cliff, the oldest of six children, relates the past year, describing the family's challenges, conflict, and tragedy when a younger brother is killed in an accident. "Fletcher captures perfectly the humor, irritations, and sadness of life in a large, close-knit family and makes Cliff a sympathetic and thoughtful narrator, occasionally bewildered by his siblings' antics but always a completely believable older brother" (*Booklist* May 15, 1995). Ages 9–12.

Forrester, Sandra. **Leo and the Lesser Lion.** New York: Random House Children's Books, Knopf Books for Young Readers, 2009. 304p. $19.99. ISBN 0-375-95616-6; 978-0-375-95616-4.

Twelve-year-old Mary Bayliss Pettigrew struggles to understand why her older brother died and whether she, miraculously, survived for some special purpose. "A Depression-era tale set in tiny Lenore, Ala., may not have immediate or obvious appeal. But Forrester creates a compelling account of how hardship can be overcome and grief survived, however grudging and reluctant our efforts may be" (*Kirkus Reviews* July 15, 2009). Ages 9–12.

Franklin, Kristine L. **Lone Wolf.** Somerville, MA: Candlewick Press, 2006. 224p. $5.99. ISBN 0-7636-2996-0; 978-0-7636-2996-0.

> Eleven-year-old Perry and his father have moved to the north woods of Minnesota following the death of Perry's baby sister. When a large family moves into a nearby house, Perry's friendship with the oldest girl helps him come to terms with his sister's death and his parents' divorce. "The writing is sure; the dovetailing of grief and memory with the events of the plot is impeccable" (*Kirkus Reviews* Mar. 1, 1997). Ages 9–13.

Graff, Lisa. **Umbrella Summer.** New York: HarperCollins, 2009. 240p. $9.99. E-book. ISBN 0-06-191260-3; 978-0-06-191260-3.

> Annie Richards's 11-year-old brother Jared recently died from a heart condition, and Annie and her parents are stricken with grief that they don't acknowledge. A welcome and sensitive addition to collections dealing with grief, this is also an appealing and moving choice for readers seeking a dose of feel-good reality fiction (*Kirkus Reviews* May 1, 2009). Ages 8–12.

Grimes, Nikki. **What Is Goodbye?** New York: Hyperion Books for Children, 2004. 64p. $15.99. ISBN 0-7868-0778-4; 978-0-7868-0778-9.

> Alternating poems by Jerilyn and Jesse, brother and sister, convey their feelings about the death of their older brother and the impact it had on their family. Jerilyn tries to keep it in and hold it together, while Jesse acts out. "Grimes handles these two voices fluently and lucidly, shaping her characters through her form. [Raul] Colon's paintings in muted colors combine imagism with realism to create an emotional dreamscape on nearly every page" (*School Library Journal* June 1, 2004). Ages 10–14.

Hemingway, Edith Morris. **Road to Tater Hill.** New York: Delacorte Press, 2009. 224p. $19.99. ISBN 0-385-90627-7; 978-0-385-90627-2.

> Ten-year-old Annie is spending the summer of 1963 with her pregnant mother on her grandparents' North Carolina farm. The baby is born prematurely and dies. Annie doesn't know how to deal with her grief, her father is stationed in Germany, and her mother becomes depressed and withdraws from the family. Annie meets an elderly woman who becomes her friend and helps her accept her loss. "True to Annie's viewpoint, the particulars tell a universal drama of childhood grief, complete in all its sadness, anger, loneliness, and healing" (*Booklist* July 1, 2009). Ages 10–14.

Henkes, Kevin. **Bird Lake Moon.** Prince Frederick, MD: Recorded Books, 2008. E-book. $27.00. ISBN 1-4356-7453-7; 978-1-4356-7453-0.

> Mitch, 12, and Spencer, 10, meet while vacationing at Bird Lake. Mitch's parents are divorcing, and Spencer's older brother drowned when Spencer was two years old. In alternating chapters we read of each boy's story, and their friendship enables them to deal with their losses. "As in his Newbery Honor Book *Olive's Ocean* (2003), every word counts, moving the story forward moment by moment....Emotions are just as carefully carved, turning characterization into portraiture; the children stand out in relief, against the deceptive tranquility of the lake" (*Booklist* Mar. 15, 2008). Ages 9–12.

Henkes, Kevin. **Bird Lake Moon.** New York: HarperCollins, HarperChildren's Audio, 2008. CD. 3 hrs. 30 min. $22.95. ISBN 0-06-155185-6; 978-0-06-155185-7.

> "Written with definitive characters and open and insightful portrayals of adolescent boys, narrator Oliver Wyman gives each character a distinctive voice, and his telling enhances the poignancy of the story" (*School Library Journal* Sept. 1, 2008). Ages 9–12.

Jackson, Aariane R. **Can You Hear Me Smiling? A Child Grieves a Sister.** Arlington, VA: Child Welfare League of America, Child and Family Press, 2004. 40p. $9.95. ISBN 0-87868-835-8; 978-0-87868-835-7.

The author, 9 years old, recounts her older sister's illness and death at age 12, and the range of emotions she experienced during this difficult time. "The mix of guilt and resentment with love, sorrow, and overwhelming loneliness is universal and will open up discussion with many children who are facing loss. The story is framed by a preface from the girls' mother and a long, clear afterword in which grief counselors speak plainly and clearly to adults about how to confront a child's anguish and help him or her feel less alone" (*Booklist* July 1, 2004). Ages 6–12.

Johnson, Patricia Polin. **Morgan's Baby Sister: A Read-Aloud Book for Families Who Have Experienced the Death of a Newborn.** Helping Children Who Hurt Series. San Jose, CA: Resource Publications, 1993. 64p. $11.95. ISBN 0-89390-257-8; 978-0-89390-257-5.

Morgan tries to understand her feelings when her family's preparations for a new baby end with the baby's premature birth and death. "The story is written simply and clearly, with a strong emphasis on Christian hope, using reunion with loved ones after death as a vehicle to help children manage bereavement. Psychological suggestions are included in an afterword to help adults deal with children in grief situations" (*School Library Journal* Mar. 1, 1994). Ages 4–7.

Johnston, Tony. **That Summer.** Boston: Houghton Mifflin Harcourt, 2007. 32p. $6.00pa. ISBN 0-15-205856-7; 978-0-15-205856-2.

A young boy's summer changes when his family finds that his younger brother is dying. "Never mawkish, Johnston's spare, understated text is emotionally eloquent and beautifully poetic in its use of simile and metaphor: hope, for example, flutters 'like a little green bird'; a needle is 'a fish, slim and silver.'...A fine choice to help children come to terms with loss" (*Booklist* May 15, 2002). Ages 6–9.

Kadohata, Cynthia. **Kira-Kira.** New York: Simon & Schuster, 2006. 272p. $6.99pa. ISBN 0-689-85640-7; 978-0-689-85640-2.

In this Newbery Award-winning book, Katie Takeshima and her family move from a Japanese community in Iowa to a small Georgia town in the 1950s. Katie loves her older sister, Lynn, who knows everything and takes care of Katie while their parents are working. It's Lynn who shows Katie the glittering beauty (kira-kira) of the stars and who prepares Katie for the prejudice she will encounter as one of the few Japanese-American children in their school. When Katie is 10, Lynn, 14, falls ill, and the roles are reversed as Katie becomes caregiver. Lynn dies, and Katie goes through all the stages of grief. "Middle school girls will relate to Katie, her heartfelt everyday concerns, and her agony when Lynn dies" (*Voice of Youth Advocates*, Aug. 1, 2004). Ages 10–14.

MacLachlan, Patricia. **Baby.** New York: Random House Audio Publishing Group, Listening Library, 1993. 2 cassettes, 2 hrs. 15 min. $15.99. ISBN 0-553-47232-1; 978-0-553-47232-5.

Blythe Danner narrates the story of 12-year-old Larkin and her family, who find baby Sophie at their home with a note indicating that her mother will return for her. They give Sophie love while concealing the grief they feel following the loss of Larkin's baby brother a few months earlier. "With simple elegance, MacLachlan relates her tale about memory, love, loss, risk, and (most of all) about the power of language. Especially impressive is her ability to invest the simplest human actions and physical events with emotion and love" (*School Library Journal* Nov. 1, 1993). Ages 10–13.

MacLachlan, Patricia. **Edward's Eyes.** New York: Simon & Schuster, 2009. 128p. $5.99pa. ISBN 1-4169-2744-1; 978-1-4169-2744-0.

Jake's younger brother Edward is special. He can make people laugh, and he teaches himself to throw a perfect knuckleball. After Edward is killed in a biking accident, his parents announce that they have donated his organs and corneas. Jake is devastated at first, but the donation of Edward's corneas to a young baseball player helps Jake accept Edward's death, and he begins to move on. "As a story of overcoming grief, it works beautifully, and the quality and brevity of the narrative will appeal to those who read it despite its actual subject" (*Kirkus Reviews* July 15, 2007). Ages 8–12.

Martin, Ann M. **Everything for a Dog.** New York: Feiwel & Friends, 2009. 224p. $16.99. ISBN 0-312-38651-6; 978-0-312-38651-1.

Ann M. Martin tells parallel stories of a stray dog (the brother of the dog featured in *A Dog's Life*), a boy dealing with the loss of his brother, and a boy whose most ardent wish is to own a dog. "These plots are seemingly unrelated, and how they ultimately fit together will defy most expectations. Plot twists, of course, are just a bonus; mostly this is a sensitive, gentle read that surrounds its occasional heartbreak with plenty of hope and warm feelings" (*Booklist* June 1, 2009). Ages 9–12.

Martino, Carmela. **Rosa, Sola.** Somerville, MA: Candlewick Press. 2005. 256p. $15.99. ISBN: 0-7636-2395-4; 978-0-7636-2395-1.

Ten-year-old Rosa prays for a sibling, and miraculously, her mother becomes pregnant. However, the pregnancy is difficult, resulting in a stillbirth that strains her mother's health and leaves her father angry and distant. Rosa learns to lean on her friends and extended family through this difficult time, finding that she isn't alone after all. Ages 9–12.

Park, Barbara. **Mick Harte Was Here.** New York: Random House Children's Books, Yearling, 1988. 96p. $5.99. ISBN 0-679-88203-0; 978-0-679-88203-9.

Phoebe, 13, works through her grief after her younger brother, Mick, is killed in a bicycle accident. The support of her family and memories of her brother's humorous antics enable her to speak about Mick at a school assembly. "The author is adept at portraying the stages of grief and the effects of this sudden tragedy on the family. The book's tone of sadness is mitigated by humor, reassurance, and hope" (*School Library Journal* May 1, 1995). Ages 9–13.

Park, Barbara, ed. **Mick Harte Was Here.** New York: Random House Listening Library, 2004. Audiocassette and paperback. 1hr. 42 min., 88p. $29.00. ISBN 0-8072-7797-5; 978-0-8072-7797-3.

"The fresh-voiced narration of Dana Lubotsky, which is both clear and sounds genuinely like that of a young teenager, puts this short, intense novel across in virtuoso style. Shedding light on the world of emotions with honesty, this will make a thought-provoking addition to libraries as well as preparing its listeners for the losses we all must bear" (*School Library Journal* Jan. 1, 1998). Ages 9–13.

Recorvits, Helen. **Goodbye, Walter Malinski.** New York: Farrar, Straus & Giroux, 1999. 96p. $15.00. ISBN 0-374-32747-5; 978-0-374-32747-7. Out of print.

Set in 1934, this family story is told from the viewpoint of fifth grader Wanda Malinski. The Great Depression has devastating effects on the family, and an accident takes the life of Wanda's brother, Walter, nearly tearing the family apart.

"Occasional pencil drawings suit the serious tone of the text, and the illustrations help to realize the unnamed mill town in which the story is set and create a feel for the era. This is a sobering but hopeful glimpse into a very different past, peopled with characters whose emotions are very much like our own" (*School Library Journal* June 1, 1999). Ages 9–12.

Roberts, Willo Davis. **The One Left Behind.** New York: Simon & Schuster, Atheneum, 2006. 144p. $16.95. ISBN 0-689-85075-1; 978-0-689-85075-2.

Mandy, 11 years old, is accidentally left behind in the family's big house on Lake Michigan. Still mourning the death of her twin sister Angel one year before, she is consumed by loneliness until she encounters two boys running away from kidnappers. After taking in teenager Zander and his toddler brother, she doesn't know how she can accept responsibility for herself and the two boys without the help of Angel. As she gains confidence, she realizes that her memories of Angel will always be there to guide and reassure her. "Mandy and Zander face troubles that leave them incomplete, and the drama of outthinking and outrunning the kidnappers imbues what might otherwise be just an 'issue book' with page-turning pacing" (*School Library Journal* May 1, 2006). Ages 8–12.

Smith, Jane D. **Mary by Myself.** New York: HarperCollins, 1994. 160p. $14.00. ISBN 0-06-024517-4; 978-0-06-024517-7. Out of print.

While adjusting to new friends and new activities at summer camp, 11-year-old Mary remembers her infant sister Felicity, who died suddenly in her sleep several months earlier. "It is a book about the loss of childhood innocence, and the recognition that people, even those we love, are not perfect. . . . Rarely is a book with such complex themes and clear voice written for this age group" (*Voice of Youth Advocates* Apr. 1, 1995). Ages 9–14.

Wallace-Brodeur, Ruth. **Blue Eyes Better.** New York: Penguin Group, Puffin, 2003. 112p. $5.99. ISBN 0-14-250086-0; 978-0-14-250086-6. Out of print.

Tessa's family is in turmoil after her 15-year-old brother is killed in a drunk-driving accident. Eleven-year-old Tessa receives little support and struggles to keep going, while her mother drifts further and further from her. "Although the book begins with the jolting darkness of confusion and devastation, its tone is one of hope. Psychological survival stories often have a more limited audience than those with more physical action, but those interested in the drama of coping and healing will find a convincing portrait of a girl and her family rebuilding their lives after tragedy" (*School Library Journal* Jan. 1, 2002). Ages 10–12.

Divorce

Adams, Eric J., and Kathleen Adams. **On the Day His Daddy Left.** Park Ridge, IL: Albert Whitman, 2000. 24p. $6.95pa. ISBN 0-8075-6073-1; 978-0-8075-6073-0.

On the day his father moves out of the house, Danny's teacher, friends, and family reassure him that his parents' divorce is not his fault. "The Adamses maintain their honesty as the book telescopes the traumatic day (and the first year), and acknowledges that only time, adjustment to the new situation, and love can temper Danny's pain. This valuable, therapeutic book speaks volumes on a few thoughtful, briefly worded pages, with [Layne] Johnson's caring, photographically realistic artwork not only mirroring the people and surroundings in Danny's life but also his intense emotions" (*Booklist* Nov. 15, 2000). Ages 4–8.

Bernhard, Durga. **To and Fro, Fast and Slow.** New York: Walker, 2001. 32p. $15.95. ISBN 0-8027-8782-7; 978-0-8027-8782-8.

> In this picture book a girl is shuttled between her mother's country home and her father's city apartment. A collection of opposites, the city features neon lights, traffic, tall buildings, people, and shopping, while the country is filled with nature, houses, few people, picnics, and children playing outdoors. The only text consists of two large words and an ampersand on each page. "In each scene, the daughter and her parent are portrayed in engaging, primitive-style, gouache illustrations. This engaging book is best shared one-on-one to appreciate the soft hues and warm, cozy details" (*School Library Journal* Sept. 1, 2001). Ages 3–7.

Brown, Susan Taylor. **Hugging the Rock.** Berkeley, CA: Ten Speed Press, Tricycle Press, 2006. 176p. $14.95. ISBN 1-58246-180-5; 978-1-58246-180-9.

> Through a series of poems, Rachel expresses her feelings about her mother's leaving the family, her awareness of her mother's mental illness, and her changing attitude toward her father. "Written in straightforward language, the text clearly reveals Rachel's emotions, describing moments both painful and reassuring. This novel will be therapeutic to children dealing with the loss of a parent or a mental illness" (*School Library Journal* Sept. 1, 2006). Ages 9–12.

Bunting, Eve. **My Mom's Wedding.** Ann Arbor, MI: Sleeping Bear Press, 2006. 32p. $16.95. ISBN 1-58536-288-3; 978-1-58536-288-2.

> Seven-year-old Pinkie has mixed feelings about her divorced mother's wedding, especially when she learns that her father will attend as a guest. She is torn by feelings of loyalty to her father and affection for the man her mother is about to marry. When Pinky accepts the reality that her parents will not get back together, she understands that it is okay to love both fathers. "While her first-person voice may be a little precocious at times, it is honest and direct in typical Bunting style. [Lisa] Papp's soft watercolors, bordered and cropped to evoke wedding photos, set up idyllic matrimonial images" (*School Library Journal* Mar. 1, 2007). Ages 4–8.

Caseley, Judith. **Priscilla Twice.** New York: HarperCollins, 1995. 32p. $14.93. ISBN 0-688-13306-1; 978-0-688-13306-1.

> After her parents' divorce, Priscilla finds that she has two of everything, including two sets of clothes, two sets of toys and books, and two places where friends can visit her. "Appealing illustrations filled with bright colors and patterns and a text injected with humor relieve some of the seriousness of the subject matter. Even so, there are still some heartbreaking episodes in which Priscilla makes it clear that divorce is no laughing matter" (*Booklist* Aug. 1, 1995). Ages 5–7.

Cleary, Beverly. **Strider.** New York: HarperCollins, 1991. 192p. $17.89. ISBN 0-688-09901-7; 978-0-688-09901-5. Also in paperback 176p. $4.50pa. ISBN 0-380-72802-8; 978-0-380-72802-2.

> Leigh Botts, 14, finds an abandoned dog he names Strider; in caring for him, Leigh passes from childhood into adolescence, learning to accept his parents' divorce and experiencing a first romance. "Although the story is centered around Leigh's relationship with Strider, this is more than just 'a boy and his dog' book. Cleary's talent for portraying the details of everyday life—both small and significant—is evident here" (*School Library Journal* Sept. 1, 1991). Ages 9–12.

Cochran, Bill. **My Parents Are Divorced, My Elbows Have Nicknames, and Other Facts about Me.** New York: HarperCollins, 2009. 32p. $17.99. ISBN 0-06-053942-9; 978-0-06-053942-9.

Ted's parents are divorced, and that makes him sad, but the things that make him weird include naming his elbows Clyde and Carl, walking around with soap in his hair, and squawking like a chicken on the phone. Illustrated by Steve Bjorkman. "The colorful cartoons add to the upbeat nature of the story and make a serious subject a little easier to swallow. Many adults will appreciate this book's message and will want to use it as a springboard for discussion in both home and school settings" (*School Library Journal* May 1, 2009). Ages 5–8.

Coffelt, Nancy. **Fred Stays with Me!** New York: Little, Brown Books for Young Readers, 2007. 32p. $16.99. ISBN 0-316-88269-0; 978-0-316-88269-9.

A young girl describes how she lives sometimes with his mother and sometimes with her father, but her dog is her constant companion. "It all sounds simple enough, but Coffelt offers a fresh, villain-free look at a split family and at a girl who finds strength, love and reassuring consistency in the dear pooch who is all her own. [Tricia] Tusa's winning, soft-edged, autumnally hued watercolor illustrations perfectly complement the quiet story, infusing humor and chaos into the more understated text" (*Kirkus Reviews* May 15, 2007). Ages 4–8.

Corriveau, Art. **How I, Nicky Flynn, Finally Got a Life (and a Dog).** New York: Abrams, Amulet Books, 2010. 288p. $16.95. ISBN 0-8109-8298-6; 978-0-8109-8298-7.

Eleven-year-old Nicky moves to inner-city Boston after his parents' divorce and struggles to cope with the changes in his life. These changes are further compounded when his mother brings home Reggie, an 80-pound German shepherd who used to be a seeing-eye dog. "The characters are vividly drawn without sentimentality, especially Mom; Nicky's Latina classmate, who tries to be his friend; and the bullies who come to respect him for running away. More than independence, it is Nicky's blindness about Dad's rejection that is the powerful theme" (*Booklist* Mar. 1, 2010). Ages 8–12.

Danziger, Paula. **You Can't Eat Your Chicken Pox, Amber Brown.** Amber Brown Series, No. 2. New York: Penguin Group, Putnam Juvenile, 1995. 112p. $15.99. ISBN 0-399-22702-4; 978-0-399-22702-8.

A sequel to *Amber Brown Is Not a Crayon* (1994). Amber visits London with her aunt while her parents are getting a divorce. She still hopes to bring her parents together, but before she gets to London, Amber finds that she has chicken pox. "She [Amber] is a convincing eight-year-old in her behavior, interests, perceptions, and penchant for gross humor. Appealing black-ink cartoons [by Tony Ross] appear throughout" (*School Library Journal* June 1, 1995). Ages 7–11.

Danziger, Paula. **Amber Brown Goes Fourth.** Amber Brown Series, No. 3. New York: Penguin Group, Putnam Juvenile, 1995. 112p. $16.99. ISBN 0-399-22849-7; 978-0-399-22849-0. Also Lexington, KY: Book Wholesalers, 2002. $12.17. ISBN 0-7587-0417-8; 978-0-7587-0417-7. Saint Louis, MO: San Val, Turtleback, 1996. 101p. $11.80. ISBN 0-613-00276-8; 978-0-613-00276-9.

In this third book in the series, Amber enters fourth grade and faces some changes in her life as her best friend moves away and her parents divorce. "Kids coping with problems similar to Amber's will find encouragement, sympathy, and an upbeat way of taking responsibility for solving them. Entertaining and satisfying, this is a first purchase, whether or not the rest of the series is owned" (*School Library Journal* Oct. 1, 1995). Ages 7–11.

Danziger, Paula. **Amber Brown Wants Extra Credit.** Amber Brown Series, No. 4. Lexington, KY: Book Wholesalers, 2002. $12.17. ISBN 0-7587-0421-6; 978-0-7587-0421-4.

Amber Brown is unhappy that she must meet her mother's new boyfriend, and she is unable to concentrate on her schoolwork. Then she meets Max, he helps her with a school project, and Amber decides that she likes him. "Danziger skillfully weaves the emotional threads into the fabric of a fourth-grader's everyday life. From the colorful jacket to the drawings throughout the book, Tony Ross' expressive and sometimes comical illustrations capture the spirit of the story" (*Booklist* June 1, 1996). Ages 7–11.

Danziger, Paula. **Forever Amber Brown.** Amber Brown Series, No.5. New York: Penguin Group, Putnam Juvenile, 1996. 112p. $15.99. ISBN 0-399-22932-9; 978-0-399-22932-9.

In this fifth book in the series, Amber's life has changed dramatically: her parents are divorced, her father lives in France, and her best friend has moved to another state. Just when Amber is accustomed to her mother's boyfriend, Max, he asks her mom to marry him. "Danziger's characterizations ring true. Her light handling of a difficult subject faced by so many youngsters will once again find a ready audience" (*School Library Journal* Feb. 1, 1997). Ages 7–11.

Danziger, Paula. **Amber Brown Sees Red.** Amber Brown Series, No. 6. Lexington, KY: Book Wholesalers, 2002. $12.17. ISBN 0-7587-0420-8; 978-0-7587-0420-7. Also Saint Louis, MO: San Val, Turtleback, 1998. $11.80 library binding. ISBN 0-613-09442-5; 978-0-613-09442-9.

Fourth grader Amber's father returns from France, and her parents' bickering escalates until she sees red. Meanwhile, Amber continues to get used to her mother's fiancé, Max. "The first-person, present-tense narrative gets exactly right the fourth-grader's mix of feelings, her focus on the trivial, the gross, and the essential. Readers will welcome the combination of farce and tenderness, the honesty about anger and hurt and love" (*Booklist* May 15, 1997). Ages 7–11.

Danziger, Paula. **Amber Brown Is Feeling Blue.** Amber Brown Series, No. 7. New York: Scholastic, 1999. 144p. $4.99pa. ISBN 0-439-07168-2; 978-0-439-07168-0.

Amber Brown must make a decision to spend Thanksgiving with her mother and boyfriend in Washington state or with her father in New York. Furthermore, Amber is no longer the only one in school with a two-color name; Kelly Green is the new girl in her class, and it's making Amber blue. "A likable nine-year-old with much common sense, she is willing to talk about her feelings openly and honestly and her first-person narration allows readers to be privy to these thoughts and emotions. Another winner in an appealing contemporary series" (*School Library Journal* Nov. 1, 1998). Ages 7–11.

Danziger, Paula. **I, Amber Brown.** Amber Brown Series, No. 8. New York: Penguin Group, Putnam Juvenile, 1999. 160p. $15.99. ISBN 0-399-23180-3; 978-0-399-23180-3.

Because her divorced parents share joint custody of her, nine-year-old Amber suffers from lack of self-esteem and feels that she is a piece of jointly owned property. In spite of her mother's objections, she gets her ears pierced when she is with her father. Illustrated with Tony Ross's black-and-white drawings. "Full of Amber's puns and laugh-out-loud situational humor, this is also a deft handling of a very difficult yet common childhood dilemma" (*Booklist* Oct. 15, 1999). Ages 7–11.

Grimes, Nikki. **Oh, Brother!** New York: HarperCollins, 2008. 32p. $17.89. ISBN 0-688-17295-4; 978-0-688-17295-4.

Xavier, a Latino boy, is unhappy when his mother remarries and he suddenly has a new stepbrother and stepfather in his home. In poetry Grimes captures the struggles of bringing together a family. "[T]his is an important topic and the blending of a Latino and an African-American family is refreshing. [Mike] Benny's artwork is bold and literal, which supports the metaphors used in the poetry" (*School Library Journal* Feb. 1, 2008). Ages 5–10.

Henkes, Kevin. **Bird Lake Moon.** Prince Frederick, MD: Recorded Books, LLC, 2008. E-book. $27.00. ISBN 1-4356-7453-7; 978-1-4356-7453-0.

Mitch, 12, and Spencer, 10, meet while vacationing at Bird Lake. Mitch's parents are divorcing, and Spencer's older brother drowned when Spencer was two years old. In alternating chapters we read of each boy's story, and their friendship enables them to deal with their losses. "As in his Newbery Honor Book *Olive's Ocean* (2003), every word counts, moving the story forward moment by moment.... Emotions are just as carefully carved, turning characterization into portraiture; the children stand out in relief, against the deceptive tranquility of the lake" (*Booklist* Mar. 15, 2008). Ages 9–12.

Henkes, Kevin. **Bird Lake Moon.** New York: HarperCollins, HarperChildren's Audio, 2008. CD. 3 hrs. 30 min. $22.95. ISBN 0-06-155185-6; 978-0-06-155185-7.

"Written with definitive characters and open and insightful portrayals of adolescent boys, narrator Oliver Wyman gives each character a distinctive voice, and his telling enhances the poignancy of the story" (*School Library Journal* Sept. 1, 2008). Ages 9–12.

Holmberg, Bo R. **A Day with Dad.** Somerville, MA: Candlewick Press, 2008. 32p. $15.99. ISBN 0-7636-3221-X; 978-0-7636-3221-2.

Tim lives with his mom, and his dad lives in another town. Today Tim's dad arrives on the train, and the two spend the day together. "[Eva] Eriksson's pastel/crayon drawings in subdued colors bring to the page Tim's emotions, which range from expectancy to joy to eagerness to uncertainty and finally to acquiescence as he recognizes a situation beyond his control. Children with similar experiences will appreciate this gentle support as they cope with the realities of divorce; the unmistakable love between child and parent is palpable" (*Kirkus Reviews* Apr. 1, 2008). Ages 4–8.

Holyoke, Nancy. **A Smart Girl's Guide to Her Parents' Divorce: How to Land on Your Feet When Your World Turns Upside Down.** Middleton, WI: American Girl Publishing, 2009. 120p. $9.95pa. ISBN 1-59369-488-1; 978-1-59369-488-3.

Divorce brings many changes to a family, and the transition can be difficult. This advice book is intended to help a girl better understand her parents' divorce. "The text has a compassionate tone, and sprinkled throughout are answers to questions that readers might have as well as snippets of advice from girls who have found what works for them. A few write-in quizzes are included" (*School Library Journal* May 1, 2009). Ages 8–10.

Hurwitz, Johanna. **One Small Dog.** New York: HarperCollins, 2000. 128p. $15.89. ISBN 0-06-029220-2; 978-0-06-029220-1.

Fourth grader Curtis gets a dog when his mother tries to compensate for their divorce, but his new dog causes problems that he did not expect. "This will be popular with Hurwitz's fans and parents of readers who are convinced that a dog will fix everything" (*Booklist* Oct. 15, 2000). "[Diane] DeGroat's realistic drawings are a bonus. A good message for aspiring or prospective pet owners" (*School Library Journal* Nov. 1, 2000). Ages 7–10.

Johnson, Angela. **Songs of Faith.** New York: Scholastic, Orchard Books, 1998. 112p. $15.95. ISBN 0-531-30023-4; 978-0-531-33023-7.

Set in a small Ohio town in 1975, this is the story of 13-year-old Doreen as she struggles to come to terms with disturbing changes in her family life. She is a child of divorce who is particularly upset at seeing her younger brother's adjustment problems after their father moves away. "Once again Johnson has set attractive and realistic African-American characters in situations in which race is not the focus. This short, sensitive book will appeal most to reflective readers" (*School Library Journal* Mar. 1, 1998). Ages 8–12.

Kimmel, Haven. **Kaline Klattermaster's Tree House.** New York: Simon & Schuster Children's Publishing, Atheneum, 2008. 160p. $15.99. ISBN 0-689-87402-2; 978-0-689-87402-4.

Third-grader Kaline Klattermaster loves his mom but thinks she's a little crazy—especially since his father left. Kaline retreats to his tree house and the imaginary friends there who give him advice for dealing with bullies and his other problems. "Kaline is a real, likable character and is reminiscent of a younger Joey Pigza. Readers will enjoy stepping into his imaginary world, empathize with his troubles, and cheer him on throughout the story" (*School Library Journal* Mar. 1, 2008). Ages 7–12.

Krementz, Jill. **How It Feels When Parents Divorce.** New York: Knopf Doubleday Publishing Group, Knopf, 1988. 128p. $16.00pa. ISBN 0-394-75855-2; 978-0-394-75855-8.

Boys and girls share their experiences with divorced parents. "The candor marking the comments of these 7-to-16-year-old young people talking about important personal feelings will touch the emotions of all readers. The text is extended by Krementz' sensitive photographs of the participants and their parents" (*Booklist* Dec. 15, 1988). Ages 7–16.

McDonald, Megan. **Happy New Year, Julie, Bk. 3.** The American Girls Collection. Middleton, WI: American Girl Publishing, 2007. 88p. $6.95pa. ISBN 1-59369-291-9; 978-1-59369-291-9.

Julie's parents have divorced, and at Christmas Julie finds comfort sharing the Chinese New Year traditions with her best friend, Ivy Ling. "Following the traditional 'American Girl' style with short chapters and a 'looking back' section at the end, the stories [in the series] are easy to read, have likable characters, and feature situations many kids will relate to. The full-color illustrations and memorabilia in the end sections enhance the realistic feel" (*School Library Journal* Jan. 1, 2008). Ages 8–12.

Murphy, Patricia J. **Divorce and Separation.** Tough Topics Series. Chicago: Heinemann-Raintree, Heinemann First Library, 2007. 32p. $26.00. ISBN 1-4034-9775-3; 978-1-4034-9775-8. Heinemann-Raintree, NA-h, 2007. 32p. $7.99pa. ISBN 1-4034-9780-X; 978-1-4034-9780-2.

Explains what happens when divorce papers are signed, explores the reasons why parents may decide to separate, and provides reassurance to any reader whose parents are splitting up. The book also describes the feelings many children experience when their parents are separating or divorcing. "The writing is frank yet sensitive enough in its approach and the accompanying full-color photographs effectively illustrate the text. A solid introduction to a tough topic" (*School Library Journal* June 1, 2008). Ages 6–10.

Newman, Lesleá. **Saturday Is Pattyday.** Chicago, IL: New Victoria, 1993. 24p. $14.95. ISBN 0-934678-52-9; 978-0-934678-52-0.

When Frankie's two moms get divorced, he is very unhappy when Patty moves into her own apartment. To address his fears, she promises that she will always be his mom and can visit her every Saturday—Pattyday. "The bibliotherapy is reassuring, especially since the words and [Annette] Hegel's expressive watercolor pictures are frank about the painful separation as well as about the parents' enduring love for their child" (*Booklist* Nov. 1, 1993). Ages 5–7.

Portnoy, Mindy Avra. **A Tale of Two Seders.** Minneapolis, MN: Lerner Publishing Group, Kar-Ben, 2010. 32p. $17.95. ISBN 0-8225-9907-4; 978-0-8225-9907-4.

After her parents' divorce, a young girl celebrates Passover seders with each parent. Illustrated by Valeria Cis. "Portnoy, a rabbi and the author of *Where Do People Go When They Die?* (2004), writes with empathy and humor of this common situation. In comparing families and charoset (a traditional Passover food made with apples, nuts, and wine), Mom makes the point that each one is different but tasty in its own way" (*Booklist* May 1, 2010). Ages 5–9.

Rogers, Fred. **Divorce.** New York: Penguin Group, Putnam Juvenile, 1998. 32p. $6.99pa. ISBN 0-698-11670-4; 978-0-698-11670-2.

Rogers assures children that adults, not children, cause divorce, and their parents will always love them. Illustrated with color photographs by Jim Judkis. "The gentle yet straightforward text validates a host of common feelings children have about divorce and thoughtfully answers many questions kids ask: 'Where will I live?' 'Is it okay to have fun sometimes?' 'Can I cry?' The photos, nicely staged to capture children and middle-class parents in warm, bright surroundings, add a positive feel" (*Booklist* May 15, 1996). Ages 4–8.

Rupp, Rebecca. **Sarah Simpson's Rules for Living.** Somerville, MA: Candlewick Press, 2008. 96p. $14.99. ISBN 0-7636-3220-1; 978-0-7636-3220-5.

Sixth-grader Sarah Simpson's life is chaotic because her parents have recently divorced, her father has moved across the country with his new young wife, and she feels betrayed by both of them. She settles on journal writing and list making as a way to organize her thoughts. "While the journal format and inclusion of lists is hardly new, Sarah's strong voice and wry humor keep this novel surprisingly fresh" (*Booklist* Feb. 15, 2008). Ages 9–12.

Rupp, Rebecca. **Sarah Simpson's Rules for Living.** Playaway Children Series. Solon, OH: Findaway World, LLC, 2008. Mixed media. $34.99. ISBN 1-60640-889-5; 978-1-60640-889-6. Grand Haven, MI: Brilliance Audio, 2008. Compact disc. 1hr. $14.95.

"Sarah's vulnerable and bewildered voice is capably captured by [reader] Emily Durante who depicts all the angst, embarrassment, and unchecked enthusiasm of a 12-year-old girl. She adds just the right amount of drama and incredulity to the reading, and projects Sarah's wry sense of humor in a matter-of-fact manner" (*School Library Journal* Nov. 1, 2008). Ages 9–12.

Santucci, Barbara. **Loon Summer.** Grand Rapids, MI: Eerdmans Publishing Co., 2004. 32p. $16.00. ISBN 0-8028-5182-7; 978-0-8028-5182-6.

After her parents' divorce, Rainie spends the summer with her father. She sees a family of loons on the lake and wishes her parents would stay together, like the family of loons. Illustrated by Andrea Shine. "Soft, watercolor washes provide a soothing backdrop to Rainie's moodiness and sorrow; bits of cut-paper collage add an intriguing dimension to the illustrations. The father-daughter relationship is beautifully and thoughtfully depicted, so the ending is a hopeful one" (*Library Journal* Aug. 1, 2001). Ages 5–9.

Schmitz, Tamara. **Standing on My Own Two Feet: A Child's Affirmation of Love in the Midst of Divorce.** New York: Penguin Group, Price Stern Sloan, 2008. 32p. $12.99. ISBN 0-8431-3221-3; 978-0-8431-3221-2.

Addison's parents are divorced, and he lives in one house with his mom and another with his dad, but he knows that both parents love him. "A simple, clearly worded text about divorce for the youngest children, this will help parents hammer home the twin messages that it is not the child's fault and that the child is loved very much by each parent, no matter what happens.... While not particularly artful, Schmitz's brightly colored, realistic illustrations portray real people with real emotions" (*Kirkus Reviews* Apr. 15, 2008). Ages 3–7.

Spelman, Cornelia Maude. **Mama and Daddy Bear's Divorce.** Park Ridge, IL: Albert Whitman,1998. 24p. $15.99. ISBN 0-8075-5221-6; 978-0-8075-5221-6.

Dinah Bear feels sad and scared when her parents say they are going to divorce, but when Daddy moves into his new home, Dinah and her sister visit him on weekends, and Dinah still takes walks with him. Illustrated by Kathy Parkinson. "The words used to describe the divorce and what it means are carefully chosen, and the expressions on the bear characters' faces are appropriately sad. However, the message of this book is that life goes on" (*School Library Journal* Sept. 1, 1998). "A sensitive book that should have wide use" (*Booklist* Dec. 1, 1998). Ages 3–6.

Spinelli, Eileen. **The Dancing Pancake.** New York: Alfred A. Knopf, 2010. 256p. $12.99. ISBN 0-375-85870-9; 978-0-375-85870-3.

After her parents separate, 11-year-old Belinda "Bindi" Winkle and her family struggle through tough times with the support of the community that emerges around their new restaurant, The Dancing Pancake. "The poetic structure of this novel succeeds in capturing the child's voice and deepest feelings. The verse also provides sound development of secondary characters. [Joanne] Lew-Vriethoff's lively pen-and-ink illustrations add texture to the story and offer touches of humor" (*School Library Journal* May 1, 2010). Ages 8–12.

Tolan, Stephanie S. **Wishworks, Inc.** New York: Scholastic, Arthur A. Levine Books, 2009. 160p. $15.99. ISBN 0-545-03154-0; 978-0-545-03154-7.

Third grader Max handles his parents' divorce, his new home and school, and a big bully by escaping into his imaginary world. He and his imaginary dog King have thrilling adventures in the woods; then Max happens upon an imaginary store called Wishworks, Inc., which promises that his wishes will come true in real life. Max is confronted with reality when he wishes for a real king, and his wish comes true. "Tolan's vivid, clean writing is deceptively uncomplicated and the many issues touched upon are handled well. This book will resonate with kids while providing parents a great jumping-off point for conversations about how to overcome some of life's obstacles" (*School Library Journal* July 1, 2009). Ages 7–10.

Zimmer, Tracie Vaughn. **42 Miles.** Boston: Houghton Mifflin Harcourt, Clarion Books, 2008. 80p. $16.00. ISBN 0-618-61867-8; 978-0-618-61867-5.

As her 13th birthday approaches, JoEllen decides to bridge the 42 miles between her two separate lives—one as Joey, who enjoys weekends with her father and other relatives on a farm, and the other as Ellen, who lives with her mother in a Cincinnati apartment near her school and friends. "Using free verse, Zimmer shows the richness in both places, while black-and-white composite illustrations bring the bits and pieces together from the baseball trophies in Dad's old room to the overview of city traffic. Casual and open, both the poetry and pictures show the fun: With Dad, one thing's for certain; nothing ever is" (*Booklist* Apr. 1, 2008). Ages 9–12.

Zimmer, Tracie Vaughn. **Sketches from a Spy Tree.** Boston: Houghton Mifflin Harcourt, Clarion Books, 2005. 64p. $16.00. ISBN 0-618-23479-9; 978-0-618-23479-0.

Anne-Marie's father suddenly leaves the family. In poetry and illustrations that include paintings, drawings, and collage, Anne-Marie takes readers through a year of change in the life of her family. With her twin sister she deals with their mother's remarriage, and the addition of a baby sister to the family. "[Andrew] Glass's multimedia illustrations, which are executed in paint, photo- and cut-paper collage and pencil, are as varied as Anne Marie's subjects and her very natural emotions. Of special interest to readers who may themselves be facing a shift in family structure" (*Kirkus Reviews* June 15, 2005). "The book uses free verse and freewheeling art with distinction" (*Booklist* Aug. 1, 2005). Ages 8–12.

Foster Children

Fogelin, Adrian. **The Sorta Sisters.** Atlanta, GA: Peachtree Publishers, 2007. 224p. $15.95. ISBN 1-56145-424-9; 978-1-56145-424-2.

Anna Casey lives in Tallahassee, Florida, and has lived in a string of foster homes since her parents' death. Mica Delano lives with her father on their boat, and when she and Anna begin corresponding, they discover they have a lot in common and call themselves the "sorta sisters." "The lively, third-person narrative alternates between each girl's perspective, and the frequently inserted letters bring intimacy and depth to the characters.... A heartfelt story that shows the many factors that create family, friends, and home" (*Booklist* Jan. 1, 2008). Ages 8–12.

Gregory, Nan. **I'll Sing You One-O.** Boston: Houghton Mifflin Harcourt, Clarion Books, 2006. 224p. $16.00. ISBN 0-618-60708-0; 978-0-618-60708-2.

Twelve-year-old Gemma is taken from a foster home she loves and is adopted by relatives she didn't know she had. After reading a book about saints, she decides to get an angel to help her. "The psychological component of the story's resolution seems less involving than the vivid portrayals and emotional nuance demonstrated throughout the story. Readers will be drawn to Gemma on the first page; she keeps them with her to the very end of this impressive first novel" (*Booklist* Aug. 1, 2006). Ages 8–13.

Grimes, Nikki. **The Road to Paris.** Logan, IA: Perfection Learning, 2008. 153p. $14.65. ISBN 0-7569-8932-9; 978-0-7569-8932-3.

Eight-year-old Paris is in another foster home. No matter how hard she tries to fit in, she feels that she never will in a town that is mostly white, while she is half black. She misses her brother, who has been sent to a boys' home. "The characters around her are not all perfectly realized, but Paris's story is touching and worth a place in most collections. Given the dearth of success stories featuring foster children and bi-racial characters, this is all the more important" (*Kirkus Reviews* Sept. 1, 2006). Ages 8–12.

Grimes, Nikki. **The Road to Paris.** Prince Frederick, MD: Recorded Books, 2007. 3 cassettes, 3 hrs. $30.75. ISBN 1-4281-6311-5; 978-1-4281-6311-9.

"Narrator Myra Lucretia Taylor admirably interprets this Coretta Scott King Honor Book (Putnam, 2006) by Nikki Grimes. A satisfying, poignant story for middle-school listeners" (*School Library Journal* Dec. 1, 2007). Ages 8–12.

Harrar, George. **Parents Wanted.** Minneapolis, MN: Milkweed Editions, 2001. 288p. $17.95. ISBN 1-57131-632-9; 978-1-57131-632-5. Paper: 320p. $6.95 ISBN 1-57131-633-7; 978-1-57131-633-2.

When 12-year-old Andy meets Laurie and Jeff at an adoption party, he has already been in eight foster homes. Andy's alcoholic mother has given him up to the state as too hard to handle, and his father is in jail. "With so much media focus on the topic of adoption, teens are becoming curious, especially those who were adopted or know someone who was. Harrar's fictional yet amazingly realistic journey of one boy's struggle through the adoption system is sure to satisfy their curiosity" (*Voice of Youth Advocates* Dec. 1, 2001). Ages 9–13.

Nixon, Joan Lowery. **A Family Apart.** Orphan Train Adventures Series, Vol. 1. New York: Random House Children's Books, Laurel Leaf, 1995. 176p. $6.50pa. ISBN 0-440-22676-7; 978-0-440-22676-5. Random House Children's Books, Dell Books for Young Readers, 1997. 176p. $4.50pa. ISBN 0-440-91309-8; 978-0-440-91309-2.

Between 1854 and 1929, more than 100,000 orphans were shipped from the East to new homes in the Midwest and Southwest. This first book of the Orphan Train series tells the story of Frances Mary, oldest of the six Kelly children. When her husband dies, Mrs. Kelly can no longer support her children, and she sends them west on the Orphan Train to be adopted by farm families. Frances masquerades as a boy so that she can be adopted with her brother, whom she promised her mother she would protect. "While the plight of the Kelly children is guaranteed to generate sympathy, the deliberate development is bothersome. The historical setting is a plus, and the book's easy consumability may make it a likely choice for recreational readers" (*Booklist* Sept. 15, 1987). Ages 10–12.

Nixon, Joan Lowery. **A Family Apart.** Orphan Train Adventures Series, Bk. 1. Prince Frederick, MD: Recorded Books, 2000. Mixed media: 4 audio cassettes & softcover. 5 hrs. $49.75. ISBN 0-7887-4331-7; 978-0-7887-4331-3.

Narrated by Barbara Caruso. "Caruso captures the personalities of the Kelly children and brings history from that time period alive. Students will be clamoring to listen to the other adventures of the Kelly children and to know more about the Orphan Train and the time period surrounding the Civil War" (*School Library Journal* Nov. 1, 2000). Ages 10–12.

Nixon, Joan Lowery. **Caught in the Act.** Orphan Train Adventures Series, Bk. 2. St. Louis, MO: San Val, Turtleback, 1999. $14.75. ISBN 0-8335-2525-5; 978-0-8335-2525-3.

In this continuation of the Orphan Train Adventures Series, 11-year-old Michael Patrick Kelly is sent from New York City to a Missouri farm with a sadistic owner and a bullying son. "Most of the figures are one-dimensional and behave predictably; it's the lively course of events that keeps the pages turning. This is undemanding fare that will appeal most to those looking for light historical fiction" (*Booklist* June 1, 1988). Ages 10–12.

Nixon, Joan Lowery. **In the Face of Danger.** Orphan Train Adventures Series, Bk. 3. New York: Random House Children's Books, Laurel Leaf, 1996. 160p. $5.99pa. ISBN 0-440-22705-4; 978-0-440-22705-2.

This third volume of the Orphan Train Adventures Series tells the story of 12-year-old Megan Kelly, who goes to live with Emma and Benjamin Browder on the Kansas prairie. Megan's belief that she carries a gypsy curse colors her perceptions of everything that happens to her until her foster mother helps her to understand that she can influence her own life. "The historical aspects of *In the Face of Danger* will have particular interest and appeal to this generation of children who hear so much about the problems of today's foster, abandoned, and street children that they will be able to relate to and understand the problems of the Kelly children and others like them 130-some odd years ago" (*School Library Journal* Dec. 1, 1988). Ages 10–12.

Nixon, Joan Lowery. **A Place to Belong.** Orphan Train Adventures Series, Bk. 4. New York: Random House Children's Books, Laurel Leaf, 1996. 160p. $5.50pa. ISBN 0-440-22696-1; 978-0-440-22696-3.

Ten-year-old Danny travels with his young sister from New York to a foster home on a farm near St. Joseph, Missouri. He plots to have his newly widowed foster father send for and marry his mother. Ages 10–12.

Nixon, Joan Lowery. **A Dangerous Promise.** Orphan Train Adventures Series, Bk. 5. New York: Random House Children's Books, Laurel Leaf, 1995. 160p. $5.99pa. ISBN 0-440-21965-5; 978-0-440-21965-1. Logan, IA: Perfection Learning, 1995. 148p. $13.65. ISBN 0-7807-5965-6; 978-0-7807-5965-7.

In 1861, 12-year-old Mike Kelly and his best friend Todd, although younger than the legal age of 16, join up with the Second Kansas Infantry and become army drummer boys. Mike is wounded at the Battle of Wilson's Creek and must begin a dangerous trek through enemy territory after Todd is killed. "Once again the Kelly family comes to life for the reader as the separated family members pursue their lives in the precarious Civil War era. Mike Kelly's relationships with those around him, the soldiers, his family, and his adopted family, as well as the people he meets on his way back to the Union Army, are well portrayed, and his adventures on the road are realistic and exciting" (*Voice of Youth Advocates* Oct. 1, 1994). Ages 10–12.

Nixon, Joan Lowery. **Keeping Secrets.** Orphan Train Adventures Series, Bk. 6. New York: Random House Children's Books, Dell Books for Young Readers, 1996. $20.95. ISBN 0-385-30994-5; 978-0-385-30994-3.

In this sixth installment about the Kelly family that was transplanted from New York to St. Joseph, Missouri, in the mid-1800s, 11-year-old Peg Kelly is drawn into the dangerous activities of a young woman who takes refuge with the Kelly family after fleeing the attack on Lawrence, Kansas, by William Quantrill and his raiders. "As the main character, Peggy is a highly believable and well rounded figure. This book is a must for middle school libraries and will appeal to some older readers also" (*Voice of Youth Advocates* Apr. 1, 1995). Ages 10–12.

Polacco, Patricia. **Welcome Comfort.** Picture Puffin Series. New York: Penguin Group, 2002. 40p. $6.99pa. ISBN 0-698-11965-7; 978-0-698-11965-9.

Overweight Welcome Comfort is a foster child who is frequently moved from home to home and gets picked on by the kids at his school. He finds friendship and acceptance when he is befriended by the school custodian, who takes a mysterious vacation every year on Christmas eve. "A touching and enjoyable story that reads well aloud" (*School Library Journal* Oct. 1, 1999). Ages 4–8.

Quattlebaum, Mary. **Grover G. Graham and Me.** St. Louis, MO: San Val, Turtleback, 2003. 179p. $12.25. ISBN 0-606-33053-4; 978-0-606-33053-4. Out of print.

Ben Watson has been shuffled from foster home to foster home since he was 5 years old—seven homes in six years. Now 11, Ben has arrived at home number eight. Here he encounters Grover G. Graham, a baby just over a year old, and Ben is convinced Grover's mother will abandon Grover again. When he has a chance to escape the foster care system, Ben takes it, and he takes Grover with him. "Ben is a likable, multilayered character, and his lively, descriptive narrative, peppered with dry wit and intimate detail, is both an engaging read and an exploration of foster care. The supporting characters and situations are somewhat stereotypical here, but taken together their stories illustrate that good hearts and homes can be found where least expected" (*Booklist* Oct. 15, 2001). Ages 8–12.

Skrypuch, Marsha. **Call Me Aram.** Markham, ON CAN: Fitzhenry & Whiteside, 2009. 86p. $16.95. ISBN 1-55455-000-9; 978-1-55455-000-5.

A sequel to *Aram's Choice* (2006), in this story Aram Davidian is one of a group of Armenian orphans brought to Canada in 1923. The boys adjust to life on a farm and Canadian customs, but they protest when told to take Canadian names. "A glossary, historical note, and lists of books, a Web site, and films are appended. Effective paintings [by Muriel Wood] help to bring this unusual chapter book to life" (*Booklist* July 1, 2009). Ages 4–8.

Stanley, Diane. **Raising Sweetness.** Pine Plains, NY: Live Oak Media, 2004. Compact disc, 14 vols., 18 min. + paperback, $39.95. ISBN 1-59112-524-3; 978-1-59112-524-2. Also audio cassette, 11 vols., 18 mins. + paperback, $16.95. ISBN1-59112-265-1; 978-1-59112-265-4. Also compact disc, 11 vols., 18 mins. + hardcover. $28.95. ISBN 1-59112-516-2; 978-1-59112-516-7.

In this mixed media sequel to *Saving Sweetness* (Putnam, 1996), Sweetness and the other orphans were adopted in the first book, and this is the story of their experiences with the kind-hearted but inept sheriff who adopted them. "This old-west story, with a touch of the tall tale, is read in a slow and easy fashion by Tom Bodet, who handles the first-person narrative with just the right level of cluelessness. Appropriate background music and occasional sound effects augment the presentation" (*School Library Journal* Mar. 1, 2004). Ages 4–8.

Warren, Andrea. **Orphan Train Rider: One Boy's True Story.** New York: Houghton Mifflin Harcourt Trade & Reference, 1996. $17.00. ISBN 0-395-69822-7; 978-0-395-69822-8. Out of Print.

For more than 75 years, orphans from the eastern seaboard were placed with Midwestern and Western families. Historians estimate the number of placed orphans at more than 200,000 from 1854 to 1930. This account focuses on one such orphan and his brothers, who rode the orphan train in 1926 to Texas. "A fascinating book about a social movement that predated today's foster homes, adoption agencies, and homeless shelters" (*School Library Journal* Aug. 1, 1998). Ages 8–12.

White, Ruth. **Way down Deep.** Waterville, ME: Thorndike Press, 2007. 239p. $23.95. ISBN 0-7862-9867-7; 978-0-7862-9867-9. New York: Farrar, Straus & Giroux, 2007. 208p. $16.99. ISBN 0-374-38251-4; 978-0-374-38251-3.

In summer 1944, a little girl is found abandoned on the steps of the courthouse in Way Down Deep, West Virginia. Miss Arbutus Ward, proprietor of the local boardinghouse, takes care of little Ruby June, and Ruby June comes to love her place in the world. "Peopled with delightfully quirky characters, this short novel captures the authentic cadences of Appalachia. Adding a hint of magical realism to this sweet and tender tale of family and friendship, White helps her readers to learn what home and family really mean for Ruby and for everyone" (*Voice of Youth Advocates* June 1, 2007). Ages 8–12.

Wolfson, Jill. **Home, and Other Big, Fat Lies.** New York: Henry Holt Books For Young Readers, 2006. 224p. $17.95. ISBN 0-8050-7670-0; 978-0-8050-7670-7.

Eleven-year-old Whitney, a foster child, arrives at her 12th foster home in a remote California town. With other foster children she leads an effort to save the biggest redwood tree in the forest. "A sweet, spirited tale told with warmth and humor about a determined misfit who finds a home at last in a family and a community" (*Kirkus Reviews* Sept. 15, 2006). Ages 10–14.

Woodson, Jacqueline. **Locomotion.** New York: Penguin Group, Puffin, 2004. 112p. $5.99pa. ISBN 0-14-240149-8; 978-0-14-240149-1. St. Louis, MO: San Val, 2005. 100p. $15.25. ISBN 1-4176-4275-0; 978-1-4176-4275-5.

Through his poetry, 11-year-old Lonnie Collins Motion shares his grief over his parents' death four years earlier and his love for his younger sister Lili, separated from him when they were placed in foster care. "Woodson continues to grow as an important writer in young adult fiction, showing that her poetic ability equals her considerable talent with fiction. A strong addition to the genre of novels in verse and recommended for public and school libraries, this title will appeal to most teens and would also be useful in conjunction with poetry groups and assignments" (*Voice of Youth Advocates* Feb. 1, 2003). Ages 9–12.

Woodson, Jacqueline. **Peace, Locomotion.** New York: Putnam, 2009.144p. $15.99. ISBN 978-0399246555. New York: Penguin Group, Puffin, 2010. 160p. $6.99pa. ISBN 9780142415122; e-book $6.99.

In this sequel to *Locomotion*, 12-year-old Lonnie is feeling at home with his foster family, but he is living apart from his little sister, Lili, and he decides to write letters to her. "Moving, thought-provoking, and brilliantly executed, this is the rare sequel that lives up to the promise of its predecessor. Serving as bookends to the body of the text are two poems in which Lonnie describes peace in everyday terms" (*School Library Journal* Jan. 1, 2009). Ages 9–12.

Woodson, Jacqueline. **Peace, Locomotion.** Grand Haven, MI: Brilliance Audio, 2009. 2 hrs. 12 CDs. $39.97. ISBN 978-1-4233-9799-12. MP3-CD. 2 hrs. $39.97. ISBN 978-1-4233-9801-11.

"Dion Graham's narration sounds exactly like that of a boy whose world is constantly shifting. His expert use of prosody makes each and every letter come alive" (*School Library Journal* Dec. 1, 2009). Ages 9–12.

SOURCES CONSULTED

Bertman, Sandra L. 1995. Using story, film, and drama to help children cope with death. In *Bereaved children and teens: A support guide for parents and professionals,* ed. Earl A. Grollman, 213–30. Boston: Beacon Press.

Corr, Charles A. 2000. What do we know about grieving children and adolescents? In *Living with grief: Children, adolescents, and loss,* ed. Kenneth J. Doka, 21–32. Washington, DC: Hospice Foundation of America.

Crenshaw, David A. 2002. The disenfranchised grief of children. In *Disenfranchised grief: New directions, challenges, and strategies for practice,* ed. Kenneth J. Doka, 293–306. Champaign, IL: Research Press.

Doka, Kenneth J., ed. 2000. *Living with grief: Children, adolescents, and loss.* Washington, DC: Hospice Foundation of America.

Doka, Kenneth J., ed. 2002. *Disenfranchised grief: New directions, challenges, and strategies for practice.* Champaign, IL: Research Press.

Donnelly, Katherine Fair. 2000. *Recovering from the loss of a sibling: When a brother or sister dies.* New York: Dodd, Mead, iUniverse.

Hooyman, Nancy R., and Betty J. Kramer. 2006. *Living through loss: Interventions across the life span.* New York: Columbia University Press.

Meyers, Barbara. 2002. Disenfranchised grief and the loss of an animal companion. In *Disenfranchised grief: New directions, challenges, and strategies for practice,* ed. Kenneth J. Doka, 251–64. Champaign, IL: Research Press.

Moody, Raymond A., Jr., and Dianne Arcangel. 2001. *Life after loss: Conquering grief and finding hope.* New York: HarperSanFrancisco.

Schreder, Maryanne. 1995. Special needs of bereaved children: Effective tools for helping. In *Bereaved children and teens: A support guide for parents and professionals,* ed. Earl A. Grollman, 195–211. Boston: Beacon Press.

Silverman, Phyllis R. 2000. When parents die. In *Living with grief: Children, adolescents, and loss,* ed. Kenneth J. Doka, 215–28. Washington, DC: Hospice Foundation of America.

Sweder, Gerri L. 1995. Talking to children about the terminal illness of a loved one. In *Bereaved children and teens: A support guide for parents and professionals,* ed. Earl A. Grollman, 47–59. Boston: Beacon Press.

U.S. Census Bureau. 2002. Newsroom Releases. Nearly 9 in 10 people may marry, but half of first marriages may end in divorce, Census Bureau Says. February 8, 2002. http://www.census.gov/Press-Release/www/releases/archives/marital_status_living_arrangements/000500.html. Accessed March 11, 2010.

Worden, J. William. 1996. *Children and grief: When a parent dies.* New York and London: Guilford Press.

4

—◆—

YOUNG ADULTS AND GRIEVING

CHAPTER OVERVIEW

As noted in chapter 3, our contemporary society does not prepare children and young adults for grieving, nor does it prepare adults for supporting youth who grieve. In this chapter we cite literature in the behavioral and social sciences that describes the grieving process of young adults so that librarians, teachers, parents, and mental health professionals can better understand the psychology underlying young adult behaviors. We then suggest ways that librarians and teachers can assist adolescents as they confront major loss. We also recommend resources appropriate for grieving older children and young adults, and for the adults who work closely with them.

MYTHS ABOUT GRIEVING CHILDREN AND ADOLESCENTS

Psychologists are in general agreement that a young person's developmental stage is a major factor influencing grief (see also chapter 3). Adults working with older children and young adults must be knowledgeable of these developmental stages as they confront grief with them. However, many popular misconceptions or myths confuse adults as they attempt to help grieving youth; we address these myths first.

Fiorini and Mullen (2006, 4–10) identify and describe several myths perpetuated in our society, and they negatively impact the ways that adults interact with children and adolescents who are experiencing loss. They also cite James and Friedman (2001). Following are popular myths, followed by statements based on behavioral research and counseling practice:

1. *Youth don't grieve*. Youth understand death, but not in the way adults do, and they do feel grief. Children and adolescents can experience strong emotions, but only for a short period of time; then they put their feelings aside. Adults seeing this reaction may believe that a youth is not grieving.
2. *It's not OK to feel bad*. Adults may want to eliminate the pain that youth are feeling and say to them, "Don't feel bad."

3. *You're supposed to feel bad.* While adults may tell children and young adults not to feel bad, they may contradict this message by suggesting there are certain responses expected by society, and they should feel bad. While it may be expected that someone should feel bad after a loss, sometimes a person feels nothing for a period of time.

4. *Replace the loss.* A common example of replacing a loss is parents who buy a young person another pet to replace one that has died. This strategy does not permit the youth time to assimilate the loss, and it suggests that the animal is replaceable. This is also true of the loss of a meaningful object or possession.

5. *Don't talk about it.* A common message adults send to young people is that grief is a private matter. The message we are sending is that no one cares what they feel, and they are alone in their grief.

6. *Brave little soldier.* Our society sends the message that we value people who face adversity with a stiff upper lip. The message is that we should suffer our grief independently and silently—exactly the opposite of what we should do.

7. *You'll get over it.* Time does not heal all wounds. Some losses produce deep wounds that leave a lasting impression.

8. *You're overreacting.* Many adults minimize the losses of young people. An adult witnessing a child's strong reaction to a loss should consider the underlying losses that the child could be associating with the current or primary loss.

9. *Just don't think about it.* An adult strategy for dealing with a loss is to keep busy so that we don't have to think about our pain. While this strategy may work for some adults, it prohibits children the opportunity and the time to work through their feelings of grief.

10. *It's time to move on.* There is no time limit on grief. Each person grieves according to circumstances.

11. *If you don't cry, you don't care.* Adults may suggest that there is a right way to grieve, but people do not grieve in the same way. Adults tend to believe if people show no emotion, or do not cry, they don't care or there is something wrong with them.

These are some of the most common myths that adversely influence adults' attempts to help grieving children and young adults. Now let's look at developmental stages, more accurate portrayals of grieving, and what adults can do to help.

GRIEVING AND DEVELOPMENTAL STAGES

A young person's age and stage of development are major factors influencing the grieving process of youth. In late childhood (ages 8 or 9 through 12) anger is less intense than adolescents' and older children do not feel the overwhelming sadness of younger children. Because of their more sophisticated concrete logical-operational thinking and problem-solving skills, older children are generally able to move ahead after a few months following a major loss, such as divorce or a parent's death. They are more capable of articulating their feelings and needs, seeking support, and making meaning of their loss (Hooyman and Kramer 2006).

By later childhood, children develop the ability to do more abstract thinking and gain independence from parents. They place an emphasis on relationships with friends and do not want to be different. They ask "what if" questions, for example,

Table 4-1 Developmental Stages and Responses to Loss

Age Range	Cognitive	Emotional	Behavioral
Ages 9 to 12 (Formal operational stage)	• More abstract thinking • Focus on peer relationships • Ask "what if" questions	• Feel responsible for the loss • Sadness, depression, anxiety, anger	• Withdrawal • Avoidance of expressing feelings • Acting out • Reduction in academic performance
Ages 13 to 18: Adolescence (Formal operations)	• Abstract thinking • Problem solving • Deductive reasoning • Comprehend concept of death • More in-depth spiritual thought	• Feel responsible for the loss • Sadness, depression, anxiety, anger	• Rebellion • Withdrawal • Avoidance of expressing feelings • Acting out • Reduction in academic performance

"What if I had been there to help Dad when he had his heart attack?" Children at this stage have feelings of sadness, depression, and anxiety (Fiorini and Mullen 2006).

Children and adolescents progress through the developmental stages at varying rates, and some may never reach the level of formal operations. Research suggests that youth of all ages experience grief, but they are able to tolerate strong grief reactions only for short periods. After a short period of grieving, they then turn back to play or some other safe activity (Corr 2000).

Table 4.1 outlines the cognitive, emotional, and behavioral characteristics of older children and adolescents.

Adolescents (ages approximately 13–18) represent a cultural group whose membership is temporary. The group maintains similar beliefs and customs based on common developmental tasks and on their relationship with adults. Adolescents realize that the rules of neither adulthood nor childhood apply to them, resulting in conflict with parents, teachers, and other authority figures. Accepted values and norms include such factors as language, dress, music, and interpersonal styles that are different than those of their authority figures' experiences (Fiorini and Mullen 2006).

For adolescents and for some older children, the behavioral, emotional, and cognitive indicators of loss may be mistaken for moodiness, hormones, or a phase. The experience of loss is unique to every individual, and external factors can compound the impact of loss. For example, a young person who has moved has few supportive friendships when there is a loss. Youth who are very sensitive to change may have difficulty with the slightest change.

FACTORS INFLUENCING YOUTHS' GRIEVING

While age and the consequent developmental age of youth have an impact on a child's reaction to loss, several other characteristics have an effect on a child's reaction. Hooyman and Kramer (2006, 89–90) identify "background characteristics and capacities" that influence resilience; the following list is an adaptation of their work. These characteristics are considered applicable for children of all ages, including adolescents.

1. Background characteristics refer to the ethnic status and socioeconomic status, as well as the urban or rural environment. Some youth living in a high-crime area of a city may be exposed frequently to violence and death, while suburban or rural children may have little experience with death, although death and violence portrayed in the media expose more children now than in the past.

2. Personal capacities are such variables as a child's age, self-esteem, problem-solving skills, gender, and attachment to the parent or other person lost. For example, a child's strong self-esteem can be very helpful in dealing with important losses.

3. Family capacities include parents' love, discipline, family routines and structure, communication patterns, and adult support. A supportive relationship with a parent or caring adult provides a sense of security to assist in dealing with a major loss.

4. Social capacities include the support of peers and adults, such as teachers, mental health professionals, church personnel, and support groups who can help the child moderate negative outcomes from a death, divorce, or victimization from violence.

5. Cultural capacities include the child's participation in such rituals as funerals and the family's cultural beliefs regarding death and afterlife.

These cultural capacities interact with the young person's developmental stage to influence reaction to loss, grief, and other occurrences during the young person's life. Furthermore, grieving is not static, and the characteristics and capacities listed above influence a child's grieving process throughout life (Hooyman and Kramer 2006).

DISENFRANCHISED GRIEF AND YOUTH

As identified in chapter 3, children and young adults may not receive permission to grieve, a phenomenon identified by Doka (2002) as "disenfranchised grief." Rowling (2002) asserts that this disenfranchised grief for adolescents is shaped primarily by the grieving rules established by parents, other adults, and peers; furthermore, Rowling (2002) identifies three areas that influence disenfranchisement of adolescents' grieving—intrapersonal, interpersonal, and environmental.

In intrapersonal disenfranchisement, the griever must give himself or herself permission to grieve. This need for permission has its basis in fear of social disapproval, and adolescents have a strong desire to be accepted by peers and to conform to peers' expectations. As a result of this peer pressure, adolescents may repress their grieving despite a significant loss because they fear they will lose peer acceptance by showing their feelings.

In the interpersonal domain, adults sometimes minimize a youth's broken friendships upon the death of friends. As youth mature and gain responsibility, they need the social web of peer and adult relationships to support them when they experience loss, but adults may not recognize that need, and other youth likewise may withhold their approval. Rowling (2002, 283) summarizes the interplay between intrapersonal and interpersonal domains in disenfranchising grief:

> [P]erceived norms for adolescent demeanor and actions—the imagined views of others—shape adolescent behavior. But this behavior is also shaped by the real actions of others and the sanctioning these actions do or do not provide.

In the environmental domain, schools and colleges can have a role in disenfranchising grief of young adults through the establishment of unhelpful policies, their practices, and their lack of preparedness to acknowledge the grief of students (Rowling 2002). Likewise, schools and other organizations can have a significant impact on counteracting the intrapersonal and interpersonal domains that can result in disenfranchisement by establishing policies and supporting youth when youth experience loss or there is a community crisis.

EMOTIONAL REACTION TO LOSS

Adolescents, because of their lack of experience and emotional maturity, often have difficulty expressing their feeling:

> It is important to understand that children, unlike adults, do not have an extensive range of labels for the emotions they feel. Therefore, it is crucial to help guide their natural efforts to communicate their loss with methods that can be tailored to their developmental level. (Fiorini and Mullen 2006, 39)

Whether a young person's loss results from loss of a major relationship, a treasured object or pet, or even a routine in a young person's life, the youth may feel frightened, lonely, angry, confused, deserted, or insecure. Often a young person feels responsible for the loss and is ridden with guilt.

Research shows that children and adolescents often experience guilt after a death or divorce. Young people may feel they should have spent more time with the loved one who has died, or they feel guilty because they were angry with the person or did not express their love to them.

Adults may have difficulty discerning the motives of adolescents by observing their behavior and listening to their verbal cues. Fiorini and Mullen (2006, 40) explain why adolescents send conflicting messages:

> Teenagers often send mixed messages regarding their needs. Some adolescents may restrict their expression of feelings, giving the impression of being unaffected. Furthermore, many teenagers see mortality and death as a natural process that is very remote from their day-to-day life and something they cannot control. The emotional consequences of loss are confusion and powerlessness, especially when a peer has died. After a significant loss, older children or young adolescents often will feel helpless and frightened.

These young people may want to retreat into childhood but have the feeling they should act like adults and suppress their emotions.

LOSS THROUGH DEATH

It is likely that a child or adolescent will experience a death-related loss. Unfortunately, adults are inept at helping youth through the grief process, abiding by the myths that accompany grieving (see above).

When a brother or sister dies, surviving siblings may receive little support or even recognition of their pain. Parents are so grief-stricken at the loss of a child that they often find themselves unable to cope with the needs of their surviving children. With family and friends concentrating on the parents' tragedy, the suffering of siblings often goes unnoticed. Some children and adolescents internalize their grief and may fantasize a relationship with the deceased. Their quiet responses may go unrecognized. Others externalize by acting out through angry outbursts, irritability, sleeping and eating disorders, persistent questioning about the loss, hypochondria, and shock.

Grieving does not end when a parent is replaced through remarriage or close family members or friends. Furthermore, children may react to their loss and experience stress during other changes that suggest separation including going to camp or staying home when a surviving parent travels (Hooyman and Kramer 2006).

Grief and loss are not only the result of something ending, such as death or a relationship. Grief is also the result of a disruption in a person's life, including divorce or moving. Even happy events in a person's life, such as marriage or graduation from school, are life-changing and can produce feelings of grief and loss.

INTERPERSONAL LOSSES

Peer relationships are not as important to younger children as they are to older children and adolescents. Adolescents frequently define their feelings and moods based on the effectiveness of their relationships with peers.

Fiorini and Mullen (2006, 98) define the importance of these relationships:

> Any parent or professional who works with adolescents on a regular basis is aware that most adolescents' worlds consist of feelings and discussions about who is mad at whom, who is dating whom, and who isn't speaking to whom. In this developmental stage of an adolescent's life, a teen learns the nuances of relationships and how they work.

Consequently, loss of a peer relationship can be devastating to older children and teens, especially relationships with the opposite sex.

TRANSITIONAL LOSSES

Adolescents are in need of support as they experience transitional losses—moving, divorce, illness or disabling condition, substance abuse, parental job loss, and military deployment (Fiorini and Mullen 2006). The most traumatic transitional losses are also addressed in chapter 3—divorce, adoption, foster children, and pet death.

Hooyman and Kramer (2006) point out that feelings of loss surface in adopted children typically at ages 11, 13, and 18—just before they become independent. These adopted children romanticize their birth families during these times and may express hatred toward their adoptive parents and themselves. They may think about suicide, and they may experiment with risky behaviors.

Reaction to divorce is similar to a young person's reaction to a parent's death; however, the stress factor is different. In a divorce the children experience anger, guilt, and sadness because of divided loyalties. These children may be hurt more by conflict, loss of economic support, guilt feelings, and a feeling of rejection. Adolescents, especially girls, have difficulty dealing with divorce (Hooyman and Kramer 2006).

Because children may have no warning that a divorce is planned, their initial response often is disbelief or denial. They may create fantasies or explanations for their parent's absence—Dad or Mom is on a trip and will come back.

TRAGIC LOSSES

Tragic losses include sudden, unexpected death, or coping with a natural disaster. Stigmatizing losses include loss related to murder, suicide, abuse or victimization, or parental incarceration. All of theses losses take a heavy toll on children and adolescents.

Sudden deaths are even more difficult for youth to grieve than an anticipated death. Baxter and Stuart (1999, 9–10) identify the following factors to consider when adolescents face a sudden death situation:

> They are likely to have an "exaggerated sense of unreality" and experience shock for a longer time period. Strong guilt feelings result because the youth believes that s/he should have done something to prevent the death. Accompanying the grief is the need to blame someone else for the tragedy, possibly a family member.

If medical or legal authorities are involved, an investigation may take an extended period of time, delaying the grieving process. A feeling of helplessness or lack of control by a survivor may result in rage directed toward physicians, hospitals, or government officials.

Suicides leave survivors with the feelings outlined above, with the additional burden of shame because of the social stigma attached to suicide. The guilt experienced by survivors is a result of the responsibility they take for not detecting warning signals and preventing the suicide. Survivors also may feel anger because they interpret the suicide as a rejection of themselves, that is, "Death is better than being with me" (Baxter and Stuart 1999, 11).

STRATEGIES FOR HELPING GRIEVING YOUTH

As we understand the reasons and reactions of grieving youth, we can more effectively determine strategies for helping them grieve. Important considerations in planning strategies is understanding the *grief tasks* that can help a young person cope with grief, then applying strategies that address those tasks.

Grief Tasks

Regardless of the type of loss children and young adults experience, they must move through certain phases or complete certain tasks, which need not be performed in a certain order:

- understand that a person has died;
- face the pain of the loss;
- cope with the occasional resurgence of the pain;
- develop new relationships;
- integrate the loss experience into a new sense of identity;
- evaluate and adjust the relationship with the person lost; and
- resume developmental tasks appropriate for the age. (Hooyman and Kramer 2006, 101)

These tasks are applicable for young adults as well as children. To address these tasks, the reader is encouraged to study the strategies below and to return to chapter 3 for review of the intervention strategies for children that can be adapted for use with adolescents.

Strategies for Addressing Grief Tasks

Silverman (2000) identifies three categories of care while assisting bereaved children and young adults. When working with youth, here are three watchwords to keep in mind:

1. Care—someone to guide them and provide feedback.
2. Continuity—providing the child a sense that the family will move ahead after the loss.
3. Connection—the child is part of the family and still is connected to the deceased through the family. (225)

It is also important to watch for problems and make referrals if necessary. Substance abuse, truancy, self-destructive behaviors, anxiety, depression, regressive behaviors, apathy, aggressiveness, delinquency, or other significant changes in behavior are indicators that a child should be referred to a mental health professional.

Rituals

As noted in chapter 3, research indicates that children who participate in rituals following a death are less likely to exhibit psychological distress than children who do not. Judaism marks death anniversaries with rituals, and Catholics and Protestants mark anniversaries with a mass. These rituals validate grief and reinforce memories for children and adolescents. See chapter 3 for suggested rituals that also are applicable for young adults.

SUMMARY

Our society does not prepare children and young adults for grieving, nor does it prepare adults for supporting youth who grieve. A young person's developmental stage is a major factor influencing grief, and adults working with older children and young adults must be knowledgeable of these developmental stages as they confront grief with them.

Among the background characteristics and capacities that influence a young person's resilience, that is, ability to handle grief, are such factors as ethnic and socioeconomic status and environment; a child's age, self-esteem, problem-solving skills, gender, and attachment to the person lost; nature of the loss; family capacities such as a parents' love, discipline, family routines and structure, communication patterns, and adult support; social capacities including the support of peers and adults; and cultural capacities such as the child's participation in rituals and the family's beliefs regarding death and the afterlife.

In addition to grieving caused by death, young people may grieve because of transitional losses such as moving, loss of relationships, and such tragic losses as a natural disaster or abuse.

When working with youth, there are three categories of care to keep in mind: (1) someone to guide youth and provide feedback; (2) continuity to provide assurance that the child and family will move ahead after the loss; and (3) connection of the child to the family. It is also important to watch for problems and make referrals if necessary.

Following are resources that are appropriate for assisting bereaved young adults, followed by recommended resources for young adults.

ADULT RESOURCES

Fiorini, Jody J., and Jodi Ann Mullen. **Counseling Children and Adolescents through Grief and Loss.** Champaign, IL: Research Press, 2006. 232p. $26.95. ISBN 0-87822-553-6; 987-0-87822-553-8.

> For a description, please see the "Adult Resources" section of chapter 3.

Wolfelt, Alan. **Healing a Teen's Grieving Heart: 100 Practical Ideas for Families, Friends and Caregivers.** Healing Your Grieving Heart Series. Fort Collins, CO: Companion Press, 2001. 128p. $11.95pa. ISBN 1-879651-24-6; 978-1-879651-24-1.

> A resource for friends, parents, relatives, teachers, volunteers, and caregivers, offering suggestions to help a grieving teen cope with the loss of a loved one. This volume addresses what to expect from grieving young people, and how to provide safe outlets for teens to express emotion. "Wolfelt encourages adults to realize that teens are 'still kids,' and that they will sometimes need to behave more like brokenhearted children than aloof teenagers. It is important to accept this dichotomy while continuing to honor the dignity of a teen's fragile maturity" (*Voice of Youth Advocates* Aug. 1, 2001).

RESOURCES FOR YOUNG ADULTS

Resources below are recommended for older children ages 10–12 and adolescents ages 13–18. The reader is also urged to consult chapter 3 for additional resources for older children.

The arrangement below is by the major categories of grief: adoption, death of a parent, death of a sibling, divorce, foster care, and suicide.

Adoption

Alvarez, Julia. **Finding Miracles.** New York: Random House Children's Books, Knopf Books for Young Readers, 2004. 272p. $15.95. ISBN 0-375-82760-9; 978-0-375-82760-0. New York: Random House Children's Books, Laurel Leaf, 2006. 288p. $6.99pa. ISBN 0-553-49406-6; 978-0-553-49406-8.

> Ninth-grader Milly Kaufman lives in Vermont and struggles to deny her adopted status in a loving family. She begins to understand her origins through a friendship with Pablo, a new student at her high school. Milly decides to travel to her homeland and discovers the story of her birth. "The author portrays the ambivalence of adopted children, the complexities of family interaction between birth and adopted children, and the ways that family members from different cultural backgrounds deal with differences. Complex multicultural characters and skillful depiction of

Latino culture raises this well-written, readable novel, which is a school story, a family story, and a love story, to far above average" (*Voice of Youth Advocates* Dec. 1, 2004). Ages 12–15.

Alvarez, Julia. **Finding Miracles.** New York: Random House Audio Publishing Group, Listening Library, 2004. 5 CDs. 4:14 hrs. $50.00. ISBN 1-4000-9489-5; 978-1-4000-9489-9.

"Daphne Rubin-Vega honestly expresses Milly's earnest teen emotions, and she narrates fluidly in both English and the occasional Spanish interjections. Sound quality is good and the case is sturdy" (*School Library Journal* Apr.1, 2005).

Bauer, Cat. **Harley, Like a Person.** New York: Winslow Press, 2000. 248p. $16.95. ISBN 1-890817-48-1; 978-1-890817-48-0. Winslow Press, 2000. 248p. $5.95pa. ISBN 1-58837-005-4; 978-1-58837-005-1.

Fourteen-year-old Harley lives with her alcoholic father and her enabling mother. Suspecting that she is adopted, she begins a search for her biological parents. "The facts of her [Harley's] life, and her emotional health, are complex. Young teens seeking stories about troubled homes and strong girls who persevere in the face of unimpressive adults will not be disappointed" (*School Library Journal* May 1, 2000). Ages 12–15.

Bauer, Cat. **Harley, Like a Person.** New York: Recorded Books, 2002. 7 cassettes. 9 hrs. $67.75. ISBN 0-7887-9402-7; 978-0-7887-9402-5.

Narrated by Carine Montbertrand. "Harley is a complicated person, and Montbertrand does not always manage to convey that complexity. Sometimes her voice is right on target in its expression; other times, she just sounds whiny when Harley should sound more confused or angry. The voices of the other characters are distinctive enough that listeners can always determine who is speaking" (*School Library Journal* June 1, 2002). Ages 12–15.

Bode, Janet. **Kids Still Having Kids: People Talk about Teen Pregnancy.** Danbury, CT: Scholastic Library, Franklin Watts, 1999. 160p. $17.25. ISBN 0-531-11588-7; 978-0-531-11588-6. Out of print.

Through interviews with teenage mothers, Bode provides information about birth control, abortion, adoption, parenting, and foster care. Faced with unplanned pregnancies, the mothers provide frank, personal accounts of their decisions and actions they took. This revised edition of the 1992 book gives updates on the individuals featured in the earlier volume. "Factual information that appears in engaging graphic blocks will satisfy students doing research. The positive, instructional narrative voice will appeal to those teens reading for more personal reasons as well" (*School Library Journal* Oct. 1, 1999). Ages 13–18.

Brinkerhoff, Shirley. **Second Choices.** Nikki Sheridan Series, Vol. 6. Bloomington, MN: Bethany House Publishers, 2000. 160p. $5.99pa. ISBN 1-56179-880-0; 978-1-56179-880-3.

Nikki has given her baby up for adoption and tries to explain her feelings about abortion to her classmates; meanwhile, she is struggling with a relationship that could lead her away from God, and she is exposed to dangerous vandalism at school. "Her [Nikki's] recent conversion to Christianity has inspired her to make wiser choices and right past mistakes, and she now recognizes that moving ahead means forgiving herself and others. The heavy messages will probably turn off some readers, but others will find comfort in Nikki's honest exploration of traditional Christian values" (*Booklist* Mar. 1, 2001). Ages 14–18.

Burg, Ann E. **All the Broken Pieces.** New York: Scholastic Press, 2009. 224p. $16.99. ISBN 0-545-08092-4; 978-0-545-08092-7.

> Vietnamese American seventh grader Matt Pin has two passions—piano and base-ball—but he feels responsible for serious injuries his little brother sustained in Viet-nam during the war. Two years after being airlifted out of Vietnam, Matt is now in a loving adoptive home in the United States, but he must confront his past to heal. He also must deal with the prejudice he faces from peers who lost loved ones in the war. "There is occasional contrivance as Matt eavesdrops on adults. But the haunting metaphors are never forced, and the intensity of the simple words, on the baseball field and in the war zone, will make readers want to rush to the end and then return to the beginning again to make connections between past and present, friends and enemies" (*Booklist* Feb. 15, 2009). Ages 10–14.

Doherty, Berlie. **The Girl Who Saw Lions.** New York: Roaring Brook Press, 2008. 256p. $16.95. ISBN 1-59643-377-9; 978-1-59643-377-9.

> Thirteen-year-old Rosa, an only child living in Sheffield, England, feels hurt and betrayed when her mother wants to adopt a little girl. Abela, nine years old, loses her mother to AIDS and is sent by her uncle to England. Eventually she is placed in foster care and finds a home with Rosa's family. "Doherty takes on multiple complex subjects including female circumcision, child trafficking, cross-culture adoption, and the death of relatives. At times, the number of issues threatens to overwhelm the story, but, ultimately, patient readers will be rewarded" (*School Library Journal* July 1, 2008). Ages 11–18.

Doherty, Berlie. **The Snake-Stone.** New York: Scholastic, Orchard Books, 1996. 176p. $15.95. ISBN 0-531-09512-6; 978-0-531-09512-6.

> Fifteen-year-old James, a champion diver, becomes obsessed with finding his birth mother. He learns the history surrounding his adoption and finally is able to un-derstand the reasons his birth mother gave him up for adoption. "*The Snake-Stone* is an important book for anyone who has wondered about the emotions surround-ing issues of adoption" (*School Library Journal* June 1, 1996). Ages 12–18.

Dudley, William, ed. **Pregnancy.** Farmington Hills, MI: Cengage Gale, Greenhaven Press, 2001. 191p. $24.95pa. ISBN 0-7377-0491-8; 978-0-7377-0491-4.

> Features the stories of pregnant teens who chose adoption, abortion, or parent-hood, and the advice they offer to others. Ages 10–18.

Ellis, Sarah. **Out of the Blue.** New York: Simon & Schuster Children's Publishing, Margaret K. McElderry, 1995. 144p. $15.00pa. ISBN 0-689-80025-8; 978-0-689-80025-2.

> Megan, 12, discovers that she has a 24-year-old half-sister whom her mother gave up for adoption years ago. "Ellis' handling of the family dynamics is quiet and sure, and her characters (with the exception of sentimental Mum) are fresh, appealing—and imperfect....No angst-filled drama here; instead, readers get a solid, credible adjust-ment story" (*Booklist* May 1, 1995). Ages 10–14.

Gravelle, Karen, and Susan Fischer. **Where Are My Birth Parents? A Guide for Teenage Adoptees.** New York: Walker, 1993. 112p. $15.85. ISBN 0-8027-8258-2; 978-0-8027-8258-8.

> Includes firsthand experiences of young people who searched for their birth fami-lies. The authors provide a variety of circumstances faced by adoptees, the responses of birth mothers, and the problems associated with subsequent relationships with birth parents. "This valuable manual is for teenagers wishing to reunite with their birth parents, those who do not want to search, and those who are unsure of their

feelings. It's of great practical and emotional benefit" (*School Library Journal* July 1, 1993). Ages 14–18.

Green, Jesse. **The Velveteen Father: An Unexpected Journey to Parenthood.** New York: Random House Publishing Group, Ballantine Books, 2000. 256p. $14.00pa. ISBN 0-345-43709-8; 978-0-345-43709-9.

A memoir of the struggles and joys that accompany a gay man's adoption of two sons. "A standout comment on the eternal and contemporary implications of family emerges from this enjoyable story that is far too good not to be true" (*Kirkus Reviews* May 1, 1999). Ages 16–adult.

Griffin, Adele. **The Other Shepards.** New York: Hyperion Books for Children, 1998. 224p. $14.95. ISBN 0-7868-0423-8; 978-0-7868-0423-8. $5.99pa. ISBN 0-7868-1333-4; 978-0-7868-1333-9.

Eighth-grader Holland and sixth-grader Geneva Shepard live in the shadow of three older siblings killed before the sisters were born. The girls struggle to establish separate identities and escape from the oppressive weight of their parents' continuing grief. "The reader can see the girls both mature and make peace with the past in the course of the story, which ends with a feeling of hope. The young characters in this book have depth and even the minor characters are not one-dimensional" (*Voice of Youth Advocates* Oct. 1, 1998). Ages 10–14.

Hicks, Betty. **Get Real.** New York: Roaring Brook Press, 2006. 192p. $16.95. ISBN 1-59643-089-3; 978-1-59643-089-1.

Destiny, a 13-year-old control freak, feels alienated in her messy, haphazard family. Her best friend Jil's adopted family is the opposite. Dez helps Jil find her birth mother and Jil decides to have a relationship with her. "The girls' friendship is a successful vehicle for unearthing the complexities of adopted children's emotions and their families' dilemmas. More than that, though, Hicks offers a solid YA novel featuring strong characters, deep friendships, supportive families, and the joy and pain of growing up" (*Booklist* Oct. 15, 2006). Ages 10–14.

Johnson, Angela. **Heaven.** New York: Simon & Schuster Children's Publishing, 1998. 144p. $16.95. ISBN 0-689-82229-4; 978-0-689-82229-2.

Marley, a 14-year-old African-American girl, has her life turned upside down when she discovers that the people she knows as her parents are really her aunt and uncle, and she must face this new reality. Heaven is the name of the Ohio town where she has grown up. "The various examples of 'family' Marley encounters make her question what's real, what's true, what makes sense, and if any of that really matters as much as the love she continues to feel for her parents in spite of their seeming betrayal. Johnson exhibits admirable stylistic control over Marley's struggle to understand a concept that is often impossible to understand or even to define" (*School Library Journal* Oct. 1, 1998). Ages 12–16.

Johnson, Angela. **Heaven.** Prince Frederick, MD: Recorded Books, 2001. 2 audio cassettes. 2 hrs. 45 min. $26.00. ISBN: 0-7887-4563-8; 978-0-7887-4563-8.

"Narrator Andrea Johnson makes the characters come alive in this Coretta Scott King Award book by giving each their own unique voice, especially the booming sound of Uncle Jack. Instructions at the beginning and end of each cassette make the transition from side to side smooth" (*School Library Journal* Dec. 1, 2000). Ages 11–15.

Kaminker, Laura. **Everything You Need to Know about Being Adopted.** Boulder, CO: NetLibrary, 1999. E-book. $17.95. ISBN 0-585-09605-8; 978-0-585-09605-6.

Kaminker provides legal facts about adoption and outlines many problems that adolescent adoptees suffer, including fear that their curiosity about their birth parents may hurt their adoptive parents' feelings, and jealousy of siblings not adopted. "The author's suggestions are sensible; for instance, a support group is strongly advised for teenagers contemplating the difficult process of searching for birth families" (*School Library Journal* Apr. 1, 1999). Ages 12–18.

Kearney, Meg. **The Secret of Me.** Karen and Michael Braziller Books. New York: Persea Books, 2007. 144p. $12.00. ISBN 0-89255-336-7; 978-0-89255-336-5.

Fourteen-year-old Lizzie was adopted as an infant and tells in poetry her desire to know about her birth mother, although her siblings, also adopted, consider her disloyal to their adopted parents. "This tenderly written book is definitely for the adopted teen but can be enjoyed by all others. It can be used within classroom poetry units with great success" (*Voice of Youth Advocates* Apr. 1, 2006). "The poems are readable and heartfelt, based in part on the author's life. Kearney creates a believable voice for her protagonist, and this book will be welcomed by adults working with young adoptees" (*School Library Journal* Jan. 1, 2006). Ages 12–18.

Lindsay, Jeanne Warren. **Pregnant? Adoption Is an Option.** Buena Park, CA: Morning Glory Press, 2003. 222p. $11.95. ISBN 1-885356-08-0; 978-1-885356-08-6.

Discusses adoption as an option for pregnant young women who do not have the resources to parent. It explores how adoption can affect the birth mother, the child, and the father. A number of birth parents share their experiences and the emotions involved. "[T]here are a great many insights here on matters such as the importance of legal advice, choosing a mediator, becoming involved in the selection of adoptive parents and staying in touch (Lindsay favors open adoptions), and the emotional cost of sticking to an adoption plan. Some of the testimonies are truly heartrending, and though the emphasis is on young mothers, Lindsay has made a concerted effort to include comments from (and information for) both birthparents" (*Booklist* Dec. 1, 1996). Ages 11–18.

Lisle, Janet Taylor. **The Crying Rocks.** New York: Simon & Schuster Children's Publishing, Atheneum/Richard Jackson Books, 2003. 208p. $16.95. ISBN 0-689-85319-X; 978-0-689-85319-7. Thorndike Press Large Print Literacy Bridge Series. Waterville, ME: Thorndike Press, 2004. 273p. $22.95. ISBN 0-7862-6140-4; 978-0-7862-6140-6. Logan, IA: Perfection Learning, 2005. 281p. $14.65. ISBN: 0-7569-5507-6; 978-0-7569-5507-6.

Thirteen-year-old Joelle wonders about her life before being adopted by Aunt Louise and Uncle Vernon. She becomes convinced that she may be related to the local Narragansett Indians. "Joelle is a well-developed character, feisty and full of bravado, which belies her vulnerability. The use of the present tense gives the narrative a sense of immediacy. The issues of ethnic identity and heritage are dealt with in a multidimensional and complex way" (*School Library Journal* Dec. 1, 2003). Ages 12–14.

Montgomery, L. M. **Anne of Green Gables.** New York: Random House, 2008. 320 p. $8.00pa. ISBN 0-8129-7903-6; 978-0-8129-7903-9. HarperCollins, Harper Festival, 2008. 464p. $9.99pa. ISBN 0-06-008138-4; 978-0-06-008138-6.

The Cuthberts hoped to adopt a boy to help them on the farm, but when Matthew Cuthbert arrived at the train station he found freckle-faced, red-headed Anne Shirley waiting for him. Anne, a talkative 11-year-old orphan, turns Green Gables upside down in this endearing classic. Ages 11–18.

Pennebaker, Ruth. **Don't Think Twice.** New York: Henry Holt Books For Young Readers, 2001. 272p. $8.99pa. ISBN 0-8050-6729-9; 978-0-8050-6729-3.

Set in 1967, 17-year-old Anne finds herself in a Texas home for unwed mothers. She believes that she can give birth to the baby and walk away, but she decides to hold the baby just once before she signs the papers. Originally published in 1996. "Pennebaker presents a compassionate, many-layered look at the complexities of teen pregnancy. The girls' desperate situations are filtered through Anne's wit and sarcasm, creating needed distance and levity" (*Booklist* May 1, 1996). Ages 12–18.

Reinhardt, Dana. **A Brief Chapter in My Impossible Life.** New York: Random House Children's Books, Wendy Lamb, 2006. 240p. $17.99. ISBN 0-385-90940-3; 978-0-385-90940-2. Out of print.

Sixteen-year-old atheist Simone Turner-Bloom's life changes when her parents convince her to contact her biological mother, an agnostic who is losing her battle with cancer. "Faith and agnosticism, drinking and puking, sex and virginity and love, Reinhardt brings it all to readers, but she does so in very realistic doses, with a sense of humor and a sense of hope. Simone's first-person voice is funny and unforgettable; a little too wise, perhaps, but her epiphanies are on target and are what readers will be looking for in this fabulous debut" (*Kirkus Reviews* Jan. 15, 2006). "It also has strong subplots that deal with friendship; with boyfriend/girlfriend relationships, both good and bad; with standing up for what one believes is right; and with struggling to keep up with academics and fit in at school when things seem to be falling apart on a personal level. The novel deals with big issues without being preachy or sappy" (*School Library Journal* Mar. 1, 2006). Ages 12–18.

Reinhardt, Dana. **A Brief Chapter in My Impossible Life.** New York: Random House Audio Publishing Group, Listening Library, 2006. 5 CDs. 6 hrs. $38.25. ISBN 0-307-28566-9; 978-0-307-28566-9.

"Simone has a secure place in a loving family and knows it, resulting in some refreshing and self-aware musing on her part which narrator Mandy Siegfried handles beautifully. Whenever appropriate, she also musters the 'whatever' tone in her voice, giving Simone an authentic teenage sound" (*School Library Journal* Aug. 1, 2006). Ages 12–18.

Sherman, Aliza. **Everything You Need to Know about Placing Your Baby for Adoption.** The Need to Know Library: Important Issues Affecting Every Teen. New York: Rosen Publishing Group, 2001. 64p. $27.95. ISBN 0-8239-3465-9; 978-0-8239-3465-2.

Provides teenage expectant parents the information needed to make an informed decision regarding placing their baby for adoption. "Sherman's slim but nevertheless substantive entry in the Need to Know Library series touches on many of the vital issues that pregnant teens need to consider—from making the difficult decision to place a baby for adoption to carrying through and handling the emotions involved" (*Booklist* Oct. 15, 1997). Ages 13–18.

Triana, Gaby. **Riding the Universe.** New York: HarperCollins, HarperTeen, 2009. 272p. $16.99. ISBN 0-06-088570-X; 978-0-06-088570-0.

Grieving over the recent death of her uncle, 17-year-old Chloe Rodriguez enjoys nothing more than riding her Harley-Davidson motorcycle that her uncle left her. Then her adoptive parents give her an ultimatum to bring up her failing chemistry grade or lose the motorcycle. She then falls in love with her tutor, Gordon. "Teens will find her dilemmas about having sex and whether or not to find her birth parents compelling, and they enjoy following Chloé as she navigates school and home life, her issues, and her discovery that opening your heart can hurt but also heal" (*Booklist* Aug. 1, 2009). Ages 14–18.

Warren, Andrea. **Escape from Saigon: How a Vietnam War Orphan Became an American Boy.** New York: Farrar, Straus and Giroux, 2004. 128p. $17.00. ISBN 0-374-32224-4; 978-0-374-32224-3.

The story of Long, orphaned in Vietnam and flown out of the country in the 1975 Operation Babylift. An American family in Ohio adopts him. "Well written and filled with many poignant and heart-wrenching photos from the era, this biography will evoke both discussion and contemplation among young teens" (*Voice of Youth Advocates* Dec. 1, 2004). "Although Warren mentions the cruelties of the communist Vietnamese government and America's abandonment of its South Vietnamese allies, this is a personal story, one that is so well written that it will be sure to hold readers' attention. An outstanding choice" (*School Library Journal* Oct. 1, 2004). Ages 10–15.

Weiss, Ann E. **Adoptions Today: Questions and Controversy.** Single Titles Series. Minneapolis, MN: Lerner, Twenty-First Century Books, 2001. 144p. $24.90. ISBN 0-7613-1914-X; 978-0-7613-1914-6.

Describes the history of adoption from ancient times to the present and explains current policies, laws, social views, and ways to adopt. Included are such issues as searches for birth parents, open adoptions, and interracial, interfaith, and international adoptions. "Students doing research on issues related to adoption, or adoptees seeking information on recent changes in the law, will appreciate this readable book.... Her [Weiss's] perspective on adoption is overwhelmingly positive (especially when she contrasts it with the foster care system), but she does offer information on the adoption black market and the problems of Internet adoptions" (*Booklist* Dec. 15, 2001). Ages 12–18.

Death of a Friend

Anderson, Laurie Halse. **Wintergirls.** New York: Penguin Group, Viking Adult, 2009. 288p. $17.99. ISBN 0-670-01110-X; 978-0-670-01110-0.

Six years after 18-year-old Cassie and her friend Lia resolved to become the skinniest girls in their school, Cassie dies. Lia struggles with grief and guilt following Cassie's death, causing her to fall deeper into her own eating disorder. "Anderson perfectly captures the isolation and motivations of the anorexic without ever suggesting that depression and eating disorders are simply things to 'get over.' Due to the author's and the subject's popularity, this should be a much-discussed book, which rises far above the standard problem novel" (*Kirkus Reviews* Feb. 1, 2009). "Struck-through sentences, incessant repetition, and even blank pages make Lia's inner turmoil tactile, and gruesome details of her decomposition will test sensitive readers. But this is necessary reading for anyone caught in a feedback loop of weight loss as well as any parent unfamiliar with the scripts teens recite so easily to escape from such deadly situations" (*Booklist* Dec. 15, 2008). Ages 14–adult.

Anderson, Laurie Halse. **Wintergirls.** Grand Haven, MI: Brilliance Audio, 2009. 1 MP3-CD. 7 hrs. $24.99. ISBN 1-4233-9188-8; 978-1-4233-9188-3. Unabridged Library ed. 6 CDs. 7 hrs. $82.97. ISBN 1-4233-9187-X; 978-1-4233-9187-6.

"Lyrically visual, this starkly truthful and chilling first-person tale is narrated convincingly by Jeannie Stith, who perfectly mimics the sarcasm and angst of a teen girl's struggle with anorexia. An interview with the author concludes the audiobook" (*School Library Journal* Aug. 1, 2009). Ages 14–adult.

Cohn, Rachel. **You Know Where to Find Me.** New York: Simon & Schuster Children's Publishing, 2008. 208p. $16.99. ISBN 0-689-87859-1; 978-0-689-87859-6. Simon & Schuster Children's Publishing, Simon Pulse, 2009. 224p. $8.99pa. ISBN 0-689-87860-5; 978-0-689-87860-2.

Cousins Miles and Laura were like sisters, and when Laura kills herself, 17-year-old Miles experiences major changes in her relationships with her parents, her best friend Jamal and his family, and her cousin's father. Miles escapes into books, food, and drugs. In the process, she learns a great deal about herself. "Teens will be riveted by Miles—intelligent, cynical, overweight, talented, and wholly authentic and her harrowing path through grief and addiction" (*Booklist* Apr. 1, 2008). Ages 14–18.

Delacre, Lulu. **Alicia Afterimage.** New York: Lee & Low Books, 2008. 144p. $19.95. ISBN 1-60060-242-8; 978-1-60060-242-9.

The author provides this fictionalized account of her daughter Alicia, a popular 16-year-old, following her death in a car crash. Her friends, family members, and others recall incidents that show her impact on their lives. "Every view of Alicia is perfect (there isn't anyone who doesn't like her), but idealization is part of the grieving process. With its messages about healing and a list of appended resources, this is an excellent title for grief counseling" (*Booklist* Dec. 15, 2008). Ages 12–18.

Draper, Sharon M. **Tears of a Tiger.** Hazelwood High Trilogy, Book 1. St. Louis, MO: San Val, Turtleback, 1996, $17.20. ISBN 0-7857-7677-X; 978-0-7857-7677-2. New York: Simon & Schuster Children's Publishing, Simon Pulse, 1996. 192p. $6.99pa. ISBN 0-689-80698-1; 978-0-689-80698-8.

Seventeen-year-old Andrew Jackson struggles with guilt after his best friend is killed in an automobile accident in which he was driving drunk. Conversations, journals, letters, and homework assignments reveal students' reactions to the high school basketball star's death. "Andy's perceptions of the racism directed toward young black males—by teachers, guidance counselors, and clerks in shopping malls—will be recognized by African American YAs. Although some heavy-handed didacticism detracts from the novel's impact, the characters and their experiences will captivate teen readers" (*Booklist* Nov. 1, 1994). Ages 14–18.

Gray, Keith. **Ostrich Boys.** New York: Random House, 2010. 304p. $17.99. ISBN 0-375-85843-1; 978-0-375-85843-7. Random House, 2011. 304p. $8.99pa. ISBN 0-375-85844-X; 978-0-375-85844-4.

After their best friend Ross dies, English teenagers Blake, Kenny, and Sim steal Ross's ashes and plan to give him a proper memorial in Ross, Scotland. During their trip they learn more about themselves, their friendship, and Ross's death. "Although it concerns death and grief, the story is never heavy-handed; Gray offers plenty of humor and grace. Understanding of the boys grows with the story; they come to know themselves better, as readers do" (*School Library Journal* Feb. 1, 2010). Ages 12–18.

Green, John. **Looking for Alaska.** New York: Penguin Group, Dutton Juvenile, 2005. 160p. $15.99. ISBN 0-525-47506-0; 978-0-525-47506-4. Penguin Group, Puffin, 2008. 256p. $9.99pa. ISBN 0-14-241221-X; 978-0-14-241221-3.

Sixteen-year-old Miles' first year at Culver Creek Preparatory School in Alabama includes good friends and great pranks. He is transfixed by Alaska Young, a sexy, unpredictable girl who is killed in a car crash. "Once the tragedy plays out, the last third of this provocative, moving, and sometimes hilarious story counts up slowly from grief as Miles tries to find his way through the fallout of depression and guilt that he suffers" (*Voice of Youth Advocates* Apr. 1, 2005). Ages 13–18.

Green, John. **Looking for Alaska.** Grand Haven, MI: Brilliance Audio, 2006. 6 CDs. 7hrs. $29.95. ISBN 1-4233-2444-7; 978-1-4233-2444-7.

"Listeners will be riveted as the friends band together to deal with the catastrophic events that plague their junior year, and rejoice at their triumphs. Jeff Woodman clearly delineates the voices for each character in an age-appropriate, smart-alecky manner, injecting great emotion while managing not to be overly sentimental" (*School Library Journal* Feb. 1, 2007). Ages 13–18.

Hawes, Louise. **Rosey in the Present Tense.** New York: Walker, 1999. 176p. $16.95. ISBN 0-8027-8685-5; 978-0-8027-8685-2.

After the death of his girlfriend, Rosey, 17-year-old Franklin can't stop living in the past until the ghost of Rosey and his family and friends help him accept his loss. "An exceptionally well-written book, *Rosey in the Present Tense* is especially appropriate for young adults who lose friends due to unnatural causes such as accidents or violence" (*Voice of Youth Advocates* Aug. 1, 1999). Ages 13–18.

Hernandez, David. **No More Us for You.** New York: HarperCollins, HarperCollins e-books, 2009. E-book. $16.99. ISBN 0-06-176139-7; 978-0-06-176139-3.

Set in Long Beach, California, the story of 17-year-olds Carlos and Isabel and how they are drawn together is told in alternating chapters. "A lot perhaps too much happens in the course of the short period covered: Isabel, who has already experienced a boyfriend's death the year before, now loses a friend in the same car accident that places Carlos' best friend in a coma; other incidents include another girl's pregnancy and vandalism at the museum where Carlos works as a guard.... These are realistic characters that teens will easily recognize and respect" (*Booklist* Jan. 1, 2009). Ages 14–18.

Hurwin, Davida Wills. **A Time for Dancing.** New York: Penguin Group, Puffin, 1997. 272p. $6.99pa. ISBN 0-14-038618-1; 978-0-14-038618-9. New York: Little, Brown, 2009. 272p. $7.99pa. ISBN 0-316-03634-X; 978-0-316-03634-4.

Seventeen-year-old best friends Samantha and Juliana tell their stories after Juliana is diagnosed with incurable cancer before their senior year of high school. "As a story of friendship and, ultimately, as a story of death and saying good-bye, *A Time for Dancing* will hold fans of this genre glued to the page and with good reason. The story is told in chapters narrated alternately by each girl; the novel's characters, plot action, and dialogue sparkle with authenticity" (*Booklist* Nov. 1, 1995). Ages 14–18.

Lion, Melissa. **Upstream.** New York: Random House Children's Books, Wendy Lamb, 2005. 160p. $17.99. ISBN 0-385-90877-6; 978-0-385-90877-1. Out of print.

After her boyfriend is killed in a hunting accident, Alaska high school senior Marty, with help from her mother and two younger sisters, tries to work through her grief and begin a new life. "Lion's imagery occasionally seems studied, but more often her descriptions, especially of emotion or moment, are resonant and truthful. Recommend this novel to savvy reluctant readers; it is an emotionally complex story told clearly, poignantly, and economically" (*School Library Journal* July 1, 2005). "The reader will come to care about Martha and grieve with her. The other characters are also well carved and authentic. Not just another teenage angst novel, this book dips into the grief that resides in anyone" (*Voice of Youth Advocates* June 1, 2005). Ages 12–18.

Mitchard, Jacquelyn. **All We Know of Heaven.** New York: HarperCollins, HarperTeen, 2008. 320p. $16.99. ISBN 0-06-134578-4; 978-0-06-134578-4. HarperTeen, 2009. 336p. $8.99pa. ISBN 0-06-134580-6; 978-0-06-134580-7. HarperCollins E-books, 2009. E-book. $16.99. ISBN 0-06-185869-2; 978-0-06-185869-7.

Maureen and Bridget, two 16-year-old best friends who look like sisters, are in a car accident and Bridget dies. At first, they are incorrectly identified at the hospital, and as Maureen achieves a remarkable recovery, she must deal with the repercussions of the accident, the mix-up in identities, and grieving the loss of her friend. "Details of her recovery are realistic—words go straight from her brain to her mouth with no filter—as is the heartbreak of families whose brain-injured children will never be normal again. Basing her tale on an actual case of mistaken identity involving two young women in Indiana, the ever-impressive Mitchard succeeds in crafting an unforgettable and intense story with the underlying and familiar message that being young does not guarantee invincibility—life may change instantly and forever" (*Voice of Youth Advocates* June 1, 2008). "Give this to readers who like descriptive stories; they'll relish the specifics and be caught up by the tabloid drama, as well as by the survivor guilt that makes Maureen feel as if she's being punished for living" (*Booklist* Mar. 15, 2008). Ages 12–18.

Ockler, Sarah. **Twenty Boy Summer.** New York: Little, Brown Books for Young Readers, 2009. E-book. ISBN 0-316-05321-X; 978-0-316-05321-1.

Matt and Anna kept their romance a secret to spare the feelings of Matt's sister, Frankie, who is Anna's best friend. When Matt dies suddenly from a heart condition, Anna is left with her secret, which causes her conflict as she mourns Matt's death. Now a year later, Anna is vacationing with Frankie and her parents, and Frankie has challenged Anna to flirt with at least 20 boys. "Often funny, this is a thoughtful, multilayered story about friendship, loss, and moving on" (*School Library Journal* June 1, 2009). Ages 14–18.

Scott, Elizabeth. **Love You Hate You Miss You.** New York: HarperCollins, HarperTeen, 2009. 288p. $16.99. ISBN 0-06-112283-1; 978-0-06-112283-5.

Amy, 16, is released from alcohol rehabilitation and must confront the strong and conflicting emotions resulting from her best friend Julia's death in a car accident for which she blames herself. "This book is not for readers in search of something light and fluffy, but those who are looking to go deeper, who are willing to engage in questions of choice and consequence, friendship and love, family and self, grief, guilt, and hope will find much within these pages" (*Voice of Youth Advocates* Oct. 1, 2009). Ages 12–18.

Shaw, Susan. **One of the Survivors.** New York: Simon & Schuster Children's Publishing, Margaret K. McElderry, 2009. 208p. $15.99. ISBN 1-4169-6129-1; 978-1-4169-6129-1.

Fourteen-year-old Joey recently lost his mother in a house fire; when his classmates die in a school fire, he is haunted by their deaths and faces the suspicion that he started the fire. "As she did in her previous novel, *Safe* (2007), Shaw again details the often agonizingly slow process of attempting to heal from an emotionally devastating experience. Joey gradually finds comfort in his journal, in an unexpected piece of music, and in a sketch he makes that may change not only his own feelings but those of his accusers" (*Booklist* Aug. 1, 2009). Ages 10–14.

Smith, Cynthia Leitich. **Rain Is Not My Indian Name.** New York: HarperCollins, 2001. 144p. $16.99. ISBN 0-688-17397-7; 978-0-688-17397-5.

Rain, a 14-year-old Native American girl, tires of staying in seclusion after the death of her best friend, and accepts a photographic assignment with her local newspaper to cover events at the Native American summer youth camp. Ages 12–16.

Stein, Tammar. **Light Years.** New York: Random House Children's Books, Laurel Leaf, 2008. 272p. $6.99pa. ISBN 0-440-23902-8; 978-0-440-23902-4.

Maya Laor, a 20-year-old Israeli woman, enrolls in an American university as she struggles to recover from her boyfriend's death in a Tel Aviv suicide bombing. "This well-paced first novel, a moving study of grief and recovery, is also a love story that should appeal particularly to students interested in other ways of seeing the world and looking forward to their own college lives" (*School Library Journal* Jan. 1, 2005). Ages 14–18.

Death of a Parent or Grandparent

Acampora, Paul. **Defining Dulcie.** New York: Penguin Group, 2006. 176p. $16.99. ISBN 0-8037-3046-2; 978-0-8037-3046-5.

Sixteen-year-old Dulcie comes from a family of janitors, and her world crumbles when her father suddenly dies. She goes to California with her mother, does not like it there, and steals her father's pickup truck to return home, where she lives with her grandfather. "Acampora's work strikes a perfect balance between the serious and the comical. His strong and delightfully human characters are sure to appeal across gender lines" (*Voice of Youth Advocates* April 1, 2006). Ages 12–16.

Almond, David. **The Savage.** Somerville, MA: Candlewick Press, 2008. 80p. $17.99. ISBN 0-7636-3932-X; 978-0-7636-3932-7.

Blue Baker's father died suddenly when Blue was younger. To cope, he wrote a comic book about a boy—a savage—who expresses his anger and loneliness through violence. Blue's comic book is part of this spare novel. "A story-within-the-story that explores the means of handling grief forms the thrust of this compact book....Avoiding sentiment, this illuminating book captures the staggering power of raw emotions on young minds, and demonstrates the ways expression can help transform and temper them" (*Booklist* Sept. 15, 2008). Ages 11–18.

Angle, Kimberly Greene. **Hummingbird.** New York: Farrar, Straus and Giroux, 2008. 256p. $16.95. ISBN 0-374-33376-9; 978-0-374-33376-8.

Twelve-year-old March Anne Tanner lives a busy life on the family pumpkin and watermelon farm in Jubilee, Georgia. When the grandmother who has raised her since her mother died also dies, March Anne finds that she must act on her feelings of loss. "Angle's story and prose are clean, lyrical, and so quaint that they sometimes feel incongruous with the contemporary setting. An overly long lead-up to what the titular hummingbird represents may deter readers not immediately taken by the meandering but heartfelt story" (*Booklist* July 1, 2008). Ages 10–14.

Blume, Judy. **Tiger Eyes.** New York: Random House Children's Books, Laurel Leaf, 1982. 224p. $6.99pa. ISBN 0-440-98469-6; 978-0-440-98469-6. New York: Simon & Schuster Children's Publishing, Atheneum/Richard Jackson Books, 2003. 206p. $18.99. ISBN 0-689-85872-8; 978-0-689-85872-7.

Davey Wexler, 15 years old, is shocked, lonely, and angry after her father is shot during a holdup. Her mother moves the family to New Mexico, where Davey meets a young man who understands her emotions and helps her to overcome her grief. "Blume skillfully deals with the stages of grief and provides a story line that will evoke much class discussion" (*Booklist* Mar. 1, 1990). Ages 12–18.

Brandis, Marianne. **The Tinderbox.** Toronto, ON: Tundra Books, 2003. 176p. $9.95pa. ISBN 0-88776-626-9; 978-0-88776-626-8.

A house fire leaves 13-year-old Emma Anderson and her younger brother orphans, and they stay with neighbors. Mrs. Harriet McPhail arrives, claiming to be a distant aunt and executor of their father's will. While the thought of city life in York is intriguing to Emma, Mrs. McPhail's strict and condescending attitude causes Emma to be doubtful. At the same time, a boy from a neighboring farm expresses an interest in marrying her, presenting a decision for Emma. "The novel, set in Upper Canada in 1830, doesn't prettify the past; instead it portrays the times and the characters with precision and finesse" (*Booklist* Sept. 1, 2003). Ages 11–14.

Brooks, Martha. **Two Moons in August.** Toronto, ON: Groundwood Books, 2008. 158p. $8.95pa. ISBN 0-88899-865-1; 978-0-88899-865-1.

A year after her mother's death, 15-year-old Sidonie is still grieving, along with her older sister and father. When 16-year-old Kieran comes to the lakeside community for the summer, she finds herself drawn into a romantic relationship with him, with conflicting emotions as she remembers her mother's illness and death. "Brooks (*Paradise Cafe,* 1990) writes beautifully; even her minor characters are well realized, while Sidonie and Bobbi's sisterly bickering, their shared grief and guilt, and their underlying affection for each another [*sic*] are exquisitely believable. The setting—small-town Canada, 1959—is authentic down to a celebratory dinner featuring melon balls in ginger ale" (*Kirkus Reviews* Dec. 1, 1991). Ages 12–18.

Butcher Kristin. **The Hemingway Tradition.** Orca Soundings Series. St. Louis, MO: San Val, Turtleback, 2003. 92p. $20.80. ISBN 0-613-62955-8; 978-0-613-62955-3.

After his father commits suicide, 16-year-old Shaw struggles to come to terms with the death. This is one of a series offering contemporary fiction for reluctant teen readers. "This book portrays true, if sometimes raw, emotions, and Shaw's character growth is impressive and believable. Students who are forced to confront loss and grieving will find comfort in the fact that they are not alone" (*School Library Journal* Apr. 1, 2003). Ages 13–18.

Cantor, Jillian. **The Life of Glass.** New York: HarperCollins, HarperTeen, 2010. 352p. $16.99. ISBN 0-06-168651-4; 978-0-06-168651-1.

Fourteen-year-old Melissa struggles to hold onto memories of her deceased father, cope with her mother's return to dating, and sort out her feelings about her best friend, Ryan. "Melissa grows and matures, but she also remains true to the person that she was at the book's start, and she is an honest narrator who describes both her own flaws, as well as the positive traits of those she dislikes. What could have been a formulaic tale of adolescent angst is instead a gentle portrait of a girl growing through her grief" (*Booklist* Dec. 15, 2009). Ages 13–18.

Chalifour, Francis. **After.** Toronto, ON: Tundra Books, 2005. 144p. $7.95pa. ISBN 0-88776-705-2; 978-0-88776-705-0.

Fifteen-year-old Francis returns to his Montreal home from a school trip to learn that his father has committed suicide. Francis at first feels terrible guilt, but the guilt turns to anger and then to a profound sadness. With the love of his mother and with counseling, Francis begins to come to terms with his father's death. "Although the story is anecdotal and occasionally slow, it is thematically unified, and the characters react as fully-realized human beings rather than a diagram of the grieving process. The book will find a place with teens who love fiction with serious themes and will resonate with readers who have lost someone they love" (*Voice of Youth Advocates* Dec. 1, 2005). "The plot is predictable, and dated pop-culture references to Ace of Base and Chia Pets are distracting. But while Chalifour's well-intentioned novel occasionally falters, teens who have experienced the death of a parent or loved one will respond to its heartfelt message: after every tragedy, there is hope" (*Booklist* Feb. 1, 2006). Ages 13–16.

Cochrane, Mick. **The Girl Who Threw Butterflies.** New York: Random House Children's Books, Knopf Books for Young Readers, 2009. 192p. $18.99. ISBN 0-375-95682-4; 978-0-375-95682-9.

Six months after her father's death, eighth-grader Molly tries out for the boys' baseball team. Her ability to throw a knuckleball earns her a spot on the team and helps her feel connected to her father, who loved baseball, and helps in other aspects of her life. "Careful to avoid pathos, the author is particularly adept at capturing just the right turn of phrase as Molly narrates her story. She sees herself as a 'brave-hearted poster girl, Miss Difficulty Overcome,' and as someone who 'had become an island'" (*Kirkus Reviews* Jan. 15, 2009). Ages 10–14.

Cooney, Caroline B. **If the Witness Lied.** New York: Random House Children's Books, Delacorte, 2009. 224p. $16.99. ISBN 0-385-73448-4; 978-0-385-73448-6.

Three orphan siblings that have been separated after the deaths of their parents reunite to save themselves from a media circus. They discover that their father did not die accidentally as thought but was murdered. "The author adds depth to this fast-paced thriller by charting the siblings' difficult emotional journeys as they try to reconnect and reconfigure their familial roles, while realizing their battered but still surviving solidarity" (*Kirkus Reviews* Apr. 15, 2009). "A Christian theme pervades as well, as the siblings each question their relationship with God as well as with one another, and inevitably resolve both issues simultaneously" (*School Library Journal* May 1, 2009). Ages 12–18.

Delaney, Mark. **Pepperland.** Atlanta, GA: Peachtree Publishers, 2004. 160p. $14.95. ISBN 1-56145-317-X; 978-1-56145-317-7.

Sixteen-year-old Beatles fan Star Cochran struggles to come to terms with her mother's death in the late 1970s, and she listens to Beatles music and plays her guitar for comfort. As she struggles to write a song for her mother, Star begins to heal and comes to the realization that people, like a guitar, can be repaired with hard work and true caring. "True guitar aficionados will appreciate the loving way in which Star helps to repair her mother's guitar, and Beatles fans will enjoy the fact that every chapter title is a Beatles' song title. Star's pain and healing sends a strong message, and Delaney is the perfect conduit" (*Voice of Youth Advocates* Oct. 1, 2004). Ages 12–18.

Dessen, Sarah. **The Truth about Forever.** New York: Penguin Group, Puffin, 2006. 400p. $8.99. ISBN 0-14-240625-2; 978-0-14-240625-0.

Macy, 16, is grieving for her recently deceased father when her boyfriend goes away for the summer, and she must make it on her own. Both Macy and her mother have repressed their feelings about the death of Macy's father until Macy discovers that she can no longer cover up her grief. "Teenagers in middle school and above will relate to Macy's emotional growth and discovery of the importance of communication in this sometimes humorous but always poignant novel" (*School Library Journal* Sept. 1, 2005). Ages 11–17.

Dessen, Sarah. **The Truth about Forever.** Prince Frederick, MD: Recorded Books, 2005. 8 CDs. 12hrs. 30 min. $111.75. ISBN1-4193-3879-X; 978-1-4193-3879-3.

> Macy and her mother, denying their grief, insist that they are "fine, just fine." "Stina Nielsen does a great job with Dessen's realistic dialogue, varying pitch, pacing, and tone to differentiate between characters. She delivers the 'Fine, just fine' mantra that is repeated throughout the novel with perfect pitch every time, varied according to speaker and occasion but always on target" (*School Library Journal* Sept. 1, 2005). Ages 11–17.

DiCamillo, Kate. **The Tiger Rising.** Somerville, MA: Candlewick Press, 2002. 128p. $5.99pa. ISBN 0-7636-1898-5; 978-0-7636-1898-8.

> After sixth-grader Rob Horton's mother dies, he and his father move to a new town to get a fresh start. Both Rob and his father are grieving, and Rob discovers that he must address the feelings he has kept within. "This short novel will be especially useful for those students dealing with the loss of a loved one, but fine stories are rare, and this one will be read eagerly by all audiences" (*Voice of Youth Advocates* Aug. 1, 2001). Ages 10–14.

Forman, Gayle. **If I Stay.** New York: Penguin Group, Dutton Juvenile, 2009. 208p. $16.99. ISBN 0-525-42103-3; 978-0-525-42103-0.

> While in a coma following an automobile accident that killed her parents and younger brother, 17-year-old Mia, a gifted cellist, struggles to decide whether to live with her grief or join her family in death. "Readers will find themselves engrossed in Mia's struggles and will race to the satisfying yet realistic conclusion. Teens will identify with Mia's honest discussion of her own insecurities and doubts" (*School Library Journal* May 1, 2009). Ages 14–18.

Fox, Paula. **The Eagle Kite.** New York: Scholastic, Orchard Books, 1995. 144p. $15.95pa. ISBN 0-531-06892-7; 978-0-531-06892-2.

> Liam's father has AIDS, and his family cannot talk about it until Liam reveals a secret that he has tried to deny since he saw his father embracing another man at the beach. "Fox writes in ordinary words about universal things: love and death and lies and also time and memory—how they seem and what they are. The story confronts our deepest fears: what if the scarecrow beggar out there on the street, the statistic in sex-ed class, the demon of the howling mob came right into our comfortable home?" (*Booklist* Feb. 1, 1995). Ages 12–16.

Friend, Natasha. **Perfect.** St. Louis, MO: San Val, Turtleback, 2004. $18.40. ISBN 1-4176-4405-2; 978-1-4176-4405-6.

> Thirteen-year-old Isabelle's father died several years ago, and she has never expressed her emotions about her loss. She fills the void by binging on junk food and forcing herself to throw up. At a group counseling session for girls with eating disorders, she befriends Ashley, the most popular girl in their middle school. "Isabelle's grief and anger are movingly and honestly portrayed, and her eventual empathy for her mother is believable and touching. Through Isabelle's wry tone and clear eye for hypocrisy, Friend elevates what could have been just another problem novel to a truly worthwhile read of great interest to many girls" (*Booklist* Jan. 1, 2005). Ages 12–14.

Friend, Natasha. **Perfect.** Prince Frederick, MD: Recorded Books, LLC, 2005. 4 CDs, 4 hrs. 30 mins. $48.75. ISBN 1-4193-7018-9; 978-1-4193-7018-2.

> "With subtle voice changes and a clear personality for each character, narrator Danielle Ferland brings listeners a convincing and compassionate portrayal of

teens struggling with self-esteem and body image, a mother struggling with life itself, and a family desperately needing to find a way to share their common grief" (*School Library Journal* Apr. 1, 2006). Ages 12–14.

Fullerton, Alma. **Walking on Glass.** New York: HarperCollins, HarperTeen, 2007. 144p. $15.99. ISBN 0-06-077851-2; 978-0-06-077851-4.

A teenage boy discovers his mother as she is attempting to hang herself. He cuts her down, but she remains hospitalized on life support. This book recounts in a free verse journal his attempts to deal with his actions and whether she should be removed from life support. "The complex, contemporary debate is always in the background, and what the boy decides is the climax of the story. This small book will take barely an hour to read, but the moral issues it raises are haunting" (*Booklist* Nov. 1, 2006). Ages 14–18.

Garsee, Jeannine. **Say the Word.** New York: Bloomsbury Publishing, Bloomsbury Children, 2009. 368p. $17.99. ISBN 1-59990-333-4; 978-1-59990-333-0.

After the death of her estranged mother, who left the family in Ohio 10 years ago to live with her lesbian partner in New York City, 17-year-old Shawna Gallagher's life is transformed by revelations about her family, her best friend, and herself. "Garsee manages to give every character depth and dimension without falling into the trap of making the children too perfect and angelic and the adults imperfect to the point where the reader loses sympathy for them, save for Shawna's father. The details of Shawna's daily life sometimes slow down the plot, but it is because of these details that readers will believe Shawna's final transition from doormat to independent thinker" (*Kirkus Reviews* Jan. 15, 2009). Ages 14–18.

Harness, Cheryl. **Just for You to Know.** New York: HarperCollins, 2006. 320p. $17.99. ISBN 0-06-078313-3; 978-0-06-078313-6.

Set in Independence, Missouri, in 1963, 13-year-old Carmen is the oldest girl in a family of eight. When her mother dies during childbirth, Carmen is thrust into a responsible role. "Emotions are brought to life as the teen believably changes from a selfish adolescent into a nurturing older sister. Although some of the characters lack development, especially bad-boy-on-the-block Ricky Scudder, Harness handles well the effect of a parent's death on a family" (*School Library Journal* Sept. 1, 2006). Ages 10–14.

Herrick, Steven. **By the River.** Honesdale, PA: Boyds Mills Press, Lemniscaat, 2006. 238p. $16.95. ISBN 1-932425-72-1; 978-1-932425-72-7.

Harry Hodby, 14 years old, describes through prose poems his life in a small Australian town in 1962. Since their mother's death, Harry and his brother have been on their own to learn about life, death, and love. "Herrick's brisk, vivid poetry, filled with precise details, creates a luminous sense of place and character, from the greasy shacks and hot, quiet riverbank to the nosy, colorful townspeople. The wistful nostalgia and languid pace may deter some readers, but the memorable scenes (many of which stand alone beautifully as individual poems) are sly and affecting as they capture timeless adolescent curiosities: his neighbor's sexual conquests, girls, God, his future, and, perhaps most of all, how to move past grief to honor and hold what he loves" (*Booklist* Aug. 1, 2006). Ages 13–18.

Hoban, Julia. **Willow: It's Hard to Keep a Secret When It's Written All Over Your Body.** New York: Penguin Group, Dial, 2009. 336p. $16.99. ISBN 0-8037-3356-9; 978-0-8037-3356-5.

Sixteen-year-old Willow was driving the car that killed both of her parents. She copes with the grief and guilt by cutting herself, until she meets a sensitive boy who is determined to help her stop. "In this unusual story of first love and redemp-tion, Hoban manages the difficult task of making the reader care about and root for a heroine with little initial self-worth and a nearly unthinkable way of dealing with her pain. Hoban does not shy away from the grisly side of cutting as Willow repeatedly mutilates herself with razor blades while worrying about scars and infec-tion" (*Voice of Youth Advocates* Apr. 1, 2009). Ages 14–18.

Johnson, Maureen G. **The Key to the Golden Firebird.** New York: HarperCollins, Harper Trophy, 2005. 304p. $8.99pa. ISBN 0-06-054140-7; 978-0-06-054140-8.

Three teenaged sisters are coping with their father's sudden death. "Told alter-nately by all three girls, with May as the primary narrator, Johnson's novel will pull readers in with its quietly complex story. May, Palmer, and Brooks each respond in separate but absolutely authentic ways, and Johnson takes readers beyond the predictable coping story by beautifully articulating each daughter's pain, gradual healing, and acceptance" (*Booklist* Sept. 1, 2004). Ages 12–18.

Kuhlman, Evan. **The Last Invisible Boy.** New York: Simon & Schuster Children's Pub-lishing, 2008. 240p. $16.99. ISBN 1-4169-5797-9; 978-1-4169-5797-3.

Following his father's sudden death, 12-year-old Finn feels he is becoming invis-ible as his hair and skin become whiter. He writes and illustrates a book to under-stand what is happening and to draw closer to his father. "While poignant and sad, the book is ultimately upbeat as they begin to heal" (*School Library Journal* Dec. 1, 2008). Ages 10–14.

López, Diana. **Confetti Girl.** New York: Little, Brown Books for Young Readers, 2010. 208p. $6.99pa. ISBN 0-316-02956-4; 978-0-316-02956-8. Little, Brown Books for Young Readers, 2009. E-book. $6.99. ISBN 0-316-05252-3; 978-0-316-05252-8.

Lina Flores, a middle school student, tries to restore her life in Corpus Christi, Texas, after her mother's death. Her father, an English teacher, has withdrawn since the loss of his wife. "López effectively portrays the Texas setting and the characters' Latino heritage; [Lina's best friend] Vanessa's mother deals with her di-vorce by obsessively making Mexican cascarones confetti-filled eggshells and Span-ish is sprinkled throughout. This debut novel puts at its center a likable girl facing realistic problems on her own terms" (*Booklist* May 15, 2009). Ages 10–14.

Lynch, Chris. **Freewill.** New York: HarperCollins, 2001. 160p. $15.95. ISBN 0-06-028176-6; 978-0-06-028176-2. HarperCollins, 2002. 160p. $8.99pa. ISBN 0-06-447202-7; 978-0-06-447202-9.

Will, 17, is trying to recover from the death of his father and stepmother and comes to believe that he is responsible for a rash of teen suicides occurring in his town. The story is written in second person, and Will, the speaker, is talking to himself. "Lynch ably carries off this complicated construct, giving the story the immediacy of experience but also the restricted perspective of a disturbed young man.... This is a dark, rich young-adult novel that offers something to think about as well as an intriguing story, and Lynch captures Will's confusion and unfolding under-standing with sensitivity and tenderness" (*Booklist* May 15, 2001). Ages 14–18.

Manning, Sarra. **Let's Get Lost.** New York: Penguin Group, Dutton Juvenile, 2006. 320p. $16.99. ISBN 0-525-47666-0; 978-0-525-47666-5. Out of print.

After her mother's death, 16-year-old Isabel hides her grief behind the facade of "Mean Girl." Her new boyfriend finally causes her to confront issues related to her mother's death. "Despite Isabel's abrasiveness, readers will see through her facade, find themselves drawn to her, and be saddened by her self-destructive downward spiral. When all appears lost, a sudden, tidy redemption ends the novel on a hopeful note" (*Booklist* Jan. 1, 2007). Ages 14–18.

Mazer, Norma Fox. **After the Rain.** Waterville, ME: Thorndike Press, 2005. 359p. $10.95pa. ISBN 0-7862-7913-3; 978-0-7862-7913-5.

Rachel, 15, cares for her difficult grandfather during the last months of his life. They gradually develop a bond, and Rachel is with him when he dies. She then must cope with her grief. "Mazer's uncomplicated prose, mostly dialogue, is effective and readable. In its portrayal of a family coalescing around an old tyrant, and of a young woman achieving adulthood, *After the Rain* sounds a resonant note" (*School Library Journal* May 1, 1987). Ages 12–16.

Mazer, Norma Fox. **Girlhearts.** New York: HarperCollins, 2001. 224p. $15.99. ISBN 0-688-13350-9; 978-0-688-13350-4.

When her mother dies suddenly leaving her an orphan, 13-year-old Sarabeth Silver is confused and at the mercy of everyone who seems to know what is best for her. Her mother's friends take Sarabeth into their home to live with them and their baby in a one-bedroom apartment, but Sarabeth soon realizes that she is intruding in their lives. "With pitch-perfect intensity, Mazer captures the fractured sense of loss, of self, of time that comes with a death in the family" (*Booklist* July 1, 2001). Ages 10–14.

McDaniel, Lurlene. **The Girl Death Left Behind.** New York: Random House Children's Books, Laurel Leaf, 1999. 192p. $6.50. ISBN 0-553-57091-9; 978-0-553-57091-5.

When an accident kills her entire family, 14-year-old Beth suddenly finds herself living with her spoiled cousin Terri. Beth faces a new family, new house, and a new school, as well as the grief from losing her parents. "Those who find tears welling up will be thankful for the periods of built-in respite. The writing, infused with imagery and nuance, lends an air of sophistication to the formulaic story line" (*School Library Journal* Mar. 1, 1999). Ages 12–15.

McDonald, Joyce. **Swallowing Stones.** New York: Random House Children's Books, Laurel Leaf, 1999. 272p. $6.99pa. ISBN 0-440-22672-4; 978-0-440-22672-7.

On his 17th birthday, Michael randomly fires a rifle that kills Jenna Ward's father. Michael tries to hide his involvement, and his guilt is related along with Jenna's grief. "A compassionate story focusing on both the killer and the family left to grieve the loss of a father and husband" (*School Library Journal* Jan. 1, 2000). Ages 12–18.

Nelson, Theresa. **Earthshine.** New York: Scholastic, Orchard Books, 1994. 192p. $17.99. ISBN 0-531-08717-4; 978-0-531-08717-6.

Twelve-year-old Slim decides to live with her father, who is dying of AIDS, and his lover. At a support group meeting, she meets Isaiah, whose pregnant mother also has AIDS. "Earthshine deals with AIDS and coping with death in a respectful, nonthreatening way that makes AIDS a little more understandable to preteens" (*Voice of Youth Advocates* Oct. 1, 1994). Ages 10–14.

Oates, Joyce Carol. **After the Wreck, I Picked Myself Up, Spread My Wings, and Flew Away.** New York: HarperCollins, HarperTeen, 2007. 320p. $8.99pa. ISBN 0-06-073527-9; 978-0-06-073527-2.

Fifteen-year-old Jenna Abbott is physically and emotionally damaged from the car accident that killed her mother. After the wreck, she is alone and desperately wants to forget the accident. When Jenna meets Crow, he begins to break down the wall that Jenna has built around her emotions. "Jenna's pain at losing the only person truly close to her and the isolation she creates for herself are poignantly drawn. Her understanding that her choices are not what her mother would want for her is especially telling and may speak to teens in comparable situations" (*School Library Journal* Oct. 1, 2006). Ages 14–18.

Patterson, Valerie O. **The Other Side of Blue.** Boston: Houghton Mifflin Harcourt, Clarion Books, 2009. 240p. $16.00. ISBN 0-547-24436-3; 978-0-547-24436-5.

The summer after her father drowned off the island of Curaçao, Cyan and her mother return to their summer house along with the daughter of her mother's fiancé. Cyan blames her mother and spends her time trying to find out what really happened to her father. "[I]n her memorable first-person voice, filled with the minute observations of a young artist, Cyan sketches out with believable detail the beautiful setting, the unspoken family tension, and her fragile recovery of hope after loss" (*Booklist* Oct. 15, 2009). Ages 12–18.

Porte, Barbara Ann. **Something Terrible Happened.** New York: Scholastic, Orchard Books, 1994. 224p. $16.95pa. ISBN 0-531-06869-2; 978-0-531-06869-4.

Twelve-year-old Gillian's mother dies of AIDS, and she is sent to live with her relatives in Tennessee. Descended from West Indian immigrants to the United States, Gillian struggles to adjust to life with her white father's family. "Porte enlivens a refreshingly cliché-free narrative with the folktales this multiracial family of strong women tell each other, carefully sourcing each one. Unusually clear-eyed; beautifully written" (*Kirkus Reviews* Oct. 15, 1994). Ages 12–16.

Rabb, Margo. **Cures for Heartbreak.** New York: Random House Children's Books, Delacorte, 2008. 256p. $8.99pa. ISBN 0-385-73403-4; 978-0-385-73403-5.

Ninth-grader Mia must deal with her mother's recent death and her father's illness while she searches for friendship and love in the world around her. "This book could easily have been overwhelming given the mother's death, Mia's recurring company of terminally ill people, and her failed romances. Instead Rabb produces a witty, matter-of-fact, and heartfelt look at what grief means to one teenager, and how the relationships and habits Mia acquires help her to accept change" (*Voice of Youth Advocates* Apr. 1, 2007). Ages 14–18.

Rapp, Adam. **Under the Wolf, under the Dog.** Somerville, MA: Candlewick Press, 2007. 320p. $8.99pa. ISBN 0-7636-3365-8; 978-0-7636-3365-3.

Steve Nugent is a 16-year-old dealing with his mother's death, brother's suicide, and father's depression. He is living in a facility for kids with substance abuse problems or suicidal tendencies and is keeping a journal as required by his therapist. "A certain grim humor sometimes relieves the heavy narrative, which does end with a gleam of hope for readers who have stuck with the long, disturbing story" (*Kirkus Reviews* Sept. 15, 2004). Ages 14–18.

Schreck, Karen Halvorsen. **Dream Journal.** New York: Hyperion Press, 2006. 256p. $15.99. ISBN 1-4231-0105-7; 978-1-4231-0105-5. Hyperion Press, 2008. 256p. $8.99pa. ISBN 1-4231-0106-5; 978-1-4231-0106-2.

Sixteen-year-old Olivia records her thoughts in a journal as she faces the impending death of her mother from cancer, grapples with the changing behavior of her best friend, and contends with her own desire to escape her problems. "Teens who have recently lost someone close to them, or know that it's about to happen, will appreciate this sincere and thoughtful novel" (*School Library Journal* Nov. 1, 2006). Ages 12–18.

Smith, Andrew. **Ghost Medicine.** New York: Feiwel and Friends, 2008. 368p. $17.95. ISBN 0-312-37557-3; 978-0-312-37557-7. New York: Random House Audio Publishing Group, 2008. E-book. $51.00. ISBN 0-7393-7246-7; 978-0-7393-7246-3.

The summer before Troy turns 17, his mother dies. Troy and his father barely speak, and Troy spends most of his time with his closest friends. The summer is a journey of loss and self-discovery as Troy and his friends try to define who they are, sometimes seeking answers from "ghost medicine," a Native American philosophy that contends that strength and signs can be drawn from nature. "Troy wishes to be lost, but his greatest hope is to be found, and *Ghost Medicine* beautifully captures that paradox in this timeless and tender coming-of-age story. Not only will it inspire readers to prod the boundaries of their own courage, but it will also remind them that life and love are precious and fleeting" (*School Library Journal* Sept. 1, 2008). Ages 14–18.

Smith, Andrew. **Ghost Medicine.** New York: Random House Audio Publishing Group, Listening Library, 2008. CD. $44.00. ISBN 0-7393-7243-2; 978-0-7393-7243-2.

Read by Mike Chamberlain. Ages 14–18.

Tilly, Meg. **Porcupine.** Toronto, ON: Tundra Books, 2007. 240p. $15.95. ISBN 0-88776-810-5; 978-0-88776-810-1.

Twelve-year-old tomboy Jack Cooper (she doesn't like to be called Jacqueline) tries to help her family adjust after her father is killed in Afghanistan. Her mother is unable to cope and moves Jack and her younger siblings across the country from their home in Halifax to Alberta, leaving them with a great-grandmother. "As with Katherine Paterson's *The Great Gilly Hopkins* (1978), this novel expands the meaning of family. There is no sentimentality in Jack's first-person narrative; she's honest about her anger, her sadness and disappointment, and her need. She also turns out to be stronger than she imagined (she even fights off a rattlesnake)" (*Booklist* Nov. 15, 2007). Ages 10–14.

Turner, Ann Warren. **Hard Hit.** New York: Scholastic, 2006. 128p. $16.99. ISBN 0-439-29680-3; 978-0-439-29680-9.

Mark, a sophomore high school baseball pitcher, faces his most difficult challenge when his father is diagnosed with and dies of pancreatic cancer. Everything Mark has ever believed in is called into question. This verse traces the physical and emotional journey of a boy in crisis, with all of the emotions that accompany loss. "Teens who have experienced serious illness and/or death in their family or with close friends will relate to Turner's profound novel that traces the journey of one young man through the stages of grief and recovery" (*School Library Journal* Feb. 1, 2006). Ages 12–18.

Vincent, Erin. **Grief Girl: My True Story.** New York: Random House Children's Books, Delacorte Books, 2007. 320p. $15.99. ISBN 0-385-73353-4; 978-0-385-73353-3. Delacorte Books, 2008. 320p. $8.99pa. ISBN 0-385-73386-0; 978-0-385-73386-1.

Australian writer Vincent recounts events of the three years following the accidental death of both parents when she was 14. "Vincent's use of the present tense makes the story more immediate, and although her prose is unremarkable, it aptly approximates her teenage self. Any adolescent going through the grieving process will tearfully embrace her book" (*Booklist* Feb. 1, 2007). Ages 14–18.

Warner, Sally. **This Isn't About the Money.** New York: Penguin Group, Viking Juvenile, 2002. 224p. $15.99. ISBN 0-670-03574-2; 978-0-670-03574-8.

Twelve-year-old Janey tries to adjust after an automobile accident that kills her parents, severely injures her face, and forces her and her younger sister to move from Arizona to California to live with their grandfather and great-aunt. "As always, Warner's dialog and characterization are rich and real. A heartbreaking coda about the family's last moments before the accident will leave readers mourning what Janey has lost while celebrating her memories" (*Booklist* Sept. 1, 2002). Ages 12–18.

Wooldridge, Frosty. **Strike Three! Take Your Base.** Sterling, VA: Brookfield Reader, 2001. 160p. $16.95. ISBN 1-930093-01-2; 978-1-930093-01-0.

Teenage brothers Bob and Rex are promising high school baseball players, and their world is turned upside down when their father dies suddenly during a baseball game. "The quickly unfolding tale will hold readers to the very end with wrenching dialogue, flashbacks that help understand the characters' behaviors and their relationships with their father, and descriptive scenes from baseball games and practices. Many readers will find that this is a difficult book to put down" (*School Library Journal* Mar. 1, 2002). Ages 11–16.

Yumoto, Kazumi. **The Letters.** Trans. Cathy Hirano. St. Louis, MO: San Val, Turtleback, 2003. 165p. $13.55. ISBN 0-613-72256-6; 978-0-613-72256-8.

Translated from Japanese, a 28-year-old woman recounts the year after her father's death, when she was ages 6 and 7. Her elderly landlady encourages her to write letters to her father and helps her cope with his death. "The particulars of young Chiaki's everyday life are specifically Japanese—the rice-ball lunches, the landlady's kimono, the tatami mats, and futons—and set this story solidly in that country, but the themes are universal. Smoothly translated into English, this title by the author of *The Friends* (Farrar, 1996) is another thought-provoking examination of the nature and meaning of death for a somewhat older readership" (*School Library Journal* May 1, 2002). Ages 14–adult.

Death of a Sibling

Averett, Edward. **The Rhyming Season.** Boston: Houghton Mifflin Harcourt, Clarion Books, 2005. 224p. $16.00. ISBN 0-618-46948-6; 978-0-618-46948-2.

In her senior year of high school, Brenda is recovering from the death of her brother Benny the year before, her basketball coach leaves, and the local mill closes. Brenda and her new English teacher-coach try to lead their team to a state basketball victory. "Brenda's is not always a convincing voice, but it is an interesting one. Her parents' separate struggles with Benny's death as well as her own sense of loss lie vividly against the small-town loss of jobs and self in a place where no one ever wants to change" (*Booklist* Sept. 1, 2005). Ages 14–18.

Banks, Kate. **Walk Softly, Rachel.** New York: Farrar, Straus and Giroux, 2003. 160p. $16.00. ISBN 0-374-38230-1; 978-0-374-38230-8.

Fourteen-year-old Rachel reads the journal of her brother Jake, who died when she was seven. Rachel's parents rarely talk about Jake, and it is through his journal that Rachel begins to know her brother and learns that his death was a suicide. "Jake's diary entries are interspersed among Rachel's first-person narrative about her life now. Both voices belong to observant, precocious young people whose self-awareness and poetic language don't always sound authentic, but Banks captures emotional truths with a subtle, intelligent sensitivity" (*Booklist* Oct. 15, 2003). Ages 12–16.

Banks, Kate. **Walk Softly, Rachel.** Prince Frederick, MD: Recorded Books, 2004. 3 audio cassettes. 3 hrs. 45 min. $28.00. ISBN 1-4025-7607-2; 978-1-4025-7607-2.

Read by Alyssa Bresnahan. "This work should definitely be included in high school and public library young adult audio collections. Middle school media specialists should use their discretion as some of the journal entries are stark" (*School Library Journal* July 1, 2004). Ages 12–16.

Beard, Philip. **Dear Zoe.** New York: Penguin Group, Plume, 2006. 208p. $14.00. ISBN 0-452-28740-5; 978-0-452-28740-2.

Fifteen-year-old Tess DeNunzio writes a letter to her little sister Zoe after Zoe's death by a hit-and-run driver on September 11, 2001.Tess begins her letter as a means of figuring out her own life. After she moves in with her real father and falls into a romance with a neighbor boy, she begins to discover herself. "Beard captures the raw emotion of a 15-year-old girl with impressive dexterity, following Tess through the many stages of grief. Everything about this moving, powerful debut rings true" (*Booklist* Feb. 1, 2005). Ages 14–adult.

Belton, Sandra. **Store-Bought Baby.** New York: HarperCollins, 2006. 256p. $15.99. ISBN 0-06-085086-8; 978-0-06-085086-9.

When her adopted brother Luce is killed in a car accident, Leah is angry and devastated, and sometimes questions her parents' love for her. Then she takes it upon herself to find Luce's biological parents. "Readers who have experienced the complex range of emotions brought on by a tragedy of this nature will appreciate Belton's sensitive depiction of loss" (*Kirkus Reviews* May 1, 2006). Ages 12–18.

Coman, Carolyn. **Many Stones.** Honesdale, PA: Boyds Mills Press, Lemniscaat, 1996. 160p. $15.95. ISBN1-886910-55-3; 978-1-886910-55-3.

After her older sister is murdered in South Africa, 16-year-old Berry and her estranged father travel there to participate in a memorial service. While working through their grief, the father and daughter confront each other with their own emotional wounds. "Coman has deftly woven together the themes of death, grieving, and reconciliation through the characters and setting of this emotionally elegant novel. Berry's tormented and disoriented thoughts are so clearly realized that readers are relieved when she finally begins to heal and allows herself to grow" (*School Library Journal* Nov. 1, 2000). Ages 12–18.

Couloumbis, Audrey. **Getting Near to Baby.** New York: Penguin Group, Putnam Juvenile, 1999. 224p. $17.99. ISBN 0-399-23389-X; 978-0-399-23389-0. Out of print.

Thirteen-year-old Willa Jo and her Aunt Patty seem to be constantly at odds while Willa Jo is staying with her and Uncle Hob, but Aunt Patty helps Willa Jo and her younger sister come to terms with the death of their family's baby. "The characters are credible, though, engaging and multidimensional. So is their grief and the ways they deal with it so they can, once again, get 'near to Baby'" (*Booklist* Nov. 1, 1999). Ages 10–14.

Dogar, Sharon. **Waves.** New York: Scholastic Paperbacks, 2009. 352p. $8.99pa. ISBN 0-545-10178-6; 978-0-545-10178-3. Scholastic, The Chicken House, 2007. 344p. $16.99. ISBN 0-439-87180-8; 978-0-439-87180-8.

Fifteen-year-old Hal is haunted by memories of his older sister's accident the year before. When his family returns to the seaside site of the tragedy, Hal tries to piece together the events that left his sister alive but in a comatose state. He also meets a girl and falls in love. "[T]eens who don't balk at nonlinear narratives will sink into Dogar's lyrical, free-associative writing, as expressive about tender romantic moments (such as the sharing of breath, sweet and close and tangling) as it is about the burden of loss, like being stuck in a half-life, like some nuclear dump, with millions of years to go before the poison burns itself away" (*Booklist* Dec. 1, 2006). Ages 12–17.

Dogar, Sharon. **Waves.** New York: Random House Audio Publishing Group, Listening Library, 2007. CD. 8 hrs. $45.00. ISBN 0-7393-3885-4; 978-0-7393-3885-8.

Read by James Clamp. Ages 12–17.

Ellis, Ann Dee. **Everything Is Fine.** New York: Little, Brown Books for Young Readers, 2010. 160p. $7.99pa. ISBN 0-316-01443-5; 978-0-316-01443-4. Little, Brown Books for Young Readers, 2009. E-book. $7.99. ISBN 0-316-04063-0; 978-0-316-04063-1.

After Mazzy's sister dies, her mother is too depressed to get out of bed, and her father moves out. Mazzy is in denial, insisting that "everything is fine." Eventually, she must face the fact that her mom is emotionally paralyzed by her daughter's death. "Ellis impressively captures the voice of a sardonic, damaged, but surviving adolescent girl....Although the ending seems hasty and perhaps unrealistically optimistic, Ellis has created a unique snapshot of family tragedy that's refreshingly devoid of melodrama" (*School Library Journal* March 1, 2009). Ages 12–16.

Ellis, Ann Dee. **Everything Is Fine.** New York: Random House Audio Publishing Group, Listening Library, 2009. Unabridged CD. $27.00. ISBN 0-7393-7906-2; 978-0-7393-7906-6.

"Short chapters and spare language are well-narrated by Carrington Macduffie" (*School Library Journal* June 1, 2009). Ages 12–16.

Foxlee, Karen. **The Anatomy of Wings.** New York: Random House Children's Books, Knopf Books for Young Readers, 2009. 368p. $19.99. ISBN 0-375-95643-3; 978-0-375-95643-0.

Set in a 1980s Australian mining town, 10-year-old Jenny struggles to understand the suicide of her troubled teenage sister. "With heart-stopping accuracy and sly symbolism, Foxlee captures the small ways that humans reveal themselves, the mysterious intensity of female adolescence, and the surreal quiet of a grieving house, which slowly and with astonishing resilience fills again with sound and music" (*Booklist* Jan. 1, 2009). Ages 10–14.

Gershow, Miriam. **The Local News.** New York: Spiegel & Grau, 2009. 368p. $24.95. ISBN 0-385-52761-6; 978-0-385-52761-3. 384p. $15.00pa. ISBN 0-385-52762-4; 978-0-385-52762-0.

Following Danny Pasternak's disappearance, his parents go into deep mourning, and his younger sister Lydia is forced to address her ambivalent grief for a brother who was sometimes cruel to her. Forgotten by her parents and drawn into the missing person investigation by her family's private investigator, Lydia struggles to find herself during Danny's absence. Lydia tells the story 10 years later, after Danny's whereabouts are revealed. "Gershow keeps her approach fresh thanks to Lydia's disarmingly unsentimental narrative voice, which allows Danny to be more than a saintly victim" (*Kirkus Reviews* Dec. 1, 2008). "Gershow's writing is fluid, her imagery of the mid-'90s concise and compelling, and her story universal" (*School Library Journal* Feb. 1, 2009). Ages 12–17.

Jacobs, Deborah Lynn. **Choices.** New York: Roaring Brook Press, 2007. 208p. $17.99. ISBN 1-59643-217-9; 978-1-59643-217-8.

Overcome with guilt over her brother's death, 17-year-old Kathleen shifts between multiple universes in an attempt to find one in which he is alive. "Kathleen's melancholic tale does justice both to the moving story of a girl coming to terms with the death of her brother and to the magical adventure of a universe-shifting girl trying to find her way home" (*Kirkus Reviews* Sept. 1, 2007). "Those looking for accurate representations of their struggles with identity, relationships, family, and high school will eagerly jump across space to enter Kathleen's world" (*School Library Journal* Oct. 1, 2007). Ages 14–18.

Johnson, Angela. **Looking for Red.** New York: Simon & Schuster Children's Publishing, Simon Pulse, 2003. 128p. $5.99pa. ISBN 0-689-86388-8; 978-0-689-86388-2.

Middle school student Mike, short for Michaela, grieves when her older brother Red suddenly dies. "In beautiful prose, the narrative moves fluidly from flashbacks to the present, and the stages of grief are represented in startling but realistic ways: Mona sits for hours near Red's home, as if awaiting his return; Mark crashes the car Red loved in what adults mistakenly perceive as a suicide attempt" (*Booklist*). "Johnson's writing is spare and lyrical. Readers care about the characters and feel their emotions" (*Voice of Youth Advocates* June 1, 2002). Ages 12–14.

Kelly, Tom. **Finn's Going.** New York: HarperCollins, Greenwillow Books, 2007. 288p. $17.89. ISBN 0-06-121454-X; 978-0-06-121454-7. HarperCollins e-books, 2009. $16.99. ISBN 0-06-185105-1; 978-0-06-185105-6.

After his identical twin brother drowns, 10-year-old Danny runs away from home because he fears that he is a negative influence on his family. He eventually returns after accepting his own grief. "Kelly handles the entire story with great care, acknowledging the impossibility of the situation and cleanly guiding the reader through it. It would be a great book for anyone who has suffered a loss, but just as important for those who have yet to deal with it" (*Voice of Youth Advocates* Aug. 1, 2007). "Immersing readers in an idiosyncratic point of view through British slang and narrative quirks (such as lists and footnotes), first-time novelist Kelly, an American who lives in England, pens a powerful novel about moving on, about being yourself no matter how hard, from the realistic perspective of a smart, funny kid who is just waking up to the larger world. Though sad, this is an ultimately life-affirming book, full of poignant insights into how people try to protect themselves and each other from tragedy, and how they cope when they fail" (*Booklist* May 1, 2007). Ages 10–16.

Lowry, Lois. **A Summer to Die.** New York: Random House Children's Books, Delacorte, 2007. 160p. $7.99pa. ISBN 0-385-73420-4; 978-0-385-73420-2.

Meg is unhappy when she must share her bedroom with her older sister Molly. The two of them are very different, and Meg resents Molly's beauty and popularity. After the family moves to a small house in the country, and the sisters begin to adjust to their new home, Molly is constantly irritable, her appearance changes, and one day Molly is rushed to the hospital with a serious illness. Ages 9–15.

Lytton, Deborah A. **Jane in Bloom.** New York: Penguin Group, Dutton Juvenile, 2009. 208p. $16.99. ISBN 0-525-42078-9; 978-0-525-42078-1.

Twelve-year-old Jane is devastated when her beautiful, older sister Lizzie dies from anorexia. Jane tells her story of recovery from the tragedy. "Characterizations are plausible in this ultimately hope-filled story. Though similar in theme to Laurie Halse Anderson's *Wintergirls* (Viking, 2009), this book can be appreciated by younger readers as it is thoughtfully revealed from Jane's perspective" (*School Library Journal* May 1, 2009). Ages 12–16.

McGhee, Alison. **All Rivers Flow to the Sea.** Somerville, MA: Candlewick Press, 2005. 176p. $15.99. ISBN 0-7636-2591-4; 978-0-7636-2591-7. Candlewick Press, 2007. 175p. $7.99pa. ISBN 0-7636-3372-0; 978-0-7636-3372-1.

Seventeen-year-old Rose struggles with her grief and guilt following a car accident that leaves her older sister Ivy brain-dead. Rose's mother denies Ivy's condition and refuses to visit her. To counteract her pain, Rose becomes sexually promiscuous. "While readers struggle along with Rose, they will gain a new perspective about the importance of family and of the grieving process" (*School Library Journal* Nov. 1, 2005). Ages 14–18.

Nelson, Jandy. **The Sky Is Everywhere.** New York: Penguin Group, Dial, 2010. 288p. $17.99. ISBN 0-8037-3495-6; 978-0-8037-3495-1.

Lennie Walker, a 17-year-old bookworm and band geek, is content to live in the shadow of her older sister, Bailey. When Bailey suddenly dies, Lennie finds herself receiving much attention from her family and peers, including two boys. "Debut author Nelson expertly and movingly chronicles the myriad, roller-coaster emotions that follow a tragedy, including Lennie's reluctance to box up her sister's belongings and her guilt over bursts of happiness. The portrayal of the teen's state of mind is believable, as are the romanticizing of her absent mother and the brief scenes of underage drinking and sexual exploration" (*School Library Journal* Mar. 1, 2010). Ages 14–18.

Runyon, Brent. **Maybe.** New York: Random House Children's Books, Knopf Books for Young Readers, 2008. 208p. $7.99pa. ISBN 0-553-49508-9; 978-0-553-49508-9.

Sixteen-year-old Brian is insecure when his family moves to a new town after the death of his older brother. Brian worries that his brother might have crashed his car on purpose, and that he might be self-destructive as well. "When at school or with friends, his grief is held at bay; however, the few scenes in which the boy interacts with his parents are particularly poignant in their portrayal of how a family tries to move forward despite their heartache. The common insecurities of adolescence, specifically of hormonally charged teenaged boys, coupled with the added drama and intrigue surrounding the brother's accident, make this an accessible work for a wide, albeit older, teen audience" (*Kirkus Reviews* Oct. 1, 2006). Ages 14–18.

Sáenz, Benjamin Alire. **Sammy and Juliana in Hollywood.** New York: HarperCollins, 2006. 368p. $8.99pa. ISBN 0-06-084374-8; 978-0-06-084374-8.

Sammy Santos, 16, recalls his first love, Juliana, killed with her siblings by her father. He also writes about the death of a friend in Vietnam, and the impact of social changes on his school life and friendships during the late 1960s. Sammy lives in a modest barrio named Hollywood in east Las Cruces, New Mexico. "Saenz, a fine storyteller, has made sure that the language, characters, and circumstances ring true, and although the Chicano and English street slangs are often crude and the Spanish terms are seldom translated, Sammy's intrinsic goodness, loyalty, and generosity of spirit make it an illuminating and edifying story. Older teens will find it emotional, a literary roller coaster" (*Voice of Youth Advocates* Dec. 1, 2004). Ages 14–18.

Sandell, Lisa Ann. **A Map of the Known World.** New York: Scholastic, 2009. 288p. $16.99. ISBN 0-545-06970-X; 978-0-545-06970-0.

Since her older brother, Nate, died in a car crash, Cora seeks solace in drawing beautiful maps, envisioning herself in exotic locales. When she falls for Damian, the handsome boy who was in the car with Nate the night he died, she uncovers her brother's secret artistic life and realizes she had more in common with him than she imagined. "This book will appeal to students who have experienced the death of someone close, although the depth of that grief is more keenly presented in Brent Runyon's *Maybe* (Knopf, 2006) or Katherine Spencer's *Saving Grace* (Harcourt, 2006)" (*School Library Journal* June 1, 2009). Ages 12–18.

Schmidt, Gary D. **Trouble.** Solon, OH: Findaway World, 2008. Audio. 9 hrs. $79.99. ISBN 1-60514-932-2; 978-1-60514-932-5.

Henry Smith's father told him that if you build your house far enough away from trouble, then trouble will never find you. But one night a pickup truck strikes Henry's older brother, Franklin. The truck was driven by a young Cambodian from Franklin's preparatory school, and the tragedy sparks racial tensions in the school and town, catching Henry between anger and grief. "Jason Culp's accomplished reading moves smoothly from a quiet and neutral narration to vivid vocal depictions of each character, complete with seamless accents. This gripping, adventure-filled journey of self discovery and exploration of themes such as discrimination and forgiveness will appeal to middle and high school students" (*School Library Journal* Feb. 1, 2009). Ages 14–18.

Stork, Francisco X. **The Last Summer of the Death Warriors.** New York: Scholastic, Arthur A. Levine Books, 2010. 342p. $17.99. ISBN 0-545-15133-3; 978-0-545-15133-7.

Seventeen-year-old Pancho Sanchez is determined to avenge the death of his sister. After he meets D.Q, who is dying of cancer, and Marisol, one of D.Q.'s caregivers, both boys find their lives changed by their interactions. "Stork (*Marcelo in the Real World*, 2008) has written another ambitious portrait of a complex teen, one that investigates the large considerations of life and death, love and hate, and faith and doubt. Though the writing occasionally tends toward the didactic, this novel, in the way of the best literary fiction, is an invitation to careful reading that rewards serious analysis and discussion" (*Booklist* Feb. 1, 2010). Ages 12–18.

Stork, Francisco X. **The Last Summer of the Death Warriors.** New York: Random House Audio Publishing Group, Listening Library, 2010. Audio. $37.00. ISBN 0-307-70699-0; 978-0-307-70699-7.

Read by Ryan Gesell.

Valentine, Jenny. **Broken Soup.** New York: HarperCollins, HarperTeen, 2009. 216p. $17.89. ISBN 0-06-085072-8; 978-0-06-085072-2. HarperCollins E-books, 2009. $16.99. 0-06-178626-8; 978-0-06-178626-6.

Following the death of her older brother, 15-year-old Rowan is left to care for her younger sister because her father is seldom present, and her mother lies in bed all day grieving. A photographic negative and two new friends become the

catalyst for Rowan's healing. "The short chapters reveal many kind and thoughtful people who are willing to help Rowan, and the dynamics among characters
ring true. Give this poignant, rewarding story to teens who need books dealing
with grief or who crave romance amid tragedy and hardship" (*School Library
Journal* Apr. 1, 2009). Ages 14–18.

Divorce

Bauer, Joan. **Stand Tall.** New York: Penguin Group, Puffin, 2005. 192p. $7.99pa. ISBN
      0-14-240427-6; 978-0-14-240427-0.

Tree is 12 years old and six feet, three and a half inches tall. He doesn't fit in at
school or on the basketball team, and since his parents' divorce, he isn't comfortable in his own home. Tree copes by helping people like his grandpa, a Vietnam
vet who's just had part of a leg amputated, and Sophie, a new girl at school who is
being teased by the popular kids. "The depictions of Tree and his colorful family
are candid and endearing, and much of the writing is leavened with the author's
special brand of humor, albeit bittersweet in this case. The story moves fluidly
as the author reminds readers of the small towns that stand tall and of the veterans
that fought in a war that not even they understood" (*School Library Journal* Aug. 1,
2002). Ages 11–14.

Bauer, Joan. **Stand Tall.** New York: Random House Audio Publishing Group, Listening
      Library, 2004. 3 cassettes. 4 hrs. 9 min. $30.00. ISBN 0-8072-1674-7; 978-0-
      8072-1674-3. 4 CDs. 4 hrs. 9 min. $35.00. ISBN 0-8072-1772-7; 978-0-8072-
      1772-6.

"Narrator Ron McLarty's voice works well as the even-keeled and wise Grandpa,
as well as the edgy, gruff-voiced Trash King, Grandpa's friend. Although he lacks
vocal variation for the other characters, it doesn't detract from the story" (*School
Library Journal* Nov. 1, 2003).

Birdsall, Olivia. **Notes on a Near-Life Experience.** New York: Random House Children's
      Books, Laurel Leaf, 2008. 272p. $6.50pa. ISBN 0-440-42161-6; 978-0-440-
      42161-0.

Fifteen-year-old Mia Day's life changes suddenly when her father moves out of
the house. Her mother works more and life is disrupted for her and her two siblings. "Written in a realistic, bright, honest, sometimes droll voice, Birdsall's debut
portrays the unfortunate side effects of divorce from the perspective of a confused
and unhappy young teen who views her parents' behavior as immature and selfish
when compared to herself and her siblings. As in life, there is no happily ever after
here, just poignant realization that life's circumstances must be worked through
and accepted with a great deal of contemplation, understanding and counseling"
(*Kirkus Reviews* Jan. 1, 2007). Ages 12–18.

Boles, Philana Marie. **Little Divas.** New York: HarperCollins, Amistad, 2006. 176p. $15.99.
      ISBN 0-06-073299-7; 978-0-06-073299-8.

The summer before seventh grade, Cassidy Carter faces living with her father, prac-
tically a stranger, as well as her relationships with her cousins. "In an easy, cool narrative, African American Cassidy (Cass), twelve, talks about coping with her parents'
recent divorce; moving in with Daddy while Mom is away volunteering somewhere
in Africa; her on-off relationship with her cousin, Rikki; her bond with her new,
white neighbor Golden, who has secrets about her mother's divorces; and Cass'
first kiss (you gotta kiss back) with the boy she thought she hated. The dialogue is

right on, a mix of anger, attraction, fear, and love" (*Booklist* Apr. 1, 2006). "Not as steamy as the author's adult work, this debut for middle-grade readers does include some kissing and a homily on condom use, without using the word. It will be particularly welcome to young African-American girls who may recognize themselves, their families and their schoolmates, and who will be eager to know how Cass gets on at Clara Ellis Academy for Girls" (*Kirkus Reviews* Nov. 15, 2005). Ages 10–14.

Brown, Jason Robert, and Dan Elish. **13.** New York: HarperCollins, Laura Geringer, 2008. 208p. $15.99. ISBN 0-06-078749-X; 978-0-06-078749-3.

Twelve-year-old Evan Goldman's parents separate, and he moves with his mother from New York City to Appleton, Indiana, just before his bar mitzvah. "Evan's social- and self-awareness get a workout as he realizes the moral edges of both his own and others' behaviors, and the concept of becoming a man is presented through both his actions and efforts to write his bar mitzvah speech. Brown and Elish keep things moving so quickly that critical questions barely have a chance to register, but *13* is ultimately a fine school story with characters that are limned with enough thoroughness to make them real" (*Booklist* Sept. 1, 2008). Ages 10–14.

Cleary, Beverly. **Dear Mr. Henshaw.** New York: HarperCollins, Harper Trophy, 2000. 176p. $5.99pa. ISBN 0-380-70958-9; 978-0-380-70958-8.

Leigh Botts has been author Boyd Henshaw's fan since second grade. Now in sixth grade, Leigh lives with his mother and is the new kid at school. His parents are divorced, he's lonely, he's troubled by the absence of his father, and angry because someone steals from his lunch bag. Through his letters to Mr. Henshaw Leigh grapples with his problems, finds comfort, and begins to recognize his talent as a writer. Ages 10–14.

Danziger, Paula. **The Divorce Express.** New York: Random House, Delacorte Press, 1982. 148p. $12.62. ISBN 0-440-02035-2; 978-0-440-02035-6. New York: Penguin Group, Puffin, 2007. 160p. $5.99pa. ISBN 0-14-240712-7; 978-0-14-240712-7.

Ninth-grader Phoebe Brooks works out problems with her divorced parents and acquires a boyfriend. She also gets involved in a committee to improve the cafeteria food at the new high school she attends after she and her father move following the divorce. Ages 10–14.

Dessen, Sarah. **Along for the Ride.** New York: Penguin Group, 2009. E-book. $19.99. ISBN 1-101-08104-X; 978-1-101-08104-4.

Seventeen-year-old Auden spent her childhood and teenage years acting like an adult. She decides to spend the summer with her dad and his new family in a small, coastal town and experiences some of the things that she missed while growing up. "It's Eli, a fellow insomniac, with whom she connects, and together they tick off items on her kid to-do list (food fights, bowling, paper-delivery route) while the rest of the town sleeps. The spark between these two sad teens and the joyful examples of girl connectivity deepen this ostensibly lighthearted, summer-fun story, which offers up complex issues—the residual effects of divorce, acceptance of imperfect parents and lip-gloss feminism" (*Kirkus Reviews* May 15, 2009). Ages 14–18.

Deuker, Carl. **Night Hoops.** Boston: Houghton Mifflin Harcourt, 2000. 224p. $15.00. ISBN 0-395-97936-6; 978-0-395-97936-5.

Nick Abbott tries to show that he is good enough to play on his high school's varsity basketball team, but he must also deal with his parents' divorce and a troubled classmate who lives across the street. "Best of all, the complexities of basketball are contrasted with the complexities of life. Nick learns how important it is to make adjustments during the course of a game, and he learns that adjustments are also important in life" (*School Library Journal* May 1, 2000). Ages 12–18.

Emond, Stephen. **Happyface.** New York: Little, Brown, 2010. 320p. $16.99. ISBN 0-316-04100-9; 978-0-316-04100-3.

Happyface is a shy, artistic sophomore who moves to a new school after his parents break up and tries to reinvent himself by putting on a happy face; however, he is forced to cope with his emotions. "Emond tells the story via the teen's illustrated journal, authentically capturing his up-and-down emotions. The pencil-and-ink sketches, comics, and doodles, paired with a disastrously small handwriting font, lend an intimate stream-of-consciousness feel to a story by turns funny, wrenching, quirky, and redemptive" (*School Library Journal* Mar. 1, 2010). Ages 12–17.

Freymann-Weyr, Garret. **When I Was Older.** Saint Louis, MO: Turtleback Books, 2002. $14.15. ISBN 0-613-62415-7; 978-0-613-62415-2. Out of print.

Fifteen-year-old Sophie learns to deal with her younger brother's death and her parents' divorce as she struggles with the transitions of adolescence in her own life. "Fast-paced, light, yet introspective, this novel of transition, love, and loss explores emotion while telling a fine story" (*School Library Journal* Oct. 1, 2000). Ages 12–17.

Goldentyer, Debra. **Parental Divorce.** Teen Hot Line Series. Chicago, IL: Heinemann-Raintree, 1995. 80p. $19.98. ISBN 0-8114-3817-1; 978-0-8114-3817-9.

Utilizing a question-and-answer format, the book addresses reasons for divorce, various reactions to it, the stages of adjustment, the legal process, custodial arrangements, and visitation rights. Parental dating, and stepfamilies are addressed as well. Ages 10–16.

Hood, Ann. **How I Saved My Father's Life: And Ruined Everything Else.** New York: Scholastic Press, 2008. 224p. $16.99. ISBN 0-439-92819-2; 978-0-439-92819-9.

Twelve-year-old Madeline believes that she is destined to become Saint Madeline because she has performed two miracles, one of which saved her father from an avalanche. After her parents' divorce, a summer trip to Italy puts her family situation in perspective. "There are shelves of books about the children of divorce, but in this novel, Hood, the author of several adult books, tells the family story with a fresh voice that stays true to the child's viewpoint. The resolution is too neat, but Madeline's narration is always funny, furious, and heartbreaking whether the girl is agonizing about religion and family or about what she should wear to school" (*Booklist* Dec. 15, 2007). Ages 10–16.

Khan, Rukhsana. **Wanting Mor.** Toronto, ON: Groundwood Books, 2009. 192p. $17.95. ISBN 0-88899-858-9; 978-0-88899-858-3.

When Jameela's mother, Mor, dies, Jameela's father decides to start a new life in Kabul. There he succumbs to alcohol and drugs. He remarries, and Jameela is treated like a slave by her stepmother. Soon her father abandons Jameela in a busy market, and she eventually is relegated to an orphanage. "Jameela's matter-of-fact, first-person narrative will awaken young readers to life and conditions in Afghanistan. The story is packed with Pushto words that may slow some readers, but a helpful glossary is included" (*Booklist* Apr. 1, 2009) Ages10–14.

Kittleson, Mark J., William Kane, and Barry Youngerman. **The Truth about Divorce.** New York: Facts On File, 2004. 192p. $35.00. ISBN 0-8160-5304-9; 978-0-8160-5304-9.

An A-to-Z guide to the facts and myths of divorce, explaining the social, legal, and personal effects of divorce. It provides readers a greater understanding of the topic while providing effective strategies for coping. Included are self-tests, sidebars, and current statistics. Topics include blended families, child support, love and marriage, and relationship challenges. Ages 11–18.

LaMotte, Elisabeth Joy. **Overcoming Your Parents' Divorce: 5 Steps to a Happy Relationship.** Far Hills, NJ: New Horizon Press, 2008. 224p. $14.95pa. ISBN 0-88282-329-9; 978-0-88282-329-4.

LaMotte, a licensed clinical social worker, offers readers five steps for building and maintaining meaningful relationships. She highlights the most common pitfalls faced by children of divorce and shows readers how to avoid making the same mistakes as their parents. "While there are other books on children of divorce, this one is positive and gives hope to those who come from broken homes. Recommended for all libraries" (*Library Journal* Aug. 1, 2008). Ages 13–18.

Ly, Many. **Home Is East.** New York: Random House Children's Books, Laurel Leaf, 2007. 304p. $6.50pa. ISBN 0-440-23900-1; 978-0-440-23900-0.

Amy, a Cambodian-American girl in fifth grade, is expected to observe the customs of her Cambodian culture while trying to fit into America. After her mother abandons the family, Amy and her father move from Florida to California. "Newcomer Ly burdens her narrative with extraneous characters and complications, and too often yields to the temptation to tell, not show, and readers may well tire of Amy before she winds up her tale. There are fine moments here, however, and those readers who stay the course will be happy to find Amy and her dad finally happy themselves" (*Kirkus Reviews* July 1, 2005). Ages 10–14.

Powell, Randy. **Swiss Mist.** New York: Farrar, Straus and Giroux, 2008. 224p. $16.95. ISBN 0-374-37356-6; 978-0-374-37356-6.

While in fifth grade, Milo's parents are divorced. He is a loner, but shares an interest in Switzerland with his fifth-grade teacher, who helps him through a difficult year. He rebels as his mother moves them from Seattle and back again. In 10th grade Milo's mother marries a wealthy businessman. "Capped by his mother's marriage to a prosperous businessman as well as eye-opening visits with his admired fifth-grade teacher and an insecure, overachieving former classmate, Milo's wry narrative will strike chords with readers engaged on similar journeys through life and family changes" (*Booklist* Dec. 1, 2008). Ages 10–16.

Reinhardt, Dana. **How to Build a House.** New York: Random House Children's Books, Wendy Lamb, 2008. 240p. $15.99. ISBN 0-375-84453-8; 978-0-375-84453-9. Random House Audio Publishing Group, 2008. E-book. $42.50. ISBN 0-7393-6413-8; 978-0-7393-6413-0.

Seventeen-year-old Harper Evans hopes to escape the effects of her father's divorce on her family and friendships by volunteering her summer to build a house in a small Tennessee town devastated by a tornado. In addition, Harper has lost her stepsister, Tess. "Although Reinhart presents an unlikely plot for a teen novel, it works. The characters and their dialogue are mostly authentic, despite the fact that the teens throw around hundred-dollar words, such as paradox, counterintuitive, and preternatural" (*Voice of Youth Advocates* Aug. 1, 2008), Ages 14–18.

Reinhardt, Dana. **How to Build a House.** New York: Random House Audio Publishing Group, Listening Library, 2008. 5 CDs. 5 hrs. 24 min. $45.00. ISBN 0-7393-6412-X; 978-0-7393-6412-3.

"Caitlin Greer voices a credible Harper, but some of her Southern accents for other characters are flat or, worse, caricatures. Pacing of both story and reading are good" (*School Library Journal* Oct. 1, 2008). Ages 14–18.

Sherrill, Martha. **The Ruins of California.** New York: Penguin Group, Riverhead Trade Paperbacks, 2007. 384p. $14.00pa. ISBN 1-59448-231-4; 978-1-59448-231-1.

Inez Ruin, the daughter of a flamenco dancer and a university professor, traces her family relationships from grade school to college. Her father is twice divorced, leaving Inez to bounce between his bohemian life in 1970s San Francisco and the more sedate world of her mother, who plays tennis and attends EST seminars in the suburbs. "Especially noteworthy among the many pleasures of this novel is the finely drawn character of Inez, whose emotional development over the years is subtly reflected in her changing assessments of the world.... Technically perfect characterization in a tale that explores an imperfect family" (*Kirkus Reviews* Nov. 1, 2005). Ages 16–adult.

Shoup, Barbara. **Wish You Were Here.** Woodbury, MN: Llewellyn Publications, Flux, 2008. 331p. $9.95pa. ISBN 0-7387-1355-4; 978-0-7387-1355-7.

Jackson (Jax) Watts is a high school senior trying to cope with his parents' divorce, his best friend's sudden departure, his mother's remarriage, and his father's nearly fatal accident. "Teens, especially boys, will identify with his [Jackson's] struggle to get in touch with his feelings while preserving an aura of being in control. Girls will see him as hiding the sensitive soul they hope is in every boy; however, the author also expresses the reality that on the road to self-discovery, even a sensitive hero may not leave the women in his life unscathed" (*Booklist* Oct. 15, 1994). Ages 14–18.

Smith, Yeardley. **I, Lorelei.** New York: HarperCollins, Laura Geringer Books, 2009. 352p. $16.99. ISBN 0-06-149344-9; 978-0-06-149344-7. HarperCollins E-books, 2009. $16.99. ISBN 0-06-173150-1; 978-0-06-173150-1.

Eleven-year-old Lorelei Connelly chronicles her sixth-grade year in a journal written for her dead cat. During this year, her parents separate, she gets a part in the school play, and she becomes friends with the cutest boy in her grade. "Recommend this read to tweens dealing with similar circumstances or those who are finally ready to see their parents as the flawed individuals they really are" (*Booklist* Jan. 1, 2009). Ages 9–13.

Trueit, Trudi Strain. **Surviving Divorce: Teens Talk about What Hurts and What Helps.** Scholastic Choices Series. Danbury, CT: Scholastic Library Publishing, 2006. 112p. $27.00. ISBN 0-531-12368-5; 978-0-531-12368-3. Scholastic Library Publishing, 2007. 112p. $8.95pa. 0-531-16726-7; 978-0-531-16726-7.

"With an open layout and reassuring text, this title in the Scholastic Choices series is an inviting guide to the facts and feelings of parental divorce. Personal stories and photos of kids begin each chapter, and frequent statistics and quizzes will help readers assess their feelings and put them into context" (*Booklist* Jan. 1, 2007). Ages 12–18.

Voigt, Cynthia. **A Solitary Blue.** Tillerman Cycle Series, Book 3. New York: Simon & Schuster Children's Publishing, Aladdin, 2003. 256p. $6.99pa. ISBN 0-689-86360-8; 978-0-689-86360-8. Simon & Schuster Children's Publishing, Simon Pulse, 2003. 256p. $6.99. ISBN 0-689-86434-5; 978-0-689-86434-6. St. Louis, MO: San Val, Turtleback, 2003. $17.20. ISBN 0-613-73441-6; 978-0-613-73441-7. Waterville, ME: Thorndike Press, 2005. 359p. $10.95pa. ISBN 0-7862-7912-5; 978-0-7862-7912-8.

Jeff Green's mother left him and his father when Jeff was only seven. When she appears again, Jeff learns some lessons about love and caring. "Jeff's own feelings at every stage are compellingly real and affecting; the growing closeness between him and his father is moving and subtly developed; and his own emotional development and growing character (that old-fashioned term is the only word for it) brings out Voigt at her best, as well" (*Kirkus Reviews* Sept. 9, 1983). Ages 11–14.

Voigt, Cynthia. **A Solitary Blue.** Prince Frederick, MD Recorded Books, n.d. Cassette $61.75. CD $77.75. ISBN 1-4237-1800-3; 978-1-4237-1800-0.

Worthen, Tom, ed. **Broken Hearts...Healing: Young Poets Speak Out on Divorce.** Logan, UT: Poet Tree Press, 2001. 248p. $26.95. ISBN 1-58876-150-9; 978-1-58876-150-7.

Poems by nearly 200 children ages 9 to 18 remind the reader that divorce ends a marriage but not the relationship with the children. Among topics addressed are the initial shock of learning of their parents' separation, feelings of abandonment, frustration and anger, stepfamilies, and acceptance. "The strength of this book lies in the charged words of youth; this is not a book about divorce written by an adult for children. Rather, it is by their peers, and readers who are going through divorce will know that they are not alone in their feelings and emotions" (*School Library Journal* Sept. 1, 2001). Ages 10–18.

Wright, Bil. **When the Black Girl Sings.** New York: Simon & Schuster Children's Publishing, 2008. 272p. $16.99. ISBN 1-4169-3995-4; 978-1-4169-3995-5. New York: Simon & Schuster Children's Publishing, Simon Pulse, 2009. 272p. $5.99pa. ISBN1-4169-4003-0; 978-1-4169-4003-6.

Lahni Schuler, 14, is an African American whose adoptive parents are white. When she finds out her parents are separating, Lahni finds that singing in a church choir gives her the confidence to compete in her school's vocal competition. "Without sugarcoating anything, Wright easily juggles the many issues found in the book with wit, compassion, and humor. The writing is clear, succinct, and never condescending" (*Voice of Youth Advocates* Feb. 1, 2008). Ages 12–16.

Foster Care

Byars, Betsy. **The Pinballs.** HarperCollins, Harper Trophy, 1996. 80p. $2.25pa. ISBN 0-06-447150-0; 978-0-06-447150-3. Out of print.

Self-named the Pinballs, three foster siblings find a family when the Masons take them in. Together they learn solidarity and trust, enabling them to deal with grief. "The sentiment throughout is as subtle as a puppy's wet kiss, but Byars' bright, flaky dialogue invites you to indulge yourself without embarrassment" (*Kirkus Reviews* Mar. 1, 1977). Ages 10–18.

Byars, Betsy. **The Pinballs.** New York: Random House Audio Publishing Group, Listening Library, 1995. 2 cassettes. 3 hrs. $23.00. ISBN 0-8072-8528-5; 978-0-8072-8528-2.

Read by Rita Gardner.

de la Pena, Matt. **Ball Don't Lie.** New York: Random House Children's Books, Delacorte Books for Young Readers, 2005. 288p. $18.99. ISBN 0-385-90258-1; 978-0-385-90258-8. Random House Children's Books, Delacorte Books for Young Readers, 2007. 288p. $7.99pa. ISBN 0-385-73425-5; 978-0-385-73425-7.

Seventeen-year-old Sticky has been removed from four foster homes. He loves to play basketball at school and a Los Angeles gym, and he dreams of becoming a pro basketball player. As he works for a college scholarship, he confronts the problem of being an outsider as a white boy. "Marked by inner-city slang and profanity, the dialogue and pacing of the story has a hip-hop rhythm much like change-of-pace moves performed on city basketball courts. Stunningly realistic, this book will hook older readers, especially urban teen males, and they will share it with friends" (*Voice of Youth Advocates* Oct. 1, 2005). Ages 14–18.

Dowd, Siobhan. **Solace of the Road.** New York: Random House Children's Books, David Fickling Books, 2009. 272p. $17.99. ISBN 0-375-84971-8; 978-0-375-84971-8.

While running away from a London foster home just before her 15th birthday, Holly considers her years of residential care and her early life with her Irish mother, whom she is now trying to reach. "Holly's character is fully developed and bright with a quirky humor, and even secondary characters with lightly sketched parts fly off the pages in three dimensions. Holly's insights and observations are completely plausible, as is her voyage of discovery, described in lovely, pitch-perfect language" (*Kirkus Reviews* Sept. 1, 2009). Ages 13–18.

Dowell, Frances O'Roark. **Where I'd Like to Be.** Waterville, ME: Thorndike Press, 2003. 162p. $22.95. ISBN 0-7862-5741-5; 978-0-7862-5741-6. New York: Simon & Schuster Children's Publishing, Aladdin, 2004. 240p. $5.99pa. ISBN 0-689-87067-1; 978-0-689-87067-5.

Eleven-year-old Maddie is a foster child who can't stop looking for a home. With her friends in the East Tennessee Children's Home they fill scrapbooks with pictures of fantasy homes, tell stories, and daydream about their futures. "Their stories, individual and collective, are poignantly told without ever becoming maudlin, and the way these lonely children come together to make their own home and family is truly lovely. . . . The talky, pie-in-the-sky resolution mars the tightness of the narrative that precedes it, but taken as a whole, this is a lovely, quietly bittersweet tale of friendship and family" (*Kirkus Reviews* Mar. 1, 2003). Ages 10–14.

Dowell, Frances O'Roark. **Where I'd Like to Be.** Old Greenwich, CT: Listening Library, Chinaberry Audio, 2003. Audio cassette. $30.00. ISBN 0-8072-1574-0; 978-0-8072-1574-6.

"The narration is lively and energetic, bringing out the story's humor and poignancy. Country flavored music plays at the beginning and end of the recording" (*School Library Journal* Sept. 1, 2003). Ages 10–14.

Frank, E. R. **America.** New York: Simon & Schuster Children's Publishing, Atheneum/ Richard Jackson Books, 2002. 224p. $18.00. ISBN 0-689-84729-7; 978-0-689-84729-5.

Fifteen-year-old America, a mixed-race boy, was abandoned by his drug-addict mother and has been in the child welfare system. He tells his story and tries to piece his life together. "Frank, the author of the much-acclaimed *Life Is Funny* (2000), exposes with compassion, clarity, and deeply unsettling detail the profound shame and horror of abuse as well as the erratic nature of a medical system that tries to reclaim the victims. She also creates an extraordinary character in America who, with the help of his doctor, confronts the deepest betrayals and, finally, lets himself be found" (*Booklist* Feb. 15, 2002). Ages 13–18.

Frank, E. R. **America.** Prince Frederick, MD: Recorded Books, 2002. 4 cassettes. 6 hrs. $40.00. ISBN 1-4025-2889-2; 978-1-4025-2889-7.

Narrated by J. D. Jackson.

Gibbons, Kaye. **Ellen Foster.** Farmington Hills, MI: Cengage Gale, Macmillan Reference, 1998. ISBN 0-7838-0116-5; 978-0-7838-0116-2.

After her mother's death, Ellen experiences abuse from her father but finds a better life in a foster home with several children. "In a winning and candid voice, spunky 11-year-old Ellen Foster recalls the day-to-day traumas she endured as a child in a very troubled family and the small measure of peace she finds when she is taken into a foster home. This humorous, unsentimental novel will stay with you long after you close the book" (*Booklist* Sept. 1, 1997). Ages 10–14.

Gibbons, Kaye. **Ellen Foster.** Prince Frederick, MD: Recorded Books, 1998. 3 cassettes. 4 hrs. $32.00. ISBN 0-7887-2019-8; 978-0-7887-2019-2.

Narrated by Ruth Ann Phimister.

Giff, Patricia Reilly. **Pictures of Hollis Woods.** Waterville, ME: Thorndike Press, 2003. 158p. $23.95. ISBN 0-7862-5094-1; 978-0-7862-5094-3. Saint Louis, MO: San Val, Turtleback, 2004. 166p. $17.20. ISBN1-4176-2441-8; 978-1-4176-2441-6. New York: Random House Children's Books, Yearling, 2004. 176p. $6.99pa. ISBN 0-440-41578-0; 978-0-440-41578-7.

Twelve-year-old Hollis is named for the place she was abandoned. She has been in numerous foster homes, but when sent to Josie, an elderly artist, she wants to stay. Flashbacks reveal Hollis's previous homes. "Giff (*All the Way Home*, 2001, etc.) expertly portrays the intense, heartfelt emotions Hollis experiences and gives her talent and spunk; she is in no way pathetic, despite her perennial foster-childhood. The secondary characters are also completely drawn and are likable without being too good to be true" (*Kirkus Reviews* Aug. 1, 2002). Ages 10–16.

Giff, Patricia Reilly. **Pictures of Hollis Woods.** New York: Random House Audio Publishing Group, Listening Library, 2004. 3 CDs. 2 hrs. 18 min. $20.40. ISBN 0-8072-1786-7; 978-0-8072-1786-3. 2 cassettes. 2 hrs. 18 min. $23.00. ISBN 0-8072-0920-1; 978-0-8072-0920-2.

"Hope Davis does a superb job narrating the story, using subtle vocal intonations to differentiate between the unusually well-drawn characters. She gives Josie a frail but lively portrayal, while Hollis is by turns sullen, defiant, and filled with guilt" (*School Library Journal* Mar. 1, 2003). Ages 10–16.

Koertge, Ronald. **Strays.** Somerville, MA: Candlewick Press, 2007. 176p. $16.99. ISBN 0-7636-2705-4; 978-0-7636-2705-8. Candlewick Press, 2010. 176p. $7.99pa. ISBN 0-7636-4377-7; 978-0-7636-4377-5.

Sixteen-year-old Ted is despondent after his parents are killed in a car accident. His foster parents are odd, but he begins to develop relationships with his foster brothers and with kids at school for the first time. "Koertge has long been renowned for his witty dialogue, and this novel does not disappoint. The themes of human and animal fostering are skillfully intertwined in this funny, fast-paced celebration of the resilience to survive loss and start anew" (*Voice of Youth Advocates* Aug. 1, 2007). Ages 14–18.

Lowell, Pamela. **Returnable Girl.** Tarrytown, NY: Marshall Cavendish Corp., 2006. 229p. $16.99. ISBN 0-7614-5317-2; 978-0-7614-5317-8. Out of print.

Ronnie Hartman, 13, was abandoned by her mother three years ago when she moved to Alaska with her boyfriend and Ronnie's younger brothers. Ronnie dreams of becoming reunited with her family and has been "returned" from foster homes 10 times because of her bad behavior. Her latest foster home is Ronnie's last chance, or she will be assigned to a residential treatment center. "As a family therapist, Lowell knows something about unhappy adolescents. Her expertise allows her to depict not only Ronnie's growing understanding of her situation and those of her friends, but also the reality of her life, all through Ronnie's eyes" (*Kirkus Reviews* Sept. 15, 2006). Ages 13–18.

McNeal, Laura, and Tom McNeal. **The Decoding of Lana Morris.** New York: Random House Children's Books, Knopf Books for Young Readers, 2007. 304p. $15.99. ISBN 0-375-83106-1; 978-0-375-83106-5.

Sixteen-year-old Lana Morris lives with a flirtatious foster father, a cold foster mother, and a houseful of special needs children. One day she ventures into an antique shop and buys a drawing set that has magical qualities—her drawings come true. "In distinct and thoughtfully crafted voices, characters reveal zany teen humor, adolescent longings, adult treachery, and youthful belief that wrongs should be righted. The touch of fantasy that drives the plot highlights a universal teen dilemma—how to use the power of personal decision" (*Voice of Youth Advocates* Aug. 1, 2007). "Give this story to your more mature readers who want some heft to their magical realism stories" (*School Library Journal* June 1, 2007). Ages 12–18.

Monninger, Joseph. **Baby.** Honesdale, PA: namelos llc, 2009. E-book. $7.95. ISBN 1-60898-005-7; 978-1-60898-005-5.

Baby, 15, has been abandoned by her alcoholic mother and winds up in a northern New Hampshire foster home. Baby's new foster parents race sled dogs, giving her an opportunity to turn her life around. "In this well-written tale, the author skillfully utilizes his love and understanding of sledding to weave a story of the redemptive and restorative power of animals. Baby learns to care for the dogs and to run them; she begins to gain a sense of responsibility and to trust again, and she is forced to make some difficult decisions about herself and her place in the world" (*School Library Journal* Nov. 1, 2007). Ages 13–18.

Paterson, Katherine. **The Great Gilly Hopkins.** New York: HarperCollins, 1978. 160p. $17.89. ISBN 0-690-03838-0; 978-0-690-03838-5. HarperCollins e-books, 2009. E-book. $5.99. ISBN 0-06-183275-8; 978-0-06-183275-8.

Gilly, a precocious 11-year-old girl, bounces from one foster home to another. She yearns for a real family and wants to find her mother and live with her instead of in the foster home where she has been placed. "Without a hint of the prevailing maudlin realism, Paterson takes up a common 'problem' situation and makes it genuinely moving, frequently funny, and sparkling with memorable encounters" (*Kirkus Reviews* Mar. 1, 1978). Ages 10–14.

Paterson, Katherine. **The Great Gilly Hopkins.** New York: Random House, 1979. Mixed media: audio cassette and hardcover book. $21.33. ISBN 0-394-78371-9; 978-0-394-78371-0. Prince Frederick, MD: Recorded Books, 1997. 4 pieces. 4 hrs. 45 min. $35.00. ISBN 0-7887-0740-X; 978-0-7887-0740-7.

Pelzer, Dave. **The Lost Boy: A Foster Child's Search for the Love of a Family.** Boulder, CO: NetLibrary, 1997. $10.95. ISBN 0-585-10493-X; 978-0-585-10493-5.

The author tells his story from the time he left his abusive mother and alcoholic father, his experiences in foster homes and juvenile detention, and his service in the Air Force. "Pelzer writes in an honest, sometimes rambling, style; he is never bitter, and his story will find many sympathetic readers. However, he leaves many questions unanswered (which may appear in the third book), dealing with his adult-life relationships, his son, the mother of that child, and the ways he turned his life around" (*Library Journal* Oct. 1, 1997). Ages 14–adult.

Rhodes-Courter, Ashley. **Three Little Words: A Memoir.** New York: Simon & Schuster Children's Publishing, Simon Pulse, 2009. 336p. $9.99pa. ISBN 1-4169-4807-4; 978-1-4169-4807-0.

This memoir by Rhodes-Courter, now in her early 20s, recounts her experiences while living in Florida's foster-care system. She was taken from her irresponsible mother and placed her in foster care when three years old. She then was placed in 13 different homes in nine years, experiencing abuse and neglect. Through the love and support of her last family, she was able to heal. "Teens will read this success story with great interest, and it will leave them feeling empowered. Ashley Rhodes-Courter, despite her difficult life, was always a good student, has graduated from college, and is quite a wonderful role model" (*Voice of Youth Advocates* June 1, 2008). Ages 12–18.

Rhodes-Courter, Ashley. **Three Little Words: A Memoir.** Ashland, OR: Blackstone Audio, 2008. CD. 30600 sec. $29.95. ISBN 1-4332-1430-X; 978-1-4332-1430-1.

Read by the author. Ages 12–18.

Sebestyen, Ouida. **Out of Nowhere.** New York: Scholastic, Orchard Books, 1994. 192p. $17.99. ISBN 0-531-08689-5; 978-0-531-08689-6.

Harley, 13, is left in the Arizona desert by his mother and her latest boyfriend. He joins four other cast-offs, including a pit bull, to form their own version of a family. This thoughtful book will have appeal to young people who feel abandoned by their parents. "Sebestyen redeems this too tidily balanced cast and too tidily contrived plot with lively dialogue, liberally laced with ironic wit. The keen depiction of Harley's obstinacy and need, and a wonderful dinner conversation in which Singer explains her views on vegetarianism and death, are ample payment for any problem of credulity" (*Booklist* n.d.). Ages 11–16.

Sweeney, Joyce. **The Guardian.** New York: Henry Holt Books for Young Readers, 2009. 192p. $16.99. ISBN 0-8050-8019-8; 978-0-8050-8019-3.

Hunter's mother gave him away when he was young, he has never known his father, his foster mother is abusive, and his foster father has died. He prays for help and believes that his prayers are answered by a guardian angel. "The peripheral characters are believable, and the religious undercurrent supports the plot. Well-paced, and with a satisfying conclusion, this book will appeal to reluctant readers and fans of contemporary realistic fiction" (*School Library Journal* June 1, 2009). Ages 13–18.

Wolfson, Jill. **What I Call Life.** New York: Square Fish, 2008. 288p. $6.99pa. ISBN 0-312-37752-5; 978-0-312-37752-6.

After her mother has a breakdown in the public library, 11-year-old Cal Lavender is taken to live in a group home that houses girls from troubled families. Cal knows she doesn't belong there at Pumpkin House, but all of the girls have much more in common than she could have imagined. "Wolfson paints her characters with delightful authenticity. Her debut novel is a treasure of quiet good humor and skillful storytelling that conveys subtle messages about kindness, compassion, and the gift of family regardless of its configuration" (*Booklist* Nov. 1, 2005). Ages 10–14.

Wolfson, Jill. **What I Call Life.** Syracuse, NY: Full Cast Audio, 2006. 6 CDs. 6 hrs. 30 min. $45.00. ISBN 1-933322-71-3; 978-1-933322-71-1. Solon, OH: Findaway World, 2007. Digital audio. $44.99. ISBN 1-59895-953-0; 978-1-59895-953-6.

"The Full Cast Family provides a splendid performance. Vaudeville style piano music punctuates the beginning and end of chapters" (*School Library Journal* Feb. 1, 2007). Ages 10–14.

Grieving (General)

Cooney, Caroline B. **Driver's Ed.** New York: Random House Children's Books, Dell Books for Young Readers, 1995. 208p. $5.99pa. ISBN 0-440-91078-1; 978-0-440-91078-7.

> Remy and Morgan, students in a high-school driver's education class, remove a street stop sign as a prank, and a young mother is killed in a car crash caused by the missing sign. The teenagers must cope with their guilt while their romance begins to unfold. "Cooney slips back and forth from Remy to Morgan, to give readers a glimpse of the different ways the teenagers handle their nightmarish burden and their families'—especially their mothers'—reactions. A poignant, realistic novel, with nicely drawn characters and a vintage metaphor that's actually refreshing: a driver's license (not first sex) is the 'ticket out of childhood'" (*Booklist* June 1, 1994). Ages 12–18.

Downham, Jenny. **Before I Die.** Waterville, ME: Thorndike Press, 2008. 409p. $23.95. ISBN 1-4104-0776-4; 978-1-4104-0776-4. New York: Random House Children's Books, David Fickling Books, 2009. 336p. $9.99pa. ISBN 0-385-75183-4; 978-0-385-75183-4. Tessa, 16 years old, has a few months to live, and she compiles a "To Do Before I Die" list. Number one is sex, and other items include drugs, breaking the law, driving, bringing her parents back together, fame, and being in love with her neighbor, Adam. "The issue of dealing with a serious illness and how it affects everyone involved, from family and friends to visiting nurses, is deftly handled and rings true. Unfortunately, much of the rest of the story does not feel as authentic, including the romance between Tessa and her neighbor, Adam, which does not begin evolving until more than halfway through the book and seems like an unnecessary afterthought" (*School Library Journal* Nov. 1, 2007). Ages 14–18.

Downham, Jenny. **Before I Die.** New York: Random House Audio Publishing Group, Listening Library, 2007. 6 CDs. 7 hrs. 10 min. $50.00. ISBN 0-7393-6290-9; 978-0-7393-6290-7.

> Narrated by Charlotte Porrus. Ages 14–18.

Fitzgerald, Helen. **The Grieving Teen: A Guide for Teenagers and Their Friends.** St. Louis, MO: San Val, Turtleback, 2000. 222p. $25.75. ISBN 1-4176-5497-X; 978-1-4176-5497-0.

> Fitzgerald addresses the needs of adolescents struggling with loss and provides the tools to help them work through their grief. Topics cover the range of situations in which teens may find themselves grieving a death, including old age, terminal illness, school violence, and suicide. "Fitzgerald, an expert in grief counseling and the author of *The Mourning Handbook*, communicates the issues clearly without oversimplifying or resorting to 'teenspeak.'...Fitzgerald provides many real-life experiences and a true sensitivity to differing religious and cultural practices" (*Library Journal* Aug. 1, 2000). Ages 13–17.

Giddens, Sandra, and Owen Giddens. **Coping with Grieving and Loss.** Coping Series. New York: Rosen Publishing Group, 2003. 124p. $31.95. ISBN 0-8239-3758-5; 978-0-8239-3758-5. Rosen Publishing Group, 2009. E-book. 192p. $31.95. ISBN 1-4358-6813-7; 978-1-4358-6813-7.

> An explanation of loss, grief, and mourning is followed by in-depth discussions of the emotions one might expect to experience at a funeral and through the recovery process. Throughout the book are reflections by teens who have experienced loss and the grieving process. Included are self-assessment tools and strategies to enhance the healing process. Ages 11–16.

Halpin, Brendan. **Forever Changes.** New York: Farrar, Straus and Giroux, 2008. 192p. $26.95. ISBN 0-374-32436-0; 978-0-374-32436-0.

> Brianna Pelletier, a mathematically gifted high school senior, has cystic fibrosis and contemplates her mortality and the unfairness of life. "A welcome touch of humor is provided in scenes with supportive friends and a geeky classmate who blossoms with Brianna's encouragement. The plot and pacing falter midway, and many of the secondary characters are one-dimensional, but Halpin's gift with dialogue and Brianna's strong voice propel this memorable inner journey to its moving, if inevitable, conclusion" (*Booklist* Oct. 15, 2008). Ages 14–18.

Hesse, Karen. **Phoenix Rising.** New York: Square Fish, 2009. 208p. $6.99pa. ISBN 0-312-53562-7; 978-0-312-53562-9.

> Following a catastrophic nuclear plant accident in rural Vermont, Nyle Sumner and her grandmother take into their home two evacuees, 15-year-old Ezra and his mother, from the area near the power plant. Nyle slowly allows herself to befriend Ezra, who is suffering from radiation sickness. "Hesse introduces important issues—environmental disaster, friendship, first love, loss, and death—in a novel that is reasonably accessible; however, the book will require effort from its intended audience, as its focus is on character growth and development, and the plot moves rather slowly" (*Booklist* May 15, 1994). Ages 10–14.

Miller, Allen R. **Living with Depression.** Teen's Guides Series. New York: Facts On File, 2007. 202p. $34.95. ISBN 0-8160-6345-1; 978-0-8160-6345-1. Facts On File, Checkmark Books, 2008. 208p. $14.95pa. ISBN 0-8160-7562-X; 978-0-8160-7562-1.

> Miller, a licensed psychologist, addresses such topics as the difference between depression and the blues, bipolar disorder, psychotherapy, antidepressants, and such self-help remedies as diet, exercise, and stress management. "*Living with Depression* is a straightforward book and a comprehensive and up-to-date resource on depression. Written in a clear and uncomplicated style, the book uses short case histories to define depression, its causes, and how it relates to other problems like bipolar, anxiety, and eating disorders" (*Voice of Youth Advocates* Apr. 1, 2008). Ages 12–18.

Myers, Edward. **When Will I Stop Hurting? Teens, Loss, and Grief.** Lanham, MD: Scarecrow Press, 2006. 176p. $14.95pa. ISBN 0-8108-5758-8; 978-0-8108-5758-2.

> A self-help guide for teenagers who are struggling with bereavement and associated emotional difficulties. It provides an overview of grief as a painful but normal process and offers insight from bereavement experts and practical suggestions for coping with loss, including personal accounts from teens. "Encouragement is offered, reminding readers that most people who have experienced such a loss will recover. However, the author also acknowledges that grief can lead to depression and thoughts of suicide and offers checklists outlining warning signs" (*School Library Journal* Nov. 1, 2004). Ages 13–18.

Peacock, Carol Antoinette. **Death and Dying.** Life Balance Series. Danbury, CT: Scholastic Library Publishing, Franklin Watts, 2005. 80p. $6.95. ISBN 0-531-16728-3; 978-0-531-16728-1.

> Child psychologist Peacock describes simple, specific actions that help to ease the pain of grieving. Chapters focus on ways to express grief, develop support, and commemorate the deceased. Other topics include religious and cultural death rituals. Ages 10–13.

Ryan, P. E. **Saints of Augustine.** New York: HarperCollins, HarperTeen, 2007. 308p. $16.99. ISBN 0-06-085810-9; 978-0-06-085810-0. HarperCollins, HarperTeen, 2008. 336p. $8.99pa. ISBN 0-06-085812-5; 978-0-06-085812-4. HarperCollins E-books, 2009. E-book. $9.99. ISBN 0-06-176746-8; 978-0-06-176746-3.

Set in St. Augustine, Florida, former best friends Charlie Perrin and Sam Findley, both 16, realize that their friendship is the only thing that will keep them afloat when each of their worlds is turned upside down through death, divorce, and other events that make their lives seem out of control. The story unfolds in alternating chapters that gradually expose each character's growing set of problems. "Although Ryan relies on third-person narration, each chapter provides Charlie's and Sam's alternating perspectives on their own stories.... Narrative focalizations aside, it is not the type of novel that screams boys' book; however, it will find readers among those who enjoy the more masculine fiction of authors such as Chris Crutcher, Randy Powell, and Ron Koertge" (*Voice of Youth Advocates* Oct. 1, 2007). Ages 14–18.

Schleifer, Jay. **Everything You Need to Know When Someone You Know Has Been Killed.** The Need to Know Library: Invaluable Knowledge. New York: Rosen Publishing Group, 1998. 64p. $29.25. ISBN 0-8239-2779-2; 978-0-8239-2779-1. Out of print.

Discusses death and the fear of death, explains the emotions experienced when someone you know is killed, describes the grieving process, and gives strategies for coping with the emotions associated with grieving. "For students seeking help for themselves or others, this resource offers a valuable first step toward identifying emotional reactions to untimely death and taking action to begin healing" (*Booklist* Oct. 1, 1998). Ages 11–18.

Winters, Paul A., ed. **Death and Dying.** Opposing Viewpoints Series. Farmington Hills, MI: Cengage Gale, Greenhaven Press, 1997. 192p. $21.20pa. ISBN 1-56510-670-9; 978-1-56510-670-3.

This anthology of articles provides differing viewpoints on such topics as the treatment of terminally ill patients, the right to die, coping with death, and whether there is life after death. Survivors' methods of grieving also are examined. Ages 14–18.

Suicide

Because suicide carries social outcast, this section includes fiction and nonfiction resources on teen suicide and parent suicide, as well as depression.

Adoff, Jaime. **The Death of Jayson Porter.** New York: Hyperion Books for Children, Jump at the Sun, 2009. 272p. $7.99pa. ISBN 1-4231-0692-X; 978-1-4231-0692-0.

For 16-year-old Jayson Porter the harsh realities of his life in the inland-Florida projects with his abusive mother never seem to change. He is biracial and tries unsuccessfully to fit in at his predominately white school, while struggling to maintain a relationship with his drug-addicted father. These pressures drive Jayson to attempt suicide. "Boys will find this book to be true and gripping, but it also needs to be read by others, including youth librarians looking for insight as well as excellent writing. It is a natural for discussion groups, but its powerful authenticity needs no intermediary to speak directly to the Jaysons of our time and their friends" (*Voice of Youth Advocates* Feb. 1, 2008). "Adoff writes candidly, with carefully chosen details carrying a wealth of insight, in a style approaching free verse that draws out the complexities of Jayson's character as he deals with sexuality, self-esteem, and identity. The ending is a bit too tidy, but Jayson is a vivid, dynamic character who will get under readers' skin" (*School Library Journal* Mar. 1, 2008). Ages 13–18.

Asher, Jay. **Thirteen Reasons Why.** New York: Penguin Group, Razorbill, 2007. 304p. $16.99. ISBN 1-59514-171-5; 978-1-59514-171-2. New York: Random House Audio Publishing Group, 2008. E-book. $38.25. ISBN 0-7393-6123-6; 978-0-7393-6123-8.

Clay Jenkins returns home from school to find a box with 13 cassette tapes recorded by classmate Hannah Baker, who committed suicide two weeks earlier. On the tapes, Hannah explains that there are 13 reasons she decided to end her life, and Clay is one of them. "Most of the novel quite literally takes place in Clay's head, as he listens to Hannah's voice pounding in his ears through his headphones, creating a very intimate feel for the reader as Hannah explains herself.... Asher has created an entrancing character study and a riveting look into the psyche of someone who would make this unfortunate choice" (*Kirkus Reviews* Sept. 1, 2007). "Short sentences make it a quick, smooth read, yet there is depth to the novel. This provocative tale touches on universal topics of interest, is genuine in its message, and would be a good choice for high school book discussions and booktalks" (*Voice of Youth Advocates* Feb. 1, 2008). Ages 14–18.

Berne, Emma Carlson, ed. **Depression.** Contemporary Issues Companion Series. Farmington Hills, MI: Cengage Gale, Greenhaven Press, 2007. 184p. $38.50pa.

An update of the 1998 edition, this volume includes chapters on such diverse topics as deep brain stimulation, alternative therapies, and antidepressants. "Thoughtfully composed, this excellent introduction to a widely recognized condition contains an extensive bibliography and support organization contact list" (*Library Journal* Dec. 1, 2007). Ages 14–adult.

Cobain, Bev. **When Nothing Matters Anymore: A Survival Guide for Depressed Teens.** Minneapolis, MN: Free Spirit Publishing, 1998. 176p. $13.95pa. ISBN 1-57542-036-8; 978-1-57542-036-3.

The author is a psychiatric nurse who works with teens and is the cousin of rock star Kurt Cobain, who took his life in 1994. "Written for teenagers with depression, as well as those who feel despondent, dejected or alone, this book offers help and information about depression and how to cope.... This positive, reassuring book should be available to all teens" (*Voice of Youth Advocates* Feb. 1, 1999). Ages 13–18.

Connors, Paul, ed. **Suicide.** Current Controversies Series. Farmington Hills, MI: Cengage Gale, Greenhaven Press, 2007. 236p. $26.75. ISBN 0-7377-2489-7; 978-0-7377-2489-9.

Includes essays and articles that present the moral, economic, political, racial, and religious dimensions of suicide. Included is a debate on whether physicians should assist terminally ill patients who wish to end their lives. A concluding chapter outlines suicide prevention. "Readers struggling with suicidal thoughts will find more direct help in books such as *Living with Depression* (2007), in the Teen's Guides series, but debaters and researchers will appreciate this title's diverse collection of primary sources, as well as the entries' concise introductions and the appended bibliography and directory of organizations" (*Booklist* Jan. 1, 2008). Ages 13–18.

Dolce, Laura. **Suicide.** Encyclopedia of Health Series. New York: Facts On File, Chelsea House, 1992. 116p. $19.95. ISBN 0-7910-0053-2; 978-0-7910-0053-3.

Discusses the social, psychological, medical, and historical facets of suicide, describing warning signs, risk factors, prevention, and other aspects. Authors are leading medical and science journalists

Ford, Michael Thomas. **Suicide Notes.** New York: HarperCollins, HarperTeen, 2008. 295p. $17.89. ISBN 0-06-073756-5; 978-0-06-073756-6.

> After 15-year-old Jeff wakes up in a hospital psychiatric ward, he won't talk about why he slit his wrists. He is convinced that he is normal and that his parents are fine; he shouldn't be in the hospital with the other teens who have problems. "Long before Jeff confronts the truth, readers will realize that he is gay, and his denial is part of the humor and sadness many readers will recognize" (*Booklist* Oct. 1, 2008). Ages 14–18.

Galas, Judith C., and Richard E. Nelson. **The Power to Prevent Suicide: A Guide for Teens Helping Teens.** Minneapolis, MN: Free Spirit Publishing, 2006. 128p. $13.95pa. ISBN 1-57542-206-9; 978-1-57542-206-0.

> Gives teens the information and insight they need to recognize the risk of suicide and how to respond appropriately. It describes the warning signs, guides teens through the steps of reaching out to a friend, and explains when and how to seek help. It also suggests ways for teens to help themselves when they're feeling stressed or depressed. "The power of this resource is in its presentation of the information. Chapters offer specific questions that teens can ask their friends to draw them out" (*Voice of Youth Advocates* June 1, 2007). Ages 12–18.

Going, K. L. **Fat Kid Rules the World.** New York: Penguin Group, Dial, 2004. 224p. $17.99. ISBN 0-8037-2948-0; 978-0-8037-2948-3. New York: Putnam Juvenile, 2004. 192p. $6.99pa. ISBN 978-0-1424-0208-5

> Troy Billings is overweight, depressed, and considering suicide. He has been killing his time by getting high—trying to avoid thinking about his family life. As Troy considers whether to end his life on a subway track, punk rocker Curt MacCrae comes along and stops him. "This book gives readers a wild ride through the mind and heart of a seventeen-year-old who contemplates suicide by imagining what his fat would look like splattered by a subway train. Going's edgy and realistic characterization of Troy and Curt will resonate with readers who themselves are struggling with image, depression, and drug abuse issues" (*Voice of Youth Advocates* June 1, 2003). "The strong language and themes make this a raw, yet immensely likable tale for older teens" (*Kirkus Reviews* May 1, 2003). Ages 15–18.

Hopkins, Ellen. **Impulse.** New York: Simon & Schuster Children's Publishing, Margaret K. McElderry, 2007. 672p. $16.99. ISBN 1-4169-0356-9; 978-1-4169-0356-7. Simon & Schuster Children's Publishing, Simon Pulse, 2008. 688p. $9.99pa. ISBN 1-4169-0357-7; 978-1-4169-0357-4.

> Three teens tell their stories in free verse from a psychiatric hospital after each has attempted suicide. Their stories are told in alternating chapters, revealing their family and peer relationships. "It is also difficult to get a real sense of each teen's character beyond his or her life circumstances, because the narrative voice varies little from one teen to another. Nevertheless readers seeking an understanding of teen suicide will surely appreciate this penetrating exploration of the topic" (*Voice of Youth Advocates* Feb. 1, 2007). "Mature fans of the verse format will devour this hefty problem novel" (*School Library Journal* Feb. 1, 2007). Ages 14–18.

Marcovitz, Hal. **Suicide.** Essential Issues Series. Edina, MN: ABDO, Essential Library, 2010. 112p. $34.22. ISBN 1-60453-958-5; 978-1-60453-958-5.

> Examines the historical background, the causes of suicide, and mental disorders. "These excellent editions combine facts and personal stories that will be of great assistance to students writing reports" (*School Library Journal* April 1, 2010). Ages 11–18.

Marcovitz, Hal. **Teens and Suicide.** Broomall, PA: Mason Crest Publishers, 2004. The Gallup Youth Survey, Major Issues and Trends Series. 112p. $22.95. ISBN 1-59084-724-5; 978-1-59084-724-4. Includes relevant statistical information, stories, and reports collected by the Gallup Youth Survey, an arm of the Gallup Organization, over the past four decades. Ages 12–15.

Maynard, Joyce. **The Cloud Chamber.** New York: Simon & Schuster Children's Publishing, Atheneum, 2005. 288p. $16.95. ISBN 0-689-87152-X; 978-0-689-87152-8.

After his father attempts suicide, 14-year-old Nate finds that he and his family have been ostracized by their small Montana community. Nate responds by entering a science fair and building a cloud chamber. "Although the story is set in rural Montana in the 1960s, it illuminates how social stigmatization, parental abuse, and suicide have universal and timeless ramifications. Maynard underscores that parents who keep their children uninformed during family crises only compound their misery" (*Voice of Youth Advocates* Feb. 1, 2006). Ages 12–16.

Maynard, Joyce. **The Cloud Chamber.** New York: Random House Audio, Books on Tape, 2005. 5 CDs. 5 hrs. 39min. ISBN 0-307-24618-3; 978-0-307-24618-9.

"Joel Johnstone's narration makes listeners hear and feel the pain, anguish, fear, and hope in the voices and hearts of the characters. Even secondary characters are brought vividly to life through Johnstone's reading of this powerful and emotionally charged coming-of-age story" (*School Library Journal* Oct. 1, 2005). Ages 12–16.

Miller, Mary Beth. **Aimee.** Logan, IA: Perfection Learning, 2004. 276p. $14.65. ISBN 0-7569-6303-6; 978-0-7569-6303-3.

Aimee committed suicide and everyone believes that her best friend Zoe helped her. Stricken by loneliness, guilt, and anger, Zoe writes in her journal and comes to realize no one could have helped Aimee, but Zoe can help herself. "A late revealing of the name of the narrator is symbolic of the healing that is beginning and indicates that all has finally been told. A fascinating character study that will intrigue readers wanting to go beyond sensationalistic headlines" (*Kirkus Reviews* May 1, 2002). Ages 14–18.

Moragne, Wendy. **Depression.** Medical Library Series. Minneapolis, MN: Lerner, Twenty-First Century Books, 2001. 112p. $33.26. ISBN 0-7613-1774-0; 978-0-7613-1774-6.

Using case histories to illustrate common forms of depression, this book covers causes, symptoms, diagnosis, treatment, and dealing with depression within a family. "Difficult medical information that might have been dull or oversimplified is presented clearly and without condescension. The chapter on depression and suicide is particularly well done" (*Booklist* May 15, 2001). Ages 12–18.

Murphy, James M. **Coping with Teen Suicide.** Coping Series: Health and Well-Being. New York: Rosen Publishing Group, 1999. 192p. $31.95. ISBN 0-8239-2824-1; 978-0-8239-2824-8. Out of print.

A psychotherapist and ordained minister, Murphy explains the causes and consequences of suicide and suggests ways of dealing with problems, preventing suicide, and coping with the suicide of a loved one. Stressful situations cited for giving rise to suicidal thinking include gender identity issues, romantic relationships, violence, ethnic differences, family issues, and abuse. "The author's style is intelligent and sympathetic. He attempts to build on the positive aspects present in every life, but he is neither dogmatic nor unrealistic" (*Library Journal* Dec. 1, 1999). Ages 12–18.

Reber, Deborah. **Chill: Stress-Reducing Techniques for a More Balanced, Peaceful You.** New York: Simon & Schuster Children's Publishing, Simon Pulse, 2008. 208p. $9.99pa. ISBN 1-4169-6555-6; 978-1-4169-6555-8.

An advice columnist and author of other books for teens, Reber provides teens a practical guide for coping with everyday pressures. She explains methods of reducing stress and makes suggestions for ways of coping with anxiety. "The text is broken up with simple line drawings, almost exclusively of white girls. Nevertheless, this helpful resource will appeal to a wide variety of young women" (*School Library Journal* May 1, 2008). Ages 13–18.

Runyon, Brent. **The Burn Journals.** New York: Random House Children's Books, Knopf Books for Young Readers, 2004. 384p. $17.95. ISBN 0-375-82621-1; 978-0-375-82621-4.

Runyon recounts the true story of setting himself on fire when he was 14 years old. He describes the suicide attempt and his recovery over the following year. "Runyon's brave willingness to relive this horrifying year in unflinching detail is perhaps even more fascinating, as is the slowly unfolding mystery of the sadness that made a smart, popular, funny, loving boy try to take his own life. Depression, regret, and rebirth are the themes that tie the narrative together, and the subtle tension among the three are beautifully related, offering no neat resolution" (*School Library Journal* Nov. 1, 2004). "Some excruciatingly painful moments notwithstanding, this can and should be read by young adults, as much for its literary merit as for its authentic perspective on what it means to attempt suicide, and, despite the resulting scars, be unable to remember why" (*Booklist* June 1, 2004). Ages 14–18.

Runyon, Brent. **The Burn Journals.** Prince Frederick, MD: Recorded Books, 2008. 7 CDs. 8 hrs. ISBN 1-4361-3876-0; 978-1-4361-3876-5.

"Christopher Evan Welch perfectly captures the naive, self-absorbed, ignorant, and angry facets of the teenager's character extremely well. Listeners alternately cringe with impatience at Runyon's thoughtlessness, empathize with his desire to please his parents and carve out a place for himself among his peers, and think about the physical and emotional pain he suffers during his long recuperation" (*School Library Journal* Jan. 1, 2009). Ages 14–18.

Scowen, Kate. **My Kind of Sad: What It's Like to Be Young and Depressed.** Toronto, ON: Annick Press, 2006. 168p. $19.95. ISBN 1-55037-941-0; 978-1-55037-941-9. $12.95pa. ISBN 1-55037-940-2; 978-1-55037-940-2.

Explores youth-specific mental health issues and offers teens expert advice on how to find help for themselves or to help a friend in need. Topics include active depression, bipolar disorder, anxiety disorders, eating disorders, self-mutilation, suicide, and treatment options. Guidance from professionals is provided along with thoughts and feelings from teens who have experienced different forms of depression. "Throughout Scowen encourages readers to pay attention to depression's warning signs. Teens won't find a quick fix here, just realistic advice—especially about seeking help" (*Booklist* Sept. 15, 2006). Ages 13–18.

Trueman, Terry. **No Right Turn.** New York: HarperCollins, HarperTeen, 2009. 176p. $8.99pa. ISBN 0-06-057493-3; 978-0-06-057493-2.

Three years after his father's suicide death, 16-year-old Jordan still cannot talk about it. When his mother starts dating a man with a Corvette, he becomes obsessed with the car and takes it for joyrides without permission. Jordan becomes enmeshed in a tangle of lies about the car but eventually is able to confront his grief and anger. "Trueman creates an affecting portrait of a teen confronting submerged pain, with Jordan's pared-down, first-person voice perhaps most authentic in his raging, private moments. Even teens who skim over the car talk will be caught by the tragic story and the reckless escapism that brings danger, hurt, and healing" (*Booklist* Feb. 1, 2006). Ages 14–18.

Vaught, Susan. **Trigger.** New York: Bloomsbury, 2007. 320p. $8.95pa. ISBN 1-59990-230-3; 978-1-59990-230-2.

A failed attempt at suicide by shooting himself in the head leaves 17-year-old Jersey Hatch with permanent neurological damage. He attempts to piece his life back together again but encounters obstacles posed by parents, teachers, and classmates. "Vaught nails Jersey's uncontrollable blurting of words looping inside his brain with remarkable sections of dialogue. But the strength of the work is allowing readers to experience the pain, anguish, and anger that Jersey's parents, friends and teachers undergo when contacting the broken shell of a once selfish and arrogant teen" (*Voice of Youth Advocates* Oct. 1, 2006). Ages 14–18.

SOURCES CONSULTED

Baxter, Grant, and Wendy Stuart. 1999. *Death and the adolescent: A resource handbook for bereavement support groups in schools.* Toronto: University of Toronto Press.

Corr, Charles A. 2000. What we know about grieving children and adolescents. In *Living with grief: Children, adolescents, and loss,* ed. Kenneth J. Doka, 21–32. Washington, DC: Hospice Foundation of America.

Doka, Kenneth J., ed. 2000. *Living with grief: Children, adolescents, and loss.* Washington, DC: Hospice Foundation of America.

Doka, Kenneth J. 2000. Using ritual with children and adolescents. In *Living with grief: Children, adolescents, and loss,* ed. Kenneth J. Doka, 153–59.Washington, DC: Hospice Foundation of America.

Doka, Kenneth J., ed. 2002. *Disenfranchised grief: New directions, challenges, and strategies for practice.* Champaign, IL: Research Press.

Fiorini, Jody J., and Jodi Ann Mullen. 2006. *Counseling children and adolescents through grief and loss.* Champaign, IL: Research Press.

Fry, Virginia Lynn. 2000. Part of me died too: Creative strategies for grieving children and adolescents. In *Living with grief: Children, adolescents, and loss,* ed. Kenneth J. Doka, 125–37. Washington, DC: Hospice Foundation of America.

Hooyman, Nancy R., and Betty J. Kramer. 2006. *Living through loss: Interventions across the life span.* New York: Columbia University Press.

James, John W., and Russell Friedman. 2001. *When children grieve.* New York: HarperCollins.

Rowling, Louise. 2002. Youth and disenfranchised grief. In *Disenfranchised grief: New directions, challenges, and strategies for practice,* ed. Kenneth J. Doka, 275–92. Champaign, IL: Research Press.

Silverman, Phyllis R. 2000. When parents die. In *Living with grief: Children, adolescents, and loss,* ed. Kenneth J. Doka, 215–28. Washington, DC: Hospice Foundation of America.

5

LOSS OF A CHILD

CHAPTER OVERVIEW

Beginning with a personal account to frame the trauma that accompanies loss of a child, we discuss the causes of prenatal and infant deaths and the psychological trauma that accompanies the loss of a child, no matter the age. The discussions of psychological effects of a child's death on siblings and other family members are followed by suggestions for parents and service providers so that they can effectively assist grieving youth. A number of books, recordings, and websites are recommended as resources.

A PERSONAL ACCOUNT

While this chapter began as an academic exercise for me, it soon became very personal. While reading the introduction to *Still to be Born* (Schwiebert and Kirk n.d., 9), I read the following:

> Most people find that it takes no more than from forty-eight hours to two weeks to get their lives back to normal routine after suffering the death of a close friend or relative not in the immediate nuclear family.
>
> For bereaved parents, however, the readjustment of one's life following a loss of a child takes approximately eighteen to twenty-four months. This does not mean that after twenty-four months the death is forgotten; it simply means that this much time is needed to come to terms with the loss.

Suddenly I was jarred with the memory—forty years ago—of my child's prenatal death. Indeed, the grieving lasted long after my wife and I returned to our daily routines. While we never met this child, who was pronounced dead by our obstetrician during the sixth month of her prenatal existence, she was a real person to us. We had shared our good news with relatives and friends, we were preparing a nursery in our home, and we were contemplating names for our daughter.

During a routine monthly examination by our obstetrician, he pronounced our baby was dead. This was shocking to us. I remember vividly the deep sorrow I immediately felt, and I recall sitting, stunned, in the car with my wife, trying to make sense of what was happening. Our dreams were suddenly dashed, and we were in disbelief—shock.

After several minutes, we drove home silently. My wife would continue carrying the fetus until the doctor performed a Caesarian Section a month later. During that time we elected to continue a charade that the pregnancy was normal—something that I would *not* recommend. We forced ourselves to live a lie for the weeks when only we knew the true story.

I also believe that we made another mistake. When the baby was born, we did not name her. Experts purport that the stillborn child should be treated as if she were born alive and lived for a time; she should be named and given a funeral. We did neither, and the adjustment to our loss undoubtedly was postponed. We did not grieve adequately. The baby rests, unnamed, in a cemetery plot near my wife, who died three years later from the diabetes that was a major contributor to the death of our baby.

What should we have done? An analysis of the effects of a child's death is provided here, along with the impact on a family.

WHY CHILDREN DIE

The death of a child is shocking to parents and family members. It is unnatural—against the expectations of adults in a society that has cures for many diseases and the technological advancement to repair or replace vital organs and limbs. It is also in opposition to laws of nature; parents are expected to outlive their children. The death of a child reverses our expectations and upsets our notions of the way the world should be.

Although the mortality rate for infants and children is relatively low especially in comparison to developing countries and to trends from this country's early years, children still die. Infants less than one year old die primarily from congenital problems, sudden infant death syndrome (SIDS), respiratory distress syndrome, disorders related to a short gestation period, pregnancy complications, and accidents. For children ages 1 to 14, the principal causes of death are accidents, cancer, congenital health problems, homicide, and legal intervention (killing by law enforcement), heart disease, pneumonia, and flu. Young people age 15–24 typically die of motor vehicle accidents, homicide, suicide, cancer, heart disease, and HIV infection (Rosof 1995, 43–44).

PSYCHOLOGICAL EFFECTS ON PARENTS

The death of a child is a catastrophe like no others, robbing parents of children with whom they have bonds of love, isolating parents from each other, and distracting them from their other children. Grieving for a dead child lasts longer and hits harder than can be imagined.

As parents struggle through the first year following a loss, the mourning consumes most of their energy. Little is left for the spouse, the other children, or

oneself. The bond of love between parent and child is the most powerful in human relationships. Rosof identifies five reasons for this bond:

1. Children invite parents' love and return it richly. From infancy, children are
   helpless and have an intense need for interaction. From this dependence and
   uncompromising love, the bond grows.
2. Children carry the hopes that are precious to the parents. Children embody
   valued parts of the parents' identity. Children give us a second chance to "set
   right what went wrong in our own childhood" (Rosof 1995, 8).
3. A child is created in the mind of the parent. While a child is a separate person, parents create a child in their minds that is a part of them. This process
   begins before the child is born, and a child becomes an intimate part of
   the parents' self-image. This image evolves through real interactions with
   the child.
4. A child gives the parent a job and an identity. During the first six years of a
   child's life, the parent has a big job requiring enormous investments of time
   and energy. Through this investment, parents grow to become more patient,
   kind, and empathetic, altering how the parents perceive themselves.
5. From the day of a child's birth, parents commit to protecting her. Without
   this protection, no child can survive, and the parents' commitment guaran-
   tees the child's survival (Rosof 1995, 6–13).

Because of this strong bond, a child's death means the beginning of a number
of losses: (1) loss of a piece of oneself; (2) loss of illusions that we can protect children, that bad things happen to other people, and that this is a safe neighborhood;
(3) loss of order—parents die before their children; and (4) loss of the future, watch-
ing the child's life unfold and their company in the years ahead (Rosof 1995).

As with any type of grief, the first reactions are shock, numbing, and denial. Like
shock, numbness is a response to a situation too painful to deal with. In this state,
a person feels in a fog, doing what needs to be done, with no connection to feelings. As the shock fades, a person starts to absorb the facts, and it still may be too
much. Denial says that this cannot be true. There has been a mistake. Although it
is irrational, denial temporarily delays the pain of the loss.

When shock, numbness, and denial are gone, acute grief remains. As a result, the
grieving parent experiences changes in perception, concentration, and memory. It
is impossible to concentrate.

Another result of acute grief is increased dependence. Ordinary routines don't
seem possible because the bereaved parent lacks the concentration and energy.
During acute grief a parent experiences physical symptoms—trouble falling asleep,
tiredness when sleep does come, lack of strength and energy, chronic fatigue, restlessness, and all-over aching.

> Your whole body misses your child, aches with your sadness. You may have
> a generalized, all-over aching or a localized pain. Grief seems to lodge in the
> chest and the gut: a strong, dull ache like an iron band around your chest or
> a hollow pain in your stomach. (Rosof 1995, 68–69)

Guilt and self-blame dominate the thoughts of parents, thinking about the things
they did and did not do in the days and weeks before the child's death. Miles and

Demi (1984, 1986) proposed a typology of six sources of guilt for parents who have suffered the loss of a child:

1. Death causation—the belief that the parent contributed to the death of the child or failed to protect it.
2. Illness related—failure in the parent's role during the child's illness or at the time of death.
3. Parents' role—belief that the parent failed in her/his role as a parent.
4. Moral guilt—the child's death was caused as punishment for the parent's immoral or unethical conduct.
5. Survival guilt—violation of the standard that children should survive their parents.
6. Grief guilt—reaction to grief following the child's death.

In addition, anger can erupt unexpectedly and sometimes at people who are helping the parent, who wants to be left alone. "Your feelings puzzle you, scare you, make you wonder if you're losing your mind. You are not. You are so spent, so depleted, that you have nothing left, even for friendship" (Rosof 1995, 70).

MAKING DECISIONS AFTER THE DEATH OF A CHILD

A parent is disabled psychologically after a child's death, yet decisions are called for. What kind of funeral is best? When? Where? How will people be informed? What should be done with the child's clothes and other possessions?

Rosof recommends a triage system of four Ds: delegate, defer, decline, and decide:

- What things can be delegated to others?
- Can something be deferred to a later time?
- Are there requests that can be declined?
- What things do you want to decide or that you must decide? (Rosof 1995, 71)

EFFECT ON SURVIVING CHILDREN

In some ways, children's grief can mirror their parents', with one key difference. Children can take a break from grieving, and parents may believe that this necessary respite from sadness is an indication that the children are not feeling the pain of their loss. Parents can benefit their children by articulating their grieving and listening to their children's grief. It is important for parents and children to keep an open line of communication during such crises.

"Initially, surviving children are more frightened by their parents' reactions and by the events of the moment than by the fact that the baby has died" (Corr et al. 1991, 89). If the child was not present when the dead child was found and was told about it, the reaction may be puzzling to adults because young children do not understand the concept of death. Consequently, the child may react without any outward sign of sadness, confusing the parents. Children's questions about a sudden infant death syndrome death may continue for months or years following the death.

PRENATAL DEATHS

In 2005, the U.S. fetal mortality rate was 6.22 fetal deaths of 20 weeks gestation or more per 1,000 live births and fetal deaths (MacDorman and Kirmeyer 2009). Although medical science has enhanced prenatal care, and the mortality rate of the United States and developed countries is much lower that a century ago, the mortality rate for fetuses and babies is significant and provides parents with trauma that stays with them through life. Mothers especially are bonded to their babies before birth. A social worker describes the devastation felt by parents of a pregnancy loss:

> Parents feel cheated out of a wondrous, natural experience that was to be theirs. Suddenly their dreams are shattered and their hope for a family is lost or temporarily put on hold. Instead of going to baby showers and decorating rooms, they are planning funerals and putting baby items away. (Seigerman 2001, 90)

Abortion, too, usually causes grieving on the part of the woman, even though she had chosen this recourse. Even when parents believed an abortion was the right decision, they may feel shock they didn't expect and are filled with grief. Mentally and spiritually a woman may question her moral values after an abortion; most women have not grown up in a family or cultural system that supported abortion (Panuthos and Romeo 1984).

The fetus is very real to the mother and to the immediate family but much less so for friends and family outside the home. The mother can feel the child move, and she may let the father and children feel the baby move. If the baby dies before birth, the child has no bond with people outside the immediate family unit.

Unfortunately, family members and friends are reluctant to talk about a baby's death. Defrain and colleagues (1986, 2) studied 350 stillborn incidents and found that a "conspiracy of silence" pervaded the families experiencing a stillbirth. As a result, families reported drug and alcohol abuse, family violence, and marital discord. The research indicated that it took years for parents to recover from the death.

Sociologists Knapp and Peppers (1980) researched the grief reactions of women to perinatal losses and, as described in Panuthos and Romeo (1984), found that "women who miscarried demonstrated grief reactions equal in intensity to those of women grieving over fetal and infant death and different only in duration" (18).

Miscarriage may create feelings of shame and failure. It can increase marital conflict after the miscarriage. Mothers tend to grieve loss of a prenatal child more than fathers, who have not known the child. Consequently, women often mourn a miscarriage alone, without a funeral, without condolences, and with little compassion expressed for her loss (Panuthos and Romeo 1984).

Ilse, a national consultant on pregnancy loss and founder of the Pregnancy and Infant Loss Center, urges parents who have experienced a stillbirth to reach out for help:

> Don't try to do this alone or only with your partner. You need people now and they need to be included. This is what family and friends are for. Call upon them; ask them for things, as hard as that might be.... Don't try to protect them by doing everything yourself. (Ilse 1990, 18)

After the baby is born, Ilse (1990) recommends holding the baby to provide memories for the days and years ahead. Seeing and holding the baby can also help to adapt to the baby's death. Some families bring in baby clothes and dress it for viewing in the hospital. Others take it home to its nursery and take pictures. (Others prefer not to see the dead baby.) Naming the baby also is recognition of the baby's importance to the family. Ilse, who has had the experience, advises, "Do what you wish to do in your heart and don't worry what others will think" (Ilse 1990, 21).

A funeral service can be helpful for family and friends to share the sorrow of the parents and to provide support for them. A funeral service does not have to be held immediately after the birth; it can be scheduled so that the mother can attend.

While some pediatricians still believe it is harmful to the parents to show a dead baby, especially a deformed one, many mental health professionals and obstetricians are convinced that parents need to hold the baby and participate in a funeral service—bond with the child and experience closure as part of the grieving process.

Memories of the baby will remain with the parents. Ilse (1990, 65) describes the long-term effects of a prenatal or perinatal loss:

> Some of the pain might always be with you, as will the memory of your baby. Continually try to express your sadness, anger and other feelings and to fondly, warmly and lovingly remember your baby.

INFANT DEATHS

The U.S. infant mortality rate generally declined throughout the 20th century. In 1900, the U.S. infant mortality rate was approximately 100 infant deaths per 1,000 live births, while in 2005, the U.S. infant mortality rate was 6.86 infant deaths per 1,000 live births (MacDorman and Mathews 2008).

Among the many causes of neonatal death are premature birth, congenital abnormalities, brain damage caused by lack of oxygen, and sudden infant death syndrome (SIDS).

SIDS is defined as follows:

> the sudden and unexpected death of an infant who has seemed well, or almost well, and whose death remains unexplained after the performance of an adequate postmortem investigation including an autopsy, examination of the death scene, and review of the case history. (Corr et al. 1991, 3)

Also called crib death, SIDS is neither predictable nor preventable, and the first symptom is a dead infant. SIDS occurs in developing countries at approximately the same rate as in North America and Europe. Indeed, SIDS occurs everywhere in the world.

Death of an infant is a painful tragedy for all who are involved—parents, family members, and friends. Parents are overcome by confusion, guilt, and loss. Friends and family feel helpless in any efforts to assist. Children in the family may have questions about the baby who died and should have their questions answered. Open communication with children provides reassurance that the same thing is not likely to happen to them (Corr et al. 1991, 93).

DEATH OF OLDER CHILDREN

Children become ill; that's expected. Relating to their own childhood illnesses, parents anticipate the usual cuts, scrapes, and even some broken bones. Chicken pox, mumps, colds, and flu are typical illnesses that befall most children. Unexpected is the trauma that accompanies diagnosis of a serious illness like cancer, heart trouble, or failure of a major organ. While the critical illness may or may not result in the child's death, the parents and other family members experience the grief similar to that of a death. Shock and denial are often the early results. A sympathetic physician can counsel the family through such crises.

Knapp (1986, 29–41) interviewed parents from 150 primarily white, middle-class families who had experienced the death of a child from a variety of deaths—illness, accident, suicide, and murder. Ages of children ranged from 1 to 28 years. Knapp listed six common characteristics from these interviews:

1. A need to remember always the child who was lost.
2. The death of an older child over the age of infancy, particularly after a sudden death, prompted parents to contemplate their own deaths.
3. A large proportion of the parents (70 %) turned to religion in searching for a reason to survive and to reassure themselves their loss was not in vain.
4. There was a shift from worldly values and worldly things to family goals as primary. For example, family took the place of jobs and career advancement as the primary value of fathers and mothers.
5. The bereaved parents became more tolerant and understanding of other people and their problems and suffering.
6. A majority of the parents in the study suffered from *shadow grief,* a type of chronic grief that can burden parents for most of their lives.

RECOVERY

A study by Defrain and colleagues (1986) showed how difficult recovery from loss of a child can be. Eventually, some parents were ready to volunteer to help others recover from their loss without reigniting their own sorrow. Defrain and colleagues suggested that the best form of counseling for parents experiencing loss is a union of professionals and volunteers. Professionals have the educational background and experience to counsel grieving parents, while volunteers have the gut-level understanding of the emotions and issues.

How long does acute grief from a child's death last? The answer depends on the length of time it requires to come to terms with the loss. This period is often six to eight weeks of acute grief for most losses, but loss of a child may require four to six months to work through the acute grief. The amount of time depends on the facts related to the child's death, the parents' relationship with the child, and prior losses experienced (Rosof 1995).

Understanding the recovery process is aided by an understanding of death as a collective experience. Our culture views death as an individual, rather than collective experience, as Shapiro (1994, 4) notes:

> In a culture that emphasizes the accomplishment of independence rather than connection and celebrates the myth of personal mastery over all adversity, the experience of grief, which exposes our deep attachments, our human

interdependence, and our true vulnerability in the hands of fate, is as unwelcome as death itself.

The tendency in American culture is to distance ourselves from death and to consider it a personal, individual experience. When death of a family member or close acquaintance occurs, we try to make sense of the death to maintain our feeling of control in our lives. As long as the death is not a close family member or friend, we can successfully maintain the distance necessary to believe that this disaster could not happen to us.

However, experience of death is *not* an individual experience. "Grief is at heart a family process, and it is within that process that the injury to an interdependent sense of self can best be understood—and healed" (Shapiro 1994,10). Shapiro (17–18) defines a systematic developmental framework for family bereavement as follows:

1. Grief is a family process interwoven with family history.
2. Grief interrupts family stability and causes the redefining of the family's identity as a group.
3. The first priority of a bereaved family is establishment of stability in order to support family development.
4. The process of shared family development is lifelong—a continuing process.
5. The greater the family's degree of stress, the greater the need to reestablish stability and restrict the change that is causing new stresses.
6. After a death, families continue integrating the reality of the death and its impact on the dynamics of the family.
7. Changing relationships within a family include transformations of relationship to the deceased.
8. The goal of family bereavement is to restore ongoing family development.

Shapiro's systemic approach to grieving explains the complexity of the process and the far-reaching nature of a child's death. This model suggests that the reconstruction of one's adult life and sense of self is a process that can take years. Consequently, the grieving process takes much longer than the layman's concept and popularly held belief that getting over the loss of a loved one—a child included—should take no more than a year. In addition to the element of time, Shapiro states that a supportive environment is needed to establish a revised sense of self.

That supportive environment should include participation in a support group. "We probably cannot overemphasize the benefits parents reap by joining a parent support group. Hearing others tell of their struggles coping with the death of a child can bring tremendous comfort to a parent. 'I am not alone' is the message" (Defrain et al. 1986, 197).

One reason that a support group is so important to parents who have lost a baby is the opportunity to talk. Death, especially death of a child, is very difficult to confront and to talk about.

IMPLICATIONS FOR SERVICE PROVIDERS

Because of the traumatic effect of a child's death on parents and family members, the best approach is to let individuals talk about their grief—if they wish. As noted above, family members and friends usually feel uncomfortable talking to parents about the death of their child, yet psychologists and social workers emphasize the need of parents to talk about their experience. Educators, mental health professionals, librarians, and other professionals who encounter grieving parents should recognize their grief and their need to talk through it. A heartfelt expression of condolence and opening the door to conversation can be very helpful to the parents.

Children who have lost a brother or sister may feel left out of the grieving because their parents are consumed by their grief and by all of the activities that a death requires. Siblings of a deceased child may be ignored by their parents because of the parents' grief. Simply talking with them, pulling them aside for a private conversation, can acknowledge the child's worth. Recommending books at an appropriate reading and comprehension level from chapter 3 can provide insight to a child.

Adults, too, may need an opportunity to tell their stories. Adult resources found here can be useful for adults seeking to know more about their feelings and remedies for recovery. Those education and library professionals not trained in therapy cannot offer therapy, nor should they feel obliged to try; however, we can offer grieving parents and children emotional support through our caring service in our field of expertise.

Because of the traumatic effect of a child's death on parents and family members, the best approach is to let the individuals talk about their grief—if they wish. Psychologists and social workers emphasize the need of parents to talk about their experience. Educators, mental health professionals, librarians, and other professionals who encounter grieving parents should recognize their grief and their need to talk through it.

SUMMARY

The death of a child is shocking to parents and family members. It is unnatural—against the expectations of adults because parents are expected to outlive their children. Death of a child reverses our expectations and upsets our notions of the way the world should be. The death of a child isolates parents from each other, and distracts them from their other children. Grieving for a dead child lasts longer and hits harder than can be imagined.

As with any type of grief, the first reactions are shock, numbing, and denial. Denial says that this cannot be true. Although it is irrational, denial temporarily delays the pain of the loss. As the shock fades, a person starts to absorb the facts, and it still may be too much.

Although medical science has enhanced prenatal care, the mortality rate for fetuses and babies is significant and provides parents with trauma that stays with them through life. The fetus is very real to the mother and to the immediate family but much less so for friends and family outside the home.

After the dead baby is born, seeing and holding the baby can help parents and immediate family members to adapt to the baby's death. Some families bring in baby clothes and dress it for viewing in the hospital. Others prefer not to see the dead baby. Parents should be guided by their feelings and should not be guided by others' expectations.

RECOMMENDED RESOURCES

Allen, Marie, and Shelly Marks. **Miscarriage: Women Sharing from the Heart.** Hoboken, NJ: Wiley, 1993. 272p. $18.95pa. ISBN 0-471-54834-0; 978-0-471-54834-8.

> The authors have experienced miscarriage and share their feelings, along with the personal stories of 100 women who relate their miscarriage experiences. Fathers also are interviewed. Advice is offered for partners, family members, and health care professionals. "Painfully moving anecdotes in the respondents' own words, combined with informed commentary, make this text a detailed and insightful guide to understanding just what a bereaved mother feels" (*Library Journal* Feb. 15, 1993).

Allende, Isabel. **Paula: A Memoir.** Trans. Margaret Sayers Peden. New York: HarperCollins, HarperPerennial, 2008. 368p. $14.99pa. ISBN 0-06-156490-7; 978-0-06-156490-1.

> Author Isabel Allende's daughter, Paula, was 28 years old in 1991 when she became gravely ill and fell into a coma. Allende then began to write her life story and family history for Paula. "Pointing out that until the 20th century, and even now in all but the most industrially advanced countries, losing a child was a common experience, she gives some insight into what it takes to bear that loss. Highly recommended" (*Library Journal* Apr. 1, 1995). "Allende has an exciting life story to tell, and while her beloved daughter was not to be the recipient, it is, nonetheless, a gift to the rest of us" (*Booklist* Mar. 15, 1995).

Bearison, David J. **When Treatment Fails: How Medicine Cares for Dying Children.** New York: Oxford University Press, 2006. 312p. $34.99. ISBN 0-19-515612-9; 978-0-19-515612-6.

> A pediatric psychologist, Bearison examines the care provided to dying children by the medical staff of a large, urban, pediatric hospital. His study is based on results of interviews with medical students, physicians, and nurses concerning care provided for 20 dying children. The results provide insight for medical, mental health, and education professionals in contact with dying children.

Beattie, Melody. **The Lessons of Love: Rediscovering Our Passion for Life When It All Seems Too Hard to Take.** New York: HarperSanFrancisco, 1994. 225p. ISBN 0-06-251072-X; 0-06-251078-9pa.

> The author of *Codependent No More* and other self-help books relates the death of her 12-year-old son and her journey through despair to an acceptance of her loss and a reawakening of her passion for living. Her sensitivity to her emotions and plain talk provide a role model for parents or any adult suffering a major loss.

Berman, Michael R., ed. **Parenthood Lost: Healing the Pain after Miscarriage, Stillbirth, and Infant Death.** Westport, CT: Praeger, 2000. 272p. $35.00. ISBN 0-89789-614-9; 978-0-89789-614-6. $25.00pa. ISBN 0-313-36093-6; 978-0-313-36093-0.

> Berman, an obstetrician, shares his original poetry, experiences, and views regarding the causes and family reactions to miscarriages, stillbirth, and infant deaths. Berman's firsthand, sensitive accounts of his interactions with grieving parents are supplemented with chapters by parents and medical professionals, who provide most frequent reasons for perinatal losses. This is an important resource for family members experiencing the tragic loss of a baby. Includes a glossary and suggested resources.

Bernstein, Judith R. **When the Bough Breaks: Forever after the Death of a Son or Daughter.** Kansas City, MO: Andrews McMeel, 1998. 256p. $16.99pa. ISBN 0-8362-5282-9; 978-0-8362-5282-8.

Documents the evolution from initial grief to an altered outlook on life. Included are excerpts from 50 interviews with parents who lost a child from ages 5 to 45. Bernstein writes from the perspectives of both bereaved parent and psychologist. She examines the stages of grief, the mourning process, the effects on family and social relationships, and the emotional differences between facing a sudden death and an anticipated death. "Compassionate and revealing, it should aid both mental-health professionals and parents dealing with this kind of devastating loss" (*Booklist* May 15, 1997).

Conrad, Bonnie H. **When a Child Has Been Murdered: Ways You Can Help the Grieving Parents.** Amityville, NY: Baywood, 1997. 152p. $51.95. ISBN 0-89503-186-8; 978-0-89503-186-0.

A guide for parents and those who work with parents whose child has been murdered. After a general discussion of types of grief, the author discusses specific emotions felt by grieving parents. Other topics include working through the grieving process, and how friends and professionals can help grieving parents.

Corr, Charles A., Helen Fuller, Carol Ann Barnickol, and Donna M. Corr, eds. **Sudden Infant Death Syndrome: Who Can Help and How.** New York: Springer, 1991. 262p. $29.95. ISBN 0-82616-720-9.

This collection of research reports reveals the nature of sudden infant death syndrome (SIDS), its causes, and its impact on parents, siblings, and extended family. Guidelines for first responders and mental health professionals are provided.

Fein, Leonard. **Against the Dying of the Light: A Parent's Story of Love, Loss and Hope.** Woodstock, VT: Jewish Lights, 2004. 176p. $15.99pa. ISBN 1-58023-197-7; 978-1-58023-197-8.

Author Leonard Fein chronicles the sudden death of his 30-year-old daughter and shares the wisdom he gained through his grief. "This work will attract readers concerned with grieving and solace as well as those wanting to learn about people who have lived through, and found hope after, tragedy. For public libraries and popular collections in academic libraries" (*Library Journal* May 15, 2001).

Green, Reg. **The Nicholas Effect: A Boy's Gift to the World.** Bloomington, IN: AuthorHouse, 2009. 270p. $14.49pa. ISBN 1-4490-0841-0; 978-1-4490-0841-3.

The story of seven-year-old Nicholas Green's killing and his parents' decision to donate their son's organs—an act that saved the lives of five Italians and restored the sight of two others. "Nicholas's story puts a human face on organ donation, much as Ryan White's did for AIDS. Highly recommended" (*Library Journal* May 1, 1999).

Hobbie, Douglas. **Being Brett: Chronicle of a Daughter's Death.** New York: Henry Holt, 1996. 332p. $15.00pa. ISBN 0-8050-7118-0; 978-0-8050-7118-4.

Novelist Hobbie recounts daughter Brett's struggle with Hodgkin's disease. Diagnosed at age 23, Brett fought the disease four years before her death. "Moving from optimism to despair to acceptance, Brett attempted to live fully in the moment, savoring every precious day as the miracle she knew it to be. Readers will feel privileged to accompany this remarkable young woman and her loving family along this anguishing and enlightening journey through life and death" (*Booklist* Dec. 15, 1995).

Hood, Ann. **Comfort: A Journey through Grief.** New York: Norton, 2008. 160p. $19.95.
     ISBN 0-393-06456-5; 978-0-393-06456-8. Norton, 2009. 192p. $12.95pa.
     ISBN 0-393-33659-X; 978-0-393-33659-7.

     In 2002 the author's five-year-old daughter died suddenly of strep throat. Hood,
     a novelist, was too devastated to do anything but reflect on her daughter's death.
     Following the suggestion of a friend, she learned to knit, an activity that soothed
     her until she was able to read and write again. "Hood's sometimes-too-painful-to-
     read memoir bares all the raw emotions, from denial to despair to anger, that she
     experienced. The grief never really leaves, she says; it just stops eclipsing all else"
     (*Booklist* April 1, 2008).

Horchler, Joani N., and Robin D. Morris. **The SIDS Survival Guide: Information and
     Comfort for Grieving Family and Friends and Professionals Who Seek to
     Help Them.** Cheverly, MD: SIDS Educational Services, 1994. 290p. $14.95pa.
     ISBN 0-9641218-7-5; 978-0-9641218-7-4.

     Provides survival suggestions for mothers, fathers, siblings, grandparents, child-
     care providers, police officers, emergency medical responders, health profession-
     als, counselors, clergy, and funeral directors when a baby dies of sudden infant
     death syndrome (SIDS). Includes chapters on anger, guilt, surviving anniversa-
     ries, home monitoring of subsequent babies, and moving forward. "Horchler,
     the mother of a baby who died of Sudden Infant Death Syndrome (SIDS), and
     Morris, a speaker on parenting issues, have compiled an outstanding collection.
     This book consists of poems, letters, diary entries, and essays written by parents,
     grandparents, professional counselors, siblings, friends, and babysitters—all of
     whom discuss their personal experiences in confronting SIDS" (*Library Journal*
     Dec. 1, 1994).

Ilse, Sherokee. 2008. **Empty Arms: Coping with Miscarriage, Stillbirth and Infant
     Death.** Rev. ed. Maple Plain, MN: Wintergreen Press, 2008. 104p. $12.95pa.
     ISBN 0-9609456-6-0 (English); 0-9609456-7-9 (Spanish).

     The author, who has experienced miscarriage, offers practical suggestions and sup-
     port at the time of the loss and during the months that follow. First published
     in 1982, the book provides an updated bibliography and resource section. This
     title and a number of other related resources are available at the author's website:
     http://wintergreenpress.com.

Johnson, Christopher. **Your Critically Ill Child: Life and Death Choices Parents Must
     Face.** Far Hills, NJ: New Horizon Press, 2007. 212p. $15.95pa. ISBN 0-888282-
     284-5; 978-0-88282-284-6.

     The cofounder of the pediatric intensive care unit at Mayo Clinic's pediatric facility
     uses case studies and relies on his 25 years of experience to describe issues related
     to children's critical illnesses and their treatment. Included is a chapter on the
     ethics concerned with ceasing treatment when the patient's condition is hopeless.
     Each chapter concludes with a brief section, "Crucial Advice for Parents." An in-
     formative and sensitive treatment of a family's challenges when a child is diagnosed
     with a critical and sometimes fatal illness or injured in an accident.

Kaplan, Louise J. **No Voice Is Ever Wholly Lost.** Collingdale, PA: Diane, 1999. 285p.
     $24.00pa. ISBN 0-7881-6402-3; 978-0-7881-6402-6.

     Psychologist Kaplan illuminates the psychological forces that form the bond be-
     tween parents and children, even following death of a child. The author bases
     her thesis on her experience as a psychoanalyst and uses cases of lost parents and
     children in art, literature, and recent history, "Occasionally bogged down in over

analysis, but generally a probing, sensitive, and finely crafted work that deserves a wide readership among clinicians and laypeople" (*Kirkus Reviews*). "Kaplan's interpretation of the mourning process is grounded in Freudian theory, and although her book is meant to offer comfort, it is too abstract to do so. It will be of most interest to psychologists and advocates of Freudian thought" (*Library Journal* Feb. 15, 1995).

Klein, Darci. **To Full Term: A Mother's Triumph over Miscarriage.** New York: Penguin Group, 2007. 288p. $19.00. ISBN 0-425-21587-3; 978-0-425-21587-6.

The memoir of Klein's pregnancy with her son, and the story of her struggle to give birth following three miscarriages. She refused to accept outmoded obstetric guidelines, confronted stubborn medical professionals, and overcame her own fears. "She [Klein] notes that nearly half of the estimated two million miscarriages per year are the results of treatable conditions and also that high-risk pregnant women must demand certain tests and interventions. She did demand them, and this journal of her pregnancy puts the authority of personal experience behind heavy-duty advice on what expectant mothers, especially those who have had one or more miscarriages, must do to ensure a full-term pregnancy" (*Booklist* June 1, 2007).

Panuthos, Claudia, and Catherine Romeo. **Ended Beginnings: Healing Childbearing Losses.** New York: Bergin & Garvey, 1984. 220p. $12.95pa. ISBN 0-89789-054-X.

The authors state that in the United States more than one-third of babies conceived will not survive—meaning that one-third of parents are touched by childbearing loss. *Ended Beginnings* is an analysis of parents' reactions to pregnancy-related loss as well as death of young babies. The guilt feelings and grief accompanying abortion, miscarriages, stillbirths, and infant deaths are described and documented by references to research. The authors' scope includes infertility, release to adoption, birth of handicapped children, and abortion. Numerous accounts of women who have experienced these types of losses enable the reader who is experiencing such grief to understand and to begin dealing with it.

Rich, Laurie A. **When Pregnancy Isn't Perfect: A Layperson's Guide to Complications in Pregnancy.** Rhinebeck, NY: Larata Press, 1996. 349p. $18.95pa. ISBN 0-9654985-0-6; 978-0-9654985-0-0.

Advice on coping with various problems experienced during pregnancy, with a special chapter for fathers. "Rich explains in easy-to-understand, thoughtful language several complications that until now have not been extensively covered by mainstream pregnancy books. A straightforward chapter on how to cope when a baby dies during a complicated pregnancy is particularly helpful and informs the reader of parental rights" (*Booklist* Jan. 15, 1991).

Rosof, Barbara D. **The Worst Loss: How Families Heal from the Death of a Child.** New York: Henry Holt, 1995. 304p. $17.99pa. ISBN: 978-0-8050-3241-3; 0-8050-3241-X.

The author, a psychotherapist with more than 25 years' experience, clearly describes the deep emotions that accompany death of a child of any age. She explores causes of neonatal, infant, and child death and characterizes the grieving process experienced by parents and siblings. The unique impact of stillbirths, infant deaths, and the sudden death of children via accidents, murders, and suicides is also discussed. Hope is provided in concluding chapters that advise readers on surviving the first year, then living the rest of life. A beneficial guide for parents and professionals who work with grieving parents and their surviving children.

Sawyers, Norma E. **A Personal Grief and a Reasonable Faith: A Mother's Journey from Tragedy to Triumph in Understanding the Christian Faith.** Bolivar, MO: Dogwood Publishing, 1992. 140p. $11.95. ISBN 0-9630031-0-0; 978-0-9630031-0-2. 156p. $11.95pa. ISBN 0-9630031-4-3; 978-0-9630031-4-0.

The accidental death of her 15-year-old daughter precipitated Sawyers' exploration into her faith. She asked the questions that many Christians ask themselves, for example, why does God permit suffering? Is Jesus really God? Answering these questions leads to a better understanding of her faith. "Her answers are somewhat simplistic and based on the assumption that everyone sees the world as she does, but for those who are struggling with these very real issues, she provides a starting point from which they may continue to grow" (*Booklist* Mar. 1, 1992).

Additional resources pertaining to grief and religion are found in chapter 8.

Scher, Jonathan, and Carol Dix. **Preventing Miscarriage: The Good News.** New York: HarperCollins, 2005. 304p. $13.99pa. ISBN 0-06-073481-7; 978-0-06-073481-7.

Dr. Jonathan Scher provides current medical information on the causes and latest treatments available for preventing miscarriages. "Between discussions of hormonal imbalances, physical anomalies, and immunological incompatibilities come poignant stories from women who have suffered numerous miscarriages and subsequent, anxiety-filled pregnancies that finally resulted in birth. Scher also acknowledges the psychological trauma of miscarriage, offering hope to those who have been struggling for years to carry to term" (*Booklist* Mar. 1, 1990).

Sears, William M. **SIDS: A Parent's Guide to Understanding and Preventing Sudden Infant Death Syndrome.** New York: Little, Brown, 1995. 256p. $19.95. ISBN 0-316-77912-1; 978-0-316-77912-8.

Pediatrician Sears outlines SIDS research and combines with his own expertise to present a practical seven-step program that reduces the worry and risk of SIDS. He also discusses grieving and coping with the death of a child. "Unlike Joanni Horchler and Robin Morris's *The SIDS Survival Guide* (LJ 12/94), which offers only psychological advice, this guide presents supportive techniques that promote health and bonding of parents and infants. Highly recommended for all collections" (*Library Journal* Aug. 1, 1995).

Vanderbilt, Gloria. **A Mother's Story.** G. K. Hall Core Series. Farmington Hills, MI: Cengage Gale, Macmillan, 1996. 170p. $23.95. ISBN 0-7838-1886-6; 978-0-7838-1886-3.

Vanderbilt, the daughter of a railroad baron, reflects on her own childhood bereft of parental love while trying to make sense of her son's suicide when he is 24. "Interspersed with excerpts from her own diaries and testimonials from friends and family, the memoir is a paean to one woman's strength and faith. Vanderbilt offers empathy to other inhabitants of glass bubbles and assurance that every tragedy harbors hope" (*Booklist* May 15, 1996). "In spare, unadorned prose Vanderbilt relates 'the loss that had no echo' and her own survival. Most public libraries will want this haunting portrayal" (*Library Journal* May 1, 1996).

SOURCES CONSULTED

Berman, Michael R., ed. 2001. *Parenthood lost: Healing the pain after miscarriage, stillbirth, and infant death.* Westport, CT: Bergin & Garvey.

Centers for Disease Control and Prevention. National Center for Health Statistics. VitalStats. Available at: http://www.cdc.gov/nchs/vitalstats.htm. Accessed September 13, 2010.

Corr, Charles A., Helen Fuller, Carol Ann Barnickol, and Donna M. Corr, eds. 1991. *Sudden Infant Death Syndrome: Who can help and how.* New York: Springer.

Defrain, John, Leona Martens, Jan Stork, and Warren Stork. 1986. *Stillborn: The invisible death.* Lexington, MA: D. C. Heath, Lexington Books.

Ilse, Sherokee. 1990. *Empty arms: Coping with miscarriage, stillbirth and infant death.* Maple Plain, MN: Wintergreen Press.

Johnson, Christopher. 2007. *Your critically ill child: Life and death choices parents must face.* Far Hills, NJ: New Horizon Press.

Knapp, Ronald J. 1986. *Beyond endurance: When a child dies.* New York: Schocken Books.

Knapp, Ronald J., and Larry G. Peppers. 1980. *Motherhood and mourning.* New York: Praeger.

MacDorman, M. F. and S. Kirmeyer. 2009. Fetal and perinatal mortality, United States 2005. *National Vital Statistics Reports,* vol. 57, no. 8. Hyattsville, MD: National Center for Health Statistics.

MacDorman, M. F., and T. J. Mathews. 2008. Recent trends in infant mortality in the United States. NCHS data brief, no 9. Hyattsville, MD: National Center for Health Statistics.

Miles, M. S., and A. S. Demi. 1984. Toward the development of a theory of bereavement guilt: Sources of guilt in bereaved parents. *Omega,* 14, 299–314.

Miles, M. S., and A. S. Demi. 1986. Guilt in bereaved parents. In *Parental loss of a child,* ed. T. A. Rando, 97–118. Champaign, IL: Research Press.

Panuthos, Claudia, and Catherine Romeo. 1984. *Ended beginnings: Healing childbearing losses.* New York: Bergin & Garvey.

Rosof, Barbara D. 1995. *The worst loss: How families heal from the death of a child.* New York: Henry Holt.

Schwiebert, Pat, and Paul Kirk. n.d. *Still to be born: A guide for bereaved parents who are making decisions about their future.* Portland, OR: Perinatal Loss.

Seigerman, Andrea. 2001. A social worker's perspective on pregnancy loss. In *Parenthood lost: Healing the pain after miscarriage, stillbirth, and infant death,* ed. Michael R. Berman, 89–93. Westport, CT: Bergin & Garvey.

Shapiro, Ester R. 1994. *Grief as a family process: A developmental approach to clinical practice.* New York: Guilford Press.

6

——✦✦✦——

DEATH OF A SPOUSE

CHAPTER OVERVIEW

Death of a spouse is traumatic. Unless a spouse dies suddenly from an undiagnosed illness or accident, the trauma begins with the recognition that death is probable. Anticipatory grief sets in when death appears imminent and becomes pronounced upon the actual passing. While friends and relatives return to their established life patterns, the grieving spouse is left without the partner who shared life's joys, sadness, and routines.

This chapter provides a description of the emotions and challenges that accompany the loss of a life partner, with implications for service professionals who work with grieving widows and widowers. An annotated bibliography of suggested resources concludes the chapter.

LOSS OF A LIFE PARTNER

Perhaps the greatest loss when a spouse dies is loss of a companion, a life partner. To this partner the grieving spouse told everything and could discuss anything. The couple shared their history, and didn't have to provide background when they talked about a situation at work. The spouse provided continuity in life, knew the other spouse's past, and helped make decisions for the present and future.

Loss of a spouse includes loss of a couple's activities together and the friends from the spouse's work and hobbies. The surviving spouse no longer fits into the world shared by the couple. Going to a favorite restaurant alone or with a friend is unfulfilling because it's not the same. Any activity shared as a couple will never feel the same.

Death of a loved one often leaves a person isolated symbolically, physically, and emotionally. For the many years of their relationship, they were together constantly; they thought of themselves as an inseparable pair. Suddenly, one of them is alone; how can they *not* feel isolated? These feelings are better understood with an explanation of the grieving process.

Considerable diversity exists among persons who experience bereavement, and some writers challenge Kübler-Ross's five stages of grief (denial, anger, bargaining, depression, and acceptance) described in chapter 2. "Recent studies have revealed that the bereavement process is more like a roller coaster ride than an orderly progression of stages with clear time frames associated with each stage" (Lund and Caserta 2002, 210). The roller coaster ride is characterized by experiencing changing emotions, learning new skills, recognizing limitations and weaknesses, developing new behavioral patterns, experiencing helplessness and loneliness, and forming new relationships.

Although less is known about loss of gay or lesbian partners, many aspects of the loss are comparable to loss of a spouse. Like traditional marriage partners, a gay or lesbian partner may have difficulty managing those tasks of daily living that were the primary responsibility of the partner who died.

A difference with gay or lesbian or cohabiting heterosexual couples that lose a partner is that often the survivor does not have the societal right to grieve. The result is disenfranchised grief (Doka 2002; see also chapter 2). Other losses that could experience disenfranchised grief are extramarital affairs and ex-spouses. The surviving partners of these relationships may be excluded from many of the rituals, losing opportunities for support as well as legal benefits of survivorship. This exclusion can add stress to an already stressful situation.

Anticipatory grief occurs before the death of a loved one. A surviving spouse may go through some or all of the stages of grief, but that does not stop their going through them all again when the loved one dies. Anticipatory grief may be experienced in that limbo when loved ones are not getting better but are not dying (Kübler-Ross and Kessler 2005).

Caregiving responsibilities are challenging. It is backbreaking, exhausting work, but it is rewarding to the caregiver. Roberts cared for her husband as he died of cancer and relates her feelings after:

> For the rest of my life I will cherish my memories of care giving, even though they were partly painful. I know Frank forgave my shortcomings and embraced my caring and love, and even my emotional strength as we daily faced his approaching death. (Roberts 2002, 53)

Men frequently are active participants in caregiving for ill wives, although they may employ a female to help with such tasks as bathing, toileting, and dressing. During an extended illness there is grieving for the loss of companionship. Reactions for men and women may include depression, fatigue, apathy, listlessness, worry, feelings of isolation, and illness. Anticipatory grief comes with the realization that the spouse is dying, and the survivor must construct a new reality (Moore and Stratton 2003).

THE EMOTIONS OF GRIEVING

The emotions experienced by bereaved persons who have lost a spouse are quite similar to other types of losses. In this section we examine the most common emotions that accompany grief.

Shock

Shock is the term used to describe trauma immediately following a death (see chapter 2), and it is the first emotion usually felt after death of a loved one. The degree of shock is related to the level of attachment to the deceased, and when, where, and how the death occurred. It also depends on the presence of others at the time of death and following. How persons deal with this shock determines the course of their grief.

Shock can last from a few minutes to many days but usually passes when the rituals are over. The initial shock following a spouse's death is a feeling of numbness. Even when the death is expected, the surviving spouse has difficulty accepting the finality of it. The full impact can be postponed by intellectual acceptance and the activity of funeral planning and nurturing of others, but the raw awareness becomes clear soon.

When a person is in shock, it is best for the individual to conduct as many usual activities as possible during the crisis to help him come out of shock and move on in the grief process. A person may come out of the initial shock and still experience times when the loss seems unreal (Westberg 1997).

Tears

Tears are a way of relieving sadness. Psychologists agree that the worst thing a person can do is to refrain from expressing their emotions. "If you have a half hour of crying to do, don't stop at twenty minutes. Let yourself cry it all out. It will stop on its own. If you cry till your last tear, you will feel released" (Kübler-Ross and Kessler 2005, 43).

It is difficult for men in our society to cry. It is instilled in boys and reinforced until some men *can't* cry. Some men think that crying is a sign of weakness, which is a disadvantage to widowers who need to release their intense feelings. Cultural and social barriers inhibit full expression of grief.

> The underlying message suggests that public displays of emotion are a breach of etiquette, even un-American. Emotional outbursts make everyone uncomfortable: the bereaved because they feel out of control and weak, and the supporters because they feel embarrassed and helpless. It is as though there is an unwritten dictum that states, "Thou shalt not grieve in public places." (Sanders 1989, 18–19)

Brothers (1990), a psychologist and widow, concurs that the first reaction following a husband's death is nearly always shock, followed by numbness. After the numbness, suffering comes accompanied by emotions including longing, panic, helplessness, loneliness, anger, resentment, depression, self-pity, denial. Not all women experience all of these emotions or with the same intensity. As Coughlin (1993) demonstrates, this second stage may last many months or several years.

> What no one ever tells you after your husband is dead is that the old chestnut about there being good days and bad days is categorically not true. There are, instead, those days that are bad, and then there are those days that are much worse. As for the nights, and very often the days, it is impossible to stop the videotape that continues to play in your mind, the months, the weeks, the last days, the last hours, the last minutes in full color. (41)

Regrets

When a loved one dies, the survivor is usually left with regrets about the things they should have said and done. Regrets are a part of grief, but when there are regrets or guilt regarding a lost loved one, one can still say the things that are in their heart. "It's never too late to say, 'I'm sorry. Forgive me and I forgive you. I love you and I thank you.' After that, what else is there to regret?" (Kübler-Ross and Kessler 2005, 41).

Loneliness

Studies underscore the difficulty loneliness poses for bereaved spouses. It is awkward for them to make new friends, and established friends are often couples; the bereaved feel out of place without a partner. The least lonely are those who have established close bonds with family and friends.

For most widows and widowers, lack of a sexual partner is not a major deprivation. Of greater concern is loneliness and separation. Lying alone in bed, getting up without someone to say good morning to, and lonely evenings constituted some of the lonely events reported by bereaved spouses (Sanders 1989). In response to his stark loneliness, Lewis wrote, "Her absence is like the sky, spread over everything" (Lewis 1996, 11).

Relief

Many people experience a period of relief amidst the sadness of loss. This is especially true if the loved one suffered before dying. When this happens, relief is recognition that the pain of the loved one has come to an end. The illness is over, and the end of the pain and suffering relieves the surviving spouse.

However, the relief is momentary, and the pain begins again. Surviving spouses can tolerate the pain of loss only for a short time. Then they must back away to recover, process their feelings, and move ahead once more. It is important to give their emotions rest. They must decide what activities give them pleasure and give rest to their emotions—TV, movies, reading, travel, or loafing. They should do what gives them relief, and they should not feel guilty about it (Kübler-Ross and Kessler 2005).

RECOVERY

As the shock of the partner's loss diminishes, the grieving person begins coping with a different lifestyle. They learn to accommodate their new status as a single person and make adjustments in their lives. Customs and rituals are an aid in making the transformation to a single lifestyle, but surviving spouses must cope with the grief that accompanies anniversaries and holidays, and they must eventually confront the dispersal of clothing and possessions of their spouse. The recovery should result in a healthy lifestyle that includes a variety of social activities. Eventually, as the healing continues, remarriage is a consideration. All of these issues are part of recovery.

Accommodating the Loss

Eventually, people who have lost a spouse accommodate the death. The grieving continues, but they develop strategies for dealing with the pain. Most mourners reach a point where they have conquered the pain, and it does not dominate them any longer. Faith and religion often play a role in this accommodation.

Human development is a lifelong process influenced by relationships with others. Bereaved adults can reflect on their behavior and the role of others in their lives. As they recognize the need to change, they can develop a new sense of self; however, this healing and accommodation process does not occur without effort. Time alone does not heal the wound of grief. Adjustments to overcome grief require effort and the support of friends and relatives.

A persons' ability to reshape a concept of self following a spouse's death is affected by the relationship while the spouse was alive. A husband or wife who embeds sense of self in a marriage loses that self when the spouse dies. Silverman quotes a widow one year after the death of her husband: "I know I am still my children's mother. I am still a grandmother. But I feel like I don't know who I am any more, now that Jim is dead. If I am not his wife, then who am I?" (Silverman 2002, 179).

Brothers describes her despair and her recovery:

> I was positive that I would never feel whole again. I would have sworn to it. But after a year and a half I have come to realize that I *am* a whole. As the months go by I feel more and more together, so much so that I feel like a different woman. (Brothers 1990, 184–85)

Religion and Rituals

Religion **is** a mainstay providing hope to many when a person's life is shaken by a spouse's death, although some report feeling anger toward God following loss of a spouse. Faith in God generally is a strong support, and the interaction of the survivor, family, and friends in religious activities will help to reduce anger, depression, and feelings of isolation. Optimism and enhanced physical health can be by-products of these activities. Sanders reports, "When there are people to supply nurturance, grief is less intense" (Sanders 1989, 194).

Research has shown that both the bereaved and the community must find a way to relate to the deceased. Rituals can help in this process. In Catholicism, mourners may offer a memorial mass on the anniversary of a death. Mourners in Judaism remember a deceased individual by participating in a synagogue ritual during the year, including the anniversary of death.

In the authors' town, the family of a prominent man in the community organized an annual walk/run scholarship fundraiser in his name. Some families remember deceased members with an empty chair or a candle at a holiday gathering, or include them in a prayer of thanksgiving before the meal.

Evidence from research shows the abandonment of some mourning customs could have negative effects on adjustment. Customs like the black armband or dark dress as signs of mourning to relieve mourners from participation in social events are changing. Although specified periods for mourning may not correspond to an individual's psychological needs, the absence of social expectations common in Western society can leave bereaved people "confused and insecure in their grief" (Parkes 1986, 179).

Adjustments

Widows sometimes feel overwhelmed by the prospect of handling the financial affairs following a husband's death, and the difficulty of tending to home maintenance and repair. Similarly, widowers feel lost preparing meals and shopping; however, widowers usually receive more nurturing for a longer period of time following death of a spouse—invitations to dinner and meals delivered—yet when a husband dies, there is not similar care with financial matters and home maintenance for widows.

Eating alone is painful for many bereaved spouses. Eating dinner before the TV is unsatisfying because it brings back memories of times when they had done so as a couple. Cooking for one can be difficult and unsatisfying. Quantities at a grocery store are not packaged for individuals, and it is difficult to learn to cook for single helpings.

Anniversaries and Holidays

The surviving spouse faces the recognition of anniversaries and holidays alone. They may remember the day of the person's death, but other anniversaries will arise that were unanticipated, such as the first date, the wedding date, and fondly remembered occasions. While these anniversaries and holidays brought happiness for a couple, they now bring painful memories of loss.

Kübler-Ross and Kessler (2005, 118) provide this advice:

> Find your own way to honor your loved one's memory. It is an occasion that may bring up your greatest sadness along with some of your best memories. It deserves its spot in your heart. Just do what feels right for you. Attend a service, visit your loved one's grave, or just talk to friends and family. Honor the love and the memories left behind.

An alternative solution is to ignore the holiday instead of going through the motions. In time, new traditions can be established. Another solution is to continue the tradition by including the missing loved one with a prayer or by lighting a candle in their memory.

Clothing and Possessions

One of the hardest things to do after the loss of a loved one is to deal with his possessions—clothing, jewelry, and other items. It is another point at which the survivor must confront the fact that the partner is gone. Most bereaved spouses accomplish this, often with the help of a relative or friend, within the first six months.

> The emotions of going through someone's things will be enormous, possibly overwhelming. With the smell or the touch of their fabric, clothes remind us of the one we love and the moments we spent together and their likes and dislikes. Their watches, rings, and other pieces of jewelry remind us of their style and personality. Most of all, their clothes and belongings emphasize their absence in our lives. (Kübler-Ross and Kessler 2005, 133)

Keeping meaningful items or giving them to relatives and friends can help the grieving process. So can giving clothing or furnishings to charities or people in need as a remembrance of the loved one.

GRIEVING AND HEALTH

A literature review reported by Silverman (2002) indicates that a relationship exists between bereavement and mortality and morbidity, and the rate was elevated for men. For example, a 23-year study indicated that bereaved men died twice as often as bereaved women—30 percent of men compared to 15 percent of women. Mortality increased most during the period 7 to 12 months after the loss and remained higher for more than two years. Furthermore, healthy men who lost their wives were twice as likely to die as healthy men who had not suffered loss of a wife (Silverman 2002, 192).

Silverman cites numerous studies suggesting that depression often follows death of a spouse, and depression can lead to other serious health problems. Studies show that depression increases mortality generally and is associated specifically with increased cardiovascular disease (CVD) mortality. Many deaths soon after death of a spouse are caused in part by CVD. Depression can lead to social isolation, which increases mortality from CVD (Silverman 2002, 194–96).

Maintaining an active social life and engaging in religious observance appear to have a positive effect on the health of bereaved individuals. Citing numerous studies of social networks and mortality, Silverman (2002) declares:

> From all these reinforcing studies, it seems clear that spending enjoyable time with other people is a hallmark of a longer life. Little evidence exists to explain this consistent finding, although considerable research links psychological stress with adverse health effects, and it seems plausible that spending pleasant time with other humans can provide substantial survival benefits. (199)

REMARRIAGE

Archer (1999) cites studies that indicate widowers remarry sooner than widows. Age appears to be a factor in the probability of remarriage. One study reported that after 25 months of a spouse's death, 61 percent of the men and 19 percent of the women were either remarried or involved in a serious relationship. Archer cites two studies with middle-aged samples, reported that the average or median times for remarriage was 3 years for men and 7 years for women. The average was 1.7 years for men and 3.5 years for women among a wider age range from 20 to over 65 years (Archer 1999, 126).

Widows outnumber widowers, and men customarily marry women younger than themselves. A study by Moore and Stratton (2003) concluded that any of the men who wanted to could have remarried; however, anxiety toward dating and preference to be alone were among reasons for not seeking a marriage partner. Because of the difference in numbers, not all women who wish to remarry have the opportunity.

A caution for considering remarriage is the temptation to fill the void caused by the death of a spouse. Instead of accommodating the change in one's life, some bereaved individuals (especially men) do not take the time to feel comfortable as a single person before inviting another person into their lives. Quick remarriage often signals that the newly bereaved has not grieved adequately, and emotional turmoil could interfere with a remarriage.

SUPPORT NETWORKS

People live within a web of relationships that provide support during difficult times. While family members assist out of a sense of obligation, friends and neighbors also participate in this support network. Other members of this network include health professionals, physicians, mental health agencies, clergy, and other care profession-als. Also, talking with others who have had similar experiences can help the be-reaved realize theirs is not a unique experience and can help in the healing process (Silverman 2002).

People who are one step ahead, that is, who have had a similar experience, can serve as a role model for those who are struggling. Social networking is a key factor in helping bereaved individuals recover from loss:

> Research has clearly demonstrated that one of the most critical factors affect-ing health is social networks. In many prospective studies, a higher level of social interrelationship and social activity is associated with a higher rate of survival and vice versa. It is not unreasonable to suppose that we can favor-ably influence our clients' will to live by providing appropriate social support. (Silverman 2002, 197)

During the first weeks or months of grieving it may be difficult to persuade bereaved people to join a support group, but many can benefit from the mutual support of a group sharing the same experience. Women are more likely to join a support group, but older men want to feel self-reliant. They are unwilling to seek help, to accept help, or to express feelings that suggest they need help. Older men are reluctant to engage in groups or activities designed for women, but they can be persuaded to join when there is little else to do.

Older men are more likely to seek informal groups of men who may only briefly acknowledge their grieving but talk about other things. Such informal discussions and activities may help a grieving widower to move on with his life. Men will at-tend a bereavement group if assured other men will be in attendance, and a male coleader makes a group more appealing to older men than a female leader alone (Moore and Stratton 2003).

Social networking enables the bereaved to tell their story. Following the death of a loved one, an individual wants and needs to tell the story of the spouse's illness or accident over and over, before and after the funeral. That telling of the story is an important part of their coping with the shocking change in their lives. Telling and retelling the story is essential for relieving their pain and for grieving. Support and bereavement groups allow bereaved individuals to associate with others who have experienced loss, and they provide a forum for telling their story (Kübler-Ross and Kessler 2005, 62–63).

ADDRESSING THE NEEDS OF BEREAVED PERSONS

Parkes (1986, 173) lists the following critical needs of newly bereaved persons:

- While in a dazed condition, they will need help making the simplest decisions.
- They need time to process what has happened and to organize their thoughts.
- They need help with those first things that need to be done, for example, noti-fication of relatives, funeral arrangements.
- They need friends, but they should be protected from too much attention from neighbors. This is particularly true during the time immediately after the death and while they are in shock.

A wide range of social support strategies can be effective for bereaved adults, in-cluding bereavement groups, churchgoing, playing cards, attending concerts, and singing. Needed is a mix of activities tailored to the needs and interests of bereaved individuals.

In addition, Sanders writes that bereavement requires "hibernation time" during the mourning period—a "holding pattern" to ponder the meaning of the loss and to let go:

> Understanding this will not necessarily reduce the despair, sadness, and sorrow felt because of missing someone who is deeply loved. But it will supply a measure of faith and hope, which promises that healing will occur eventually. (Sanders 1989, 195)

Helping Widows

Brothers (1990), a widow and psychologist, issues the following advice for widows:

1. Stay in charge of your life; do not let children or others try to run your life.
2. Avoid hasty decisions. If possible, a widow should not make major decisions for at least a year after her husband's death.
3. Plan for the future. Consider your physical condition and where you should live.
4. Maintain a regular routine. Get up at the usual hour and follow the daily and weekly routines followed for years.
5. Plan ahead for holidays, anniversaries, and weekends. These special days can be very emotional and should be spent with family or friends.
6. Get out of the house. Get involved in activities, do volunteer work.
7. Be good to yourself. Visit the hairdresser, get a massage.
8. Exercise makes you feel better and benefits your health.
9. Cry when you feel like it. Don't repress your tears.
10. Beware of pills and alcohol. Don't rely on them for relief. Follow your doctor's advice.
11. Check your progress regularly. Do you feel better than you did three months ago?

Brothers (1990) also offers the following advice for friends and relatives. Her points are a summary of other literature for supporting widows.

1. Write to her. Recall memories of the husband. Other widows can share their experiences to help her understand she is not the only one going through this terrible experience.
2. Follow the golden rule of comforting. Try to put yourself in the widow's place.
3. Avoid the impossible question: "How are you?" "How are you doing?" or "How are you bearing up?" They are impossible to answer. Instead, say that you've been thinking of her and would like to visit. Ask if there's something you can do for her. Ask if she's getting enough sleep; she probably has not, and this question is easier to answer.
4. Encourage her to talk. Most widows want and need to talk about their loss, although it may make you uncomfortable. By reviewing her memories of the illness or circumstances of his death, she is gradually ending these important years of her life.
5. Let her cry. "Tears are a kind of first aid for grief" (Brothers 1990, 251).

6. Stick with her. Loneliness is a difficult part of grief. A widow needs family and friends to stay in touch with her. Keep calling to see how she is and invite to her dinner.

7. Show your love. Her husband's companionship is missing, and she needs a hug or pat on the shoulder or kiss on the cheek.

8. Refrain from giving advice. Don't make suggestions about her life unless asked.

Helping Widowers

The advice for widows above generally holds true for widowers. Additional advice for widowers comes from research by Moore and Stratton (2003), who studied 51 older widowed men over seven years. Men in this study gave the following cogent advice to widowed men: "Stay busy and involved. Have interests. Develop new interests. Rely on religion to help with acceptance of the loss. Get professional help. Look for another companion" (Moore and Stratton 2003, 216).

Urging widowers to get professional help or to join a support groups is good advice, but men tend to prefer self-reliance or informal group discussions.

Perhaps Roberts, writing about her own experience, offers the best advice for both widows and widowers:

If you are questioning whether it is okay to grieve in your own way, then I give you permission to weep, weep loudly. Take his sweatshirt to bed. Talk about her and to her. Keep pictures in the living room and set an empty place at the table. Watch old movies and videotapes that show that familiar face. Hug a pillow and rock yourself. Put your feet in his shoes or wear her ring on a chain under your clothing next to your skin. Cry out his name in the night, visit her grave as often as you need to. Do the things that help you through a night, a day, a week, a year, two years. Through all of this remember, "It will take as long as it takes." (Roberts 2002, 7)

Advice for Professionals Working with Bereaved Adults

How should professionals help grieving adults who have lost their life partners? Research and published personal accounts suggest the following strategies:

• Bereaved persons want and need to tell their stories. If you are acquainted with the individual, it is especially important to inquire about their loss.

• Listen carefully to determine their state of grieving. Early after the death of a spouse, many prefer solitude, and reading is an excellent escape.

• If they are looking for personal accounts of others who have grieved and survived, consult the bibliography below for resources in your library's collection.

• *If* they ask, show them a list of mental health professionals or support groups in your community. As noted above, women are more likely to request such help.

• *Don't* say, "I know how you feel." You can't know how another person feels at any given time. You might say that you have lost close relatives, and the loss is very painful. It is okay to share your experiences and your feelings with them, but don't presume you know how they feel now.

- You could engage them in conversation about their favorite pastimes in order to provide them with books and other resources.

- Generally speaking, any sincere expression of condolence is appropriate.

SUMMARY

Perhaps the greatest loss when a spouse dies is loss of a companion, a life partner. To this partner the grieving spouse told everything and could discuss anything. Loss of a spouse includes loss of a couple's activities together and the friends resulting from the spouse's work and hobbies. The surviving spouse no longer fits into the world shared by the couple.

Shock is the term used to describe trauma immediately following the death of a loved one. Shock can last from a few minutes to many days but usually passes when the rituals are over.

After a loss, tears are a way of relieving sadness. Psychologists agree that the worst thing a person can do is to refrain from expressing emotions. Many people experience a period of relief amidst the sadness of loss. This is especially true if the loved one suffered before dying. When this happens, relief is recognition that the pain of the loved one has come to an end.

Eventually, people who have lost a spouse accommodate the death. The grieving continues, but they develop strategies for dealing with the pain. Most mourners reach a point where they have conquered the pain, and it does not dominate them any longer. Faith and religion often play a role in this accommodation.

A relationship exists between bereavement and mortality and morbidity, and the rate is elevated for men. Furthermore, healthy men who lost their wives were twice as likely to die as healthy men who had not suffered loss of a wife.

People live within a web of relationships that provide support during difficult times. While family members assist out of a sense of obligation, friends and neighbors also participate in this support network. A wide range of social support strategies can be effective for bereaved adults, including bereavement groups, churchgoing, playing cards, attending concerts, and singing. Needed is a mix of activities tailored to the needs and interests of bereaved individuals.

Suggestions for supporting bereaved adults conclude this section.

SUGGESTED RESOURCES

The books listed here are recommended for persons who have lost life partners and for professionals who work with them.

Archer, John. **The Nature of Grief; the Evolution and Psychology of Reactions to Loss.** London and New York: Routledge, 1998. 336p. $110.00; $39.95pa. ISBN 978-0-415-17857-0; 978-0-415-17858-7pa.

> A synthesis of research on grief by a professor of psychology at the University of Central Lancashire. An historical account of grief research is followed by a review of grief accounts from ethnographic and historical sources, as well as from the arts and biological sciences. Focused on psychological studies, this is a scholarly, authoritative, and readable resource that can serve as a basis for any adult collection of resources on grief. A valuable resource for people in the helping professions.

Brooke, Jill. **Don't Let Death Ruin Your Life: A Practical Guide to Reclaiming Happiness after the Death of a Loved One.** New York: Penguin Group, Plume, 2002. 288p. $15.00pa. ISBN 0-452-28298-5; 978-0-452-28298-8.

Former CNN correspondent Brooke, who lost her father at 16 and later lost an unborn child, interviewed hundreds of people about their loss of loved ones for this guide for transforming grief into healing. "This is truly a practical book in that death is viewed as a normal part of life and dealing with it constructively should be a more common reaction. The book includes such particular issues as a child's grief, seeking professional help, and dealing with the deceased's possessions" (*Booklist* Feb. 1, 2001).

Brothers, Dr. Joyce. **Widowed.** New York: Random House/Ballantine, 1992. 224p. $6.99pa. ISBN 0-345-37400-2pa.

The noted psychologist describes the death of Milton, her husband of 39 years. She reflects on the events leading to his death caused by bladder cancer and the devastating grief and loneliness she felt after. "The stages of grief may be predictable, but there is very little that is orderly about a widow's emotions in the weeks and months— sometimes years—following her husband's death. She is caught up on a passionate and painful maelstrom" (82). She concludes her personal account with advice for widows and for those relatives and friends who want to support them. A sensitive and thoughtful memoir that will help other widows and widowers to deal with their grief.

Caine, Lynn. **Being a Widow.** New York: Penguin, 1990. 272p. $16.00. ISBN 0-14-013025-X; 978-0-14-013025-6.

Practical advice and guidance to women experiencing the loneliness and stress of widowhood. This book was written following the death from cancer of Caine's husband of 17 years. Includes a section advising families and friends on what to do and what not to do for a grieving widow. "Completed just before her untimely death, this powerful book by the author of *Widow* provides solace, guidance, and direction for widows everywhere" (*Library Journal* Oct. 1, 1988).

Coughlin, Ruth. **Grieving: A Love Story.** New York: Random House, 1993. 176p. $17.00. ISBN 0-679-42696-5; 0-8129-9260-1.

After a romance of 14 years, including 9 years of marriage, cancer intruded on the lives of Ruth and Bill Coughlin, claiming his life. Ruth recalls in vivid detail her deep feelings during his illness and following his death. An enlightening and inspirational memoir for men and women who have experienced loss of a loved one.

Crain, Mary Beth. **A Widow, a Chihuahua and Harry Truman: A Story of Love, Loss and Love Again.** New York: HarperCollins, 2000. 224p. $22.00. ISBN 0-06-251672-8; 978-0-06-251672-5.

After Crain lost her husband of three years to cancer, she fell into a deep depression. She describes how she resigned herself to loss, worked through anger and guilt, and rediscovered a sense of purpose. She was assisted in her transition by a Chihuahua puppy she named Truman, after the president she admired for his down-to-earth character, his integrity, his energy, and his fortitude in the face of adversity. She drew upon President Truman's character and the companionship of furry Truman to brighten her world. The story offers many insights into the grieving process.

Daily, Art, and Allison Daily. **Out of the Canyon: A True Story of Loss and Love.** New York: Crown Publishing Group, Harmony, 2009. 288p. $24.00. ISBN 0-307-40940-6; 978-0-307-40940-9.

Driving home from a youth hockey game, Art Daily's wife and two young sons were killed when a boulder struck his car on Interstate 70. Art received love and support from family, friends, and strangers, one of whom was Allison. Art sent a response to her, which led to a friendship and a romance. "A powerful account of our ability to recover from emotional devastation and love again, this book will appeal to anyone who has experienced personal tragedy, those who can appreciate finding a life partner under unexpected circumstances, and those who don't mind a good cry" (*Library Journal* May 11, 2009).

Didion, Joan. **The Year of Magical Thinking.** New York: Random House, 2005, 2008. 368p. $23.95. ISBN: 0-7393-2779-8; 978-0-7393-2779-1pa.

Novelist, essayist, and screenwriter Joan Didion shares the year following her husband's untimely death in unvarnished truth, describing her denial, guilt, and drive to get a precise account of his passing. At the same time, her daughter was dealing with a life-threatening illness. Didion and her husband John Gregory Dunne had just sat down to dinner after visiting their daughter in the hospital when Dunne had a sudden, massive coronary. While her daughter did recover, Didion found herself deep in mourning, stuck in these stressful events.

Dodge, Hiroko H. **Poverty Transitions among Elderly Widows.** Studies on the Elderly in America Series. New York: Garland, 1996. 164p. $145.00. ISBN 0-8153-2280-1; 978-0-8153-2280-1.

Among the aged in the United States, the risk of falling into poverty is highest following a husband's death. This book investigates causes of poverty among widows and means for overcoming that poverty despite their fixed income. This is a revision of the author's PhD dissertation (Penn State University, 1992). Recommended for scholarly or professional collections.

Dumm, Thomas L. **Loneliness as a Way of Life.** Cambridge, MA: Harvard University Press, 2008. 208p. $23.95. ISBN 0-674-03113-X; 978-0-674-03113-5.

Dumm, professor of political science at Amherst College, asks what it means to be lonely, using the works of writers and philosophers such as Shakespeare, Thoreau, and Foucault, along with personal reflections on his feelings after the death of his wife. "Dumm's straightforward writing style and ability to combine scholarly analysis with personal reflections will make his book appealing to both scholars and general readers. Highly recommended for public and academic libraries" (*Library Journal* Sept. 1, 2008).

Ginsburg, Genevieve Davis. **Widow to Widow: Thoughtful, Practical Ideas for Rebuilding Your Life.** New York: Basic Books, 2004. 240p. $15.95pa. ISBN 0-7382-0996-1; 978-0-7382-0996-8.

Widow, author, and therapist Genevieve Davis Ginsburg offers widows, their families, and their friends advice for coping with life after the loss of a husband. Topics include traveling and eating alone, surviving holidays and anniversaries, managing finances, and dating again. Testimonies from widows address these and other challenges to building a new life.

Greene, Phyllis. **It Must Have Been Moonglow: Reflections on the First Years of Widowhood.** New York: Random House, Villard Books, 2003. 192p. $10.95pa. ISBN 0-8129-6784-4; 978-0-8129-6784-5.

After Greene's husband of 56 years died, she kept a journal for the two years following his death. This memoir chronicles her sleepless nights and the challenges posed by making decisions, traveling alone, and adjusting to her new life without her husband's companionship. She writes how she found satisfaction in volunteer work and her socializing with friends and family. "For the woman who has recently joined the bereft sisterhood, reading Greene's book is akin to having someone to share a sigh and a knowing smile with" (*Kirkus* Aug. 1, 2001).

James, John W., and Russell Friedman. **The Grief Recovery Handbook: The Action Program for Moving Beyond Death, Divorce, and Other Losses.** 20th Anniversary Expanded Edition. New York: HarperCollins, 2009. 208p. $16.99. ISBN 0-06-095273-3; 0-06-019279-8.

James founded the Grief Recovery Institute more than 30 years ago, an agency that offers grief counseling and support in the United States and Canada. First published in 1988, this edition has been revised and updated to provide an easily understood guide for grief recovery. A readable account intended for general adult audiences.

Jamison, Kay Redfield. **Nothing Was the Same: A Memoir.** New York: Knopf Doubleday, Knopf, 2009. 224p. $25.00. ISBN 0-307-26537-4; 978-0-307-26537-1.

Psychologist Jamison, author of *An Unquiet Mind,* recounts slowly losing her husband to cancer. "A superb read guaranteed to appeal to those who have survived the loss of a spouse, with insights into differentiating depression from grief" (*Library Journal* Aug. 10, 2009).

Jenkins, Carol Lynn, ed. **Widows and Divorcees in Later Life: On Their Own Again.** Journal of Women and Aging Series. New York: Routledge. 2003. 208p. $100.00. ISBN: 0-7890-2191-9; 978-0-7890-2191-5.

Geared toward the mental health professional, *Widows and Divorcees in Later Life* draws on a multidisciplinary panel to provide perspectives on the problems older women face adjusting to life without a spouse. The book examines the transition from the togetherness of marriage to the solitude of being suddenly single, exploring how older widows and divorcees adapt, including issues of physical and psychological well-being (clinical depression, nutrition), economics (reduced Social Security benefits, loss of pension income, health care costs), social support (public policy, counseling), and living arrangements. Copublished simultaneously as *Journal of Women and Aging,* vol. 15, nos. 2/3, 2003.

Kaimann, Diane S. **Common Threads: Nine Widows' Journeys Through Love, Loss and Healing.** Amityville, NY: Baywood, 2001. 190p. $51.95. ISBN 0-89503-264-3; 978-0-89503-264-5.

Kaimann's husband died suddenly at age 61, and she tells the story of her painful journey as a widow. Included are the stories of nine other middle-aged women who experienced a similar loss. The index facilitates the book's use as a reference for widows.

Kübler-Ross, Elisabeth, and David Kessler. **On Grief and Grieving: Finding the Meaning of Grief through the Five Stages of Loss.** New York and London: Scribner, 2005. 235p. ISBN 978-0-7432-6628-4; 0-7432-6628-5.

Kübler-Ross, the author of several books on death and dying, collaborated before her death in 2004 with David Kessler to author this book devoted to grief following death of a loved one. Beginning with the Kübler-Ross model for the five stages of grief, the authors address the deep feelings accompanying loss and present coping strategies. A chapter is devoted to challenges of grieving spouses, including anniversaries, health, clothes and possessions of a deceased loved one, holidays, and finances. An easily read, informative source for adults recovering from loss of a dear one. Highly recommended.

Latham, Aaron. **The Ballad of Gussie and Clyde: A True Story of True Love.** Waterville, ME: Thorndike Press, 1997. 232p. $26.95. ISBN 0-7862-1237-3; 978-0-7862-1237-8.

Latham, a novelist and author of the screenplay *Urban Cowboy,* relates how his father found love at age 84. When his wife died after more than 50 years of marriage, Clyde Latham, a retired high school football coach in Spur, Texas, was lonely until Gussie Lancaster arrived from California. She was widowed and, much earlier, had known Clyde and had grown up with him. When Gussie returned to California, Clyde followed her the next day, and a week later the couple was married. "Their love led to engagement and elopement and a son's lessons about his own marriage, the need to accept a parent's remarriage, and the marvelous possibilities of 'new love in old bottles.' A captivating memoir" (*Booklist* June 15, 1997).

Lewis , C. S. **A Grief Observed.** New York: HarperCollins, HarperOne, 2009. 96p. $16.99. ISBN 978-0-06-06527-39; 0-06065-273-X. New York: HarperCollins, HarperOne, 2009. 112p. $11.99pa. ISBN 978-0-06-06523-88; 0-06065-238-1.

Originally published in 1961 and written after his wife's death, *A Grief Observed* is Lewis's reflection on the fundamental issues of life, death, and faith in the midst of his grief. In his forthright and vivid description of his churning feelings, he questions God's presence and leads us through his tortured grieving. One of the few memoirs by a widower, it is highly recommended, especially for men. See chapter 8 for additional editions of this work.

Lieberman, Morton. **Doors Close, Doors Open: Widows, Grieving and Growing.** New York: G. P. Putnam's Sons, 1996. 287p. ISBN 0-399-14141-3.

Lieberman, a professor of psychology at the University of California San Francisco, reports a study of 600 widows over a period of seven years and compares those results with a study of 100 widowers. This is a study of grief, the early months following death of a husband, the role of friends and family, the value of support grownups, and the growth that can occur through this journey. A chapter is devoted to the differences experienced by widowers. An informative, scholarly report for adult readers.

Mays, June B. **Women's Guide to Financial Self-Defense.** New York: Grand Central, 1997. 176p. $17.99. ISBN 0-446-67264-5; 978-0-446-67264-1.

Investment expert Mays combines case histories of women who were experiencing financial hardship after their husband's death with detailed suggestions for handling a wide variety of financial situations. Provides good advice for widows facing common financial problems.

Moore, Alinde J., and Dorothy C. Stratton. **Resilient Widowers: Older Men Adjusting to a New Life.** Amherst, NY: Prometheus Books. 2003. 260p. $20.98. ISBN: 1-59102-082-4; 978-1-59102-082-0.

Based on a qualitative study of 51 widowers, the authors cite services needed to help widowers adjust and achieve independence. Among the topics discussed are models of resilience, marriage and illness of the spouse, caregiving and communication, death of the wife, grief and adjustment, living alone and remarriage, life values carried forward, adult children and other social support, and cohorts and the future. This volume is highly regarded and recommended for any collection.

Roberts, Barbara K. **Death without Denial, Grief without Apology: A Guide for Facing Death and Loss.** Troutdale, OR: NewSage Press, 2002. 116p. $12.00pa. ISBN 0-939165-43-0.

Barbara Roberts was Oregon governor and her husband Frank was an Oregon State senator when he suffered a recurrence of lung cancer. This is the story of how they faced the challenges of his illness, and how they turned to hospice for assistance when they determined that his fight for life was futile. Suggested reading for the individual facing death as well as for the life partner providing care and support.

Robinson, Eric. **One Dark Mile: A Widower's Story.** Amherst, MA: University of Massachusetts Press, 1990. 200p. $35.00. ISBN 0-87023-684-9; 978-0-87023-684-6.

An account of the last two years of a dying woman's life, told by her husband, a professor of history at the University of Massachusetts. When Robinson married his second wife, he was aware of the prognosis of her ovarian cancer. He chronicles her battle for life through several health complications, and his experiences caring for her. "Not for the squeamish, but one of the most honest and eloquent accounts yet written of terminal illness and death" (*Kirkus Reviews* Dec. 1, 1989).

Roiphe, Anne. **Epilogue: A Memoir.** New York: HarperCollins, HarperLuxe, 2008. 288p. $24.95pa. ISBN 0-06-166857-5; 978-0-06-166857-9.

Author Roiphe's husband died suddenly after 39 years of marriage. This memoir is an account of her heartbreak and her attempts to find a new life. "Through crystalline observations that startle with their unassuming honesty, Roiphe recounts the joys and disappointments of not only her marriage, but also her life, trying to reconcile the virtual helplessness she feels with the literal tenets of feminism to which she always held true. No one can really prepare a woman for this passage in life, but Roiphe's luminous memoir is a beacon of help and, ultimately, hope" (*Booklist* June 1, 2008).

Silverman, Phyllis R. **Widow to Widow: How the Bereaved Help One Another.** Death, Dying and Bereavement Series. Philadelphia, PA: Brunner-Routledge, 2004. 259p. $ 34.95pa. ISBN 0-415-94749-9; 978-0-415-94749-7.

This second edition presents the updated theory, research, and findings of the Widow-to-Widow Project, a mutual help program started by the author in the 1960s. This approach emphasizes the social and psychological transitions that accompany widowhood. In this edition, Silverman surveys the success of the widow-to-widow model, with new chapters on issues faced by older widows and widows with young children, and a how-to section concludes the book with useful resources and suggestions for forming community support groups and committees. Silverman is associate professor in social welfare, Department of Psychiatry, Massachusetts General Hospital, Harvard Medical School. For a general adult audience.

Torres, Alissa R., and Sungyoon Choi. **American Widow.** New York: Random House, 2008. 224p. $22.00. ISBN 0-345-50069-5; 978-0-345-50069-4.

Eddie Torres started his new job in the North Tower of the World Trade Center on September 10, 2001. The following day a hijacked plane crashed into his office building, turning Alissa's life upside down. His widow tells the couple's story as well as how she dealt with Eddie's tragic death, her motherhood, and being a "terrorist widow." *American Widow* has generally positive reviews, touching readers from all walks of life. The book provides a close-up view of young widowhood under very public circumstances.

van den Hoonaard, Deborah Kestin. **The Widowed Self: The Older Woman's Journey through Widowhood.** Waterloo, ON: Wilfrid Laurier University Press, 2001. 186p. $32.95. ISBN 0-88920-346-6; 978-0-88920-346-4.

> Dr. van den Hoonaard, associate professor of gerontology at St. Thomas University, combines theory with personal stories to express the emotional and personal challenges facing widows. Both younger and older widows' stories are told—how they relate to their children, their friends, to men, and they describe their husbands' illnesses and deaths. A valuable resource for widows, their families, and professionals working with older adults.

Weaver, Frances. **I'm Not As Old As I Used to Be: Reclaiming Your Life in the Second Half.** Waterville, ME: Thorndike Press, 1997. 208p. $25.95. ISBN 0-7862-1248-9; 978-0-7862-1248-4.

> The author of *The Girls with the Grandmother Faces* presents her experience adapting to widowhood and offers practical suggestions for self-development. After her husband's death, Weaver drank excessively and relates how she retreated into alcoholism until her family and friends convinced her to check into a treatment center. She was then able to adjust to widowhood and to build a new life by returning to school, traveling, and writing. "A feisty, flamboyant yet poignant account of life after 70" (*Booklist* July 1, 1997).

Whipple, Vicky. **Lesbian Widows.** New York: Routledge, 2006. 216p. $110. ISBN 1-56023-330-3; 978-1-56023-330-5.

> Whipple explores the grieving and recovery of lesbian widows. Twenty-five women, including the author, reveal their challenges when widowed at a young age. The widows give their accounts of their efforts to resume their lives, and the legal and financial discrimination they encountered as lesbians. An insightful look into the grieving and recovery process that offers practical advice for coping, whether in or out during the process.

SOURCES CONSULTED

Archer, John. 1999. *The nature of grief: The evolution and psychology of reactions to loss.* London and New York: Routledge.

Beattie, Melody. 1994. *The lessons of love: Rediscovering our passion for life when it all seems too hard to take.* New York: HarperSanFrancisco.

Brothers, Dr. Joyce. 1990. *Widowed.* New York: Simon and Schuster.

Coughlin, Ruth. 1993. *Grieving: A love story.* New York: Random House.

Doka, Kenneth J., ed. 2002. *Disenfranchised grief: New directions, challenges, and strategies for practice.* Champaign, IL: Research Press.

Kübler-Ross, Elisabeth, and Kessler, David. 2000. *Life lessons.* New York: Scribner.

Kübler-Ross, Elisabeth and David Kessler. 2005. *On grief and grieving: Finding the meaning of grief through the five stages of loss.* New York and London: Scribner.

Lewis, C. S. 1996. *A grief observed.* New York: HarperCollins.

Lieberman, Morton. 1996. *Doors close, doors open: Widows, grieving and growing.* New York: G. P. Putnam's Sons.

Loconte, Joe. 2003. Hospice care improves end-of-life care. In *Death and dying*, ed. James Haley, 17–27. Opposing Viewpoints Series. San Diego: Greenhaven Press.

Luebering, Carol. 2004. *Giving yourself permission to grieve*. CareNotes. St. Meinrad, IN: Abbey Press.

Lund, Dale A., and Michael S. Caserta. 2002. Facing life alone: loss of a significant other in later life. In *Living with grief: Loss in later life*, ed. Kenneth J. Doka, 207–24. Living with Grief Series. Washington, DC: Hospice Foundation of America.

Moore, Alinde J., and Dorothy C. Stratton. 2003. *Resilient widowers: Older men adjusting to a new life*. Amherst, NY: Prometheus Books.

Parkes, Colin Murray. 1986. *Bereavement: Studies of grief in adult life*. 2nd American ed. Madison, CN: International Universities Press.

Roberts, Barbara K. 2002. *Death without denial, grief without apology: A guide for facing death and loss*. Troutdale, OR: NewSage Press.

Sanders, Catherine M. 1989. *Grief: The mourning after: Dealing with adult bereavement*. New York: Wiley.

Silverman, Phyllis R. 2002. Loss and transition in later life. In *Living with grief: Loss in later life*, ed. Kenneth J. Doka, 173–87. Living with Grief Series. Washington, DC: Hospice Foundation of America,

Westberg, Granger E. 1997. *Good grief: A constructive approach to the problem of loss*. Minneapolis: Fortress Press.

7

GRIEVING AS WE AGE

CHAPTER OVERVIEW

The aging process causes changes in one's perspective on grieving, and it is helpful for service professionals to understand how the aging process influences perspectives on death and grieving. This chapter explores the aging process and how it influences grieving and attitudes toward life's losses. The impact of grieving on health is followed by suggestions for serving aging bereaved adults. The chapter concludes with a list of recommended resources.

AGING

Thanatologists study death and usually focus on out-of-order death, such as the death of a child and traumatic deaths. Gerontologists study aging and usually focus on the aging process. Often neglected by both thanatologists and gerontologists is attention to loss in later life.

Although aging may be viewed as a journey to self-reconciliation with God or nature in spiritual literature, it is not a theme found in the scientific literature on aging. While many writers, gerontologists, and laypersons think of aging as a series of losses, Noyes (2002) uses the framework of Martha Rogers (1970, 1986).

Rogers's theory of aging describes human development as an ongoing process that does not end with death. Rather, death is just an event in the continuous growth and development of a human being. Humans continue on into infinity even though the body dies (39).

Rogers does not place a value on the losses that people experience as they age. Such losses are considered value-neutral because bodies are not taken with a person after death. Consequently, loss of hearing or sight need not be considered a handicap but rather preparation for future growth.

Noyes' in-depth study of four oldest-old (85 and older) individuals supported Rogers' theories. All four expressed a purpose for their lives, had taken on new roles and responsibilities, and had future plans for their lives. "Growth was mainly in the area of creativity and development of a more inclusive worldview of people and circumstances" (Noyes 2002, 45). The four subjects had prepared for death and accepted death as a reality, but they wanted to enjoy the life that they had left. They all felt that life was given to them to be enjoyed, and they wanted to stay connected to the things they considered important.

We can no longer limit the horizons of the oldest-old with an outdated social construct that holds that life in old age is only a downhill ride. Older people need the opportunity to talk about what death and dying will be like for them. Using an optimistic framework will help the oldest-old find growth in previously unexplored areas to balance the losses they may be experiencing (Noyes 2002, 51).

UNDERSTANDING DEATH

Children can begin to grasp the concept of death, and older children can understand death, but they do not personalize it. In midlife people learn to accept their mortality; a child primarily looks to the future and measures time from date of birth, but in midlife, adults not only measure time by looking to the past and measuring time from birth, they also start thinking of time left to live.

In later life people understand that life is nearing an end. Awareness of death can also be ignored early in the adult years; the young adult is concerned with starting a career and beginning a family. As they accumulate assets and establish a family, young adults usually begin to take legal steps to ensure against unexpected death, heightening the awareness of their mortality.

As adults reach their 30s, 40s, and 50s, they experience physical and sensory declines that serve as reminders of their aging and eventual death:

- One has a loss of speed and endurance.
- One needs more sleep.
- Vision and hearing begin to falter.
- It's harder to learn large amounts of information.
- Women experience menopause.
- Men and women experience a lessening of sexual prowess.
- Death of peers, from accidents or illnesses, are reminders of one's mortality.
- Parents age and die.
- Grandparenthood is a mark of aging.
- Preparing for retirement marks the passage of time. (Doka 2002a, 20–22)

The awareness of mortality gained in midlife influences how we look at the passage of time, and it also leads to the desire to seek meaning in life. Doka (2002a) notes that midlife awareness of mortality may lead to an assessment of one's life goals and may result in revising priorities, such as spending more time with family. Other people who have a troubled past may find that the awareness of death causes panic and the realization that living a meaningful life is no longer possible. Still others cannot face the reality of death and may employ escape or coping mechanisms.

Eventually, a person reaches an understanding that he or she will die, although it may not be any time soon. This awareness of finitude means that persons understand that they are in the final stages of life, and time is viewed through the past. Awareness of finitude prompts the review of one's life to ascertain if his or her life has been meaningful and worthwhile. If the life review determines that the life has been wasted, the result can be despair.

Onset of an awareness of finitude and life review can be hastened with a chronic health condition, commitment to a nursing home, or any situation that leads to the expectation of a shortened life span. Awareness of finitude, in addition to prompting a life review, can also encourage persons to plan for the administration of their estate and for a funeral.

In conclusion, there are three related and overlapping processes concerning death: (1) children begin to comprehend death; (2) older children and middle-aged adults personalize death—it will happen to them; (3) the older adult concedes that death will occur soon and that life is near an end.

The Grief Process in Later Years

Increasing age is often accompanied by the loss of important social relationships, and loss of a spouse is especially important in understanding successful aging. Widowhood is associated with higher mortality rates for both men and women, although the mortality rate for men is higher, especially in the six months following death of a wife. Research shows that the bereaved consult physicians more often, consume more alcohol, tobacco, and tranquilizers, and show more symptoms of illness (Wortman and Silver 1990).

Loss of a Spouse

Widowhood in later life poses different readjustments than those faced by younger widows and widowers (see also chapter 4). Recent U.S. Census Bureau data (2006–2008) indicates that 6.3 percent of the general population is widowed, but the number of widows and widowers is 31.1 percent of the population age 65 and over. Among the population 65 and older, 45 percent of women and 15 percent of men are widowed; 2 percent of widowed women remarry, while approximately 20 percent of widowed men do so (Carr and Ha 2006, 398).

Research shows a clear relationship between bereavement and mortality and morbidity (see the section "Bereavement and Health" further on), but research on whether men or women are more affected by loss of a spouse is inconclusive. Conditions surrounding a spouse's death can influence the depth of grieving. Knowledge that a spouse will die in the near future enables the couple to address emotional and practical issues before the death; however, a prolonged chronic illness may be accompanied by difficult caregiving, financial strain, isolation from other family and friends, and neglect of the caregiver's health (Carr and Ha 2006).

Men and women may react differently to conditions of a spouse's death. According to Carr and Ha (2006), women experience greater psychological distress following a sudden death of a spouse, while men mourn more when their wives died after a prolonged illness. Men usually have less social support than women and bond more closely to their spouse during the final weeks. Women typically may call upon female friends' experience with death of their spouses in preparation for the dying process.

Loss by Minorities

Little research has been conducted on the reactions of African American, Hispanic/Latino, Asian American, and Native American older widows in the United States. Likewise, little research has been done on the resilience of African American, Hispanic, Asian American, and Native American older widows in the United States. Little comparative research has been conducted, although research on ethnic and racial differences in stress and coping suggest that older African American women are more likely to participate in formal religions than white women. Also, research has suggested that African American married women are less dependent on their spouses for emotional support and dependency on household tasks, so African American widows may experience less distress when they lose a spouse. In addition, African American women go beyond the immediate family for emotional support to help their adjustment after a loss (Carr and Ha 2006).

BEREAVEMENT AND HEALTH

Williams' (2002) review of literature revealed that while bereavement effects health, level of depression and stress also are factors in the rise in mortality following a spouse's death. Maintaining an active social life and religious observance can have a positive effect on the health of the bereaved. Williams draws the following conclusions from published data:

• Many deaths after losing a spouse are caused by CVD (cardiovascular disease).

• Depression increases mortality generally.

• Depression is associated specifically with increased CVD mortality.

• Social isolation increases mortality specifically from CVD, although it is proving difficult to determine how. (Williams 2002, 194)

Research shows that social networks and social activity play a critical role in survival after a loss (Williams 2002). In a survey of more than 12,000 couples over a 23-year period, twice as many bereaved men died as bereaved women (30% of men versus 15% of women) (Schaefer, Quesenberry, and Wi 1995).

Sheehy (1998) also discusses research showing a link between exposure to loss and physical and psychological illnesses. Numerous losses accumulate in the second half of life; for example, children leaving home, sudden death of friends, loss of social status. Often people suffering from such stresses, especially men, are unaware of the stress and its impact. Stress is especially a problem for men who expect to be strong and to overcome any obstacle alone.

Sheehy (1998, 126) identifies research results that indicate that unexpressed grief—a false front—is one of the most stressful things a man can do to invite a heart attack. Furthermore, she notes that depression manifests itself differently in men than in women. While women show their emotions by crying and using food to insulate themselves against the emotions, men cover their feelings with drinking and drug use—much more destructive actions.

Women are more likely to attend to changes in their bodies over their life span than are men, and they are more likely to seek medical help when they encounter health problems. Also, lifestyle risk factors influence the risk for developing illnesses. For example, men's risk behaviors include smoking, alcohol consumption, hazardous occupations, and driving fast. Women experience stress because of competing demands on their time and feeling stressed. Gender differences in health in later life are the result of cumulative effects of biology, lifestyle, and behavior, the latter strongly influenced by societal forces (Morgan and Kunkel 2007).

Emotional Reactions

Lund and Caserta (2002) recognized that while 15 to 25 percent of bereaved spouses have difficulty long term coping with their loss, older adults are more resilient than younger persons because death is more expected in later years, and older adults have had opportunities to manage successfully losses in their lives and have developed strategies for coping. Lund and Caserta (2002) state that recent research has revealed that the bereavement process is less an orderly progression of stages than a roller coaster ride with rapidly changing emotions, recognizing personal weaknesses, learning new skills, experiencing feelings of loneliness and fatigue, and forming new relationships. "Our own research has also documented that there is considerable diversity among and within bereaved persons. Not all people experience the same feeling, thoughts, and actions as they move through the process" (Lund and Caserta 2002, 210).

Typically there is a direct correlation between intensity of grief reactions and the emotional commitment in a relationship. Whether partners are married or not, intense commitment typically results in a stronger grief response.

Loss of a grandchild is an extremely difficult loss for an older person. Bereaved grandparents express feelings of shock and disbelief and a need to restructure their relationships with other grandchildren and family members. They have a "shattered belief system" and feel that life is unfair. They also feel guilt for surviving (deVries, Blieszner, and Blando 2002, 231).

Death of a sibling in later life also is felt deeply by older people. Siblings experience a unique bond because of their shared generation and experiences over time. While they may have been competitive and rivals earlier in life, the attachment of older siblings can grow stronger in later years. Siblings frequently rely on each other for emotional support and share each other's life story (deVries, Blieszner, and Blando 2002).

Friends assume their position in a person's life by choice. They share values, interests, and experiences while offering companionship, empathy, and affection. Friendships may remain intact despite changes in family relationships and work roles. Death of a friend evokes not only the loss of a relationship but the fear that "it could have been me" with the feeling of relief that it wasn't. "For older gay men and lesbians, the role of friendship may be even more pronounced" (deVries Blieszner, and Blando 2002, 234).

Although it is expected that older people will die, Knight notes that in his clinical experience, older people do not anticipate the death of others; it is a surprise emotionally. In many cases the death of loved ones is more difficult for older adults because of the longer relationships (Knight 2004,142).

Depression

Approximately 15 percent of older people in the community and 25 percent in nursing homes suffer from depression. Depression is more common among

Hispanic and black older people than among whites, although racial/ethnic differences disappeared when researchers examined differences in education, health insurance coverage, income, and physical health status. Another study showed that people with a lower level of education were more likely to experience depression (Morgan and Kunkel 2007). Sheehy (1998) also cites medical research that suggests that depression may be a strong predictor of heart attack and stoke, similar to the prediction capability of high blood pressure and high cholesterol count.

DISENFRANCHISED GRIEF

Doka has defined disenfranchised grief as "grief that is experienced when a loss cannot be openly acknowledged, socially sanctioned, or publicly mourned" (Doka 2002b, 160). When a person experiences such a loss, no one else recognizes that it is a cause for grief.

Sources of disenfranchised grief for older people are losses within same-sex relationships, unmarried cohabiting heterosexual relationships, partner loss due to aids, and partners in extramarital affairs. In all of these types of relationships, the bereavement is similar to loss of a spouse—loss of companionship, loneliness, depression, and distress associated with assumption of new daily tasks (Lund and Caserta 2002).

Ageism in American society places a lesser value on older persons and can be a factor in disenfranchisement. Fear or shame also cause a person experiencing loss to believe they are unworthy of support or refuse to acknowledge and share their loss. An example is elder abuse, when persons have lost safety and a relationship yet fear appearing frail or facing judgments about their support, family, or abilities. Also, multiple losses over time inhibit an individual from acknowledging all of the losses. Unrecognized losses include the loss of siblings, companionship relationships, nursing home friends or staff, and close relatives—children, grandchildren, or great-grandchildren. In the latter case, the needs of older family members may be overlooked as people focus on surviving children and spouses. Also, because of ageism, the death of a parent is discounted when a child is older (Doka 2002b).

Other unacknowledged losses include developmental losses such as youth, roles—including work and leisure roles—abilities and independence that can result in loss of home, neighbors, and community. Some people as they age may lose their native culture as descendants assimilate into a new culture. Onset of dementia can result in loss of a relationship because the personality can be so changed that the loved one is perceived as dead, though the individual remains physically alive. Another unacknowledged loss can be a pet who provides companionship, protection, and opportunities for interaction with others. Unacknowledged loss can also result when a life review brings up a miscarriage or abortion that was not mourned. In later life, that loss can be mourned (Doka 2002b).

Sometimes older people are denied the opportunity to grieve when loss of friends or relatives are kept from them because they are considered too frail to bear the loss. Unfortunately, grief for a friend may be disenfranchised because society tends to reserve the grieving role to family members. "Friends are largely unsupported in a world of grief; health care facilities, employers, and other social institutions often exclude friends during the dying process and grieving ritual" (deVries, Blieszner, and Blando 2002, 235).

GRIEF INTERVENTION

Doka (2002b) suggests that disenfranchised grief should be treated like any other type of grief. Those working with older persons should be aware of the range of losses encountered later in life. Also, loss is individually evaluated and perceived; retirement may be welcomed by some and considered a major loss by others. In any case, a professional working with a disenfranchised griever must assist the grieving person to understand the factor disenfranchising the grief.

Transition after Loss

People dealing with loss of a loved one often treat it like an illness that a person can get over. "Yet, particularly in later life, bereavement is a normal transition in the life cycle, and, it is hoped, one from which the grieving person can grow" (Silverman 2002, 173).

Silverman (2002, 173) identifies three factors that are critical to a healthy transition after loss of a loved one: (1) the bereaved must change how they relate to others as well as themselves; (2) their relationship with the deceased must change; and (3) they must receive support from friends, family, and their community.

Knight (2004) points out that grief work with older adults may be complicated by multiple deaths within a relatively short period of time. Since one loss can remind us of others, older adults have a long history and may rework several losses both past and more recent.

Older people may lose a spouse, siblings, friends, and members of the extended family. With each loss, the transition continues because each death is unique, and the bereaved person continues to address loss and continues to order and make meaning out of a changing world. In the process, they learn new coping skills (Silverman 2002).

After the initial period of shock following a death, the numbing dissipates, and the bereaved persons realize that life will be different without the person who died. Most friends and relatives have returned to their lives, and grieving persons may feel inadequate because they are asked why they are not over their grief.

One of the most difficult things that all mourners need to do is to bear the pain—the strong, upsetting, and strange feelings that they are experiencing. They may look for ways of avoiding the feelings to give themselves respite. Learning to cope with these feelings will take time, education, and an ability to acknowledge the changed context of their lives (Silverman 2001, 177).

In time, a bereaved person accommodates the death of a loved one, but there is not an end to the grieving. People develop a sense of their ability to prevail and deal with the pain. Pain is no longer the driving force in their lives. Faith and religion can play a role in comforting mourners.

When people are widowed late in life and after a long life together, they must find a way to keep the deceased alive in their lives through activities that memorialize them. However, a person cannot live in the past because the deceased is both present and absent. Life goes on with a place for the deceased in memory, but life is different. "It becomes clear that grief is not something from which people recover. They do not get over it. There is no closure. They do not live life as they once lived it" (Silverman 2002, 182).

Support for the Bereaved

The first support for bereaved persons will be family, friends, and neighbors who can help plan the funeral, provide food, and help with some of the physical and emotional needs of the bereaved. A clergy member and funeral director and staff can help with funeral arrangements. As time progresses, mourners may need professional help as their needs change from clergy, physicians, or mental health professionals.

Another source of help is anyone who has lived through a similar personal experience. People who have gone before, who have lost loved ones, can share their experiences with the newly bereaved, including life style changes. Men especially may have to learn to do housework, cook, and shop for the first time, while women must learn to pay bills and do minor home repairs. Mutual help organizations like clubs or service organizations can help peers make decisions through social activities, newsletters, meetings, group discussions, telephone hotlines, and one-on-one contact.

Throughout the process of working with a grieving older adult, the mental health professional or helping professional should validate the person's grief and assist in developing effective interventions, such as therapy, bibliotherapy, support groups, self-help programs, and use of therapeutic rituals. "Therapeutic rituals also can be validating by affirming either publicly or privately the legitimacy of grief. Such rituals can be conducted in a variety of places where older persons frequent and reside, including nursing homes and senior centers" (Doka 2002b, 166).

Since reactions to bereavement are so diverse, a variety of intervention formats and professionals should be available. Some feel that they need one-on-one counseling, while others benefit from a self-help group. For many, reading about similar people who have experienced grief can be a beneficial experience.

Following is good advice for teachers, mental health professionals, and library and information professionals who encounter grieving older adults: "The best way to help bereaved persons is to be educated about the process; assess the context in which it occurs; become familiar with a wide range of resources; and be patient, nonjudgmental, and a good listener" (Lund and Caserta 2002, 220).

SUMMARY

Loss in later life is often neglected as a topic of study and concern. Essential is an understanding of death, which begins in childhood, is personalized among older children and middle-aged adults, and accepted by older adults.

Increasing age is often accompanied by the loss of important social relationships, including loss of a spouse. Typically there is a direct correlation between intensity of grief reactions and the emotional commitment in a relationship, whether partners are married or not.

Disenfranchised grief is experienced when a loss cannot be "openly acknowledged, socially sanctioned, or publicly mourned" (Doka 2002b, 160). When a person experiences such a loss, no one else recognizes that it is a cause for grief, yet disenfranchised grief should be treated like any other type of grief. Those working with older persons should be aware of the range of losses encountered later in life.

The first support for bereaved persons will be family, friends, and neighbors who can help with some of the physical and emotional needs of the bereaved. As time progresses, the mourner may need professional help from clergy, physicians, or mental health professionals.

The best way to help bereaved aging persons is to be educated about the grieving process, assess the context in which it occurs, become familiar with pertinent resources available, and be a nonjudgmental listener.

RECOMMENDED RESOURCES

In addition to the resources listed here, see also the resources recommended in chapter 6.

Albom, Mitch. **Tuesdays with Morrie: An Old Man, a Young Man, and Life's Greatest Lesson.** New York: Knopf Doubleday Publishing Group, Doubleday, 1997. 208p. $23.95. ISBN 0-385-48451-8; 978-0-385-48451-0.

> The true story of Albom and the discussions he had with his dying sociology professor and mentor, Morrie Schwartz. Albom calls these sessions a class, the topic is Life, and the book is his final exam. "This book, small and easily digested, stopping just short of the maudlin and the mawkish, is on the whole sincere, sentimental, and skillful. . . . Place it under the heading 'Inspirational'" (*Kirkus Reviews* July 1, 1997).

Berman, Claire. **When a Brother or Sister Dies: Looking Back, Moving Forward.** Portsmouth, NH: Greenwood, Praeger, 2009. 140p. $34.95. ISBN 0-313-35528-2; 978-0-313-35528-8.

> When a brother or sister dies, we lose a lifetime companion, someone who shares a family history. In most cases of sibling loss, there are conflicted feelings of pride and jealousy, as well as love and hate. Making peace with the death of the sibling can be very difficult for an adult. Berman interviewed a number of bereavement scholars to explore the phenomenon of sibling loss and she uses her findings, along with her own experience of losing a sister to heart disease, to show the reader how to understand and navigate a loss that causes so much emotional confusion and pain.

Bernardin, Joseph Louis. **The Gift of Peace.** Chicago: Loyola Press, 1997. 156p. $17.95. ISBN 0-8294-0955-6; 978-0-8294-0955-0.

> The Chicago cardinal recounts the events and emotions of his last three years before his death in November 1996. He sustained a false accusation of sexual misconduct as well as the traumatic diagnosis and suffering from cancer. "Bernardin also accepted his own imminent death from pancreatic cancer as a true lesson of the cross, writing here about his mixed sense of abandonment and hope with a profound awareness of the meaning of shared suffering and Christian love. A very moving last testament, written with simplicity and deep wisdom" (*Library Journal* May 1, 1997).

Bevington, Helen S. **The Third and Only Way: Reflections on Staying Alive.** Durham, NC: Duke University Press, 1996. 224p. $34.95. ISBN 0-8223-1850-4; 978-0-8223-1850-7.

> Bevington seeks an alternative way to deal with old age and death instead of the solitude her mother accepted and the despair of her father. She discusses a number of literary and historical figures, including such diverse characters as Chekhov, Marcus Aurelius, Beatrix Potter, Thoreau, and Alexander the Great. "Her work is an entertaining but not profound meditation on life and the acceptance of death" (*Library Journal* Oct. 15, 1996).

Chittister, Joan. **The Gift of Years: Growing Older Gracefully.** New York: BlueBridge, 2008. 240p. $19.95. ISBN 1-933346-10-8; 978-1-933346-10-6.

"Benedictine sister Chittister beautifully downplays regrets and accents the rewards of a mature life. While she acknowledges the pain of old age, she focuses on the new beginnings that life can offer at this stage and discusses the need to stay involved, to put one's affairs in order, and to be open to new relationships" (*Library Journal* May 15, 2008).

Furman, Joan, and David McNabb. **The Dying Time: Practical Wisdom for the Dying and Their Caregivers.** New York: Crown, Harmony/Bell Tower, 1997. 224p. $14.95pa. ISBN 0-609-80003-5; 978-0-609-80003-4.

A nurse practitioner and lawyer collaborate to produce this useful guide to caregiving for the elderly. The authors provide suggestions for the mental and spiritual peace of both the dying and the caregiver. "Overall, the messages in this concise little book are practical, clear, and comforting" (*Library Journal* Oct. 1, 1997).

Hansson, Robert O., and Margaret S. Stroebe. **Bereavement in Late Life: Coping, Adaptation, and Developmental Influences.** Washington, DC: American Psychological Association, 2007. 219p. $59.95. ISBN 1-59147-472-8; 978-1-59147-472-2.

In an individual's later years, bereavement poses an array of difficult issues for coping. Hansson and Stroebe, professors of psychology, present a critical review of the literature and dominant theories in the field of bereavement and examine how aging affects the experience of bereavement in late life. The authors also present a path for future research on the bereavement experiences of older adults. "This volume will be particularly valuable to developmental psychologists, gerontologists, and medical practitioners, but it will also serve those in training" (*Choice* Mar. 1, 2007).

Heinz, Donald. **The Last Passage: Recovering a Death of Our Own.** New York: Oxford University Press, 1998. 320p. $45.00. ISBN 0-19-511643-7; 978-0-19-511643-4.

Heinz, dean of the College of Humanities and Fine Arts at California State University, argues that we should reconceptualize death and to give it meaning beyond that of a biological event. He discusses models for such a reconstruction by offering an overview of the ways death has been viewed throughout human history. "Heinz admits that his own Christian beliefs color his discussion, but he compensates by devoting ample consideration to other religious traditions. In conclusion, he looks to music, the visual arts, dance, theater, and language to help invigorate the connection between the living and the dead" (*Library Journal* Dec. 1, 1998).

Hope, Mary. **Towards Evening: Reflections on Aging, Illness and the Soul's Union with God.** Ed. LaVonne Neff. Orleans, MA: Paraclete Press, 1997. 200p. $10.95pa. ISBN 1-55725-183-5; 978-1-55725-183-1.

Daisy Haywood Moseley kept a journal that she later published under the name Mary Hope. "Hope, as she entered her 60s more than 40 years ago, began contemplating her relationship with God. The published author and devout Catholic's observations may offer comfort for others who are aging" (*Library Journal* May 1, 1997).

Kastenbaum, Robert. **On Our Way—The Final Passage Through Life and Death.** University of California Press, 2004. 466p. $31.95. ISBN 0-520-21880-9; 978-0-520-21880-2.

Kastenbaum, professor emeritus at Arizona State University, explores the role of death rituals in human lives. Using interviews, case studies, and sociological findings, he reflects on biological, anthropological, theological, and psychological understandings of death and how these ideas influence how people live. He also surveys religious beliefs and practices from a variety of cultures. "The question that pervades this book is 'How can one determine the place of death in life and live one's life with the awareness that the body may be ultimately 'food for worms' or continue in an afterlife?'" (*Choice* Nov. 1, 2004).

Lawrence-Lightfoot, Sara. **The Third Chapter: Passion, Risk, and Adventure in the 25 Years after 50.** New York: Farrar, Straus and Giroux, 2009. 272p. $25.00. ISBN 0-374-27549-1; 978-0-374-27549-5.

An exploration of life's third chapter, profiling 40 individuals who had successful careers but, for various reasons, embarked on a different life course after age 50. "Although she references psychologists and other social scientists, the book is not dryly academic. It's a collection of powerful stories by a gifted interpreter and story-teller" (*Library Journal* Feb. 1, 2009). "Heady, fruitful explorations of ill-charted terrain destined for a population explosion" (*Kirkus Reviews* Oct. 15, 2008).

Pipher, Mary. **Another Country: Navigating the Emotional Terrain of Our Elders.** New York: Penguin Group, Riverhead Trade, 2000. 352p. $15.00pa. ISBN 1-57322-784-6; 978-1-57322-784-1.

Psychologist Mary Pipher suggests strategies that can help bridge the gaps that separate younger people from a growing generation of elders. "Full of insight and compassion, this provides a vivid glimpse into the other country for those seeing their elders go there, as well as those people preparing for their own journey" (*Library Journal* Aug. 1, 1999).

SOURCES CONSULTED

Carr, Deborah, and Jung-Hwa Ha. 2006. Bereavement. In *Handbook of girls' and women's psychological health,* ed. Judith Worell and Carol D. Goodheart, 397–401. Oxford: Oxford University Press.

deVries, Brian, Rosemary Blieszner, and John A. Blando. 2002. Faces of grief and intimacy in later life. In *Living with grief: Loss in later life,* ed. Kenneth J. Doka, 225–41. Washington, DC: Hospice Foundation of America.

Doka, Kenneth J., ed. 2002a. *Living with grief: Loss in later life.* Washington, DC: Hospice Foundation of America.

Doka, Kenneth J. 2002b. Disenfranchised grief. In *Living with grief: Loss in later life,* ed. Kenneth J. Doka, 159–68. Washington, DC: Hospice Foundation of America,

Knight, Bob G. 2004. *Psychotherapy with older adults.* Thousand Oaks, CA: Sage.

Lund, Dale A., and Michael S. Caserta. 2002. Facing life alone: Loss of a significant other in later life. In *Living with grief: Loss in later life,* ed. Kenneth J. Doka, 207–23. Washington, DC: Hospice Foundation of America,

Morgan, Leslie A., and Suzanne R. Kunkel. 2007. *Aging, society, and the life course.* 3rd ed. New York: Springer.

Noyes, Lin E. 2002. Stories of the oldest-old as they face death. In *Living with grief: Loss in later life,* ed. Kenneth J. Doka, 37–54. Washington, DC: Hospice Foundation of America.

Rogers, M. E. 1970. *An introduction to the theoretical basis of nursing.* Philadelphia: Davis.

Rogers, M. E. 1986. Science of unitary human beings. In *Exploration on Martha Rogers' science of unitary human beings,* ed. V. M. Malinski, 3–8. Norwalk: Appleton-Century-Croft.

Schaefer, C., C. P. Quesenberry, Jr., and S. Wi. 1995. Mortality following conjugal bereavement and the effects of a shared environment. *American Journal of Epidemiology* 141: 1142–52.

Sheehy, Gail. 1998. *Understanding men's passages: Discovering the new map of men's lives.* New York: Random House.

Silverman, Phyllis R. 2002. Loss and transition in later life. In *Living with grief: Loss in later life,* ed. Kenneth J. Doka, 173–90. Washington, DC: Hospice Foundation of America.

U.S. Bureau of the Census. American FactFinder. *2006–2008 American Community Survey 3-year estimates.* Available at: http://factfinder.census.gov/servlet/STTable?_bm = y&-geo_id = 01000US&-qr_name = ACS_2008_3YR_G00_S0103&-ds_name = ACS_2008_3YR_G00. Accessed November 23, 2010.

Williams, J. Richard. 2002. Effects of grief on a survivor's health. In *Living with grief: Loss in later life,* ed. Kenneth J. Doka, 191–206. Washington, DC: Hospice Foundation of America.

Wortman, Camille B., and Roxanne Cohen Silver. 1990. Successful mastery of bereavement and widowhood: A life-course perspective. In *Successful aging: Perspectives from the behavioral sciences,* ed. Paul B. Baltes and Margret M. Baltes, 225–37. Cambridge: Cambridge University Press.

8

---•◆•---

GRIEF AND RELIGION

CHAPTER OVERVIEW

The United States is a diverse population, one that shares equally diverse religions. Self-identified Christians make up the largest number of the population, while adherents to Judaism, Islam, Hinduism, Buddhism, paganism, and atheism represent the broad spectrum of religious freedom guaranteed by the First Amendment to the U.S. Constitution.

The role of religion in the grief experience varies. For some, faith in God is shaken when a loved one unexpectedly dies, or a marriage suddenly dissolves. For others, those same experiences result in a closer relationship that is often described as joy in the midst of deep pain. The role of faith, and especially the supernatural, is a delicate subject. Unless one is close to the bereaved and is certain of his or her beliefs, attempts to share one's faith may not be welcome.

For those whose faith beliefs are known, we present this brief collection of materials from the major world religions: Buddhism, Christianity, Judaism, and Islam. Despite copious attempts to locate materials from all major religions, the mainstream literature tends to avoid the subject of religion and grief. Therefore, this selection is briefer than other chapters in this book, and some titles were chosen based on popular, rather than professional, reviews.

While materials have been sorted in alphabetical order of their corresponding religion, it is hoped that readers will keep an open mind and be willing to read outside of their own faith experience. Many of these resources have universal truth and application. In addition to religion headings, "Multifaith" and "New Age" were added for those materials that either apply to more than one religion, or reflect a postmodern application of established religions. Again, the reader would do well to look at all materials despite the organizational heading.

Unfortunately, we were able to locate only a very few Islamic resources, most likely due to the West's continued lack of understanding of this major religion. In addition to the two titles located, we have listed a few publishers in this section for the reader to investigate further. This is not a comprehensive list, nor is there any guarantee that books on grief will be found.

Unless otherwise indicated, materials are best suited for adults.

BUDDHISM

Becker, Carl B. **Breaking the Circle: Death and the Afterlife in Buddhism.** Boulder, CO: NetLibrary, 1993. E-book. $21.00. ISBN 0-585-03949-6; 978-0-585-03949-7.

The author covers the concept of rebirth in Buddhism, including chapters that provide background for the issues of suicide and euthanasia from a Buddhist perspective. General critique is that Becker does not consult the standard text G. R. Welbon's *The Buddhist Nirvana and Its Western Interpreters* (1969). Consequently, Becker's coverage of alternative interpretations of Nirvana is dismissed, as well as his lapse into personal observation rather than scholarly objectivity (*Choice* Apr. 1, 1994).

Coberly, Margaret. **Sacred Passage: How to Provide Fearless, Compassionate Care for the Dying.** Collingdale, PA: Diane, 2006. 162p. $16.00pa. ISBN 0-7567-9940-6; 978-0-7567-9940-3.

Coberly was an experienced RN when her brother was diagnosed with terminal cancer. Through helping him, Coberly found the Tibetan Buddhism's view of death as a natural happening to be helpful, especially when compared with the Western health care view of death. Coberly's book also provides advice on what to expect during the dying process. "Recommended for public and academic libraries, and as a gift for anyone who may be in contact with a terminally ill friend, relative, or patient" (*Library Journal* Apr. 15, 2002).

Cuevas, Bryan J. **Travels in the Netherworld: Buddhist Popular Narratives of Death and the Afterlife in Tibet.** New York, NY: Oxford University Press, 2008. 216p. $65.00. ISBN 0-19-534116-3; 978-0-19-534116-4.

Cuevas examines a little-known genre of Tibetan narrative literature about the delok, ordinary men and women who claim to have died, traveled through hell, and then returned from the afterlife. Their accounts emphasize the universal Buddhist principles of impermanence and worldly suffering, the fluctuations of karma, and the feasibility of obtaining a favorable rebirth through virtue and merit. Cuevas argues that these narratives express ideas about death and the afterlife that held wide currency among all classes of faithful Buddhists in Tibet.

Mullin, Glenn H. **Living in the Face of Death: Advice from the Tibetan Masters.** Ithaca, NY: Snow Lion, 1998. 238p. $16.95pa. ISBN 1-55939-100-6; 978-1-55939-100-9.

Covers topics such as meditation techniques to prepare for death, inspirational accounts of the deaths of saints and yogis, methods to facilitate the transition to new modes of consciousness, and a clear introduction that explains the concepts of karma and reincarnation. Whereas Western society views death as the final taboo, the Tibetan tradition incorporates meditation on death into everyday life. "Mullin tends to consider Tibetan thinking and behavior better than Western rather than just different. The reader may make the opposite judgment. Recommended for academic and public libraries with strong collections in religion and philosophy" (*Library Journal* Dec. 1, 1998).

CHRISTIANITY

A Place Prepared: Helping Children Understand Death and Heaven. Orleans, MA: Paraclete Press, 2000. DVD. 40 min. $34.95. ISBN 1-55725-241-6; 978-1-55725-241-8.

By helping adults come to terms with their thoughts and feelings about death, they can in turn help children do the same. Children have different ideas about death and the afterlife, often dependent on their age and developmental stage. This video helps not only approach the subject of death, but also anticipates children's emotions when death does occur, and help them walk through it. "An excellent product for both group and individual viewing, it will be useful for parenting seminars, continuing education programs, and general population viewing. In-service programs for educators would find the first two segments of the video particularly beneficial" (*School Library Journal* July 1, 2000).

Bregman, Lucy. **Beyond Silence and Denial: Death and Dying Reconsidered.** Boulder, CO: NetLibrary, 1999. E-book. $18.00. ISBN 0-585-27258-1; 978-0-585-27258-0.

Bregman discusses the historical approach Christianity has had toward death and suggests that the death-awareness and hospice movement has changed Christianity's view of death and dying to being natural.

Carmody, John T. **God Is No Illusion: Meditations on the End of Life.** London, UK: Continuum International, Burns & Oates, 1997. 128p. ISBN 1-56338-188-5; 978-1-56338-188-1.

The author, a multiple myeloma patient, shares psalms that focus on the end of life. Whether the reader is suffering from terminal cancer, AIDS, or heart disease, Carmody shares the insight he gained through his illness with people facing their end of life.

Davies, Douglas. **The Theology of Death.** London, UK: Continuum International, T&T Clark, 2007. 208p. $120.00. ISBN 0-567-03048-2; 978-0-567-03048-1.

Aimed at Christians, Davies explores the historical view of life after death, in particular, as Christian thought has evolved over the last two thousand years. Davies is willing to embrace all possibilities—life after death, eternal life in the now, and points in between. The topic of hope is a key element and the book explores the birth and fostering of hope within Christian traditions. Best suited for scholars.

Hope, Mary, and LaVonne Neff, ed. **Towards Evening: Reflections on Aging, Illness and the Soul's Union with God.** Orleans, MA: Paraclete Press, 1997. 200p. $10.95pa. ISBN 1-55725-183-5; 978-1-55725-183-1.

Daisy Haywood Moseley first published her journal in 1949 under the pen name of Mary Hope. Deeply influenced by her devout Catholic faith, she wrote forthrightly about the pain and loneliness of old age, but always with the greater vision of God's continuous blessings. Also recommended for caregivers.

Lewis, C. S. **A Grief Observed.** New York: Harper Collins Publishers, 2009. E-book. $11.99. ISBN: 0-06-194934-5; 978-0-06-194934-0. New York: Random House, 1999. ISBN 0-553-23539-7; 978-0-553-23539-5. Grand Rapids, MI: Zondervan. 1994. 96p. $11.00pa. ISBN: 0-06-065284-5; 978-0-06-065284-5.

Ashland, OR: Blackstone Audio, Incorporated. 2005. 120min. $24.00. ISBN: 0-7861-7586-9; 978-0-7861-7586-4. 120min. $29.95. ISBN: 0-7861-7861-2; 978-0-7861-7861-2.

Lewis, a confirmed bachelor, was married to Joy Davidman, an American poet with two small children, for four years before Davidman succumbed to cancer. In this journal Lewis honestly states his doubts, his rage, and his awareness of human frailty. An enduring classic by one of the most brilliant Christian apologists of the 20th century.

Meyer, Roger. **Fighting Grief with F-Cubed: Faith, Family and Friends.** Mustang, OK: Tate, 2008. 75p. $8.95pa. ISBN 1-60247-796-5; 978-1-60247-796-4.

Whether one needs to react to or prepare for the wrenching loss of a loved one, this brief book can help. The author wrote this book after losing his 19-year-old son in order to help others deal with the grief that comes with such a loss. Meyer encourages mourners to fall back on their faith, family, and friends to carry them through the very trying times that come with losing a loved one

Sawyers, Norma E. **A Personal Grief and a Reasonable Faith: A Mother's Journey from Tragedy to Triumph in Understanding the Christian Faith.** Bolivar, MO: Dogwood, 1992. 140p. $11.95pa. ISBN 0-9630031-0-0; 978-0-9630031-0-2.

The accidental death of Sawyer's daughter at the age of 15 provides the springboard for her journey into faith. Sawyer asks many of the questions Christians face in this situation: Is it wrong to doubt and question? Why does God allow evil and suffering? and other questions of faith. This work could be helpful for those who approach grief through the Christian framework.

Wangerin, Walter, Jr. **Mourning into Dancing.** Grand Rapids, MI: Zondervan, 1996. 304p. $19.99pa. ISBN 0-310-20765-7; 978-0-310-20765-8.

"Death doesn't wait till the ends of our lives to meet us and to make an end," writes Walter Wangerin. "Instead, we die a hundred times before we die; and all the little endings on the way are like a slowly growing echo of the final BANG!" *Mourning into Dancing* defines the stages of grief, names the many kinds of loss we suffer, shows how to help the grief-stricken, gives a new vision of Christ's sacrifice, and shows how a loving God shares our grief. We learn from this book that the way to dancing is through the valley of mourning—that grief is a poignant reminder of the fullness of life Christ obtained for us through his resurrection. "Wangerin depicts human feeling convincingly; his theology that all death is related to the first (primal fall and original sin) supports his hopeful and confident faith in the purpose of grief as leading to renewal, healing, and resurrection. For public and seminary libraries" (*Library Journal* Aug. 1, 1984).

Waters, Brent. **Dying and Death: A Resource for Christian Reflection.** Cleveland, OH: Pilgrim Press, The United Church Press, 1996. 168p. $12.95pa. ISBN 0-8298-1121-4; 978-0-8298-1121-6.

Waters invites congregations "to study, discuss, and discern how we might give a wise and responsible witness to our faith in the face of death." Waters addresses the personal and social issues of when and how one should die—not from a legal or political point of view, but from a carefully considered theological and moral perspective. "Although the book is a specific response to resolutions on dying and death adopted by the United Church of Christ, it is not an official document, and its usefulness is not limited to UCC congregations. The appendix on resources and the bibliography are rich sources for readers who wish to pursue the issues in more depth" (*Booklist* Apr. 15, 1996).

Weaver, Andrew J., and Howard W. Stone. **Reflections on Grief and Spiritual Growth.** Nashville, TN: Abingdon Press, 2005. 183p. $13.00pa. ISBN 0-687-06508-9; 978-0-687-06508-0.

A series of 16 essays by Catholic and Protestant writers. Reflecting on their experiences with grief and loss as a part of their faith journey, these writers share the lessons they have learned and the wisdom they have gleaned from their personal experiences. An included study guide helps individuals and groups grapple with the reality of grief and loss in the context of their Christian faith so that we may better learn to grieve as those who have hope.

Westberg, Granger E. **Good Grief.** Minneapolis, MN: Augsburg Fortress, Augsburg Books, 2009. E-book. $4.99. ISBN 1-102-04060-6; 978-1-102-04060-6. 2004. $8.99. ISBN 0-8066-5150-4; 978-0-8066-5150-7. 2004. $8.99pa. ISBN: 0-8006-1361-9; 978-0-8006-1361-7.

A classic, in the same league as C. S. Lewis' *A Grief Observed,* that comforts the bereft by explaining the natural state of grieving and the different stages we go through. The decision to work through one's grief can result in significant personal growth.

ISLAM

Al-Jibali, Muhammad. **The Inevitable Journey: Sickness, Death, and the Grave.** Arlington, TX: Al-Qur'an was-Sunnah Society, 1997. 225p. $10.00pa. ISBN 1-886451-06-0; 978-1-886451-06-3.

Halevi, Leor. **Muhammad's Grave: Death Rites and the Making of Islamic Society.** New York: Columbia University Press, 2007. 416p. $45.00. ISBN 0-231-13742-7; 978-0-231-13742-3.

An historical account of early, premodern Islam. Halevi reveals that religious scholars of the early Islamic period produced codes of funerary law not only to define the handling of a Muslim corpse but also to transform everyday urban practices. The real and imaginary relationships between husbands and wives, prayer leaders and mourners, and even dreamers and the dead are presented. Recommended for scholars.

Other Islamic Publishers

Al-Saadawi Publications. 20 S. Quaker Lane, Ste. 120, Alexandria, VA 22314. 703-751-4800; 703-751-4833 fax.

Amana Publications. 10710 Tucker Street, Beltsville, MD 20705. http://www.amana-publications.com.

Dar-us-Salam. 1111 Conrad Sauer Dr., Houston, TX 77043. P.O. Box 79194, Houston, TX 77279. 713-722-0419; 713-722-0431 fax.

Ta-Ha Publishers Ltd. Unit 4, The Windsor Centre, Windsor Grove, West Norwood, London SE27 9NT. +44-208-670-1888; +44-208-670-1998 fax. http://www.taha.co.uk/index.php.

Tahrike Tarsile Qur'an, Inc. 80-08 51st Ave., Elmhurst, New York 11373. 718-446-6472; 718-446-4370 fax.

JUDAISM

Gillman, Neil. **The Death of Death: Resurrection and Immortality in Jewish Thought.** Woodstock, VT: Jewish Lights, 2000. 336p. $18.95pa. ISBN 1-58023-081-4; 978-1-58023-081-0

Theologian Neil Gillman offers readers an original and compelling argument that Judaism, a religion often thought to pay little attention to the afterlife, not only presents us with rich ideas on this subject but submits that Jewish thought includes bodily resurrection and spiritual immortality. "Gillman's writing style is work-manlike, but his organization and knowledge of history are excellent, making this a good starting point for anyone interested in the topic. His own personal conclusion—a belief in bodily resurrection—makes for an intriguing summation" (*Booklist* May 15, 1997).

Goldman, Ari L. **Living a Year of Kaddish.** New York: Schocken Books, 2006. 224p. $14.00pa. ISBN 0805211314; 978-0805211313.

Traces the author's experience during the Jewish ritual year of mourning after the loss of his father. Despite his parents' divorce at age six, which left his father as a "distant presence," Goldman felt the obligation of saying kaddish daily for 11 months to honor his father. With him were nine other men, the number required to form an minyan. "The book is a poignant chronicle of bereavement and solace to be read by Jews and non-Jews alike who mourn the loss of a loved one" (*Booklist* Aug. 2003).

Kamin, Ben. **The Path of the Soul: Making Peace with Mortality.** Bloomington, IN: iUniverse, 2009. 164pa. $15.95. ISBN 1-4401-0998-2; 978-1-4401-0998-0.

Senior rabbi at Temple Tifereth Israel in Cleveland, Kamin offers a compassionate and well-reasoned tour through modern Jewish interpretations of death. There is not so much explanation as the promise of life itself and "the universe and its elusive yet comforting concept of a God," as well as the duty to live our lives on earth in a way that uplifts spiritual values and does honor to the memory of the departed. Intelligent and consoling, Kamin's work should be well received by most readers (*Library Journal* July 1, 1999).

Kushner, Harold S. **The Lord Is My Shepherd: Healing Wisdom of the Twenty-third Psalm.** New York: Knopf Doubleday, 2003. 192p. $19.95. ISBN 1-4000-4056-6; 978-1-4000-4056-8.

Kushner discusses one line of the Twenty-third Psalm in each chapter. In the process, he expands our understanding of this uncommonly powerful biblical work and helps us benefit from its everyday wisdom. "Perhaps the greatest overarching message of the psalm that Kushner wishes to inculcate is that it tells us that, though God does not prevent evil and suffering, He is always with each person who is wronged, each person who is suffering, and He will provide the resources of spirit to transcend fear and experience the ongoing holiness of life" (*Booklist* June 1, 2003).

Lamm, Maurice. **Consolation: The Spiritual Journey beyond Grief.** Philadelphia: Jewish Publication Society, 2005. 360p. $30.00. ISBN 0-8276-0764-4; 978-0-8276-0764-4. 2005. 340p. $18.00pa. ISBN 0-8276-0815-2; 978-0-8276-0815-3.

The author of *The Jewish Way in Death and Mourning* helps mourners grow through their grief and he shows consolers how to listen and speak with their hearts so that they can provide real comfort to others. His marvelous insights on the days of shiva, the year of kaddish, and the loving-kindness of others reveal the richness and true purpose of Jewish mourning rituals and customs. They prepare us to receive consolation and ready us for the journey that will take us beyond grief. "A very wise and helpful guide, this book will have crossover appeal for non-Jewish readers and is highly recommended for public libraries. It is also recommended for academic libraries as a vital companion to *The Jewish Way in Death*" (*Library Journal* Feb. 1, 2004).

Solomon, Lewis D. **The Jewish Tradition and Choices at the End of Life: A New Judaic Approach to Illness and Dying.** Lanham, MD: University Press of America, 2001. 328p. $79.50. ISBN 0-7618-1959-2; 978-0-7618-1959-2.

While he treats medical ethics and legalities relevant to terminal and chronic debilitating illnesses, this author of other books on Jewish living and dying focuses more on tools for making decisions "informed, but not straitjacketed, by the Jewish tradition." Patients' tools include not blaming oneself, prayers of different types, meditations, taking more responsibility, cultivating a positive, lighthearted attitude, social support, and creating a life map. The perspective of loved ones and differences of opinion on Jewish law are also considered (*Reference & Research Book News* Aug. 1, 2001).

Wolpe, David J. **Making Loss Matter: Creating Meaning in Difficult Times.** New York: Penguin Group, 2000. 240p. $17.95pa. ISBN 1-57322-820-6; 978-1-57322-820-6.

Rabbi Wolpe helps us decide how we will respond to loss, which can often be a new source of strength. Wolpe explores the meaning of loss, and creates a remarkably fluid account of how we might find a way out of overwhelming feelings of helplessness and instead create meaning in difficult times. "This is a book to pass on to those who are grieving—i.e., to every single person we know" (*Kirkus Reviews* July 1, 1999).

MULTIFAITH

Bowker, John. **The Meanings of Death.** New York: Cambridge University Press, 1993. 257p. $30.99pa. ISBN 0-521-44773-9; 978-0-521-44773-7.

Bowker digs deep into the origins of religion to contradict accepted modern myth regarding the fear of death and promise of an afterlife. He draws on Jewish, Christian, Muslim, Hindu, and Buddhist texts and concludes that the origins of religion were to extend life, and the afterlife was a product of religious belief, not its origin. "Appropriate for college and university libraries" (*Choice* Jan. 1, 1992).

Bregman, Lucy, ed. **Religion, Death, and Dying.** Portsmouth, NH: Greenwood, Praeger, 2009. 715p. $154.95. ISBN 0-313-35173-2; 978-0-313-35173-0.

A wide-ranging anthology that covers many religious, ethical, and spiritual aspects of death, dying, and bereavement in American society. This three-volume set approaches the role of religion in death and dying in an academic manner. As such, it may be most useful for scholars and clergy rather than the casual reader.

Brookes, Tim. **Signs of Life: A Memoir of Dying and Discovery.** Hinesburg, VT: Upper Access, 2000. 269p. $18.95pa. ISBN 0-942679-22-9; 978-0-942679-22-9.

Brookes turns an account of the death of his mother into a work hailed as literature by book critics, and as moving testimony of the value of hospice care by leaders of the hospice movement. "An incredibly personal, detailed account of the process of death. General readers; lower-division undergraduates" (*Choice* Jan. 1, 1998).

Heinz, Donald. **The Last Passage: Recovering a Death of Our Own.** New York: Oxford University Press, 1998. 320p. $45.00. ISBN 0-19-511643-7; 978-0-19-511643-4.

Heinz argues that we need to rethink death to save it from becoming a meaningless biological event. Heinz draws on an overview of the many ways death has been envisioned and ritualized throughout human history, from the Tibetan Book of the Dead to 15th-century Christian *ars moriendi*—manuals on the art of dying—and from

Jean-Paul Sartre to Elizabeth Kübler-Ross. This scholarly analysis includes a rich bibliography and is recommended for all libraries (*Library Journal* Dec. 1, 1998).

James, John W., and Russell Friedman. **Grief Recovery Handbook: The Action Program for Moving Beyond Death, Divorce, and Other Losses Including Health, Career, and Faith.** New York: HarperCollins Publishers. 2009. 224p. $16.99pa. ISBN: 0-06-168607-7; 978-0-06-168607-8.

This classic resource helps people complete the grieving process and move toward recovery and happiness. Incomplete recovery from grief can have a lifelong negative effect on the capacity for happiness. Drawing from their own histories as well as from others', the authors illustrate how it is possible to recover from grief and regain energy and spontaneity. "Highly recommended for public library and other self-help collections" (*Library Journal* Mar. 2, 2009).

Kastenbaum, Robert. **On Our Way—The Final Passage through Life and Death.** Berkeley, CA: University of California Press, 2004. 466p. $31.95. ISBN 0-520-21880-9; 978-0-520-21880-2.

A look at how death and dying is understood, negotiated, and experienced by different cultures. The author of one of the primary textbooks in the field, here he approaches death from a variety of different perspectives: anthropological, biological, psychological, spiritual, and personal reflection (includes discussions about his own brush with death).

McCurley, Foster R., and Alan Weitzman. **Making Sense Out of Sorrow: A Journey of Faith.** London, UK: Continuum International, Burns & Oates. 1995. 96p. $17.95pa. ISBN 1-56338-113-3; 978-1-56338-113-3.

This book is intended for people who are grieving, specifically for those who are searching for answers to questions that might be called religious, and for those who want to find hope when their world appears to be falling apart. For persons of Christian or Jewish tradition.

Rosen, Steven. **Ultimate Journey: Death and Dying in the World's Major Religions.** Portsmouth, NH: Greenwood, 2008. E-Book. $44.95. ISBN 0-313-35609-2; 978-0-313-35609-4.

Recommended by *MultiCultural Review* and *Choice* for the comparative study of religions, for persons working in hospice settings, and for those seeking to offer support in dying to persons of diverse faith and cultures.

Vanduivendyk, Tim P. **The Unwanted Gift of Grief: A Ministry Approach.** New York: Routledge, 2006. 192p. $42.50. ISBN 0-7890-2949-9; 978-0-7890-2949-2.

A passionate, practical guide through the grieving process for those who have suffered loss—and those who suffer with them. *The Unwanted Gift of Grief* helps those who grieve to walk through their pain rather than avoid it. The book presents sophisticated but simple methods of embracing grief and using it as a path to emotional and spiritual growth and profound transformation and healing. Equally valuable as a professional guide for ministers and counselors, a training resource for lay ministers and congregations, and as a gift to a grieving person.

York, Sarah. **Remembering Well: Rituals for Celebrating Life and Mourning Death.** Hoboken, NJ: Wiley, Jossey-Bass, 2002. E-book. $22.95. ISBN 0-7879-5865-4; 978-0-7879-5865-7.

Planning the funeral often falls to the survivors, who may already be overcome with mourning. Whether the family and loved one have a strong faith life or want to honor traditional rituals, this book can help readers create the funeral service appropriate to their situation. York, a Unitarian minister, also includes funeral services for specific situations, such as suicides or the death of heavily religious individuals.

NEW AGE

Carmody, John. **How to Handle Trouble.** Farmington Hills, MI: Gale, Macmillan Reference USA, 1994. $20.95. ISBN 0-8161-5912-2; 978-0-8161-5912-3.

Carmody, a multiple myeloma patient who died in 1995, offers advice on how to handle all types of trouble, whether minor or major. Carmody outlines a five-point technique of thinking, feeling, sharing, determination, and prayer.

Spong, John Shelby. **Eternal Life: A New Vision—Beyond Religion, beyond Theism, beyond Heaven and Hell.** New York: HarperCollins, HarperOne, 2009. 288p. $24.99. ISBN 0-06-076206-3; 978-0-06-076206-3.

God, says Spong, is ultimately one, and each of us is part of that oneness. We do not live on after death as children who have been rewarded with heaven or punished with hell but as part of the life and being of God, sharing in God's eternity, which is beyond the barriers of time and space. Spong argues that the discovery of the eternal can be found within each of us if we go deeply into ourselves, transcend our limits, and become fully human. By seeking God within, by living each day to its fullest, we will come to understand how we live eternally. "For conservative Christians, Spong's views are heretical; for many other readers, Christian and non-Christian, Spong's writing here as elsewhere is intelligent, engaged, comforting, and uplifting. Verdict: Spong's thought and theology are crucial stimulants for every thinking Christian; an important book" (*Library Journal* July 1, 2009).

Van Praagh, James. **Healing Grief: Reclaiming Life after Any Loss.** New York: Penguin Group, 2001. 304p. $15.00pa. ISBN 0-451-20169-8; 978-0-451-20169-0. Collingdale, PA: Diane, 2000. 286p. $24.00. ISBN 0-7567-5920-X; 978-0-7567-5920-9.

The medium and author of the *New York Times* bestsellers *Talking to Heaven* and *Reaching to Heaven* reveals how the devastating sorrow of a loss can lead to incredible opportunities for spiritual growth—and bring a sense of renewal and focus to our lives. Van Praagh shares many insightful spiritual messages from deceased loved ones, who shed new light on grief and loss. These stories, along with accounts of his own personal experiences, assist us in viewing our losses as steppingstones on our soul's evolving spiritual journey.

APPENDIX: ORGANIZATIONS

The organizations listed below are generally national in scope, providing listings or access to helpful resources for those grieving a loss. Forums or bulletin boards enabling interaction, important in the recovery process, are included. The authors recommend all. We recommend consulting the website as a first step in soliciting information or assistance.

AARP. 601 E Street, NW, Washington, DC 20049. 888-687-2277. E-mail: member@aarp.org. http://www.aarp.org.

Dedicated to enriching the experience of aging, AARP provides information on such topics as caregiving, bereavement, and a variety of topics related to aging.

The American Academy of Child and Adolescent Psychiatry. 3615 Wisconsin Avenue, NW, Washington, DC 20016-3007. 202-966-7300; 202-966-2891 fax. http://www.aacap.org.

A national professional medical association dedicated to treating and improving the quality of life for children, adolescents, and families. "Facts for Families" on the website provides concise, current information on issues affecting children, teenagers, and their families. Included is information on bereavement and such topics as adoption, foster care, and companion pet loss. The online resource centers provide readings, video clips, and links to information on a variety of topics.

American Childhood Cancer Organization. 10400 Connecticut Ave., Kensington, MD 20895-0498. 800-366-2223; 301-962-3520; 301-962-3521 fax. E-mail: staff@acco.org. http://acco.org.

American Childhood Cancer Organization (ACCO) began in 1970 as Candlelighters Childhood Cancer Foundation, established by a group of parents whose children had been diagnosed with cancer. The organization is comprised of families of children and adolescents who are in treatment or have

been treated for cancer, survivors of childhood and adolescent cancer, bereaved families, and health care professionals and educators who work with
cancer patients and survivors. Books, newsletters, and links to related websites are among the types of information provided.

American Foundation for Suicide Prevention. 120 Wall Street, 22nd Floor,
New York, NY 10005. 888-333-AFSP (2377); 212-363-3500; 212-363-
6237 fax. www.afsp.org.

Founded in 1987, AFSP is a national not-for-profit organization "exclusively
dedicated to understanding and preventing suicide through research, education and advocacy, and to reaching out to people with mental disorders
and those impacted by suicide" (website). Among the foundation's activities
are research and providing education and information about depression and
suicide to professionals, the media, and the public through workshops, train-
ings, the AFSP website, videos, publications, brochures, and public service
announcements.

Association for Death Education and Counseling. 111 Deer Lake Road,
Suite 100, Deerfield, IL 60015. 847-509-0403; 847-480-9282 fax. http://
www.adec.org.

An international, interdisciplinary professional organization promoting excel-
lence in death education, care of the dying, grief counseling, and research in
thanatology. Provides CDs, online publications, and links to other resources
on death and grief.

Centering Corporation, 7230 Maple Street, Omaha, NE 68134. Phone 866-
218-0101; 402-553-0507 fax. http://www.centering.org.

Founded in 1977, a nonprofit organization providing education on grief and
loss for professionals and the families they serve. It has a catalog of more than
five hundred resources for grief and loss including the magazine *Grief Digest.*
Includes numerous titles related to infant and child death.

Children's Grief Education Association. 6883 Wyman Way, Westminster, CO
80030. 303-246-3826. E-mail: mlyles@childgrief.org. http://childgrief.org.

The mission of the Children's Grief Education Association is to provide grief
education and support to bereaved children, their families, and professionals
in schools and community organizations through local, national, and international outreach and training. On the website is a bibliography for children
of all ages, along with links to other resources. Includes material on suicide.

The Compassionate Friends. 900 Jorie Blvd., Suite 78, Oak Brook, IL 60523.
877-969-0010 or 630-990-0010; 630-990-0246 fax. http://www.compas
sionatefriends.org.

"The mission of The Compassionate Friends is to assist families toward the positive resolution of grief following the death of a child of any age and to provide information to help others be supportive" (website). The Compassionate
Friends was established in the United States in1978 and offers "friendship,
understanding, and hope to bereaved parents, siblings, grandparents, and other family members during the natural grieving process after a child has died."

Chapters are found in more than 30 countries. Resources available include online resources, audio and video programs, media kits, and brochures.

Daily Strength. Widow and Widowers Support Group. 3280 Peachtree Road, Suite 600, Atlanta, GA 30305. http://www.dailystrength.org/c/Widows-Widowers/support-group.

Daily Strength lists more than five hundred online support groups for health and other life issues. The Widow and Widowers Support Group is dedicated to those who have lost a husband, wife, or partner. "Anything is open for discussion here, with the hope that we can focus on grief, bereavement, life after loss, and continuing on after a great loss." The "Ask an Expert" page allows anyone to pose questions to doctors and other experts.

The Dougy Center. PO Box 86852, Portland, OR 97286. 503-775-5683; toll free 866-775-5683. E-mail: help@dougy.org. http://www.dougy.org.

Provides support for children, teens, young adults, and their families grieving a death. "We provide support and training locally, nationally and internationally to individuals and organizations seeking to assist children in grief." Books, brochures, and DVDs are available for purchase.

Grief Recovery Online—Widows and Widowers (GROWW). http://www.groww.org.

Provides support for widowed and other persons grieving the loss of a loved one. Offers a large variety of chat rooms run by volunteers and dealing with specific issues (e.g., loss of a child, sibling, significant other, or parent). The website also provides gateways to organizations or agencies that can provide assistance to the bereaved.

GriefNet. PO Box 3272, Ann Arbor, MI, 48106-3272. E-mail: cendra@griefnet.org. http://www.griefnet.org.

An Internet community dealing with grief, death, and major loss. Sponsors 50 e-mail support groups and two websites, including KIDSAID.com. A rich source of books and online resources for death and bereavement.

Grief Watch. 2116 NE 18th Avenue, Portland, OR 97212. 503-284-7426; 503-282-8985 fax. E-mail: webmaster@griefwatch.com. http://www.griefwatch.com.

A ministry of Metanoia Peace Community, a congregation of the United Methodist Church in Portland, Oregon; its mission is to offer spiritual, emotional, and other support to persons who are grieving. Grief Watch and its companion program, Perinatal Loss, publish books, videotapes, audiotapes, and other helpful resources aimed at persons who have suffered loss. These resources are distributed by mail order to hospitals, schools, and individuals throughout the United States and Canada.

Growthhouse.org. 2261 Market Street, #199A, San Francisco, CA 94114. 415-863-3045. E-mail: info@growthhouse.org. http://www.growthhouse.org.

Provides education and printed and online resources about life-threatening illness and end-of-life care. Hosts the Inter-Institutional Collaborating Network On

End Of Life Care (IICN), a partnership effort by more than 40 educational organizations in the United States, Canada, the United Kingdom, and other countries. The network maintains full-text educational materials about end-of-life care in a shared database. Included are specialized resources on such topics as bereaved families, helping children grieve, pregnancy and infant loss, and suicide.

GROWW. 11877 Douglas Road, #102-PMB101, Alpharetta, GA 30005. E-mail: Staff@GROWW.org. http://www.groww.org.
GROWW is an acronym for "Grief Recovery Online (founded by) Widows & Widowers," but it is now a support community for all bereaved. GROWW provides a website link to a variety of other support resources, gateways to organizations or agencies that provide assistance to the bereaved, a bulletin board, a message center, a locator service to direct individuals to appropriate services, and chat areas.

Hospice Foundation of America. 1710 Rhode Island Ave., NW, Suite 400, Washington, DC 20036. 202-457-5811; 800-854-3402; 202-457-5815 fax. E-mail: hfaoffice@hospicefoundation.org. http://www.hospicefoundation.org.
Provides leadership in the development and application of hospice and its philosophy of care to enhance the U.S. health care system. Offers newsletters, books, brochures, DVDs, and downloadable publications.

Hospice Net. 401 Bowling Avenue, Suite 51, Nashville, TN 37205-5124. E-mail: info@hospicenet.org. http://www.hospicenet.org/html.
Hospice Net provides information and support to patients and families facing life-threatening illnesses, including online information and links to other helpful organizations and services. The website is a rich source of information for caregivers and family members who are facing the imminent death of a loved one.

KIDSAID.com. PO Box 3272, Ann Arbor, MI, 48106-3272. E-mail: cendra@griefnet.org. http://kidsaid.com.
Gives children a place to deal with their feelings with other kids who have suffered major losses. Posts stories, comments, and artwork as well as an online support group.

MedlinePlus. U.S. National Library of Medicine, 8600 Rockville Pike, Bethesda, MD 20894. http://www.nlm.nih.gov/medlineplus.
MedlinePlus pages contain links to Web resources with health information on more than 800 topics, including diseases, conditions, and wellness issues. Includes information on death and bereavement.

Mothers Against Drunk Driving (MADD). 511 E. John Carpenter Freeway, Suite 700, Irving, TX 75062. 800-GET-MADD, 800-438-6233; 972-869-2206/07 fax. http://www.madd.org.
"The mission of Mothers Against Drunk Driving is to stop drunk driving, support the victims of this violent crime and prevent underage drinking." Begun in

1980, MADD has offices in most states and works with law enforcement agencies to support law enforcement to catch drunk drivers and to pass legislation requiring ignition interlock devices or in-car breathalyzers to stop drunk driving.

National Association of People with AIDS. 1413 K Street NW, Washington, DC 20005. 202-898-0414. www.napwa.org.
Provides information and resources about HIV, stigma, testing, and policy.

National Hospice & Palliative Care Organization (NHPCO). 1731 King Street, Suite 100, Alexandria, VA 22314. 703-837-1500; 703-837-1233 fax. E-mail: nhpco_info@nhpco.org. http://www.nhpco.org.
Devoted to hospice and palliative care, NHPCO provides health care professionals and the general public with information about hospice and palliative care through publications and links to related sources on its website.

National Sudden and Unexpected Infant/Child Death and Pregnancy Loss Resource Center. Georgetown University, Box 571272, Washington, DC 20057-1272. 866-866-7437; 202-687-7466; 202-784-9777 fax. http://www.sidscenter.org.
This national consortium's program includes pregnancy loss (i.e., miscarriage) and stillbirth, as well as sudden and unexpected infant and child death. The Resource Center provides a toll-free information line and e-mail service to answer requests for information or publications, maintains an accessible website with continuously updated information, resources, and links to programs and services, develops print and Web-based materials for professionals and the public, publishes a monthly electronic newsletter, maintains searchable databases, and makes direct referrals.

Rainbows. 1360 Hamilton Parkway, Itasca, IL 60143. 847-952-1770 or 800-266-3206; 847-952-1774 fax. E-mail: info@rainbows.org. http://www.rainbows.org.
An international, nonprofit organization that fosters emotional healing among children grieving a loss from a life-altering crisis. The website provides brochures, informative articles, and links to other resources.

The Sibling Connection. E-mail: info@counselingstlouis.net. http://www.counselingstlouis.net/
A resource for anyone who has lost a sister or brother. Based in St. Louis, Missouri, the stated mission "is to provide resources to grieving siblings through counseling, the SiblingConnection web site, education, research, writing, and to raise public awareness about the profound impact of sibling loss." Links are provided for people of various age groups who have lost siblings, as well as a message board and listing of resources.

Society of Military Widows. 2486 N. Camino Valle Verde, Tucson, AZ 85715. 800-842-3451. E-mail: mshdgirl@comcast.net. http://www.militarywidows.org.
The organization seeks to benefits widows of members of all branches of the armed services of the United States. It provides moral support, advice, referral

service, and general help so that widows can resume their lives. Military survivors often face problems a civilian counterpart does not—for example, change of residence and separation from the support network of the armed forces. SMW provides support to help widows overcome their grief.

Twinless Twins Support Group International. PO Box 980481, Ypsilanti, MI 48198-0481. 888-205-8962. E-mail: contact@twinlesstwins.org. http://www.twinlesstwins.org.

A support group for people of all ages who have lost through death or estrangement a twin or other sibling of a multiple birth. Books are available for purchase in the store, and a list of recommended books is available.

WidowNet. http://www.widownet.org.

Established in 1995, this site is an online information and self-help resource for and by widows and widowers. Topics covered include grief, bereavement, recovery, and other information helpful to people of all ages, religious backgrounds, and sexual orientations. Provides links to helpful websites and lists recommended books. There's nothing fancy about the website, but it is informative.

WidowSpeak. 707-824-8030. E-mail: annmarie@widow-speak.org. http://widow-speak.org.

WidowSpeak is a literary project and a humanitarian effort where one can read widows' stories, see widows in the news and the arts, visit a photo gallery of widows, learn about widows' projects, and participate in the discourse of widowhood.

Young Widow.org. http://www.youngwidow.org.

Sponsored by Young Widow—Chapter 2, a nonprofit organization dedicated to young widows and widowers. The website provides a list of books, links to helpful websites, a bulletin board for discussions with peers, and links to support groups across the nation.

AUTHOR INDEX

SUBJECT INDEX

TITLE INDEX

ABOUT THE AUTHORS

ROBERT J. (BOB) GROVER is retired associate vice president for academic affairs and dean of graduate studies at Emporia State University, and former dean and professor in the School of Library and Information Management. He now serves as lay pastor of a small membership church in Bazaar, Kansas. His MLS and PhD in Library and Information Science are from Indiana University. In addition to authoring numerous professional journal articles, he co-edited *The Handy Five; Planning and Assessing Integrated Information Skills Instruction* (2001), co-authored *Introduction to the Library and Information Professions* (2007), and co-authored *Assessing Information Needs: Managing Transformative Library Services* (2010). He has worked in school library media centers at the elementary, middle school, and high school levels. His awards include the Association for Library and Information Science Education Outstanding Teaching Award, Beta Phi Mu International Library and Information Science Honorary Society, Pi Lambda Theta Education Honorary Society, Phi Kappa Phi, and Phi Eta Sigma.

SUSAN G. FOWLER remains active in the information consulting business she founded immediately after earning her MLS from Emporia State University in 1993. Her expertise includes managing special libraries, research and analysis, and the design and implementation of information infrastructures. She authored *Information Entrepreneurship: Information Services Based on the Information Lifecycle* (2005) and coauthored *Introduction to the Library and Information Professions* (2007) in addition to a number of articles. Her clients include organizations in the fields of law, health care, and philanthropy. Ms. Fowler is a member of the library and information science honor society Beta Phi Mu, Association of American Law Libraries (AALL), and the Kansas Library Association (KLA). She serves her local and state community through membership on a variety of committees. Her biography is listed in the 2006 Marquis *Who's Who in America*.

Bob and Susan are married and share a country home near Emporia, Kansas, with five idiosyncratic cats and two spoiled Cavalier King Charles Spaniels.